# THE LAW OF PARKS, RECREATION RESOURCES, AND LEISURE SERVICES

# THE LAW OF PARKS, RECREATION RESOURCES, AND LEISURE SERVICES

**ARTHUR S. FRAKT**

*Rutgers University School of Law—Camden*

**JANNA S. RANKIN**

*Temple University*

**BRIGHTON PUBLISHING COMPANY**
P.O. Box 6235
Salt Lake City, Utah 84106

**BRIGHTON SERIES IN RECREATION AND LEISURE**
Joel F. Meier, University of Montana, Editor

*High Adventure Outdoor Pursuits: Organization and Leadership*, Meier, Morash, and Welton, 1980, ISBN 0-89832-019-4

*Public Parks and Recreation Administration: Behavior and Dynamics*, Rockwood, 1982, ISBN 0-89832-021-6

*The Law of Parks, Recreation Resources, and Leisure Services*, Frakt and Rankin, 1982, ISBN 0-89832-022-4

**Library of Congress Cataloging in Publication Data**

Frakt, Arthur N., 1939-
    The law of parks, recreation resources, and leisure services.

    (Brighton series in recreation and leisure)
    Bibliography: p.
    Includes index.
    1.  Parks—Law and legislation—United States.
2.  Recreation areas—Law and legislation—United
States.  3.  Recreation—Law and legislation—
United States.  I.Rankin, Janna S.  II.  Title.
III.  Series.
KF5635.F73        344.73'099        82-4217
ISBN 0-89832-022-4    347.30499        AACR2

ISBN 0-89832-022-4

*This book is dedicated to our children,*
*Alex and David*

# Contents

# Preface

The purpose of this book is to provide students enrolled in professional parks and recreation curricula and related disciplines with a basic understanding of the role of the law and the legal system in the creation and management of parks, recreation facilities, and leisure services and programs. It should also be a valuable tool for professional park and leisure service administrators who must deal with legal aspects of parks and recreation management problems on a routine basis.

Although leisure service agency attorneys may find this book valuable for review purposes, it is not a manual on how to deal with specific legal questions, nor does it approach the often complex legal issues from the point of view of an advocate gathering precedents and arguments in order to reach a particular representational goal. Rather, the aim is to help the reader gain a sufficient appreciation for and understanding of legal reasoning so that when substantial legal problems arise his or her* role as a leisure service professional will be a constructive and creative one. Attorneys representing parks and recreation agencies are often not fully appreciative of the management goals and objectives of the park professional. To put it bluntly, the primary responsibility of an attorney is to keep the client agency out of court by minimizing the risk of liability. Thus, whether the issue is one of undertaking a major capital expansion program, extending recreation opportunities for special populations, sponsoring adventure programming, or any of the myriad functions to which the parks administrator is dedicated by profession and philosophy, it may be expected that the attorney will be a voice of caution and conservatism. Perhaps this is as it should be, but frequently the attorney will rely on a

*To avoid the awkwardness of the phrase "his or her," the authors have chosen to randomly select one or the other pronoun throughout the text.

superior knowledge of law to dictate rather than advise. "You can't do this!" and "The law won't permit that!" are statements heard all too often by the innovative parks and recreation administrator or programmer. When such statements are presented with a barrage of impressive legal jargon and a string of citations to cases and laws mysteriously plucked from the dusty and forbidding volumes that always surround the working attorney, it is no wonder that all but the boldest nonlawyer will be intimidated and will retreat.

We cannot emphasize too strongly that the preceding scenario is not inevitable. Armed with an understanding of how the law actually works and the ways in which attorneys investigate questions, the informed leisure service professional will see that the law is not necessarily a concrete barrier to innovation, but can be a tool that may be used to build progressive programs. The lawyer, rather than being either dictator or sage, is a resource whose advice and information should be carefully evaluated and utilized as opposed to blindly followed.

Basically, constructive and intelligent use of law and lawyers is necessary so that the philosophical goals of the profession can be achieved in the most economical, safe, secure, and democratic manner.

It is certainly not necessary for the leisure service professional to be aware of every case, statute, ordinance, or administrative ruling that might have some implication for parks and recreation. This is clearly the job of the attorney. On the other hand, since law is a dynamic and evolving social force, the readers who restrict themselves to the principles and materials within these pages will eventually find that much of their knowledge is stale and, to the extent that it may form the basis of decision making, possibly even destructive. To avoid this eventuality, the general principles set forth here should be considered only a background to an understanding of a legal problem, not as providing hard and fast rules that must be applied.

In order to be able to maintain an understanding of contemporary legal issues affecting professional life, the reader is strongly urged to become familiar with the basic legal research methods explained in Appendix A. With a bit of practice, any reasonably well-educated individual can learn to do sufficient legal research to keep current on all but the most technical and esoteric areas of the law and, most important, to eliminate the aura of impenetrability surrounding law and lawyers.

As will be readily apparent from a brief examination of the table of contents, the main thrust of this book is toward public parks and recreation services; nevertheless, those interested in voluntary agencies, commercial and private programs, athletic administration, and physical education will encounter many similar if not identical legal problems. The breakdown of governmental immunity from personal injury actions, the increase in cooperative efforts and joint ventures between public and private enterprises, and the proliferation of statutes and regulations concerning employment, civil rights, and environmental and occupational safety have resulted in a general blurring of distinctions and have created a substantial overlap of the legal problems of public and private sectors of our society.

The organization of this book reflects our belief that the reader must first have a general understanding of the legal system before he or she can fully understand those portions of the law that directly affect the parks and leisure service profession. Therefore, the first portion of Chapter 1 covers such basics as the organization of the court systems, the separation of powers, and the role of the Supreme Court.

Beyond these basics we have organized the material in the most logical manner for nonlawyers. That is, rather than use the typical law-school approach, we have chosen a modified chronological organization structure. Before any leisure service system is established there must be the legal authority, the enabling acts, to allow the government to be involved in the business of providing parks and recreation opportunities. After the agency has been established, it must acquire property and protect existing open space. Therefore the sections on land acquisition and environmental protection are next in the progression.

The subsequent actions of the leisure service professional will be to provide programs and equipment for the clients or participants. One major legal concern in program provision involves liability for injuries to the recipients of the services. Another programming concern involves constitutional and civil liberties issues—political and religious activities in the parks, discrimination in the use of facilities, and so on.

Finally, there are a number of concerns that fall within the general province of the administration of parks and recreation. Among other things, these include employment-related issues (labor law, workers' compensation, unemployment compensation, job discrimination, etc.), other administrative matters such as contracts and private and public cooperation, and finally some general areas of the law that are important to all areas of endeavor including leisure services, such as criminal law. Copyright law is also briefly discussed because of the expanding use of photocopying machinery and tape recorders.

Because we chose to organize the book in this way, some issues are developed in more than one chapter. For example, the constitutional issue of government's taking private property for public use without just compensation is covered in the "Property" portion of Chapter 2, while the constitutional issues dealing with the standards for the issuance of park permits to religious groups are included in Chapter 5.

We would like to acknowledge the assistance of friends, family, and colleagues who encouraged and supported us in this endeavor—particularly Bernadine Rankin and Jane and Charles Gilliland, who cared for our children during the most hectic periods of our research and writing. We must also note the contributions to our educations made by recreation professors Charles Brightbill, Edith Ball, and Adah Parker Strobell and by law professors Bob Knowlton and Tom Cowan. Their examples inspire and challenge us.

*Medford, New Jersey*                                          A. N. F.
*March 1982*                                                   J. S. R.

# 1

# An Overview

## THE AMERICAN LEGAL SYSTEM

All societies are rooted in some form of law. The term *law* encompasses the rules and regulations established for the governance of any group of human beings, from the basic family unit to international organizations like the United Nations. A society's collection of laws, or its legal system, reflects the history, tradition, needs, and desires of the peoples being governed and served by this system.

Naturally, then, law in the United States is as unique, complex, volatile, and adaptable as the individuals and groups who make up our society. Therefore there are very few generalizations concerning our legal system and our laws that are not subject to qualification and partial contradiction.

This is, in part, due to the fact that our laws come from a number of sources. For example, civil (noncriminal) law in the United States has its roots in English common law, which was in turn based on the customs and traditions of England. Beginning in the twelfth century, royal judges would travel from town to town settling disputes on the basis of community custom. This commonly accepted law continued to develop, and as the law came to be professionally administered, it reflected not only the custom of the land but also the custom of the court. Judges would look to past decisions to see how other courts had decided when they were faced with similar facts.

This pragmatic approach was adopted by colonial America because it was flexible and could accommodate new circumstances. After the Revolution, the various states continued to look to the established principles of both British common law and the newly developing American common law.

By contrast, most of Europe and Latin America is governed by a system of statutory civil codes that are much more specific, precise, and narrowly focused than the common law. The most famous of these civil codes were promulgated under the authority of great rulers, most notably Napoleon of France. This legislative system leaves less room for flexible interpretation or modification to meet changing situations or the unique needs of a particular dispute.

When we remember the settlement patterns of the United States, it makes sense that the French civil codes formed the basis of law in Louisiana, and that in California and most of the far West, Spanish law is influential.

To further complicate things, several states, including California, Montana, the Dakotas, Idaho, and Oklahoma, have largely *codified* their common law; that is, they have consolidated and summarized common law into a written code that has been adopted by statute. In most states criminal laws and most commercial laws have been codified as well. In fact, legislative enactments or statutes in all states coexist with or modify the common law in anticipating or responding to problems affecting society.

Even where legislatures have transformed and modified judicial tradition and have set forth the law in statutory codes and other enactments, American courts have remained resourceful and creative in rendering judicial opinions that interpret and apply the laws in keeping with the common-law heritage and the factual and moral imperatives of the cases under consideration.

With the necessary caution that it is impossible to discuss many of the exceptions and complications in this brief survey, we shall describe the framework of the American legal system.

### The Constitution

The Constitution of the United States is the basic charter of our government. It sets forth those underlying principles that the founders of the country held most important for the organization of a just society.

The Constitution was originally adopted in 1787. The first ten amendments, popularly called the Bill of Rights, were proposed by Congress and ratified by the states in 1791. These amendments established a charter of essential liberties with which the federal government could not interfere. Since then, the Constitution has been amended only sixteen times, with two of these amendments, the Eighteenth (prohibition) and the Twenty-first (repeal) essentially canceling each other out. The most significant of these later amendments were the Thirteenth, Fourteenth, and Fifteenth, which were adopted in the wake of the Civil War. They substantially extended the reach of essential liberties to members of all races and eventually led to the guarantee of most basic rights against infringement by the states, as well as by the federal government. The Nineteenth Amendment, which guarantees voting rights to women, is the most important modification in this century.

The Constitution is not only responsible for the structure and much of the operational form of our national government, but also has had a profound influence on the social and intellectual environment of almost every family and individual in the United States. Many dramatic changes in the way we live have had at least part of their beginnings in interpretive constitutional decisions by the Supreme Court. Just since World War II, decisions on segregation, obscenity and censorship, abortion, school prayer and aid to religious schools, presidential privilege and power, and right to counsel in criminal trials, to name just some areas of great constitutional activity, have profoundly altered our society.

Constitutional issues of particular importance to parks and leisure services will be discussed in Chapter 5, but a basic understanding of the system of law and government created by the Constitution is a prerequuisite to consideration of any legal issue arising in the United States.

The most important principle is that the United States Constitution is the ultimate authority from which we derive the powers and limitations of our government. All state constitutions, local, state and federal statutes, ordinances, regulations, and administrative rulings, all judicial determinations regardless of level of court, and, in fact, every governmental action regardless of how informal or seemingly unimportant, must comply and not conflict with the constitutional plan.

Article VI of the Constitution states:

> This Constitution and the Laws of the United States which shall be made in Pursuance thereof; and all Treaties made, or which shall be made, under the Authority of the United States, shall be the *supreme law of the Land;* and the Judges in every State shall be bound thereby, any Thing in the Constitution or Laws of any State to the Contrary notwithstanding. [emphasis added]

The federal government is limited to those powers expressly granted to it by the Constitution, with basic responsibility for health, safety, and welfare of the people theoretically left to the states. Nevertheless, the federal government's powers have been interpreted by the courts to be very broad and far-reaching. In large part this has been based on those powers expressly set forth in article I, section 8, which includes the power to tax and spend for the general welfare, conduct foreign policy, provide for defense and the conduct of warfare, and most critically, "to regulate commerce with foreign nations, and among the several states . . . ." The final clause of this section empowers Congress "to make all Laws which shall be *necessary and proper* for carrying into Execution the foregoing Powers . . ." (emphasis added). Judicial interpretations of these and other provisions of the Constitution have permitted federal action in virtually all significant areas of public and private activity.

## State and Federal Powers and Functions

Despite the fact that federal authority has continually expanded throughout the twentieth century, the states have retained residual powers to deal with government matters not expressly delegated to federal responsibility. The states also act where the courts and Congress have determined that specific federal standards and national uniformity are not required. The states have substantial authority to legislate and regulate matters of health, safety, morals, and welfare through what is known as their general *police power.* The creation and maintenance of parks and leisure services falls within this police power.

Because we have two fundamental authority structures, federal and state, with complementary and at times overlapping power, there is considerable complexity in government. This is particularly true in the judicial system. Most of the common law and the day-to-day legal management of society is within control of the state courts except insofar as their opinions may transgress Constitutional boundaries. The federal judiciary interprets and applies federal law and regulations. At the same time, federal courts often must apply state law and vice versa. All courts must look to state supreme courts for guidance on state statutory and constitutional matters, and to the United States Supreme Court with regard to federal laws and the Constitution.

We are all familiar with the fact that the Constitution establishes a tripartite federal structure including legislative, executive, and judicial branches. Different aspects of this government structure and state and local counterparts are dealt with throughout this book. In general it may be said that the trend is toward enacting state and federal legislation that sets forth principles and policy in broad strokes and delegates to executive departments both the task of spelling out details through regulations and administrative rulings and the supervision of the functioning of the legislative plan. Administrative determinations have the force of law and are generally subject to judicial review and interpretation in the same manner as legislation. In considering such rulings and procedures, the courts generally restrict themselves to determining whether or not the administrative or executive agency was operating within the legislative mandate, and if it was, whether its actions were rational and constitutionally sound. Thus the burgeoning governmental agencies have broad discretionary powers.

In addition to executive and legislative departments, the states also delegate considerable powers to counties, cities, towns, boroughs, villages, or other *municipal corporations* as they are collectively known in law, as well as to other more specialized political subdivisions such as special water or education districts, and, in some states, independent park districts. These subdivisions, in turn, govern through local laws, generally known as *ordinances* and *regulations*. Ordinances are the local equivalent of statutes. Regulations usually require less formal procedures for adoption and involve routine management.

Obviously a substantial proportion of the administration and funding of parks and leisure services and the bulk of recreation programming is done by and through local government units. Yet it is important to remember that all municipalities and local government units, from Two Dot, Montana, to New York City, are creatures of the state. They have no sovereignty or residual governmental powers and function only under whatever charter (and these vary widely) the state constitution and legislature may dictate.

Having outlined the broad bases of our government, we shall more closely examine the legal and judicial system.

### The Federal Judiciary

Article III, sections 1 and 2, of the Constitution delineate the structure and jurisdiction of the federal courts. A solid understanding of this system is valuable, not only because of the importance of the federal judicial branch but also because the structures of all of the state court systems roughly parallel the federal, although not necessarily with the same degree of complexity.

The only court specifically required by the Constitution is "one Supreme Court." Although during its debates the Constitutional Convention considered naming other courts, it finally compromised in article III on language that gave Congress power to "ordain and establish" inferior courts. Congress has done that from the time of the Judiciary Act of 1789. The current structure of the federal judiciary is as follows.

**Federal District Courts.**   Federal district courts are the basic federal trial courts. Each state, the District of Columbia, Puerto Rico, the Virgin

Islands, and other territories, has at least one federal judicial district, and larger or more populous states have several. The number of district judges is determined by Congress on the basis of population and the amount of federal business in the district.

Although Congress has created some specialized court systems (for example, the United States Tax Court and the Court of Military Appeals), the federal district courts nevertheless hold the bulk of criminal and civil trials, make findings of fact and law, and render judgments in cases brought before them under the federal civil and criminal codes.

In addition to hearing federal issues, the district courts are also required to hear many state law issues. There are two reasons for this. First, state law issues may be subordinate or attached to the federal issues, and it would be costly and time-consuming for them to be tried separately. Similar considerations and the supremacy of the federal constitution often result in federal questions being litigated in state courts. Even where there are no issues of federal law, Congress has determined that under article III, section 2, which extends judicial power to controversies "between Citizens of different states" the federal courts should be open to litigation by citizens of one state against citizens of another. This is called "diversity" jurisdiction. The technical complexities of this jurisdiction are beyond the scope of this book. Suffice it to say that the historical justification is that local courts might be prejudiced against the interests of outsiders from other states. In recent years, this rationale has come under considerable attack, not the least being from some Supreme Court justices who feel that the federal courts are unduly burdened with diversity cases. Thus it is possible that such jurisdiction may be restricted or eliminated in the future. In any event, federal courts when interpreting state law are bound to follow and apply the interpretation of that law set forth by the highest court of the state, and not to create a competing federal-state jurisprudence.

Most federal district court cases are tried by a single judge with or without a jury, depending on the preference of the litigants. Under the Constitution, individuals have the right of jury trial in all criminal and most civil cases. This constitutional right to trial by jury has been extended to the states insofar as criminal, but not necessarily civil, trials are concerned. Even in criminal cases, the states have been permitted under the Supreme Court's constitutional interpretations to experiment with nonunanimous criminal verdicts and juries of less than the traditional twelve members.

As noted earlier, most federal district court trials are presided over by a federal district court judge with life tenure appointed by the President, although in a limited but growing number of instances, a federal magistrate may preside. He is a lesser official not given the same powers or protection as an article III judge. In a few instances, as prescribed by Congress, three-judge district court panels are constituted to determine important constitutional questions. The advantage to the litigants of such a procedure is that direct appeals from a three-judge court may be taken to the Supreme Court.

**Federal Circuit Courts of Appeals.** Normally, if a litigant is not satisfied with the result of a federal trial or district court ruling, he or she may appeal to a circuit court of appeals. Such appeals are generally based upon contentions that the trial judge has misinterpreted and misapplied the law, that constitutional requirements have been violated, or, in some instances, that the findings of fact are so totally unsupported by the evidence that to accept them would violate the appellant's right to justice.

It may surprise the reader to learn that although the majority of trial court rulings are upheld on appeal, a large number are reversed. This does not signify lack of judicial knowledge on the part of trial judges. Rather, they must work in haste under pressure-laden circumstances. Appeals courts have the luxury of examining a complete record in quiet circumstances when the passions of the moment have died down. They therefore stand as a necessary corrective force against the errors of trial courts.

There are eleven federal judicial *circuits,* so called because, just like frontier ministers and doctors in the nineteenth century, judges, including those of the Supreme Court, at one time rode a circuit, stopping to hold court sessions in towns and villages throughout their assigned region. The federal circuits cover all regions of the country and the territories. They range in geographic scope from the District of Columbia circuit, hearing cases arising in the capital, to the Ninth Circuit, which encompasses Alaska, Arizona, California, Hawaii, Idaho, Montana, Nevada, Oregon, Washington, and Guam. There are always proposals to redistribute and increase the number of circuits. The number of judges in each circuit is, as in the district courts, dependent upon size, population, and amount of judicial business. For example, the Ninth Circuit currently has thirteen appeals judges, while the Fourth Circuit, covering Maryland, North Carolina, South Carolina, and Virgina, has only seven. In addition, retired federal circuit or district court judges may be called upon to participate in certain cases.

Most appeals are heard by three-judge panels, although occasionally where there has been prior disagreement among judges within a circuit on a legal issue or when a case is very important, all of the judges in a circuit may hear and decide the matter (the legal phrase for this is *en banc*). Unlike many district court decisions, which are based on factual findings at a trial and which therefore may result only in a brief decision or order, many of the circuit court determinations interpret matters of law and are utilized to explain the law to the trial courts as well as to correct errors in the procedure of lower courts. Because of this explanatory or teaching function, whenever the appeals courts do more than routinely uphold or affirm a lower court decision, there will be a written opinion. These may vary in length from a few paragraphs to hundreds of pages, depending on the complexity of the issues. Because the circuit courts have more than one judge, there may also be *concurring* and *dissenting* opinions, the former agreeing with the result of the court majority but not necessarily with the reasoning upon which the result was based. Dissenting opinions obviously express disagreement with the actual decision or the *holding* in the case. There may also be partial dissents and concurrences as well as opinions that merely reemphasize or add to the weight of either a majority or dissenting opinion.

The written opinions of the circuit courts, along with those of district courts when the trial judge is making formal rulings on legal questions, make up the bulk of our federal jurisprudence. Dozens of new volumes of reports of decisions in the circuit and district courts are published annually, adding up to well over a thousand lengthy volumes since the formal reporting of federal cases began.

This rich harvest of legal knowledge, along with corresponding volumes from state appellate and supreme courts, forms the backbone of our law libraries and the major resource (along with statutes) for original research in American law. Yet as important as all of these opinions are, the few formal decisions rendered annually by the nine members of the United States Supreme Court are the ones that gain the greatest recognition and, except in state common law and statutory matters, largely determine the paths that American law will follow.

## The Supreme Court

Although in the early days of the Republic the Supreme Court briefly had five, then six and seven members, except for the Civil War and Reconstruction periods, the number of jurists has remained at nine since 1837. In 1937, President Roosevelt, frustrated by the rejection on constitutional grounds of much of his "New Deal" legislation, introduced a plan to "pack" the Court as well as the rest of the federal bench with younger, more sympathetic judges, by naming a new judge for every federal judge over seventy years old.

Despite Roosevelt's enormous popular mandate and dominance of Congress, his plan was rejected, and all other proposals for expanding the court, restructuring it, or diminishing its authority have also failed. Thus, despite occasional political threats brought on by unpopular decisions such as school prayer, abortion, and the "one person-one vote" cases, it apears that the nine-member Supreme Court is secure for the foreseeable future.

Although attorneys seek hearings for several thousand cases annually, the Supreme Court will formally hear only a couple of hundred, and about a hundred of these will ultimately result in formal opinions. For the most part the court determines which cases it will hear in one of two ways, both of which involve rather complex processes. They can either review a case as "of right" or by granting *certiorari.*

While a few state court decisions concerning the constitutional validity of federal and state laws are theoretically appealable as of right, most state court cases heard by the Supreme Court arrive through the discretionary *certiorari* method. Both of these methods require that four justices agree that there is "probable jurisdiction" (in the few cases where there is a right to appeal at the Supreme Court level), or "certify" that there are certain constitutional aspects of a case that merit its being considered by the full court (in cases where they grant *certiorari*).

The procedures for appeal of federal court decisions to the Supreme Court differ slightly, but the general result is the same. *Certiorari* and appeals procedures result in the formal consideration of only a few cases.

It may seem unfair that most litigants are unable to have their cases heard by the highest court in the land, but the reader should reflect on the fact that, in most instances, a case has not only been tried but also reviewed by at least one and sometimes two tribunals before reaching the Supreme Court and that several judges have considered its merits. Thus litigants have had a large measure of justice afforded them. A case that the Supreme Court does hear and decide usually reflects issues of substantial significance whose importance extends far beyond the boundaries of the immediate controversy and the parties to it.

The Court applies various criteria to determine which cases it will actually hear. For our purposes it is sufficient to know that they involve a blend of constitutional requirements and policy considerations. The word for this blend is *justiciability,* and even law professors have a difficult time determining just what it is that makes a case "ripe" for the Court. A complex combination of legal controversy (the Court will not give advisory opinions), public pressures, societal changes, and political and moral considerations with a substantial measure of mere chance and fortuitousness may result in one case being heard while hundreds with similar issues and fact patterns have been ignored in the past.

We have already referred to the fact that Supreme Court decisions are of paramount importance in our constitutional scheme. When Chief Justice John Marshall wrote his landmark opinion in the case of *Marbury v. Madison*[1] in 1803, the young Court with very little historic precedent and authority ruled that an act of Congress violated the Constitution and was therefore void and unenforceable. This established the right of the Supreme Court to judge the workings of Congress. This was followed in 1816 by the almost equally important opinion of Justice Joseph Story in *Martin v. Hunter's Lessee,*[2] which said that the Court's constitutional powers allowed them to ensure compliance by the state courts and laws. Since then, the Supreme Court has maintained its ultimate authority to require that all government officers and agencies conform to its determination of the requirements of the Constitution, and all courts follow its rulings on constitutional and other federal matters.

This enormous and largely self-created power, when considered in conjunction with the lifetime tenure of the Supreme Court justices, could give rise to judicial tyranny. That it never has is attributed by legal scholars to the unique nature of the judicial authority. Commanding no army and appropriating no funds, the Court is dependent on the goodwill and cooperation of the legislative and executive branches. Furthermore, the Anglo-American judicial tradition of conservative responses to the realities of political life and social pressures has generally (but not invariably) ensured that the Court will not be so far ahead or behind the emerging positions of the society at large that its opinions would provoke widespread resistance or refusal to obey.

### The State Judiciary

Under our unique system of dual sovereignty, each state has a judicial system roughly paralleling the federal court system. The state courts exercise the primary judicial power over the personal and business lives of Americans, and even where actions between citizens of different states are initiated or removed to federal courts under "diversity" jurisdiction, the supremacy of the state's highest judicial tribunal in the interpretation and application of state statutory and common law is unchallengeable.

Twenty of the state court systems have three principal tiers as does the federal system, but in many of the less populous states, appeals are taken directly from the trial court to the state supreme court. It should also be noted that the basic trial courts or courts of general jurisdiction have a variety of names, including superior court, circuit court, county court, court of common pleas, and most confusingly in New York State, the supreme court. Although in most states the highest court is known as the supreme court, in Maryland, New York, and the District of Columbia, the highest court is the court of appeals. Because of the confusion surrounding court titles, it is important to know the jurisdiction and authority of a court and the level at which an opinion has been rendered. Obviously, the higher the court, the greater the likelihood of finality and the larger the impact of the court's reasoning.

In addition to the courts of general jurisdiction, there may be lesser or specialized courts, such as a small claims court, created to determine minor civil matters at low cost to the litigants, often without the need for representation by a lawyer, or municipal or justice of the peace courts, which hear lesser criminal or disorderly persons and traffic offenses. At the lower limits, often the judges are not attorneys and the likelihood of judicial error is substantial. Therefore, very extensive appeals rights are usually afforded from decisions of such courts, although most litigants do not avail themselves of these opportunities. Furthermore, though decisions of minor courts are obviously very important to the parties involved, they have little or no weight as precedent and cannot be relied on to predict the ultimate resolution of a legal issue.

Since the majority of state judges are elected, unlike members of the federal bench, the screening process for candidates or appointees is often not as rigorous as for potential federal judges. Questions concerning the competence, impartiality, and even the honesty of state and local judges are more likely to arise than has been the case (with a few notable exceptions) with the federal bench, but on the whole, judges are honest.

What may appear to litigants as partiality and favoritism may almost always be explained by considering the reality that judges are human beings who have usually had successful and often lengthy careers before their elevation to the bench. Thus they must inevitably filter the law and the facts of controversies before them through a screen of their own experiences and perceptions.

How, then, are we assured of a fair and reasonably consistent judicial response to legal questions presented to the courts? This is a critical issue, particularly since even with most elected state judges, terms are long and nominations are often bipartisan, so that the public rarely has the opportunity to respond to a judge's performance in the same manner as with most public servants. In order to answer the question, a closer examination of the judicial process is required.

## The Judicial Process

The simplest statement of the function of the courts is that they judicially enforce the laws. Of course, this is anything but a simple process!

Since much of our law is not legislatively enacted but comes to us through the common-law tradition, it must constantly be reinterpreted by the courts to meet the changing needs of society fairly while at the same time remaining true to an underlying body of Anglo-American and Western legal and philosophical principles.

Statutes and ordinances may provide legislative instruction to the courts, but much legislation is the result of compromise, and consequently the meaning of the terms of an enactment may be obscure and ambiguous. Even when legislative intent is plain, circumstances may arise that have not been anticipated in the legislation. Furthermore, our language is imprecise by its very nature, and courts may be required to determine which of several possible constructions to give to a word or phrase, or even, as is often the case, to consider the placing and use of commas and semicolons in determining which of two competing meanings was intended.

Consider for example the question of the exclusion of "private clubs" from coverage of civil rights statutes concerning public accommodations. What is a "private" club? Is it one that is member owned and nonprofit, or would a profit-making business such as an indoor tennis center qualify if it charged an annual membership fee and limited the number of people who used its facilities? Suppose a swimming club was nonprofit but essentially was an adjunct to a housing development? Think of the various recreational facilities with which you are familiar. Which, if any, would you consider to be private clubs, and how would you articulate the distinction between those and "public" facilities? As one can see, there are almost endless possibilities for dispute revolving around the use of two words "private club" and, as shall be demonstrated when they are considered in the material on constitutional law and civil rights in Chapter 5, the judicial responses have been varied and often surprising!

Similarly, consider a Minnesota statute that was the subject of litigation concerning whether a business was required to pay a worker's compensation claim to an injured employee of another firm. The argument of the worker's attorney was that the defendant company had avoided covering its workers by contracting for other companies to have their employees do work that was essentially part of its own business. A Minnesota statute provided that under certain circumstances, a business would still be responsible for worker's compensation for employees of other companies:

> Any person who creates or carries into operation any fraudulent scheme, artifice or device to enable him to execute work without himself being responsible to the workman . . . [would be liable].

The majority found that the employer was responsible because he used a "device" to contract away his responsibilities. To reach this conclusion, they determined that the word "fraudulent" modified only "scheme" because there was a comma after "scheme" and before "artifice or device." Thus the fact that the "device" used by the business was not fraudulent was irrelevant. There was a strong dissenting opinion by one judge, who read the statute as requiring "fraudulent" to modify all three following words "scheme, artifice or device."[3] What is your opinion of the proper grammatical construction? Is it appropriate for the court to take into consideration the fact that depending on how it interpreted the statute, an injured employee might receive no compensation at all for his or her injuries?

Beyond the immediate problems of the interpretation of language, courts often face an underlying requirement of trying to conform legislative enactments to the Supreme Court's interpretation of U.S. Constitutional requirements, or in many cases, a state court's interpretation of its own constitutional provisions. Since courts are extremely reluctant to totally strike down a legislative enactment, they will often strain to come up with a narrow or creative interpretation of legislative language to conform it to constitutional needs.

The principles of judicial interpretation are broad and sometimes contradictory. It is said, for example, that laws that are in derogation of the common law should be strictly or narrowly construed. Translated into ordinary language, this means that when a law is enacted that changes or limits the way judge-made common law principles have operated, the courts should limit its effect to the specific circumstances considered by the legislature. The theory is that the developed wisdom of the common law experience should not be readily overthrown. On the other hand, it is often stated that laws whose purpose is to enforce constitutional requirements or that are in aid of socially beneficial goals and principles should be given liberal and broad interpretation in order to further the legislative purpose.

There would be no purpose here to relate all of the arcane and contradictory maxims utilized by lawyers and judges to give broad or narrow interpretations to statutes, ordinances, and regulations. What is important to understand is that the judicial function is rarely a mechanical one in anything but the most routine of matters. The subtleties of language, the varying demands of public policy, and the infinite variety of fact patterns inevitably result in a complex and often seemingly contradictory pattern of judicial decisions across the country even on issues of great similarity. A more pertinent question is what, if anything, limits judges' exercise of discretion so that they do not become petty tyrants, using their judicial powers to impose their own personal value systems on the law governing our lives.

Obviously, the system of appellate judicial review serves to introduce a large measure of consistency in our judicial system. A judge who is too far out of step will regularly find his or her decisions reversed. But what limits are there on higher courts beyond the need to conform to the constitutional and federal statutory determinations of the relatively few issues that reach the United States Supreme Court?

One major conservative factor is the principle of *stare decisis*, or the requirement to adhere to previously decided issues of law. Under this principle, lower courts are bound to follow the precedent of earlier decisions of higher courts in the same jurisdiction when they are confronted with similar fact situations and legal issues. Similarly, although a court such as a supreme court of a state is not absolutely bound to follow its own prior decisions, *stare decisis* dictates that courts should not depart from their own previous determinations or "overrule" them unless compelled to do so by greatly changed circumstances or highly persuasive reasoning. Thus judges are restrained from following the dictates of their own socioeconomic preferences and constrained to give considerable deference to past judicial wisdom, not only because history and experience is a wise teacher to be ignored at our peril, but also because law should be predictable. People, businesses, and organizations should be able to plan their courses of action based upon a relatively stable understanding of what the law demands.

Because of the search for guidance from prior decisions, *stare decisis* also dictates that the reasoning or *precedent* of courts in other jurisdictions, whether federal, state, or at times foreign nations with similar legal systems, although not binding, may be considered worthy of substantial reflection and may be persuasive.

Given the strong value placed on the principle of *stare decisis* and *precedent*, how do attorneys seek to have the courts reach conclusions contradictory to what may have been decided in the past? Although sometimes there will be a direct argument that a prior decision is wrong and should be ignored, or, if the court has the power, overruled, more often than not a lawyer's argument and ultimately a judge's decision in his favor will combine a distinction of the facts with a subtle reinterpretation of the law. In fact, the process of *distinguishing* contradictory opinions is at the heart of much legal argument. Lawyers for one side will say that the facts of a previously decided case are different, and therefore application of the same legal principles will provide a different result, or that the difference in facts calls forth other legal principles not fully considered in the earlier case in question, and so on. Lawyers for the opposition, are of course, arguing that the situations are essentially the same and *stare decisis* requires a similar conclusion. Usually, lawyers on both sides of an issue find it necessary to distinguish some cases, while asking the court to follow the reasoning of others.

To a nonlawyer, many of the arguments about language and the attempts to distinguish cases may look like foolish quibbling (and it sometimes is!). What must be borne in mind, however, is that, in the process of distinguishing cases, attorneys are often also attempting to justify different results on a social policy basis. Clearly, there is a great reluctance to flatly overrule substantial legal precedent, and there is a desire for consistency and continuity. In the case of recent decisions, the courts have a strong interest in avoiding a sense that judicial opinions are ephemeral or not based on sound principles. Thus the process of distinguishing cases is a way to gradually but continually restructure and rebuild the law to conform to changing needs and perceptions, while at the same time continuing to honor that past experience and understanding which is the essence of judicial wisdom.

## Conclusion

What has been briefly outlined in this section is the stuff of which legal education is made. Law students spend three years essentially learning how the processes of change and distinction in the law operate. Therefore we must reiterate what we said in the preface of this book. Whatever statements may be made about the law in this or any other text should not be taken as reflecting irrefutable, unchangeable rules. The search for the "black letter" (the basic rules of the law) or the simple immutable explanation will usually be an unrewarding and misleading one. On the other hand, as an introduction to legal processes and to current and historic approaches to legal issues in the field of parks and leisure services administration, this work may aid not only in comprehending the law and lawyers but also in permitting the lay reader to contribute to the resolution of the legal controversies that inevitably will arise in the course of a professional career.

One further note of caution: The reader may find that much of what is discussed here bears little resemblance to the reality of how law operates at the ordinary day-to-day level. The local park commission, the park police officer, the justice of the peace or magistrate may seem to be operating on the basis of a seat-of-the-pants interpretation of immediate needs, desires, passions, and prejudices, not on the loftier or more neutral principles that we discuss. Manipulation of law caused by greed, favoritism, or even outright dishonesty is a fact of life with which we are

all familiar. Yet recognition of this reality should not lead to cynical rejection of the proper uses of law and legal principles. The justice system
has been used in the past to correct even the most blatant excesses of
political power and local prejudice, and though much error and injustice
has and will be undetected and uncorrected, a great deal more has been
alleviated through intelligent and persistent application of law.

## LEGISLATION ESTABLISHING PARK AND LEISURE SERVICE AGENCIES

### Federal Agencies

The primary source of authority for federal involvement in the provision
of parks can be found in article IV of the Constitution, which says, "The
Congress shall have Power to dispose of and make all needful Rules and
Regulations respecting the Territory or other Property belonging to the
United States."

While the charters of several of the original colonies extended their
boundaries to the Mississippi, after the Revolution these new states
ceded most of their claims on land beyond their present borders to the
United States. Therefore, while much of what is now the United States
was held by the federal government in what was called the "public domain," the federal government never held significant amounts of land
within the boundaries of the original states. This marked the beginnings
of federal land use patterns that still affect us today; that is, private
ownership in the eastern portion of the United States with the majority
of the public lands in the western portion.

From the Louisiana Purchase in 1803 to the Alaska purchase in 1867,
substantial lands were added to the public domain. As these lands were
opened for settlement and development, the federal land policy was one
of divestment—to sell or give the land to people who agreed to cultivate
and use it. This disposition of land grants did not go smoothly, and the
original claims were frequently tainted with fraud and deceit.[4]

Toward the end of this period of frontier movement when most settlers in the far West were still exploring, trying to avoid hostile natives,
staking out claims, and generally struggling to survive, a few influential
Montana citizens decided to explore the rugged Yellowstone region to see
if the fantastic stories of the early trappers were true. The Washburn-
Langford-Doane expedition in 1870 is generally credited with the idea of
the national park. Whether or not the story is true that the concept of a
national park came to these men while gathered around a campfire in
Yellowstone, their intensive lobbying efforts strongly influenced Congress which, on March 1, 1872, Congress established Yellowstone National Park.[5]

This first national park legislation is significant for at least two reasons. First, it marked the embryonic stage of a progressive new attitude toward retention rather than disposal of federal lands. Second, as the notes on the debate in the Senate over this bill make clear, many of the same arguments concerning the desirability of private development versus expansion of federal park lands which can be found wafting over Capitol Hill today were raised then. As Justice Oliver Wendell Holmes once said, "Upon this point a page of history is worth a volume of logic."

For example, Senator Cole of California is reported to have given the following speech in opposition to Yellowstone:

I have grave doubts about the propriety of passing this bill. The natural curiosities there cannot be interfered with by anything that man can do. The geysers will remain, no matter where the ownership of the land may be, and I do not know why settlers should be excluded from a tract of land forty miles square, as I understand this to be, in the Rocky Mountains or any other place. . . . I do not see the reason or propriety of setting apart a large tract of land of that kind in the Territories of the United States for a public park. There is abundance of public park ground in the Rocky Mountains that will never be occupied. It is all one great park, and never can be anything else; large portions of it at all events. There are some places, perhaps this is one, where persons can and would go and settle and improve and cultivate the grounds, if there be ground fit for cultivation.[6]

In spite of this invective, the bill passed and was promptly signed by President Grant.

The act that established Yellowstone National Park states that the land is

dedicated and set apart as a public park or pleasuring ground for the benefit and enjoyment of the people.[7]

Although Congress set aside the land, they did not appropriate any funds to protect and maintain the park. John Ise, in *Our National Park Policy: A Critical History,* explains why:

It was assumed at the time the park was established that it would be self-supporting, that concessioners would pay as rents enough to provide for administration and protection, and that there would be no need for Congressional appropriations.[8]

The early years of the park were not trouble-free. The boundaries were ill-defined, trappers and hunters continued to slaughter vast numbers of the "protected" wildlife, tourists carted away specimens of geyser cones, there were no rangers or guards, the nearest courts were 150 miles away, and the only punishment available was to eject an unruly individual from the park. Ise reports that "in desperation the Superintendent once confiscated the firearms and outfits of poachers, but the Attorney General ruled that this was illegal, and ordered the property returned to the poachers."[9] In addition, there are reports that early guides were lying in wait to separate the tourist from his money. These fellows are generally portrayed as unscrupulous exploiters, incapable of honorable employment.

This foreboding theme would be repeated through the years. Two major dangers for the national parks are commercial exploitation and deterioration from the park visitors' abuse.

From 1872 to the turn of the century, four more national parks were established by Congress. Additionally, the executive branch (the President or a delegated administrative agency) had the authority to "withdraw" or "reserve" land from the public domain, thereby making it unavailable for exploitation and preserving its current status. This power has been exercised for a number of purposes: to reserve public lands covered with timber, to withdraw lands from development pending congressional disposition and classification, to establish Indian or military reservations, or to establish wildlife reserves. One case states that prior to 1910 this power had been exercised at least 252 times, and that the right of the president to withdraw land from private acquisition was appropriate and in the public interest.[10]

In the Antiquities Act of 1906,[11] Congress specifically authorized the president to reserve lands containing scenic and scientific curiosities. Many national monuments have been created in this way from the 1892 reservation of the Casa Grande Native American ruins to the 1978 preservation of Alaska's federal lands by President Carter.

The method of establishment is a principle difference between national parks and national monuments. National parks can only be created by an act of Congress, while national monuments can be created by Congress *or* by presidential proclamation. Both are administered today by the National Park Service. Congress has decreed that because of the specific focus of national monuments upon particular scientific, historic, or cultural phenomena, their size should "be confined to the smallest area compatible with the proper care and management of the objects to be protected."[12] Thus there exist the Craters of the Moon National Monument in Idaho, which preserves a volcanic region, the Statue of Liberty National Memorial in New York Harbor, a cultural and sociological monument, and the Johnstown Flood National Memorial in Pennsylvania, commemorating a major disaster, to name just a few.

**The National Park Service.** As early as 1900 Representative John Lacey of Iowa introduced a bill to administer the national parks. The bill did not pass, and the parks continued to be administered individually, some by the Army, some by the Department of the Interior. Finally, in 1916, forty-four years after the establishment of Yellowstone National Park (and five years after Canada's Park Service was established), Congress created the National Park Service.

The purpose of the Park Service is to

> promote and regulate the use of Federal areas known as national parks, monuments, and reservations . . . by such means and measures as conform to the fundamental purpose . . . which purpose is to conserve the scenery and the natural and historic objects and the wild life therein and to provide for the enjoyment of the same in such manner and by such means as will leave them unimpaired for the enjoyment of future generations.[13]

Congress did not appropriate any money for the National Park Service until 1917, when $4500 was made available to hire Steven T. Mather as its director. Mather believed that one of his first jobs was to convince people that they should visit the national parks because park visitors would be more supportive of badly needed congressional appropriations for the parks. Early parks had few visitors. To get to Yellowstone from the East, one had to travel by steamboat up the Missouri to Clarks Fork, an arduous, time-consuming journey, and then by coach to Bozeman, Montana, where an outfitter could be hired to guide the visitor by horseback into the park some fifty miles away.

In the summer of 1920 Mather arranged a trip for eleven members of the House Committee on Appropriations to visit a number of national parks. Ise says, "Only one . . . of the committee had ever seen the parks, which no doubt explains in part the common indifference of Congress to national park problems."[14]

During the twelve years of Mather's leadership the Park Service became known to millions of people. He improved the facilities, added new parks, and fought with a number of special-interest groups. When poor health forced Mather to retire in 1928, he was succeeded by his assistant, Horace Albright. Albright was a lawyer who specialized in legal work connected with the national parks. He is credited with efficiently organizing the service; with continued park expansion, particularly historical sites and monuments; with the development of master plans for many of the parks; and with the establishment of Grand Teton National Park, a project that he had been involved in for a number of years as Mather's assistant.

When President Franklin Roosevelt appointed Harold Ickes to be Secretary of the Interior, Albright knew that the Park Service would have the necessary support and protection, and he resigned his post to Arno B. Cammerer, who had been associate director.

Through the years Congress continued to establish additional units of the park system, and it gave the Secretary of the Interior both general directives to be applied to all of the system and specific instructions with regard to specific parks. These laws are collected in Title 16 of the U.S. Code. (All of the various areas that come under the jurisdiction of the National Park Service are listed in National Park Service, U.S. Department of Interior, *Index of National Park System and Related Areas.*[15])

For example, 16 United States Code Annotated (U.S.C.A.) § 407m established Independence National Historic Park and authorized the Secretary of the Interior to acquire the appropriate properties. When the condemnation of one of these properties was challenged, the court upheld the park acquisition and praised the congressional intent of providing "a permanent memorial to the principles on which the nation is founded."[16]

One of the more recent additions to the park system is Channel Islands National Park in California. When Congress established this park on March 5, 1980, the lawmakers specified that it was

> to protect the nationally significant natural, scenic, wildlife, marine, ecological, archaeological, cultural, and scientific values of the Channel Islands ... including ... the brown pelican nesting area; ... the only breeding colony for northern fur seals south of Alaska; ... the presumed burial place of Juan Rodriguez Cabrillo; and the archaeological evidence of substantial populations of Native Americans ....[17]

To accomplish these goals, and recognizing the fragility of park's resources, the law requires the Secretary of the Interior to establish the appropriate visitor carrying capacity[18] and to submit a comprehensive management plan for the park. The law also requires the secretary to consult and seek advice of the scientific community and to conduct public hearings in nearby counties. This statute is more specific with regard to these requirements than are most of the others that rely on regulations promulgated by the administrators.

Some of the general directives from Congress to the Secretary of the Interior include the creation of a Volunteers in Parks Program,[19] the requirement that the secretary maintain a continuing inventory and evaluation of outdoor recreation needs and resources in the United States,[20] and the requirement that the secretary investigate, study, and continually monitor areas of national significance for potential inclusion in the National Park System.[21]

**The Forest Service.** When the Forest Service was conceived in 1876, recreation was not included as a primary function of the forest reserves. The public concern was over the importance of a continual supply of timber and of a forest cover to prevent floods and retain water for useful purposes.[22]

Gifford Pinchot, the father of professional forestry, believed that forest resources should be actively managed to benefit the greatest number of people. He is reported to have said:

> The object of our forest policy is not to preserve the forests because they are beautiful ... or because they are refuges for wild creatures ... but ... [is] the making of prosperous homes ... Every other consideration comes as secondary.[23]

At the same time, it is safe for us to assume that the national forests were used for hunting and fishing, and, in fact, Pinchot noted in his "Use Book" (later to become the *Forest Service Manual*) that "quite incidentally, also the National Forests serve a good purpose as playgrounds for the people ... and their value in this respect is well worth considering."[24]

The first appropriation to the Forest Service for recreational facilities was in 1923, and in 1924 a large part of what is now the Gila Wilderness in New Mexico was set aside for the preservation of wilderness.

Led by foresters like Aldo Leopold, Robert Marshall, and Arthur Carhart, and by Congress through the Multiple-Use Sustained-Yield Act of 1960[25] and the Wilderness Act of 1964,[26] the utilitarian philosophy became broadened to include recreational uses. This legislation is explored in detail in Chapter 3, which deals with the current recreational status of federal lands.

**Other Federal Agencies.** Throughout the years a good number of other agencies have developed programs and policies that involve responsibility for some form of recreation or leisure interests. Some of these have evolved from administrative directives, while others have been brought about by actions of Congress. These agencies include the Bureau of Land Management, the Bureau of Sport Fisheries and Wildlife, the Bureau of Reclamation, the Corps of Engineers, and the Tennessee Valley Authority, among others.

### State Systems

Since the federal government has specified, limited powers, the framers of the Constitution left all residual powers (those not specifically assigned to the federal government) to the various states. It is appropriate, therefore, for the state legislatures to exercise this power to establish state park systems. The names of the administrative agencies vary from state to state, but their mandates are generally similar to those of Montana's Department of Fish, Wildlife, and Parks:

> [The Department is established] for the purpose of conserving the scenic, historic, archaeologic, scientific, and recreational resources of the state and providing for their use and enjoyment, thereby contributing to the cultural, recreational, and economic life of the people and their health.[27]

Historically the state park systems had their beginnings in the mid-nineteenth century. Shortly after designing and supervising the development of Central Park in New York City, Frederick Law Olmstead visited Yosemite Valley and initiated plans to make it a public park. The next year, 1864, Congress granted the valley to the state of California, and it became one of the first areas set aside for "public use, resort and recreation." The park was managed by a commission appointed by the governor. Olmsted was appointed chairman of the commission, but he soon left California to go back to New York.

Yosemite park management put a severe financial strain on the sparsely populated state, and sheepherders, poachers, mining prospectors, commercial entrepreneurs, and tourists were not well controlled. As a result, much of the valley was abused, and there were numerous complaints and suggestions that the park should be receded to the federal government.

John Muir and his Sierra Club were in the forefront of the movement to give the state park back to the federal authorities. In 1903 Muir took President Theodore Roosevelt on a pack trip to the valley and convinced him to use his influence to persuade Congress to accept the land. In 1905 the valley was returned to the federal government and became a national park.

By this time, however, California had purchased Redwood State Park in the Santa Cruz Mountains, and after this the Save-the-Redwoods League worked diligently toward the establishment of a state park system.

Another early state park was created by the New York legislature in 1892. The language establishing the Adirondack Park and Forest

Preserve became incorporated into the state constitution, which was adopted in 1894. The constitution specified that the park lands were to

be forever kept as wild forest lands. They shall not be leased, sold or exchanged, or be taken by any corporation, public or private, nor shall the timber thereon be sold, removed or destroyed.[28]

Over the years both private and public organizations have tried to develop areas within the Adirondack Park, efforts which have parallels in every state park system. For example in preparation for the 1932 winter Olympic Games, the legislature authorized the conservation commissioner to construct a bobsled run on state lands. This would involve removing the trees on about four and one-half acres of the almost two-million-acre preserve. An association of people who wanted to protect the Adirondacks sued the commissioner and sought to have the 1929 law authorizing the construction voided because it was unconstitutional.

The attorney for the Olympic planners argued that the underlying purpose of the park lands was for the use of the people for their health and pleasure, and that the erection of a bobsled run was within this purpose.

The highest court in New York, the Court of Appeals, under the leadership of Chief Judge Cardozo, disagreed and found in favor of the association. The opinion said:

The framers of the [state] Constitution . . . intended to stop the willful destruction of trees upon the forest lands, and to preserve these in the wild state now existing; they adopted a measure forbidding the cutting down of these trees . . . for any purpose.[29]

The judiciary has generally been responsive to arguments that park land should be preserved for its intended purposes, and not subject to the demands for more economically advantageous uses.

The first director of the National Park Service, Stephen Mather, also gave state park development a boost. During the early years of the National Park System every congressperson seemed to want a national park in his or her district. While many of these areas were suitable for local or regional parks, they were not all of significant national interest. It occurred to Mather, therefore, that the states should purchase these sites for the use and enjoyment of the populace. With this in mind, he initiated the National Conference on State Parks in 1921.

Although it is inappropriate for us to attempt a complete history of the continued development of state parks, it is important that we note the impact of the depression-era relief work funds.

During the first months following his inauguration, President Franklin Roosevelt (who, incidentally, as a state senator in New York had fought to protect the Adirondack Park and Forest Preserve) convinced Congress to pass the Emergency Conservation Act. This gave the president the authority to establish the Civilian Conservation Corps (CCC) to provide employment in national forests, national parks and monuments, and state and local parks. The CCC existed from 1933 to 1942 and did a substantial amount of work in the park systems.

Other relief programs, like the Works Progress Administration (WPA), gave appropriations for employment benefiting state and local parks. Under the WPA, many buildings, swimming pools, tennis courts, bridges, playgrounds, and park sites were developed at the state, county, and local levels.

Prior to the Depression, in 1926, Congress had authorized the Secretary of the Interior to identify federal lands that were chiefly valuable for recreational purposes and to sell or lease them to the states.[30] Twenty-nine states established state park agencies between 1917 and 1930.[31] Roosevelt further encouraged the development of state parks when he created the National Resources Board in 1934 to study the problem of natural resources, including national and state parks. A large number of state and county park sites and roadside picnic areas were acquired during his administration.

Today every state has a system of parks and related recreational areas. These systems operate under the state legislature, which authorizes such necessary activities as property acquisition, law enforcement, and so forth. The day-to-day operation is delegated to an administrative agency.

Quite obviously, recreation statutes vary from state to state—one would hardly expect Louisiana, for example, to include a comprehensive section on snowmobile regulation, nor would Nebraska be concerned with the regulation of beaches and seagoing vessels.

Although we have concentrated on public recreational opportunities, the states also regulate private and commercial recreation. Many states, for example, have camp safety acts that prescribe the requirements for camps within their jurisdiction. All states have licensing requirements—for recreation vehicles, for hunting or fishing, for food and beverage operations, for ski lifts, and so on. Many states license professions that are closely aligned with some aspects of recreation; for example, occupational therapy or family counseling. This broad regulatory power exercised by the states has an impact upon every form of leisure service enterprise.

Because it is impossible for us to list each of these statutes for every state, it is important for both the student and the administrator to refer to the laws of her or his own state and to become familiar with those that are applicable to his or her area of interest. The material on legal research in the appendix will assist you in finding the appropriate sections of your state statutes.

## County and Local Leisure Service Provision

Prior to any of the state or federal interest in recreational opportunities, the New England towns of the Colonial period set aside open areas in the center of town. These areas were to be shared by all of the townsfolk for grazing, military drilling, public displays, and, not incidentally, for socializing. The Boston Common, established in 1634, is an early example of a muncipal public area.

During the planning stages of many early American cities, the founders thought to include parks and open space. In 1682, for example, William Penn designated a number of spots for parks for the Philadelphia public. James Oglethorpe, when he planned Savannah in 1733, established public squares spread evenly throughout the city. Brigham Young remembered the need for public squares a century later as he planned Salt Lake City.

The late nineteenth century saw the development of Central Park in New York City, the prototype of the large urban park, the expansion of YMCA programming, Boys' Clubs, the first professional baseball, and the first city park systems. In 1893 the Illinois legislature passed an enabling law permitting the establishment of park districts, and in 1895 Essex County, New Jersey, established the nation's first county park system. By 1920 about eight hundred cities had municipal park systems, although only a few were fully supported by public funds. Civic-minded individuals and conservation leaders were in the forefront in making recreation available for the masses, and much park development depended upon private contributions and voluntary activities.

The provision of parks and leisure services has traditionally been a grassroots operation. Since county and local governmental units can only provide those functions that have been authorized, what is the source of this authorization?

As we have already stated, the constitutional form of government of the United States centers those powers that are not specifically reserved for the federal government within the individual states. The states, in turn, may parcel out or delegate various responsibilities to the county and local governmental units. This delegation of police powers and the responsibilities for public health, safety, morals, and welfare is accomplished in one of several basic ways.

Some state constitutions give the authority directly to localities through grants of home-rule powers. For example, article XI, section 11 of the California constitution provides that any county or city may make and enforce within its area of authority local police, sanitary, and other regulations that are not in conflict with the general laws. This language restricts the grant of power by specifying that whenever the state legislature passes a law on a particular subject it takes precedence in this area and the local government must operate only within the bounds of this state legislation. Nevertheless, home-rule provisions are the broadest grant of state powers to local authorities. Although the provision of recreational opportunities is not specifically mentioned, it has been held by the courts to be an appropriate function of government and to be a valid exercise of police powers in home-rule cities.

A second way in which local governments attain the authority to operate parks and recreation is through state legislation that grants specific powers to all units of local government within a certain category, such as "cities of more than 500,000," or with the delegation of power included in a grant of a municipal charter to a specific locality. These general legislative enactments, like home-rule powers, are limited by the state and federal constitutions.

Another form of state legislation that affects local agencies is mandatory legislation. Mandatory legislation requires, prohibits, or regulates specific activity. An example of mandatory legislation would be a state statute prohibiting local park and recreation agencies from charging fees in excess of the amount necessary to provide the service. We are all familiar with other forms of mandatory legislation: the regulatory statute that requires licensing of recreational vehicles, a statute that sets limits on fish and game, or a statute that establishes health and safety regulations for camps and swimming pools.

Generally, localities are not mandated to provide parks and recreation, although they may be encouraged to do so by the availability of state grants or matching funds.

Finally, local exercise of police power can be authorized through enabling acts passed by the state legislature to give localities the power to function in particular areas. This permissive legislation enables the governmental units to establish various systems to deliver public services. An example of permissive legislation would be a statute that would allow the local subdivision control board to require a housing developer to dedicate a certain portion of his or her proposed project for public park use as a condition of the subdivision approval.

In some states, establishment of special park districts, units of government with taxing powers established solely to provide park and recreation opportunities for the residents within their jurisdiction, is made possible through special enabling laws.

Permissive legislative authorization may be phrased in general or specific terms, depending upon the legislative objectives. The following are examples of permissive legislation from New Jersey:

Public parks on beach or ocean front;

1. That it shall be lawful for the common council or other governing body of any city in this state, located on or near the ocean, and embracing within its limits or jurisdiction any beach or ocean front, to open and lay out on and along such beach or ocean front, a public park or place for public resort and recreation, and to devote the lands within the limits of such park or place of resort, when established as herein directed, to such use exclusively.[32]

And from the section of the statutes dealing with county parks:

Park police system;

The county park commission may establish a constabulary to preserve order in the parks, parkways, playgrounds and recreation places under its control, and to secure enforcement of the rules and regulations enacted by it . . . .[33]

The authority given to the local or county governmental unit to provide parks and recreation is generally delegated to a board or commission. This body, hopefully working closely with the professional staff, can adopt rules and regulations for the day-to-day use and operation of the system. When adopted according to specific legal requirements, these regulations take the form of an ordinance. An ordinance has the effect of a law and can be enforced accordingly. As a practical matter and to ensure efficient enforcement, all of the ordinances of a system should be kept together in a codified form and should be periodically updated to keep them in line with current policies and practices; unfortunately, most are not.

For example, one park commission still has a prohibition against "cutting ice from any stream or lake within any park without the previous license of the Commission." This rule obviously was an effort to keep the formerly important ice house and home ice industry from profiting from the public without paying a fee for the privilege. (Or perhaps the commission wished to keep competing ice companies from going at it with hammer and tongs.) The same ordinance instructs the park user that "no person shall enter a retiring house set apart for the use of the opposite sex." How many people would understand that "retiring house" was a euphemism for toilet?

Of course, no one would think of taking the most outrageously outdated ordinances seriously, but if park ordinances are to be enforced in an evenhanded manner, it is important that they be reviewed on a regular basis.

## Conclusion

Very few writings conceived by human ingenuity, are drier or duller than the documents ordaining and establishing government agencies and services. With parks and leisure services, as with other activities, the excitement and the interest is in the doing, not the ordaining. With this in mind, we have attempted to provide an outline and a representative sampling of these processes and structures without overly burdensome detail. The reader should bear in mind, however, that without the appropriate legislative and administrative authorization and procedures, none of the activities of the public leisure services field would be possible. In many instances, the ability to offer or afford innovative services or significant programs depends upon the amount of authority delegated, particularly with regard to fiscal resources. Furthermore, the specificity and detail of legislative authority may determine whether, on the one hand, an important program will withstand administrative indifference or opposition, or on the other hand, if creative administrators will have the flexibility to adapt to changing needs and conditions.

## NOTES

The authors realize that the citation form used throughout this text may be unfamiliar to some readers. Therefore, legal citations are fully explained in Appendix A.

1. 5 U.S. 137 (1803).
2. 14 U.S. 304 (1816).
3. *Washel v. Tankar Gas,* 2 N.W.2d 43 (Minn. 1941).
4. See generally, Paul Gates, *History of Public Land Law Development* (Washington, D.C.: U.S. Government Printing Office, 1967).
5. For a detailed history of Yellowstone, see Aubrey L. Haines, *Yellowstone National Park—Its Exploration and Establishment* (Washington, D.C.: U.S. Government Printing Office, 1974).

6. *Congressional Globe,* January 30, 1872, at 697.
7. 16 U.S.C.A. § 21. The U.S.C.A. is the United States Code Annotated. This code is the restatement of the laws of the United States in convenient form. It is divided into a number of volumes according to subject matter. The number 16 indicates the title, and § 21 indicates the particular section where this can be found.
8. John Ise, *Our National Park Policy: A Critical History* (Baltimore: John Hopkins University Press for Resources for the Future, 1961).
9. *Id.* at 24. At this point (in 1886) the park superintendent called upon the War Department to have the Army protect the park. They were there until 1916.
10. *United States v. Midwest Oil Co.,* 236 U.S. 459 (1915).
11. 16 U.S.C.A. §§ 431-433. The Antiquities Act is frequently called the Lacey Act because Representative John F. Lacey, a parks supporter from Iowa, was the moving force behind the bill.
12. 16 U.S.C.A. § 431.
13. 16 U.S.C.A. § 1.
14. Ise, *supra* note 8, at 197.
15. Washington, D.C.: U.S. Government Printing Office, 1979.
16. *U.S. v. Certain Parcels of Land in City of Philadelphia, Pa.,* 99 F. Supp. 714 (D.C. Pa., 1951).
17. 16 U.S.C.A. § 410ff.
18. The concept of carrying capacity is a critical one for all recreation and leisure service personnel. See generally, Richard L. Bury, "Recreation Carrying Capacity—Hypothesis or Reality?" *Parks & Recreation,* January 1976; and George H. Stankey and David W. Lime, *Recreation Carrying Capacity: An Annotated Bibliography,* U.S. Forest Service, General Technical Report INT-3 (Ogden, Utah: Intermountain Forest and Range Experiment Station, U.S. Forest Service, 1973).
19. 16 U.S.C.A. § 18g.
20. 16 U.S.C.A. § 460L-1(a). This Outdoor Recreation Act of 1963, or P.L. 88-29, was the focus of the "Washington Scene" column in November 1981 *Parks & Recreation.* The column emphasized that P.L. 88-29 is still "good law" although the Secretary of the Interior has a great deal of discretionary power in deciding how to enforce the Congressional intent.
21. 16 U.S.C.A. § 1a-5.
22. See generally Glen O. Robinson, *The Forest Service, A Study in Public Land Management* (Baltimore: John Hopkins University Press for Resources for the Future, 1975).
23. Samuel Hayes, *Conservation and the Gospel of Efficiency: The Progressive Conservation Movement* (Cambridge, Mass.: Harvard University Press, 1959), at 42.
24. Quoted in Michael Frome, *Whose Woods These Are: The Story of the National Forests* (Garden City, NY: Doubleday, 1962), at 330.
25. 16 U.S.C.A. § 528.
26. 16 U.S.C.A. §§ 1131-36.

27. 23 M.C.A. § 1-101.
28. New York Constitution, art. VII § 7 (1894).
29. *Association for the Protection of the Adirondacks v. MacDonald,* 253 N.Y. 234, 170 N.E. 902 (1930).
30. Ise, *supra* note 8, at 296.
31. Clifford Hynning, "State Conservation of Resources: A Study Made for the National Resources Committee," 1939, at 32, as cited in Ise, *supra* note 8, at 295.
32. N.J.S.A. 40:179-98. This law was passed in 1894, which explains the unconventional language.
33. N.J.S.A. 40:37-95. 40.

# 2

# Property
# and Parks

## HISTORY OF LAND USE CONTROLS

No area of law is more arcane and encumbered with ritual, ancient forms, and legalistic phraseology than the law of property. Much of our modern property law stems from English tradition, and, long before that, from early Roman law. In fact, the earliest Roman Code (450 B.C.) provided for appropriate distances between trees and boundaries and setback lines from the property boundary to any dwelling.

It is a popular notion that the possessor of property has absolute dominion over it. Much of the tradition of Western culture is based on possessive attitudes toward the ownership of land, or "real property," as it is legally known. It may be that the tragic history of Native American relations with the Western European immigrants can largely be explained by the Indians' inability to understand or appreciate the European concept of land ownership. Why shouldn't a chief take a few trinkets or blankets for a meaningless signature? The Indians believed that the land was eternal, and that no one could own it. In the same way, much of the Western revulsion against Communism is related to the destruction of private-property rights.

Actually, while the right of individuals to own property may be absolute in Anglo-American law, this has never included total control over the use of the property. From medieval times some forms of restrictions on property use for health, safety, and even aesthetic reasons have been imposed. For example, under a statute of Edward I, (1239-1307), parsons were forbidden to cut down trees in churchyards. With the rise of urban centers, controls were established over the maintenance of odorous and unsightly conditions in inappropriate populous areas. Piggeries were controlled and the practice of dumping garbage in public streets was prohibited. The use of flammable thatch for roofing was also restricted. The greatest impetus for both sanitary and building controls was provided by the twin tragedies that struck London in 1665 and 1666, the Great Plague and the Great Fire. Out of the devastation caused by these cataclysms, land use planning was born.

Although visionaries like Penn and Oglethorpe saw the need for planning, as demonstrated by their work in Philadelphia and Savannah respectively, in general there were few restrictions on land use in the colonies. Where they did exist, they were designed to meet specific problems. Slaughterhouses and other nuisance activities were not permitted in certain areas of Boston and Charlestown, and there were regulations concerning the keeping of animals and the construction materials that could be used in heavily populated residential areas. In general, however, since land was plentiful and people were few, only a minimal need for controls was perceived. As our society has become more complex, as technology has expanded the potential for environmental disasters with far-reaching impact, and as the population has increased and become more urbanized, complex patterns of land use regulations over private as well as public property have become the rule rather than the exception. Still, in much of the West, traditional antipathy to governmental control over the land remains strong.

## COMMON-LAW DEVICES FOR REGULATION

Considering the crucial role that property played in Anglo-American society, it is hardly surprising that many of the disputes that judges were called upon to resolve, as they made their circuits around the countryside, involved land ownership, possession, and use. Few things in life are as likely to enrage the ordinary citizen as much as disturbance of his home, whether it comes from direct physical invasion or through noise, odor, or even the interference with sunlight through obstruction.

Inevitably, the great number of property disputes led to a mass of complicated and often contradictory decisions. Although much of this complexity remains today, most common-law physical land use disputes roughly fall into two general categories, *trespass* and *nuisance*.

*Trespass* refers to the physical invasion of a person's exclusive possession of property. A *nuisance* is a substantial and unreasonable interference with the possessors' use and enjoyment of their property. Historically the principle distinction was that trespass was always a physical invasion, while a nuisance did not necessarily involve an actual presence on the property. Climbing over a fence to use a neighbor's swimming pool without permission is a trespass, while having a noisy swimming party at 3:00 a.m. in your own pool might constitute a nuisance against your neighbor.

Despite the connotations, trespasses are not always consciously intentional or surreptitious. Having a driveway overlap a property line without formal permission may be a trespass. Today many of the elements of trespass and nuisance are intermingled; the terms are often used interchangeably, and distinctions in the actions and remedy have become "wavering and uncertain."[1]

Since both trespass and nuisance are *torts* or civil wrongs (although there may be criminal liability for intentional harm), they are also dealt with in Chapter 4 on liability. Our focus here is on why these common-law forms are not particularly well suited for dealing with today's major land use and environmental problems, but still may have viability where the conflicts are relatively clear cut and don't involve major economic disruption.

The most important limitation results from the fact that nuisance and trespass suits usually deal with existing conditions and problems rather than anticipating and planning for future needs as intelligent land use planning requires. Related to this is the fact that in common-law actions the court's authority is limited to the parties and disputes before it. Judges are very reluctant to afford remedies that will have significant effects upon aspects of the community not directly involved in the immediate problem.

A good example of this is found in the case of *Boomer v. Atlantic Cement Company*,[2] where the neighboring landowners wanted the court to shut down a cement company that was polluting the air. They argued that the pollution constituted a nuisance. The court agreed that the company was emitting hazardous pollution, that Mr. Boomer and his neighbors had been substantially damaged, and that this was indeed a nuisance. The court did not, however, decide to close the cement plant. Rather, it took into consideration the "large disparity in economic consequences of the nuisance and of the injunction."

Not only was Atlantic Cement a major industry with a forty-million-dollar investment in plant and equipment and three hundred employees, but it was also an important economic factor in the community. Furthermore, if Atlantic was closed, cases might be brought against other companies in similar businesses, turning the Hudson Valley into a severely depressed area. Recognizing the public welfare value of a major industry, the *Boomer* court allowed Atlantic to permanently lower the value of its residential neighbor properties by paying them a mandatory fee. The one-time payment to the plaintiffs was in fact a judicial recognition of a kind of private condemnation procedure.

In delivering the *Boomer* decision, the court emphasized the principle of judicial restraint that holds that it is the responsibility of the legislative branch of government, not of the courts, to promote the general welfare by developing pollution control laws, and it is the responsibility of the administrative branch to enforce these laws in a fair and comprehensive manner.

In contrast to the *Boomer* decision, there are occasions when the economic and social balance will fall in favor of the recreational or residential land users, and they will, in effect, be permitted to require a noxious industry to close down or modify its operations. The foremost example is the case of *Spur Industries Inc. v. Del Webb Development Co.*[3]

A major recreation-retirement community, Sun City, located some distance from Phoenix, was developed on relatively cheap ranch land. At least to some degree, the low price for the land reflected the presence of an adjacent cattle feedlot that produced a million pounds of manure a day. (We will refrain from commenting on the ethics of establishing a vacation and retirement community in such an area.) Despite the fact that the feedlot was a legitimate use in what had been a desolate area, the time came when the courts had to take some action to protect the health and investments of the thousands of Sun City residents. Nevertheless, why should the developer get the benefit of a judicial decision that would enhance the value of several hundred otherwise unsalable lots?

The court solved this dilemma by requiring Del Webb to pay damages or "buy out" the feedlot operation so that it could move to a new location. This type of judicial solution may have some viability in conflicts over polluting industries and other societally useful but damaging enterprises. (The complexities of these and other environmental issues are considered further in Chapter 3.)

The *Spur* court recognized that the common-law concepts of trespass and nuisance have limited value in terms of their ability to deal with current land use problems. On the other hand, a New York court relied exclusively on the nuisance doctrine to enjoin commercial recreation entrepreneurs when they proposed a springtime open-air rock music festival at a ski resort. The court found that the festival, if conducted, would "interfere substantially with the rights of the general public in the vicinity, and would obstruct the exercise of rights common to all . . . ."[4]

A third common-law concept with potentially significant applicability to parks and leisure service professionals is the *public trust doctrine.* A trust is a right of property, real or personal, held and administered by the trustee(s) for the benefit of a third party. In our field, the public trust doctrine essentially recognizes that the government holds and administers the parks and other natural resources for the proper use and enjoyment of the citizens.

Historically, the public trust doctrine developed along the tidal waterways in England, where the Crown held the shoreline (as well as the submerged land) for the use and benefit of all.

In *Neptune City v. Avon-By-The-Sea,*[5] the New Jersey Supreme Court utilized the public trust doctrine to decide a parks and recreation case. In 1970 Avon amended its beach user fee ordinance to require higher fees from nonresidents than from residents. Justice Hall, writing the majority opinion, mentioned two important aspects of the public trust doctrine: the extent to which a legislature could alienate or sell trust lands to private parties and the idea of public accessibility to and use of such lands for recreation. "Both," he writes, "are of prime importance in this day and age." While this particular case did not involve improper alienation, he cautioned that such conveyances must be consistent with the public rights and public good.

With regard to the question presented in the case—nonresident fees and charges—Justice Hall writes:

> [A] modern court must take the view that the public trust doctrine dictates that the beach and ocean waters must be open to all on equal terms and without preference and that any contrary state or municipal action is impermissible.[6]

New Jersey courts have since carved out an exception when local tax money is involved in maintaining facilities such as a pool or bath house, but Wisconsin courts have applied the public trust doctrine to all waters in the state.[7] The Oregon Supreme Court found a public right to the use of ocean beaches in custom, holding that long-standing beach and ocean recreational activities vested a continuing right in the public.[8]

Another common law control on land use involves a concept called *waste.* A lawsuit predicated on waste customarily involves two people, or two groups of people, who possess interests in the same piece of land. This could mean landlords and tenants, mortgagors and mortgagees, or in the case of public parks, beneficiaries and trustees. The allegation of waste occurs when the party in possession commits certain acts upon the land that are harmful to the rights of the party not in possession. These acts can be either voluntary (unreasonably destroying something which diminishes the value of the nonpossessor's interest, such as clear-cutting of timber) or permissive (such as failure to utilize good husbandry techniques in caring for the property).

The party bringing the lawsuit will seek either monetary damages or injunctive relief, or a combination of the two. The damages would be based on the amount by which the acts of the possessor have diminished the value of the property. Injunctive relief simply means that the court would order the person or agency to stop doing whatever acts of waste are being committed. In some instances it may be possible to get a restraint order if acts of waste are threatened which would seriously damage the plaintiff's interest.

The final common-law principle relating to land use controls has to do with *strict liability for abnormally dangerous activities.* The most important decision is an English case, *Rylands v. Fletcher.*[9] This mid-nineteenth century action involved the escape of water from a mill dam pond or reservoir into the subterranean shafts of an adjacent coal mine. It was acknowledged that the mill owners were not at fault; nevertheless, probably influenced by the suspicion harbored by the landed gentry toward the new industrial enterprises dotting the countryside, the English courts held the mill strictly liable. There were two significant opinions. The first was rendered by Justice Blackburn in the Exchequer Chamber, who wrote:

> We think that the true rule of law is that the person who for his own purposes brings on his land and collects and keeps there anything likely to do mischief if it escapes, must keep it at his peril, and if he does not do so, is prima facie answerable for all the damage which is the natural consequence of its escape.[10]

On appeal in the House of Lords, Lord Cairns took a somewhat less sweeping view, condemning the mill owners' reservoir as a "non-natural use" of the land as distinguished from activity "for which it might in the ordinary course of the enjoyment of the land be used."[11]

Although most American courts initially rejected the *Rylands v. Fletcher* doctrine, they were in fact reacting to Justice Blackburn's sweeping condemnation. Later, Lord Cairns' views concerning "natural" versus nonnatural uses were found more compatible with developing American industry.

While *Rylands v. Fletcher* would seem to put a potent tool in the hands of the conservationists with the language "non-natural use of land," this is not always the case. For example, in a Texas case the courts refused to impose strict liability for escape of salt water into the drinking water supply from ponds constructed for use with oil well drilling. The rationale used was one of balancing economic interests; as the court put it, "producing oil is one of our major industries."[12] There have been similar results in Delaware with chemicals.

## POTENTIAL OF COMMON-LAW TECHNIQUES FOR LAND USE CONTROL

Obviously a number of problems in the parks and leisure services field could be approached through the use of these common-law land use remedies, particularly where no major economic or social dislocations are at stake. In some instances considerable legal imaginative boldness would have to be shown both by litigants and the judiciary. For example, why couldn't the public trust doctrine and the waste doctrine be combined by conservation groups to argue that federal or state land management practices destructive of the public's permanent interests should be enjoined? Such a concept could be applied to overuse of fragile river ecosystems by commercial raft and boat companies or to destruction of the grizzly bear population in national parks and forests.

In *Neptune City v. Avon-By-The-Sea* the court addressed the extension of common-law actions for modern problems:

> In this latter half of the twentieth century, the public rights . . . are not limited to the ancient prerogatives . . . but extend as well to recreational uses. . . . The public trust doctrine, like all common law principles, should not be considered fixed or static, but should be molded and extended to meet changing conditions and needs of the public it was created to benefit.[13]

Although many such common-law actions are still largely theoretical, the nuisance doctrine is a very practical way to deal with local conflicts over land use for recreational purposes. Where residential and commercial interests conflict with recreation and leisure, judicial wisdom may often prove more sophisticated and subtle in reaching an appropriate solution than the heavy hand of legislation or regulation. For example, consider the common problem of conflict between residential neighbors of a park who value it for open space and scenic beauty and park users who desire extensive recreational programming both in the day and evening. The variables in each situation, such as the character of the neighborhood, the availability of alternatives, the degree of disturbance, parking, and so on, are so extensive that a general rule such as "All ball fields in the park district shall be lighted and available for league play until 9:00 p.m." may prove overly restrictive in some areas and unfair to the neighbors in others.

In *Kasala v. Kalispell Pee Wee Baseball League*,[14] for example, Justice Harrison of the Montana Supreme Court stated:

> The development of parks and playgrounds equipped for the enjoyment of the working public, whose recreation is necessarily taken after working hours, and frequently after dark, is a significant phenomenon in

thousands of urban communities. The court takes judicial knowledge that many lighted parks and fields are located adjacent to residential property and must to some extent interfere with the full enjoyment of darkness (if desired), by the residents.[15]

After setting forth this principle, the court went on to painstakingly evaluate the conflicting interests and the degree of disturbance. The court found that "it was possible to have eliminated the objectionable features" without closing down the ball field, and concluded with the inelegant but appropriate poem:

Oh, somewhere in this favored land
dark clouds may hide the sun.
And somewhere bands no longer play
and children have no fun.
And somewhere over blighted lives
there hangs a heavy pall.
But in Kalispell, hearts are happy now,
for the Pee Wee's can play ball.[16]

It is hard to imagine some anonymous bureaucrat so aptly concluding a controversy.

## GOVERNMENT AND LAND USE

The basic source of authority for the elected officials to govern and regulate land use is the police power. As noted in Chapter 1, this is the authority to regulate for the health, safety, morals, and general welfare of the community. There are a number of ways in which government can use the police power to affect land use. Some are more restrictive than others. We look at a variety of these techniques in this section.

### Fee Simple Acquisition

One of the ways for government to create and control parkland is through an outright purchase. Interests in land may be thought of as a bundle of sticks—that is, a group of rights tied together by a geographic boundary. Property rights include air rights, mineral rights, water rights, development rights, and so forth. Purchase of the whole bundle is called *fee simple absolute*, because, subject to government restrictions, the owner enjoys complete control of all aspects of the property, including the right to sell it or any part of it and to bequeath it to whomever she chooses. The term *fee* has its origins in feudalism and is derived from the ancient term *fief,* which was an estate granted by a feudal lord. Obviously, today the owner of a fee simple no longer has to perform services for a superior lord or nobleman, but it might be argued that taxes paid on land to the government are a modern version of those customs.

There are occasions when the person who owns the property does not wish to sell it. When this happens the government has, as a prime attribute of sovereignty, the power to command its transfer through *eminent domain.* Prior to the Magna Charta in 1215, the sovereign had unlimited power to take any property he chose. The Magna Charta put a limitation on this power by requiring due process of law before the land could be condemned. The United States Constitution further limited this power in the Fifth Amendment, as applied to the states through the Fourteenth Amendment, which prohibits the taking of private property for public use without just compensation.

The principles that fair value must be paid for the taking of private lands and that property may be condemned only when there is a clear "public use" are strong testaments to the value that the founding fathers placed on the sanctity of private property rights.

Obviously there will be at least two issues regarding the property taken through the power of eminent domain. First, what constitutes "public use"; second, what is "just compensation"?

It is sufficient for our purposes to state that the taking through eminent domain of real property for parks is clearly a public use; the Supreme Court has upheld a variety of instances when land has been condemned in order to create parks. Even when government assembled real property in order to lease or sell it to private developers as part of an urban redevelopment plan, the Supreme Court, in *Berman v. Parker,* upheld condemnation as a legitimate exercise of the police power. In that case the court stated:

> The concept of the public welfare is broad and inclusive. The values it represents are spiritual as well as physical, aesthetic as well as monetary. It is within the power of the legislature to determine that the community should be beautiful as well as healthy, spacious as well as clean, well-balanced as well as carefully patrolled.[17]

This broad view of public use—whatever tends to enlarge the resources and generally contribute to public welfare—is the approach most often adopted by the courts.

The measure of compensation when a person's land is taken is the fair market value of the property at the time of the condemnation. The fair market value is the amount that a property would reasonably be worth on the market in a cash sale to a willing buyer, under no obligation to buy, if offered for sale by a prudent willing seller who is under no obligation to sell. Implied in this "willing buyer-willing seller" formula is that the price will be what a buyer would pay for the highest and best use of the land. If, for example, the highest (or most lucrative) use of the land is for high-rise condominiums, and the land is zoned for the condominiums, then that is probably the price the buyer must pay even though the present use may be unimproved open space. The evaluation to establish the fair market value will not consider the use to which the government will put the land.

How does a local park commission determine the fair market value? Generally through a professional appraiser. Although appraisers consider many elements in determining the fair market value, the approach most often used is that of comparable sales. That is, they look at the prices paid for similar land in the same general area which was sold voluntarily. The appraiser takes into account any inflationary trends and allows for any discrepancies in the characteristics of the land itself.

Warren Kershow, in his monograph *Land Acquisition*,[18] points out that appraisers have different "emphasis areas, abilities, general slants, and prejudices" and that it is critical to choose those who are adept at handling the type of land which is in question. Furthermore, because appraisals are often rough estimates, particularly in undeveloped areas, and rely on instinct and guesswork as much as science, it should be standard practice to use at least two appraisers on a case. The difference between their appraisals will give the agency a feel for the range in which it should negotiate.

If the situation is one in which the governmental agency is exercising its power of eminent domain and has condemned the property, the landowners may go into court to say that more property is being condemned than is necessary for the public use, or that the compensation offered is inadequate. At this point it is extremely important to have a professional appraiser who is prepared to defend her findings in court. Whether required by laws or not, wisdom always dictates that governmental authorities should make an effort to purchase through negotiation prior to or concurrent with condemnation proceedings.

Plainly, there are times when the need for park property is so pressing that there is no substitute for the purchase or condemnation of property. A full-service park with varied recreational facilities demands nothing less than full ownership or a very long-term lease.[19] Very often, however, public needs may be satisfied by something less than complete or fee simple ownership of property. Furthermore, there are a number of legally permissible strategies for obtaining governmental interests in land or securing the aid of private agencies and individuals in creating parks and recreational opportunities that do not necessitate the outlay of large amounts of the taxpayer's cash. We shall explore some of these methods. Although many may seem novel or questionable, the value of real property in an ever-shrinking world will, in the long run, increase in almost geometric progression. If there are to be new parks in the future, both in urban areas as well as in vanishing wilderness settings, imaginative methods of land preservation must be utilized. If we refer back to the "bundle of sticks" analogy, these innovative techniques require the purchase of only some of the sticks, not the entire bundle.

## Easements

By acquiring only certain rights pertaining to the use of the land, either private conservation organizations or governmental agencies may still achieve their goal of preserving open space. This acquisition of some of the rights is called an easement. An easement is an interest in the land of another person that is created by the transfer of some attributes of the property. In the past, most easements were "affirmative" and granted certain rights to one party upon the land of another party. For example, a utility company might purchase an easement to run power lines across the landowner's property. More recently, there has been a movement to use easements for the preservation of open space and the protection of natural resources and scenic views. These easements are generally "negative" in that they prevent the landowner from doing something on his or her own land.

Two attorneys employed by the former Heritage Conservation and Recreation Service, Timothy Fox and Glenn Tiedt, were instrumental in communicating the value of conservation easements as a land use tool for parks and leisure service professionals.[20] In explaining the nature of conservation easements Mr. Fox says:

> In effect, the landowner transfers certain development rights for the purpose of preventing future development of the property. The easement owner may prevent the uses specified in the easement, but generally he, himself, may not engage in any activities on the property.[21]

Typical conservation easements might prohibit any type of construction, alterations of the vegetation or topography, any nonnatural substance like toxic sprays or billboards, or in the case of historic conservation easements, any change in the exterior of the building. Each restriction will be specifically developed to the purposes or interests of the agency purchasing the easement and the needs of the landowner.

The price that the purchasing agency will have to pay for the easement is directly related to the magnitude of the restrictions the easement will place on the landowner. If a restriction is not burdensome, as for example, the right to use a preexisting private pathway to gain access to a fishing area, the price will be lower than if the rights surrendered by the landowner are substantial, such as an easement that prohibits all cutting of timber or creation of subdivisions.

Because the rights and restrictions included in an easement vary so widely, the value of an easement will also vary. The rule that has been adopted by the Internal Revenue Service to determine the value of a conservation easement is the difference between the fair market value of the property before the restrictions and the fair market value of the property with the restrictions.[22]

Easements are said to "run with the land," which means that, while they do not restrict the right of the landowner to sell the property, they *do* continue to restrict the use of the property when a new landowner acquires the underlying fee simple. While easements are generally in perpetuity, there can be "term" easements that run for a predetermined number of years.

Frequently a conservation easement is a way for the landowner to perpetuate his or her own present interest in preserving the property. If a family has always allowed the public to fish along a stream, then they can continue this practice and gain attractive tax benefits by donating a conservation easement along the stream to a public agency or an appropriate charitable organization (such as the Nature Conservancy, the Trust for Public Lands, or a local landholding organization). Federal tax laws provide that where easements are donated in perpetuity, deductions of the fair market value may be made from adjusted gross income (subject to certain technical qualifications) for income tax purposes. Furthermore, under the Tax Reform Act of 1969, gifts of easements in real estate for conservation purposes may not be subject to federal gift taxes.[23] Beyond this, the value of property may be substantially decreased for purposes of property and estate taxes by the granting of a conservation easement. Consider an historic family farm being encroached upon by suburban sprawl. By donating a conservation easement in the land, the donor may be able to preserve the property for future generations by eliminating that portion of estate taxes based on the developmental value of the property. Of course tax laws are extremely complex and subject to rapid change, and recent modifications have eliminated federal inheritance taxes for estates with substantial value; nevertheless the park planner must be aware of possible tax advantages and be able to work with park attorneys in presenting and perfecting the opportunities to acquire valuable property rights at a minimal cost.

### Zoning and Regulation

Often the funds for the purchase of even an easement may not be available. A developing community has many competing demands on its budget. There may be a strong temptation for government officials to try to have their needs for parks and open space met without substantial cost. One of the ways to do this is through zoning requirements.

**Constitutional Background.** Historically there has been a clash between the need for regulation under the police power and the requirement of payment or compensation for a "taking" under the Fifth Amendment (or the Fourteenth Amendment when the regulation is by the states). Despite the old cliches "A man's home is his castle" and "I can do what I want with my own property" it is obvious that many restrictions are necessary to protect the public interest. Fire codes, maximum occupancy rules, and limitations on obnoxious usages are all readily accepted restrictions on property use; it is easy to understand the relationship between these restrictions and public health and safety.

On the other hand, there may come a point at which the restrictions are so severe that the property owner is left with little or no economic value to his property. Thus, in a famous case arising in the Pennsylvania coal country, *Pennsylvania Coal Co. v. Mahon*,[24] Justice Oliver Wendell Holmes railed against what he considered "the petty larceny of the police power." In that case the state had passed a law prohibiting coal mining where subsidence would cause damage to dwellings and buildings on the surface. The coal company argued that the mining rights that it had retained when it sold the surface rights had no value under the statute. The Court agreed and held that this state regulation went so far as to amount to a "taking."

A more modern case illustrating the point is *United States v. Causby*,[25] where the army built an airport immediately next to Causby's chicken farm. The planes flew directly overhead at a height of eighty-three feet, forcing the chicken business to be discontinued. The Court held that the frequent low flights had, in effect, created an easement in the property and the government would have to compensate for this "taking." Despite these instances, the vast majority of cases involving governmental restriction on land use have been upheld as being legitimate regulations, not requiring compensation through condemnation proceedings.

The historic case in which comprehensive zoning was first approved by the Supreme Court was *Euclid v. Ambler Realty Co.*[26] The village of Euclid had adopted a typical zoning ordinance regulating the location of businesses, industries, and different kinds of housing units as well as restricting building sizes and requiring minimum lot sizes. The Court held that although the ordinance would severely limit the uses of a property by its owner, there was substantial governmental interest under the police power in separating incompatible land uses and protecting the public health and welfare. Furthermore, the economic value of property was not totally destroyed, and the government did not impose some public use on the property. Since *Euclid*, the Court has consistently upheld zoning requirements, including one that restricted a residential zone to "traditional" family units, *Village of Belle Terre v. Borass*,[27] and another that essentially prohibited continuance of a quarry operation by restricting all excavations below the waterline. In this case, *Goldblatt v. Town of Hempstead*,[28] the Court found that, although the quarry had been in existence for thirty years, the changed conditions caused by the town growing up around the quarry justified the restrictions even though the quarry owner suffered a major loss. Prohibition was the only way to achieve the legitimate safety and welfare purposes.

The only exceptions to the Supreme Court's general approval of zoning restrictions have been when some fundamental right is being substantially eroded or if there are racial or other discriminating restrictions. Thus, in *Moore v. City of East Cleveland*,[29] an ordinance that would not permit blood relatives who were not in the immediate family to live together in a one-family dwelling was held unconstitutional. It would have separated a grandmother from her grandson.

The obvious question that arises is whether zoning and related regulations can be utilized to achieve some of the goals of parks and recreation professionals. The answer is a qualified yes.

**Zoning to Preserve Open Space.**    Land use planners have criticized the traditional form of rigid "Euclidian" zoning that has shaped most of our cities. The resulting gridlike layout of streets and homes does not encourage open space for leisure pursuits. One alternative is a form of planning called "cluster zoning." This permits residential uses to be grouped together, leaving substantial areas to be devoted to open space, parks, bike paths, and wooded areas for the common use and enjoyment of the residents. The population density of the area remains the same, and there are advantages for both the developer and the homeowners.

A major recent innovation is *planned unit developments* (called PUDs). PUDs are broader in scope than cluster zoning, frequently involve more acreage, and include mixed uses of the land. For example, there may be commercial enclaves, mixed single and multifamily housing, and possibly even light industry. The idea is that all of these uses should blend harmoniously since the entire unit was planned at one time to maintain both property and aesthetic values. Parks and recreation facilities are almost always an integral part of PUDs.

A more common approach to open space preservation uses the zoning ordinance to designate the land as being available for only low-density uses such as large-lot single-family homes, agriculture, or recreation. While the courts are generally supportive of communities that are trying to plan their development, they will not uphold plans that, through large lot zoning, tend to "lock up" the communities and keep out the less affluent. One such plan severely restricted the growth of a municipality within a major developing area within commuting distance of Philadelphia. It was rejected by the New Jersey Supreme Court because of the failure of municipal officials to consider the housing needs of the entire region and the discriminatory effect which the plan would have on people with low or moderate incomes.[30] On the other hand, in *Golden v. Planning Board of Ramapo*,[31] a New York community passed an ordinance that limited and slowed growth by utilizing such criteria as the availability of five essential services (including "improved parks or recreation facilities") to determine whether or not to issue subdivision permits. This plan was upheld as a legitimate land use planning tool.

In a controversial decision the Supreme Court has supported the view that under certain conditions, zoning requirements to preserve historic landmarks may be permitted without requiring government compensation. In *Penn Central Transp. Co. v. New York City*[32] the court held that the City Landmarks Preservation Commission could deny a request to build a multistory office building on top of the "Beaux Arts" Grand Central terminal, which would have impaired its historic architectural quality. The court pointed out that the terminal still retained value as a railroad station. Furthermore, the city law permitted transfer of the air development rights to other properties. On balance, the restrictions were not so severe as to amount to a taking.

The *transfer of development rights* is one of a series of newly emerging zoning and land development strategies useful not only for preservation of historic sites, but also for preservation of farm land and open space. How does the scheme work?

A zoning plan in a developing area would specify which areas could be subjected to intensive development and which would be required to be preserved as farmland or open space. To simply tell a property owner that his land must remain completely undeveloped would obviously be unfair and could amount to a taking. But suppose someone in the development zone wants to construct a high-density townhouse development. By forcing such a developer to pay for the development rights by purchasing them from the open space or farm owner, the latter is being compensated, and an open space easement is effectively created. Using such a scheme, land less suitable for high-intensity development could be preserved for open space or agricultural use, while at the same time officials could meet concerns that land use restrictions requiring large maximum lots would effectively squeeze out the middle class, the poor, and minorities from developing communities. Development rights could also be "banked" by a community to be sold when pressures for development make them valuable. That is, they could be purchased when land was still inexpensive and sold at higher prices later, generating revenue for the community.

**Subdivision Controls.**   When a landowner decides to divide his property, or to sell portions of it as building lots, he generally must get subdivision approval from the local officials. The landowner/developer prepares a plat map indicating his intentions, and submits it to the local planning or zoning board for approval. As one condition for granting this approval, the governmental body may require the developer to dedicate portions of his property for streets, sewers, and utility facilities. These dedications, called *exactions,* are seldom controversial since such facilities are necessary to sell the lots, and by giving them to the municipality the developer can avoid the cost of maintenance.

   Many states have passed the necessary enabling statutes to allow municipalities to require the developer to donate a certain portion of the total development area for park purposes. This technique of open space acquisition is called *mandatory dedication.* Frequently if there is no area suitable for park development, if the area to be dedicated is too small to be a useful park, or if there is already an abundance of parks in the surrounding neighborhood, the municipality may require the developer to pay a certain amount of money per unit or acre in lieu of the donation of land.

   In *Krughoff v. City of Naperville,*[33] the Illinois Supreme Court upheld the mandatory exaction under the police power only when the exactment is "specifically and uniquely attributable" to the needs generated by the subdivision. In other words, park or school dedications could only be required for the purposes of meeting the additional burden generated by the new development or it would be considered a "taking" and would require compensation.

On the other hand, a number of courts have upheld exactions that were "reasonably related" to a subdivision even if the new park would benefit the population at large. In the leading case, *Associated Home Builders of Greater East Bay, Inc. v. City of Walnut Creek*,[34] the California Supreme Court said:

We see no persuasive reason in the face of these urgent needs caused by present and anticipated future population growth on the one hand and the disappearance of open land on the other to hold that a statute requiring the dedication of land by a subdivider may be justified only upon the ground that the particular subdivider upon whom an exaction has been imposed will, solely by the development of his subdivision, increase the need for recreational facilities to such an extent that additional land for such facilities will be required.[35]

When the association of developers argued that only those exactions directly related to the health and safety of the subdivision residents should be imposed, the court responded that recreation *is* directly related to these salutary purposes and is not merely a frill. To the claim that the dedication requirements would cause the price of the individual lots to be higher, and would therefore exclude low-income families from the community, the court responded:

The desirability of encouraging subdividers to build low-cost housing cannot be denied and unreasonable exactions could defeat this object, but these considerations must be balanced against the phenomenon of the appallingly rapid disappearance of open areas in and around our cities.[36]

It is important to note that Walnut Creek had a detailed set of principles and standards regarding the amount of parkland required for the city's population and for different types of parks and the various facilities which each type of park should contain. These standards were incorporated into the city's general plan and no doubt were significant in the determination of the outcome of the case.

After the initial dispute regarding the constitutionality of mandatory dedication, arguments generally revolve around the amount of land or money involved. How much is too much? A Montana court upheld an exaction of one-ninth of a subdivision for park purposes.[37] Typical ordinances require something on the order of an acre of land per fifty dwelling units, or ten acres per thousand residents, or 5 percent of the total land.[38] Financial alternatives may be in the range of 5 percent of the value of the development or a specific dollar amount per lot. A municipality can go too far. In *East Neck Estates Ltd. v. Luchinger*[39] the municipality required the waterfront area of a development to be dedicated. This amounted to 40 percent of the total value and was held to be confiscatory.

Although there is not a great deal of case law yet, in states with appropriate enabling statutes mandatory dedication provisions are a promising alternative to the purchase or condemnation of property in developing areas.

### Tax Policy

A matter involving tax laws (along with maritime law and other esoteric specialties) is one in which the parks and leisure services professional should immediately consult with an attorney who specializes in the field. Not only are the tax laws complex, with regulations and rulings filling volumes with information on highly technical matters, but just when a person has finally achieved a secure grasp on relevant technicalities, Congress, the IRS, or local agencies invariably seem to change the rules. Therefore, our purpose in this section is merely to acquaint you with situations that may have significant tax implications. Some of these have already been alluded to in our discussion of property acquisition.

**Property Tax.** Property tax has been called the "backbone of local government finance"[40] and is therefore extremely significant in the provision of parks and recreational opportunities. Beyond this, however, the property tax can be viewed as one of the tools available to the state and the political subdivision to assist in the preservation of open space.

Tax assessments, the methods used to determine how much property tax an individual will pay, are based on potential use of the land rather than on actual use. If the local officials have chosen to "down zone" (restricting the use of property to what already exists, such as farming) or zone areas for open space and recreation, then it is unfair for those property owners to continue to be taxed as if their land were suitable for intensive development. One answer for this problem would be a legislative directive to the tax assessor to presume that the current zoning patterns represent a permanent condition and to assess the property at this lower potential.

Another solution is a policy of *tax deferral.* This involves postponing the amount of taxes due in excess of the currently zoned or restricted condition of the land. If the landowner changes the use of the land, or if the regulation is removed, then the deferred taxes become due. The obvious intent is to encourage the preservation of the undeveloped land.

A similar, less drastic, alternative is called *preferential assessment*, which assesses open land at its value for the present use but does not assume that the land is permanently in this condition. When the land ceases to qualify for the preferential assessment because the use has changed, then the regular property tax will be charged. This technique has generally been utilized to encourage farmers to continue to farm their property rather than sell it for nonagricultural uses. It serves to slow the rate of subdivision rather than to ensure permanent reservation of open space.

Another property tax device available in some states is the granting of *tax exemptions* to certain kinds of privately owned space. A New Jersey statute states:

> Any owner of a fresh water lake . . . may propose an agreement . . . by which he shall retain title to the property, but grant to the citizens of this state access to and the free use of the waters of such lake or pond for boating and fishing subject to a reasonable charge to be made for the use of boats belonging to the owner of such lake or pond. If . . . the board shall be satisfied that the public interest will be as well served by the freedom to use the lake or pond for boating or fishing, as it would be if the property were conveyed to the state, the board shall enter into an agreement with the owner of such lake or pond, which agreement shall provide that, in consideration of the free use by the public of the waters of such lake or pond for boating and fishing, the property shall be exempt from taxation so long as the agreement remains in force, the same as it would if the state acquired title thereto.[41]

In this way the property owner could retain title to her land and the state could assure the retention of open space.

Of course one of the most basic ways for a property owner to avoid paying real estate taxes is to donate the property to a qualified recipient. In this instance the donor no longer owns the land and therefore pays no tax. There are additional tax benefits that accompany gifts of land.

**Income Tax.**   There are two kinds of property, real (land and buildings affixed to the land) and personal (all other property). Gifts of property, either real or personal, to governmental bodies or other qualified charitable or nonprofit recipients are deductible for federal income tax purposes and for most state income taxes. In this way the government has encouraged private individuals to donate property. The amount of tax deduction that an individual is entitled to take varies for different types of gifts—cash, securities, or other personal property are treated differently than gifts of real property. Corporations are also allowed to deduct the fair market value of a donation from their before-tax income.

Frequently there are a number of options available for the donor with regard to the method of calculating the deduction. An attorney who is a tax specialist should be consulted to be certain that the donor is receiving all of the tax benefits possible from his or her donation.

The tax laws place limitations on what constitutes a deductible gift. For example, the granting of a perpetual conservation easement to the Trust for Public Lands, a qualifying § 501(c) (3)[42] organization, would be eligible for an exemption, but the same grant to a commercial whitewater rafting company would not. Similarly, a term easement would probably not qualify since it is a limited gift with no permanent benefits.

Gifts of cash are fully deductible up to certain limitations (50 percent of the adjusted gross income for individuals, and up to 5 percent of a corporation's net income), and there are "carryover provisions" that allow for tax deductions in succeeding years for gifts that exceed the maximum allowable deduction in one tax year.

Another aspect of the income tax law that affects parks and leisure services has to do with the special tax rate due on *long-term capital gains.* A long-term capital gain is income from the sale of capital assets that have been held for more than one year. A capital asset could be real estate, securities, or other long-term investments.

In recent years, taxes on such income have been reduced to the point where, currently, the maximum rate is only 20 percent of the profits from the sale of capital assets. Another provision of the law exempts all capital gains from the sale of a residential home up to $125,000 for persons over the age of fifty-five. This provision is coupled with other provisions that permit the payment of capital gains tax on the sale of personal homes to be deferred indefinitely when there is a replacement home of equal or greater cost. Since, for many middle-class Americans, the home is the principal capital asset, the likelihood that they will need to consider the various contribution schemes discussed here in order to avoid excess taxation is limited or eliminated by these changes.

When an individual donates capital gain property to a public agency or a qualifying charitable organization, she may generally take the fair market value of the property as a deduction. The combination of this deduction, reduction of taxable income, and the exemption from having to pay capital gains taxes gives substantial encouragement to wealthy property owners to donate land for public purposes. Often the donor will actually receive so great a tax advantage that he will be in a more advantageous financial position than had he sold or retained the property. The Department of the Interior publication *Land Conservation and Preserva-*

*tion Techniques*[43] gives detailed examples of the tax results from a donation, from the gift of a conservation easement, from a fair market sale, and from a bargain sale where a portion of the value of the property is discounted before purchase by a public agency. The case studies in this publication will assist the practitioner who needs a more thorough understanding of the intricacies of these acquisition alternatives, although it is important to remember that it was published before the 1981 Tax Act and does not reflect significant tax changes. Presumably the publication will be updated.

**Estate Taxes.** Another tax incentive that has encouraged people to donate property for public open space has been the estate tax. Charitable gifts made by bequest, through the donor's will, are deducted from the donor's taxable estate. Until recently, there was an exemption of $175,625 on estates; that is, an estate worth $160,000, for example, was not subject to the estate tax. With the 1981 Tax Act that exemption is gradually being raised to $600,000 by 1987. The effect of this change, when coupled with the new lower tax rates on capital gains and "unearned" income, will probably discourage some potential donors who might have been inclined to give a bargain sale or a donation of land for a park. Families who want to pass along their holdings to their heirs will find it easier. Since the estate tax has been reduced, they will worry less about the children having to sell the property to pay taxes on it. When the heir does decide to sell, the capital gain on the property will be taxed at a reduced rate. On the other hand, those with substantial estates and property will still seek tax relief, and continued inflation will boost many individuals above the maximum exemption levels.

**Effect of Changes in Tax Laws.**   It should be readily apparent to the student that one of the ways for government to influence land use patterns is through revisions of tax policies and laws. Parks and recreation projects in every area of the profession will be affected by the changes in the tax laws that were proposed by President Reagan and approved in August 1981 by Congress.

In the public sector, not only will direct support of new programs not be forthcoming, but drastic reductions in social programs are virtually assured.[44] One researcher has concluded that rather than tolling the death knell for parks and recreation, this period of austerity will encourage local leisure service agencies to implement a variety of innovative fiscal strategies.[45] In spite of the innovations, however, new facility development will probably be retarded. This is due to the fact that the market for tax-exempt bonds, the principal means of funding major governmental expenditures, will quite likely be depressed. This is partly because of the new temporary laws designed to help the banks and savings industry. More importantly, the permanent elimination of distinctions between ordinary employment income and "unearned" interest income when combined with predicted continued high interest rates on federal treasury notes and money-market instruments make the tax-free municipal bonds a less attractive investment instrument. Wealthy investors formerly had to pay up to 70 percent of their interest income in taxes. With a maximum 50 percent rate now, the relatively low interest and other undesirable aspects of tax-free municipal bonds will create substantial difficulties in utilizing them as the dominant funding source for capital improvement for cities.

Voluntary agencies will also feel the effects of the new tax laws. One article reported that private charities stand to lose more than $18 billion during the next four years, "as the tax cuts give wealthy people less incentive to contribute."[46] This loss in donations, when coupled with the federal budget cuts, could amount to a total loss in charitable funding of over $45 billion through 1984. As could be expected, corporations report that they are receiving many more requests for aid than in previous years, which would lead one to expect increased competition for these limited corporate contributions.

It is to be hoped that in the private sector of recreation enterprise, reductions in capital gains and corporate taxes may encourage new development, growth, and investments. That is, of course, a principal justification for the drastic changes in tax law and policy.

## CONCLUSION

In this brief survey of the legal aspects of property and its relationship to parks and leisure services, we have touched upon a rich and varied complex of laws, judicial decisions, and planning strategies. Perhaps more than any other legal subject, the subtleties and technicalities appear overwhelming to the layperson. Although as we stated at the outset, this is partly the result of historic events, in a deeper sense, that history only reflects the unique place that land and the property developments related to it have in our culture.

Obviously, this carries over into parks and leisure services. We are not by nature a contemplative people in the Eastern sense. Not only do we seek active outlets for our energies, which require land, buildings, and other physical facilities and equipment, but many of our more spiritual pleasures are inextricably tied to the physical world—the mountains, lakes, and rivers in which we seek true re-creation. Since law is an inevitable and necessary adjunct to our use and possession of property for all these purposes, the parks professional should make every effort to understand it sufficiently to make it an ally and a useful tool rather than a confusing, frustrating obstacle. Whether the particular concern is explaining to an elderly couple how they can preserve their property for their families while benefiting the public as well, ensuring the legality and freedom from harassing lawsuits of a community group home for retarded adults, or properly evaluating and assembling properties for the creation of a new regional park, the difference between success and failure may depend upon your ability to work as a liaison between lawyers, officials, and the public.

## NOTES

1. W. L. Prosser, *Law of Torts*, 4th ed. (St. Paul: West Publishing Co., 1971), at 594.
2. 26 N.Y.2d 219, 257 N.E.2d 870, 309 N.Y.S. 2d 312 (1970).
3. 108 Ariz. 178, 494 P.2d 700 (1972).
4. *Town of Preble v. Song Mountain, Inc.*, 62 Misc.2d 353, 308 N.Y.S. 2d 1001 (Sup. Ct. 1970).
5. 61 N.J. 296, 294 A.2d 47 (1972).
6. *Id.* at 309. 294 A.2d at 54.
7. *Hixon v. Public Service Commission*, 32 Wis.2d 608, 146 N.W.2d 577 (1966).
8. *State Ex Rel. Thornton v. Hay*, 254 Or. 584, 462 P.2d 671 (1969).
9. L.R. 1 Ex. 265 (1866), aff'd. L.R. 3 H.L. 330 (1868).
10. *Id.*
11. *Id.*
12. *Turner v. Big Lake Oil Co.*, 128 Tex. 155, 166, 96 S.W.2d 221 (1936).
13. 61 N.J. at 309. 294 A.2d at 54 (1972).
14. *Kasala v. Kalispell Pee Wee Baseball League*, 151 Mont. 109, 439 P.2d 65, 32 A.L.R. 3d 1120 (1968).
15. *Id.* at 114-115, 439 P.2d at 68.
16. *Id.* at 116-117, 439 P.2d at 69.
17. 348 U.S. 26 (1954).
18. Arlington, Va: National Recreation and Park Association, Special Publication Series No. 15002 (1975).
19. Sometimes a corporation or other entity has reason to retain actual title to property for tax purposes or future use, but is willing to grant a long-term lease of fifteen, twenty, or even ninety-nine years. Such an extensive lease would make development of substantial capital improvements practical.
20. See Timothy Fox, *Land Conservation and Preservation Techniques* Heritage Conservation and Recreation Service, Department of the Interior, March,

1979; and Glenn F. Tiedt, "Conservation Easements in Colorado," *The Colorado Lawyer,* vol. 5, at 1265 (September 1976).
21. Fox, *Supra* note 20, at 15.
22. Rev. Rul. 76-376.
23. Internal Revenue Code § 2522.
24. 260 U.S. 393 (1922).
25. 328 U.S. 256 (1946).
26. 272 U.S. 365 (1926).
27. 416 U.S. 1 (1974).
28. 369 U.S. 590 (1962).
29. 431 U.S. 494 (1977).
30. *Southern Burlington Cty. N.A.A.C.P. v. Township of Mt. Laurel,* 67 N.J. 151, 336 A.2d 713 (1975).
31. 30 N.Y.S.2d 138, 285 N.E.2d 291 (1972).
32. 438 U.S. 104 (1978).
33. 68 Ill.2d 352, 369 N.E.2d 892 (1977).
34. 4 Cal.3d 633, 94 Cal. Rptr. 630, 484 P.2d 606 (1971), appeal dismissed 404 U.S. 878.
35. *Id.*
36. *Id.*
37. *Billings Properties Inc. v. Yellowstone County,* 144 Mont. 251, 394 P.2d 182 (1964).
38. See J. P. Karp, "Subdivision Exactions for Parks and Open Space," 16 *American Business Law Journal* 277 (1979).
39. 305 N.Y. Supp. 922 (1969).
40. Dennis Howard and John Crompton, *Financing, Managing and Marketing Recreation and Park Resources* (Dubuque: Wm. C. Brown, 1980), at 8.
41. N.J.S.A. 13:8-23.
42. § 501 (c) (3) refers to that section of the Internal Revenue Code which defines charitable organizations.
43. Fox, *supra* note 20.
44. *Newsweek,* August 10, 1981, at 16.
45. Martin P. Schwartz, "An Analysis of Innovative Fiscal Strategies in Local Public Recreation and Park Agencies," unpublished doctoral dissertation, Temple University, 1981.
46. *The Philadelphia Inquirer,* August 28, 1981, at 1.

# 3

# Environmental, Natural Resources, and Public Lands Law

## OVERVIEW

Much of this chapter is devoted to a discussion of the complex statutory, administrative, and judicial doctrines and practices that govern the recreational uses of federal lands and natural resources. Although we do not specifically discuss state laws, there are state and local equivalents to at least some of the statutory and administrative schemes detailed here. We should further note that consideration of the federal system for recreational land use is, of necessity, selective and illustrative rather than comprehensive. Students seeking greater detail should consult the outstanding book in the field of public land law, *Federal Public Land and Resources Law*, by George Cameron Coggins and Charles F. Wilkinson (Foundation Press, 1981).

The connection between such federal land use as national parks, wildlife preserves, national forests, hiking and horse trails, and wild and scenic rivers and the interests of the professional in parks and recreation is clear and direct. On the other hand, it might be argued that environmental law is no more closely related to parks and leisure services than it is to, say, industrial development or residential land use.

In one sense, that is true. Society has a ubiquitous interest in breathable air, potable water, and poison-free land. In another sense, however, the particular impact of environmental pollutants upon parks and recreation is so dramatic and indisputable that recreational opportunity and environmental protection may be viewed as interdependent concerns. Consider these increasingly common phenomena: beaches are closed at the height of summer heat and tension because of the polluting effects of sewage dumped untreated into the sea; magnificent vistas in isolated national parks are obscured to the point of near invisibility because of the persistence of smog generated by automobiles or power plants; a fisherman reels in an empty line in frustration because the placid waters of a wilderness lake in Ontario are as acidic and barren of fish as a huge pitcher of grandma's lemonade. One need not even look to outlying parks for examples. In a number of urban centers, particularly in Southern California, there are several days each year when children are not permitted to go out of school at recess to play jump-rope or tag because an air inversion has turned the sky brown and threatened hearts and lungs with oxygen insufficiency.

Because we believe it is imperative that everyone in the parks and leisure services profession have a basic understanding of environmental laws both as members of an affected field and simply as human beings concerned with life and breath, a brief review of major developments is included in the latter part of this chapter. One statute, however, is so significant in the consideration of any federally related natural resources development program that it must be described before proceeding. That is the *National Environmental Policy Act of 1969 (NEPA)*.[1] Not only is NEPA the basic expression of congressional concern for the environment, it is also a good example of the way in which modern legislation sets forth broad principles and general guidelines, leaving specific detailed regulation and interpretation to administrative agencies with some judicial supervision.

Although some of the environmental and natural resources statutes are much more detailed and specific than NEPA, all depend upon good-faith enforcement by administrators in the executive branch of government. Some depend equally upon cooperation by state governments. Because of the technical and complex nature of these laws, their enforcement is not a simple matter of police action or voluntary compliance. Rather, effective enforcement requires substantial numbers of dedicated highly trained personnel and continued adequate funding. Thus, regardless of the merits of the laws, cutbacks in appropriation or lack of administrative enthusiasm may cripple enforcement and make a mockery of the idealistic purposes set forth in the statutory language.

## NEPA AND ENVIRONMENTAL ADMINISTRATION

The philosophy of NEPA is set forth in Title I of the act.[2]

It is the . . . continuing policy of the Federal Government . . . to use all possible means and measures . . . . to create and maintain conditions under which man and nature can exist in productive harmony, and fulfill the social, economic and other requirements of present and future generations of Americans.

Lest the philosophy be too utilitarian, the statute also acknowledges that each generation has a responsibility, "as trustee of the environment for succeeding generations," that there should be protection of "safe, healthful, productive, and esthetically and culturally pleasing surroundings" and that "important historical, cultural and natural aspects of our national heritage" should be preserved.[3]

Certainly, these goals and objectives are in complete harmony with many of the principles of the parks and leisure services movement. How are they implemented by NEPA?

Although the act mandates a number of actions, by far the most significant and controversial is the requirement of § 102(2) (c) that "in every recommendation or report on proposals for legislation and other major Federal actions significantly affecting the quality of the human environment"[4] there be included a detailed statement concerning *"the environmental impact of the proposed action."* (emphasis added).

## Environmental Impact Statements

Environmental impact statements (EIS's) are to be widely circulated to interested agencies and individuals and must accompany projects and proposals through all review processes.

In addition to the federally mandated EIS's, a number of states have similar requirements under statutes modeled upon the Michigan Environmental Protection Act of 1970.[5] These are known as "SEPAs" or "little NEPAs." Local park agencies and municipalities may also enact requirements for some environmental assessments before licensing the use of their lands and waters for such intrusions as runoffs, increased traffic, and so on, stemming from actions of private developers.[6]

To ensure compliance with both the letter and spirit of NEPA, Title II created the *Council on Environmental Quality* (CEQ). The council prepares a massive annual report to the president and the people covering all aspects of the environment. It also serves along with the National Academy of Sciences and the Office of Technology Assessment as an advisor to Congress and the government on the effects of technology on the environment and in a general supervisory and consulting role.

Under the Environmental Quality Improvement Act of 1970,[7] the CEQ assists all federal departments and agencies in developing and coordinating environmental quality criteria and standards. Under federal executive order,[8] it is given the important task of issuing guidelines for the preparation of EIS's.

The requirements and purposes of EIS's are widely misunderstood.

In fact, the EIS is the butt of many jokes about governmental red tape and inefficiency. Despite all that, the EIS is a most significant tool in the struggle for environmental protection.

Much of the disdain for EIS's results from confusion over their form, their size, and their role in the development of programs. Initially, Congress viewed the EIS as an informational tool, a means of collecting pertinent environmental data that would assist planners to reach the most environmentally sound decision. Unfortunately, some governmental agencies now see the EIS as an annoying impediment to the fulfillment of their primary missions. This is probably inevitable since, on the whole, environmental protection is more likely to be served by a passive or protectionist attitude, which conflicts with well-documented bureaucratic tendencies to expand power and importance through increased development.

Adding to the dilemma, a few environmental groups have used the EIS requirement as a basis for drawn-out administrative and judicial challenges. Their questions concerning the adequacy of the information gathered or the procedures followed have sometimes caused projects to be abandoned or modified because of the time and cost of the legal confrontation rather than on substantive grounds.

The abandonment of a project because it did not meet procedural requirements—those specifics regarding public hearings, the elements which must be included in the EIS, and so on—seems unfair because the substantive merits of the project, those considerations that go to the heart of whether or not the project should be developed, are not given full consideration. Furthermore, these attempts to reach environmental goals through NEPA's procedural requirements tend to short-circuit our governmental processes. Environmental activists respond that they do seek specific legislation to protect environmental values, but legislative proposals to protect environmental values and limit development are met with intensive opposition from powerful lobbies representing both industry and labor. The environmentalists argue that NEPA is the major tool they have, even if it is not entirely substantive.

While the frustration of the environmentalists is understandable, the protracted litigation has at times resulted in decisions that are not based upon an objective evaluation of the relevant environmental and substantive merits of a proposal. It is clear that even if some ill-conceived projects are eliminated by these delaying tactics, in the long run this is a counterproductive strategy which may lead to "environmental backlash" or antienvironmentalist sentiment. Just as the recreation movement seeks a balanced life-style, so must the environmental movement recognize the need for cooperation and mediation so that ultimately environmental factors will not merely be grudgingly accepted but enthusiastically pursued as a positive cost-effective element in all major planning.

A number of agencies have become involved in mediating environmental conflicts.[9] These include the Office of Environmental Mediation of the Institute of Environmental Studies at the University of Washington, the Environmental Mediation Project at the Wisconsin Center for Public Policy in Madison, and Environmental Mediation International in Washington, D.C. Such organizations may often be effective in closing the gap between seemingly irreconcilable development and conservative positions.

Recently, the CEQ has attempted to simplify and clarify the entire EIS process.[10] If applied in good faith, these procedures should at least provide information for sound decision making. As a preliminary step, an agency considering or proposing an action must determine whether it is "major," thus requiring an EIS. Those proposals not instantly recognizable and being either "major" or at the other extreme having "no significant environmental impact" will necessitate an "environmental assessment" that will gather and analyze sufficient information to determine whether a full-fledged EIS should be required.

Once an EIS requirement is found by the "lead" agency,[11] the public and interested agencies are informed and the "scoping" process begins.[12] This process determines not only the scope of the issues to be addressed but also which agencies are to participate in the gathering of information and the preparation of the EIS. Frequently parks and recreation agencies play an important role at this stage.

Following completion and circulation of a draft EIS, agency and public comments are assessed and, where warranted, the final EIS is modified. In any event, all substantive comments are appended to the EIS whether or not included in the final statement.[13] If there are important changes in a proposed action, or if there are new circumstances and significant new information, the EIS must be supplemented right up to the project's completion.

A final determination on a project must include a record of considerations specifying *all alternatives that were environmentally preferable* and must explain and justify failure to use all practicable means of minimizing environmental harm.[14]

Although formerly some EIS's were so lengthy as to be virtually unreadable, the new regulations limit final texts to 150 pages (plus supplements) or, in case of "unusual scope or complexity," up to 300 pages.[15] The regulations note that the EIS is to be "analytic, not encyclopedic."

Having outlined the procedures in the development of the EIS, 'we shall selectively consider some of the aspects of NEPA and the EIS that have raised the most serious interpretive problems.

## Judicial Interpretation of NEPA

The requirement that an EIS be prepared for any *"major Federal action significantly affecting the quality of the human environment"*[16] has generated controversy over virtually every substantive word.

Some kinds of actions have been exempted from EIS requirements. Among these are general revenue sharing, judicial or administrative law enforcement,[17] and requests for legislative appropriations.[18] EIS's are required for most projects that are potentially subject to federal control or responsibility, that are partially federally funded, or that involve more than minimal federal planning assistance.[19] Even where a state withdrew a highway construction project from federal funding, it was held that federal involvement in the planning of the road was sufficient to render the entire project a federal action requiring an EIS.[20]

This liberal interpretation has been applied to other requirements for EIS preparation. Very few actions have been found too insignificant to be "major." The Second Circuit Court of Appeals suggested two criteria to determine what "significantly" affects the quality of the environment. The first is to consider the extent of adverse environmental effects in excess of what already exists in the area to determine if there is substantial incremental impact. The second criterion is to measure the quantitative adverse effects of the proposed action itself in relation to the total cumulative harm done to the environment.[21]

Examples of limited or "insignificant" developments that did not require an EIS are the construction of 4.3 miles of one-lane gravel road that was to be built in a national forest in which there were already over 700 miles of road in use[22] and the rerouting of three miles of a hiking trail in an Alabama national forest.[23]

Among the "major" federal actions requiring an EIS have been a grizzly bear management program in Yellowstone National Park;[24] a Federal Housing Authority loan for completion of a golf course and park;[25] National Park Service repair and expansion of the towpath along the C. and O. Barge Canal, an historical recreational area near Washington, D.C.;[26] the exchange of 10,200 acres of national forest land for 20,500 acres of land owned by Big Sky of Montana, Inc., preparatory to the construction of a vacation community;[27] and most recently, the widening of a highway through national forest land adjacent to Glacier National Park.[28]

The regulations recognize the difficulty in separating "major" from "significantly affecting" and suggest that both the "context" and "intensity" of a proposed project are to be considered in prescribing environmental remedies.

The regulations further put these rather vague terms in context by suggesting a number of criteria and considerations. Among those most relevant to parks and leisure services are:

> Unique characterists of the geographic area such as the proximity to historic or cultural resources, park lands, . . . wetlands, wild and scenic rivers, or ecologically critical areas . . . .
>
> The degree to which the action may adversely affect . . . [places] listed in the National Register of Historic Places or may cause loss or destruction of significant scientific, cultural, or historical resources . . . .
>
> The degree to which an action may adversely affect an endangered or threatened species or its habitat . . . .[29]

The time frame for preparation of an EIS presents some major conflicts. The process must not be an afterthought used to justify a predetermined project; on the other hand, it has to be fully developed "late enough in the development process to contain meaningful information,"[30] or as the regulations put it, "when an agency . . . has a goal and is actively preparing to make a decision on one or more alternative means of accomplishing that goal and the effects can be meaningfully evaluated."[31]

The Supreme Court has recently taken a rather narrow view of EIS requirements. In one case, the Court rejected a contention that a full EIS was required when a low-income housing project was proposed for a New York City neighborhood. It also held that a lower court was not justified in ruling that the Department of Housing and Urban Development (HUD) had failed to properly consider alternatives. Implying impatience with the use of environmental law for social and cultural purposes, the Court rejected any "contention that an agency . . . must elevate environmental concerns over other appropriate considerations."[32]

More importantly, the Court has upheld agency conclusions rejecting calls for overall or "programmatic" EIS's. In *Kleppe v. Sierra Club,*[33] environmentalists sought to bar further coal mining on federal land in the Northern Great Plains until the Department of the Interior completed an EIS for the region as a whole. The department had issued impact statements covering individual coal leases as well as a nationwide EIS on the environmental effects of coal-leasing policy.

The Sierra Club contended that both EIS's were misleading and violative of the purposes of NEPA. Each coal mine might have only a minimal local impact by itself. On a national scale, the dislocation and pollution caused by the presence of a number of leases in one isolated area might be considered a small price to pay for additional energy. On the other hand, a regional EIS might show that the large number of coalfields and their accompanying power plants would have a devastating effect on the region's environment.

Essentially, the Supreme Court ruled that since there was "no evidence in the record of an action or proposal for an action of regional scope," it should defer to the Interior Department's rejection of a regional EIS.

Although the regulations require a comprehensive EIS if a number of actions are "related to each other closely enough to be, in effect, a single course of action,"[34] the efficacy of such a planning tool remains in doubt. Yet in many instances the piecemeal or step-at-a-time approach will not afford a true picture of the potential for environmental change represented by a proposed action.

Consider, for example, the number of factors that may be related to the proposed development of a single ski area, Ski-Yellowstone, which would partly be on United States Forest Service land near West Yellowstone, Montana.[35] Beyond the obvious removal of trees and placement of trails and ski lifts, a comprehensive EIS would consider such complementary developments as condominium construction at the base area; the increased traffic resulting in pressure for enlarged or new highways; the expansion of regional airports at West Yellowstone and Bozeman, Montana; the need for increased power capacity resulting in extensive disruption of formerly pristine primitive areas so that high voltage transmission lines may be constructed; the increased demand for more strip mining and mine-mouth generating plants to power not only Ski-Yellowstone but also other ski and vacation areas such as Big Sky, Montana, and Jackson Hole, Wyoming, which would presumably also benefit from airport expansion and the creation of a European style ski circus of several interlinked major ski areas. The list could go on and on.

There are other requirements and potential problems related to the drafting of a useful, comprehensive EIS that are dealt with either in CEQ regulations or by the courts. For example, regulations attempt to ensure that the EIS preparation will be supervised by responsible, reasonably objective officials.

Under the current regulations, contractors may have no financial interest in the outcome of the agency's EIS decision making. Furthermore, the agency must actually oversee and set guidelines for the EIS.[36] Presumably this would eliminate the direct conflict of interest allowed by *Life of the Land v. Brinegar*,[37] a circuit court case that permitted an EIS for a construction project to be prepared by the engineering firm that had the actual construction contract.

With regard to the adequacy of the EIS's information and analysis, there is some disagreement concerning the degree of detail and the intensity of critical analysis to be applied both by the agency preparing the EIS and by the reviewing courts. Some courts concerned that an agency would be only superficial or cosmetic in considering the environmental effects of proposed actions have mandated what has come to be known as the "hard look" doctrine, which holds that an intense scrutiny should be given to proposals with a full consideration of less damaging alternatives. Similarly, reviewing courts themselves must cast the same "hard look" at an EIS to ensure full compliance with NEPA's mandate.[38]

The Supreme Court has had a confusing and inconsistent response to demands for tough standards of judicial review of environmental actions by governmental agencies. In a classic case that presents a direct conflict between parks and recreation and the road-building establishment, *Citizens to Preserve Overton Park, Inc. v. Volpe*,[39] the Court reviewed a decision upholding the Secretary of Transportation's determination that a federal highway should be built on park land. This decision was made despite provisions of the Department of Transportation Act of 1966 and the Federal-Aid Highway Act of 1968[40] barring highway construction through parks if a "feasible and prudent" alternative route exists, and even when there is no alternative route, permitting construction only if "all possible planning to minimize harm" to the park has been utilized.

The Court held that although a trial-type hearing was not required of the Department of Transportation and that the courts could not engage in their own fact finding, the reviewing judges nevertheless had an obligation to examine very carefully the actions of the agency to determine whether they fully complied with the requirements of the law. Furthermore, under the Administrative Procedure Act,[41] which is generally applicable to judicial review of agency actions, a reviewing court must determine on the basis of a "searching and careful" inquiry "whether the decision was based on a consideration of the relevant factors and whether there has been a clear error of judgment." The Supreme Court thereupon reversed the decision to build the road through Overton Park because the reviewing court's scrutiny of the administrative actions had been inadequate. The Court *remanded* or sent the decision back to the lower court with instructions to more thoroughly consider whether the statutory mandates had been met.

More recently the Supreme Court has shown impatience with judges who appear to be utilizing judicial review to thwart or ameliorate programs they dislike. Thus in *Vermont Yankee Nuclear Power Corp. v. Natural Resources Defense Council, Inc.*,[42] the Court reversed a court of appeals decision and indicated that courts were not authorized to set up stricter EIS review procedures even if they had doubts about nuclear power policies that were within the authority of Congress and state legislatures.

What all of this means to the parks professional and, indeed, to any environmentally concerned citizen is that without very specific statutory mandates such as those in the Transportation Act, judicial relief from environmentally questionable agency decisions will be available only when there has been a substantial abuse of discretion and where formal requirements for the development of an EIS have been violated or ignored. As agencies become more sophisticated in drafting and developing EIS's, and as they become sensitized to the need to pay at least some attention to environmental objectives in their decision-making processes, the likelihood of effective judicial action in eliminating all but the most destructive development is diminished.

A related and critical unresolved area of concern under NEPA is the question of what, if any, actual effect must be given to an EIS that does fully and faithfully detail the short- and long-term environmental consequences of proposed actions.

Some courts have taken the position that an EIS is strictly procedural.[43] In other words, an agency must collect environmental information but need not use it unless there is a specific statutory mandate. Most courts have not followed this reasoning, nor, on the other hand, have they required the adoption of the least damaging alternative (often one that calls for the abandonment of a project). Instead a middle ground has developed in which a court will

> first determine if the agency reached its decision after a full, good faith consideration and balancing of environmental factors. The court must then determine . . . whether the actual balance of costs and benefits that was struck was arbitrary or clearly gave insufficient weight to environmental values.[44]

The regulations adopt a similar position with even greater emphasis on the need

> to the fullest extent possible . . . use all practicable means consistent with . . . other essential considerations of national policy, to restore and enhance the quality of the human environment and avoid or minimize any possible adverse effects of their action . . . .[45]

The courts are bound to ensure that the agencies have taken their roles under NEPA seriously. Even where the primary mission is to develop activities and structures that are inevitably detrimental to the environment, the courts insist that the results of the EIS and the course of action adopted must be reasonable and defensible.[46]

Certainly, it is unfair to view NEPA and the EIS requirements as obstacles to progress. Rather, they serve as a kind of insurance that environmental concerns and effects will be an integral part of the administrative decision-making process and that costs and benefits will not be exclusively viewed in short-term economic and service-related contexts.

At the time of this writing there is distressing evidence that the political winds are blowing strongly against environmental protection. The Council on Environmental Quality has had severe budget limitations imposed, the Environmental Protection Agency is under seige, and there is substantial danger that necessarily complex environmental regulations will be eliminated in a fever of government simplification and a laissez-faire philosophy. This text is not on politics and in any event, political fashion is so evanescent that by the time this is read environmentalists may once again be enjoying the prestige they had in the early 1970s. It is, nevertheless, an obvious and eternal truth that, regardless of political philosophy, protection of natural resources is necessary to the health and well-being of humanity, and even if temporarily eclipsed, NEPA, the EIS, or similar legislative and regulatory provisions will reemerge.

## FEDERAL LANDS, NATURAL RESOURCES, AND LEISURE SERVICES

Natural resources and the use of public lands is a subject of concern to all of us as citizens and consumers; however, it is obviously not within the scope of coverage of this work to directly consider such complex matters as oil and gas leases or the use of rivers and streams for the generation of hydroelectric power. Nevertheless, there is a very substantial body of natural resource law with a direct impact upon recreation and leisure services. Much of this has been developed in connection with federal lands.

Although we are all aware that the National Park system is a major recreational resource, it has been only in the last few years that most Americans have begun to appreciate the importance of other federal land holdings. This is partially due to the growth of population in the western states, where the majority of federal land is located. Beyond this, the preeminent importance of energy resources and the related emergence of cowboy-accented states' rights and private enterprise lobbies and pressure groups collectively known as the "Sagebrush Rebellion" have forced the realization that the future of a great deal of our national territory is still undetermined.

Fully one-third of the land area of the United States, something in the realm of 760 million acres, is presently owned by the federal government. (Another 136 million acres is in the hands of state and local government.)[47] As mind-boggling as that figure is, remember that it was once much greater. Almost from the time of the nation's birth, and particularly through the years of the great western expansion, the federal government was extremely generous, indeed profligate, in giving away huge amounts of territory to encourage development and settlement.

Much of the public argument today is centered on the issue of whether we should treat federal lands as simply another resource for maximum development and exploitation or whether we should deal with them conservatively and permit only that development that would not degrade the essential value and quality of the lands and would preserve them intact for future generations.

It is difficult to discuss the issues involved without resorting to emotionally loaded terms. "Locking up" of resources, "elitist" preservationist, "rape of the land," and "wild-eyed environmentalist" are phrases bandied about with abandon. Selfishness, greed, and the desire for short-term economic advantage are attributes that preservationists ascribe to many developers, while they in turn are accused of seeking to impose their own narrow philosophical views on an unwilling and unconvinced populace.

Complex religious and philosophical attitudes have certainly played an important role in determining how humans relate to the environment. James Watt, the most relentlessly prodevelopment Secretary of the Interior since the 1920s, appears to base his philosophy on a fundamentalist ethic that teaches that "the earth was put here by the Lord for his people to subdue and to use for profitable purpose on the way to the hereafter."[48] Yet it is a gross overgeneralization to argue that as Western religious and philosophical thought emphasizes human domination over nature, Eastern or Oriental thinking sees humanity as just one aspect of the totality of life and experience.[49] Landowners and the nobility indiscriminately deforested much of China and Japan with dire consequences in terms of flooding and soil erosion despite, or at times because, of the philosophical attitudes of Taoism and Buddhism.[50]

Whatever the underlying philosophical, religious, and psychological attitudes may be, it is almost a truism that those in the parks and leisure services profession are in favor of preservation and conservation of natural resources, land, water, and air and opposed to excess development. Of course, this also is a gross oversimplification.

Historically, much of what we see as passive, buccolic park preservation has really involved considerable development and alteration of the natural environment. Only the most dogmatic purist would denigrate such monuments to Victorian park planning as New York City's Central Park, where every pond and the placement of virtually every rock and shrub resulted from intensive planning and landscaping by Frederick Law Olmstead and his associates. After all, untrammeled nature had disappeared from most of Manhattan by that time, and the light, air, recreation, and inspiration Central Park affords to millions is certainly enhanced by the creative and intelligent planning that went into it.

On the other hand, consider some of the "recreational communities" created in recent years. In many, lakes and lagoons are cunningly disguised drainage ditches or "borrow pits,"[51] maintained only at the cost of constant dredging; golf courses necessitate substantial tree removal and require excessive fertilizing and watering of greens and fairways; and acre upon acre is paved over with concrete and asphalt for tennis courts and parking areas, creating significant drainage problems.

More critical than the ecological disruption caused by particular activities is the fact that recreational communities are often situated in previously undisturbed areas of extreme ecological sensitivity. Developers continue to introduce hundreds or thousands of homes and condominiums with accompanying roads, parking lots, vehicles, commercial and service centers, and sewage, water, and power developments along previously virgin shorelines and in isolated mountain valleys and desert oases. This modern phenomenon has the grave potential to permanently diminish much of the natural reserve necessary to support our vast population and its industrial and agricultural base. In fact, it is no exaggeration to say that some of our most severe existing and potential ecological and pollution problems stem from the relocation of millions of people from the humid, temperate zones of the Northeast to the dry, warm Southwest. Although one could hardly characterize such cities as Los Angeles, Phoenix, and San Diego as leisure communities, obviously the desire for a more benign recreation oriented life-style has played a major role in attracting people and capital to these areas, which are climatologically ill-suited to support massive populations.

It is probably safe to proclaim that there are few, if any, in the parks and leisure services field who are total preservationists, since preservation in its purest sense would involve a complete denial of access and exploitation of nature to humankind unless we were willing or required to leave all of the aids and accoutrements of civilization and industrialization behind us. The solitary nomadic hunter clad in moccasins and armed only with his wit and a stone-age bow and arrow is probably the last human figure whose use of nature did not result in some degree of disturbance of the ecological balance.

Law deals in the realities and problems of life; it attempts to order priorities and set forth rules for the realization of agreed-upon goals in accordance with acknowledged principles. The law of the environment and natural resources, therefore, reflects the tensions and conflicts of today's emerging consciousness of the limits as well as the potential for development and exploitation. In relation to recreation and leisure, law not only must accommodate competing resource needs but must also resolve internal conflicts prompted by differences in philosophy and mission within the field.

An example of the former is found in attempts to legally structure the use of our vast national forest lands so that the requirements for timber and forest products, preservation of wildlife, rangeland for livestock, water resources, soil conservation and recreational activities may all be accommodated in a complementary fashion.

A good illustration of the latter problem, the conflict in recreational uses, is described in Joseph Sax's monograph *Mountains Without Handrails.*[52] Sax focuses on the differences and tensions caused by a desire to promote traditional sightseeing and tourism in the national parks, on the one hand, and efforts to modify accessibility and services within the parks to provide a different, less ecologically disturbing, and more profound recreation experience, on the other.

### The National Forests

The United States Forest Service supervises over 187 million acres of federal land. The principle law governing this vast empire is the Multiple Use-Sustained Yield Act of 1960.[53] As its title indicates, this statute recognizes the importance of the forests for a variety of uses and the necessity of balancing exploitation with conservation.

The Forest Service as it is now organized was formally created in 1905, when responsibility for the forests was transferred from the Interior Department to the Agriculture Department under the leadership of the preeminent but development-minded conservationist and first chief forester, Gifford Pinchot.

Among the many Forest Service employees through the years whose work preserved the vision of the forests as more than a resource for timber, two men stand out. Aldo Leopold early saw the need for the preservation of the forest reserve for wilderness and recreational values. His principle work, *A Sand Country Almanac* (1949), is certainly required reading for anyone who wishes to comprehend the wilderness-recreation ethic. Bob Marshall, founder of the Wilderness Society, became the head of the Forest Service's Division of Recreation in 1937. Among others contributing to the appreciation of wilderness and natural preservation as a positive recreational value were Stephen Mather, pioneer administrator of the National Park Service; John Muir, the founder of the Sierra Club and great philosopher of the wilderness; and more recently, Roderick Nash, author of *Wilderness and the American Mind.*

It is instructive that even the giants of the conservation movement differed substantially over the uses of resources. Foresters fight many of the same battles today. Pinchot perhaps best represents the principled advocate of development for the utilitarian service of humanity. The most famous example was his strong and ultimately successful advocacy of the flooding of the Hetch Hetchy Valley in Yosemite National Park for use as a reservoir for the city of San Francisco.

Although John Muir argued that they might "as well dam for water tanks the people's cathedrals and churches, for no holier temple [than Hetch Hetchy] has ever been consecrated by the heart of man,"[54] Pinchot believed that "the highest possible use . . . would be to supply pure water to a great center of population."[55]

While Stephen Mather had a running struggle with Pinchot and other utilitarians over the exploitation of parks resources, he nevertheless saw a need to promote tourist use of the national parks. Thus, he supported railroad lines up to the boundaries, but not within Yellowstone and Glacier National Parks. He provided for hotels and other tourist accommodations within the parks. At the same time, when the Great Northern Railroad was recalcitrant in closing down a sawmill that had been built for the purpose of providing wood for hotel construction in Glacier National Park, Mather personally supervised the blowing up of the mill. Ironically, a number of modern parks and wilderness authorities such as Sax see the tourist hotels that Mather encouraged as being just as detrimental and contrary to the purpose of national parks as the unlamented sawmill.

At this point, the reader may ask (if she has not done so already), "Well, this is all very interesting, but what has it to do with the law?" The answer is that an understanding of the Multiple Use-Sustained Yield Act and its historically inconsistent administrative applications may come about only through an appreciation of the seemingly irreconcilable conflicts over the use of the forests and other natural resources.

The statute states: "It is the policy of the Congress that the national forests are established and shall be administered for outdoor recreation, range, timber, watershed, and wildlife and fish purposes . . . ."[56]

In defining "multiple use" the statute speaks of the "combination that will best meet the needs of the American people"[57] and of consideration being given to the relative values of the various resources, and not necessarily the combination of uses that will give the greatest dollar return or the greatest unit output.

Sometimes different uses may be complementary. Wildlife and primitive back-country hiking are essentially complementary, as long as the inevitable, if rare, confrontation between human and beast (such as the grizzly bear) does not result in drastic measures against the animal population. Similarly, rafting and kayaking are normally compatible with watershed and fish preservation, unless the human activities are carried on excessively and carelessly, causing pollution and overfishing. Equally clear is the fact that under a multiple use concept, a great deal of scope for creative and evolving management must be permitted. Judicial intervention in the discretionary administrative processes must be restricted to clear and flagrant abuses of statutory authority.

Much of the litigation under the statute involves the issue of *sustained yield* of forest products. The concept of sustained yield involves the maintenance in perpetuity of the various renewable resources without impairing the productivity of the land.

The most important case involving this issue is *West Virginia Div. of the Izaac Walton League of America, Inc. v. Butz,*[58] popularly known as the *Monongahela* decision because the area involved was the Monongahela National Forest. In this 1975 case, the practice of clear-cutting timber was challenged. Clear-cutting basically involves completely leveling all of the trees within a given area as opposed to selectively harvesting the most mature specimens. This policy of even-aged management is sometimes an appropriate silviculture tool, but appeared to be in conflict with the original congressional directives to the Forest Service. This statute, the Organic Act of 1897, required selective cutting. When the court upheld the continued vitality of the Organic Act, they stated that the courts do not have a "license to rewrite a statute" and that it was up to Congress to resolve this controversial matter.

The technical issues of whether, when, and where one or another method is most appropriate in timber management are complex, but the decision prompted a surge of lobbying by the timber industry for Congress to repeal the Organic Act and permit at least some clear-cutting. Environmentalists also lobbied heavily for even greater protection of wilderness resources. The resulting National Forest Management Act of 1976,[59] as well as related statutes such as the Forest and Rangeland Renewable Resource Planning Act of 1978,[60] are highly detailed forestry planning tools of primary interest to professional foresters and timber managers; nevertheless, it should be recognized that all of these laws acknowledge the recreation resource as a significant element in forest use planning.

## Rangeland

By far the largest portion of federal property is under control of the Bureau of Land Management (BLM). More than one-fifth of the nation, some 470 million acres, is supervised by this agency within the Department of the Interior. Although "range" for livestock is one of the multiple uses of the national forests and grasslands under the Forest Service, the bulk of rangeland is managed by the BLM. This land is generally among the least productive in the United States. Dry or semiarid, largely devoid of specific dramatic scenic vistas or areas of high recreational interest, these lands nevertheless still contain leisure resources. They also contain many of the most significant archeological and historic sites in the West and Southwest.

The basic rangeland statute is the Taylor Grazing Act of 1934.[61] The BLM came into being in 1946 when it absorbed land from both the General Land Office and the Grazing Service of the Department of Interior.

Although the BLM evolved a multiple use philosophy of its own,[62] the agency directed most of its attention to grazing and mining, and most legal conflicts arose over leases and licenses for these activities. The lack of recreational concern was understandable considering the poor condition of much of the land controlled by the BLM.

In recent years, however, the public has had a renewed interest in BLM lands for recreational uses. This is due to the growth of such activities as cross-country motorcycling, snowmobiling, rock climbing, and desert camping. In 1976 the multiple use-sustained yield concept was formally applied to BLM lands under the Federal Land Policy and Management Act.[63] With specific reference to our concerns, the Act provides that land management should "protect the quality of scientific, scenic, historical, ecological, environmental, air and atmospheric, water resource, and archeological values . . . and . . . provide for outdoor recreation and human occupancy use."[64]

## Wildlife

Wildlife and the lands and waters in which they abound are obviously spread throughout the areas of jurisdiction of the Forest Service, the National Park Service, and the BLM. In recent years, a number of special statutory provisions have cut across agency and departmental jurisdictions to provide protection for our dwindling wildlife.

Prior to considering those statutes, however, we must briefly note the major Supreme Court decisions that set forth the dimensions of state authority over wildlife under our federal constitution.

**Constitutional Aspects of Wildlife Law.** In an 1896 case, *Geer v. Connecticut,*[65] the Supreme Court held that under traditional concepts of state ownership or "trusteeship" of wildlife, basic authority to regulate the movement of wild animals, herds, and fish rested with the state, not the federal government. This marked the start of a tension between state and federal authorities regarding the control over wildlife.

Courts modified the *Geer* holding over the years, and it was finally overruled in a 1979 case, *Hughes v. Oklahoma,*[66] in which the Supreme Court struck down a law forbidding out-of-state shipment of minnows gathered in Oklahoma waters. This complete ban had clearly violated the principle allowing free movement of commercial goods, which was preserved by the Commerce Clause of the Constitution. Nevertheless, the Supreme Court observed that it would make "ample allowance for preserving in ways not inconsistent with the Commerce Clause, the legitimate state concerns on conservation and protection of wild animals underlying the 19th century legal fiction of state ownership."

Although a state may limit the removal of "inordinate numbers" of wild animals and fish to maintain an ecological balance, it may not do so by discriminating against those outside the state if "equally effective nondiscriminatory conservation measures are available."

The *Hughes* decision does not mean that all distinctions between state residents and out-of-staters must be eliminated. For example, in 1978, the Supreme Court considered the constitutionality of Montana's licensing system for hunters in *Baldwin v. Montana Fish & Game Comm.*[67]

The Montana commission charged fees that were greatly disparate depending on where the applicant lived. In 1976, a Montana resident could purchase an elk license for $9. A nonresident had to purchase a combination elk, deer, bear, and bird and fish license for $225. A similar combination would cost the Montanan $30.

The United States Constitution has a clause stating that the "privileges and immunities" of citizenship may not be restricted by any of the states. Similarly, another clause in the Fourteenth Amendment says that the states cannot make distinctions among different classes of citizens with regard to these fundamental rights. Unfortunately, the Supreme Court has been very reluctant to define "privileges and immunities." Therefore, we cannot know exactly which fundamental rights fall under this protection. Several justices found the right to travel from state to state to be a privilege of citizenship, but generally the Supreme Court has relied upon either the Commerce Clause or the Equal Protection Clause of the Fourteenth Amendment and has rarely invoked "privileges and immunities."

In the Montana case, the Supreme Court ruled that the hunting license fee differential was prohibited by neither the Equal Protection Clause nor the Privileges and Immunities Clause of Article IV, Section 2, of the Constitution.

Only those privileges and immunities "bearing upon the vitality of the Nation as a single entity" were protected, and since out-of-state hunters were only in Montana for "recreation and a sport," and not as a means of livelihood or basic subsistence, "equality in access to Montana elk is not basic to the maintenance or well being of the Union."

With regard to the Equal Protection Clause, the Court held that differential treatment was reasonably "related to the preservation of a finite resource and a substantial regulatory interest of the State."

Since the *Baldwin* decision does not exactly square with other decisions on discrimination in business and employment between local and out-of-state residents, it may be seen, as Lawrence Tribe suggests, as a recognition by the Supreme Court of the "efforts by the states to protect the environmental . . . needs of their citizens."[68]

While these cases concerned state authority, the classic case of *Missouri v. Holland* outlined the justification for the federal government's continuing involvement in the protection of wildlife. In this case the court upheld the Migratory Bird Treaty Act of 1918,[69] which implemented a treaty with Great Britain (acting on behalf of Canada). Justice Oliver Wendell Holmes wrote that the state's power over wildlife was not exclusive and, in fact: "Wild birds are not in possession of anyone, and possession is the beginning of ownership . . . . But for the treaty and the statute there might be no birds for any powers to deal with . . . . It is not sufficient to rely upon the states. The reliance is vain."[70]

**Legislation Relating to Wildlife.**   Federal wildlife protection efforts mirror the confusion reflected in judicial decisions concerning wildlife. They are a patchwork quilt of different legislative and administrative concerns and methods from the turn of the century until the present. Furthermore, since wildlife is not cognizant of international boundaries, there have been numerous treaties and agreements that have been negotiated between the United States and other nations for the protection and management of the world's animal population.

Federal wildlife law got its start in a modest statute, the Lacey Act of 1900,[71] which prohibited interstate shipment of birds or wild animals killed in violation of state law. The act also authorized the secretary of agriculture to adopt measures consistent with state law to preserve and restore game and wild bird populations. This was partially in response to the awareness of the depletion of game birds.

In 1903 President Roosevelt designated Pelican Island in Florida as a refuge for nesting birds. In 1905 and 1906 wildlife refuges were designated under congressional authority in the Wichita and Grand Canyon National Forests, and in 1908 Congress established a National Bison Range in western Montana to preserve this formerly dominant species, the symbol of the high plains.

In our discussion of *Missouri v. Holland* we referred to the Migratory Bird Treaty Act. This act and its successors created "inviolate" sanctuaries; amendments eventually permitting hunting in these refuges if "compatible with the major purposes for which such areas were established."[72]

In 1966, the National Wildlife Refuge System Administration Act[73] consolidated and clarified the different statutory refuge units within the Department of Interior in order to implement a multiple use concept including "hunting, fishing, public recreation, accommodation and access," again with the provision that such activities be compatible with the dominant purpose of wildlife protection.

Today, there are approximately 30 million acres of National Wildlife Refuges in more than 380 locations under the jurisdiction of the U.S. Fish and Wildlife Service within the Interior Department. As you might imagine, the conflict between active recreation and related uses, on the one hand, and the primary purpose of wildlife propagation, on the other, has created substantial conflict.

Perhaps no case better exemplifies the nexus between law and recreational-preservation management conflicts than *Defenders of Wildlife v. Andrus,*[74] which concerned a challenge to the Fish and Wildlife Service for permitting recreational boating in the Ruby Lake National Wildlife Refuge in Nevada.

This refuge was created in 1938 by President Roosevelt under the authority of the Migratory Bird Conservation Act.[75] The specific management objectives of the sanctuary involved the breeding and protection of canvasback and redhead ducks. General objectives were to preserve and protect a variety of other wildlife, to educate humans concerning ecology, and "to provide visitors with high quality, safe, wholesome, and enjoyable recreation which is fully compatible with the area's primary purpose as a refuge and breeding ground for migratory birds and other wildlife."[76]

In 1978 the secretary of the interior promulgated "Ruby Lake Special Regulations," which permitted a variety of boats in limited zones of the refuge, including, in some areas, internal-combustion-engined boats with speeds of up to twenty miles per hour. Water skiing was also among the permitted uses.

The district court found that under the Refuge Recreation Act of 1962, public recreation is an appropriate incidental or secondary use of wildlife refuges *if it is not harmful to the basic purpose.* Nevertheless, the court held that past recreational uses of the refuge had caused the wildlife aspects to deteriorate and that further degradation could not be justified. In fact, such abuses could require the secretary of the interior to impose more substantial curtailments of recreation.

Courts generally defer to the judgment of the administrative agency. In this case, however, the court found that the recreational uses compromised the refuge's primary purpose. The clear legislative mandate left no question regarding the intended primary purpose of the refuge. The court's conclusion was bolstered by the fact that a number of Fish and Wildlife Service officers disagreed with the Ruby Lake regulations.

Despite the judicial reprimand, the Interior Department was not deterred and the secretary issued new recreational regulations, which were also rejected by the court as posing a threat of "immediate and irreparable damage" to the wildlife resource.[77] It should be noted that this judicial-administrative conflict involved a relatively conservation-minded secretary of the interior. Obviously, an increasing number of court challenges will ensue from the actions of a prodevelopment interior secretary. The primary use plan for a particular area, as outlined in the governing statute, will largely determine whether or not there will be judicial intervention. In areas that are most efficiently managed for exploitation of natural resources, conflicting recreational uses will, in all likelihood, be relegated to a secondary position.

With regard to the regulation and control of wildlife on federal land, the most authoritative statement is found in *Kleppe v. New Mexico,*[78] which interpreted the Wild Free Roaming Horses and Burro Act of 1971.[79] Ironically, this controversial statute does not actually protect wildlife. Rather, the animals are feral; that is, they are descended from escaped livestock or domesticated animals. The argument stemmed from the impact of the rapidly growing herds of these beasts on BLM grazing lands. The New Mexico Livestock Board had argued that it had the power to remove burros from BLM land in response to complaints from ranchers with grazing permits. The state took the position that the federal government lacked the power to regulate animal populations on federal lands unless they were involved in interstate commerce or threatening to damage the land itself. The board therefore seized a number of animals and auctioned them. The BLM demanded their recovery and return.

The Supreme Court ruled unanimously that the Property Clause of the Constitution,[80] which authorizes Congress to dispose of and regulate the territory or other property belonging to the United States, "necessarily includes the power to regulate and protect the wildlife living there." Furthermore, Congress has "the power to protect wildlife on the public lands, state law notwithstanding."

The Court did not reach the thorny issue of whether federal jurisdiction extended to animals that stray onto adjacent private lands.

With the support of decisions like these, Congress has enacted numerous statutes and approved treaties protecting wildlife. A few examples follow.

The Bald Eagle Protection Act[81] bans the killing of this rare national symbol except under extremely limited circumstances such as for feathers for Native American religious ceremonies. The Andromous Fish Conservation Act of 1965[82] affords some protection to spawning fish returning from the sea. The Fish and Wildlife Coordination Act of 1958[83] amends an act originally passed in 1934 and requires wildlife conservation and enhancement to be given equal consideration with other goals in water resource development. The Federal Aid in Wildlife Restoration Act[84] and the Federal Aid in Fish Restoration Act[85] provide federal assistance to states for acquiring, maintaining, and managing wildlife resources and to research related problems.

The Marine Mammal Protection Act of 1972[86] places responsibility for the protection of whales, porpoises, and most seals in the National Marine Fisheries Service under the Commerce Department, and such diverse animals as walruses, polar bears, and sea otters in the hands of the secretary of the interior. Protection is less than total, however, since Native Americans of the Northwest and Arctic may hunt these protected marine mammals for subsistence as well as for the continued practice of folk arts.

International protection for migrating species is far from complete, although such understandings as the Agreement on the Conservation of Polar Bears (1973) and the Convention for the Conservation of Antarctic Seals (1972) attempt to afford some degree of assurance of continuing vitality for the increasingly threatened international animal population.

The statutes and treaties are complex, politically compromised documents, usually riddled with exceptions that call into question their effectiveness. Even if hunting and fishing limits are rigidly enforced, the continued increase of worldwide development with its accompanying air and water pollution will likely destroy many species and of course ultimately threaten the continued viability of the human race.

The boldest and therefore most controversial of all of these measures is the Endangered Species Act of 1973.[87] The background and status of this legislation is worth considering in some detail.

The Endangered Species Preservation Act of 1966[88] set forth a congressional policy to encourage the secretary of the interior to conserve and restore threatened species of wildlife; however, the law actually provided little practical assistance for carrying out its mandate. It authorized the use of existing land acquisition laws for protection purposes and also permitted the use of a relatively small amount of money from the Land and Water Conservation Fund[89] for wildlife protection.

In 1969, an amended Endangered Species Conservation Act[90] authorized the secretary of the interior to publish a list of wildlife threatened with extinction and to largely prohibit the importation of such animals into the United States. Other changes supplemented and systemetized procedures for identifying threatened species within the United States.

A Convention on International Trade in Endangered Species of Wild Fauna and Flora in 1973[91] first listed endangered species in three separate lists or appendices:

APPENDIX I—species threatened with extinction;

APPENDIX II—species which may become threatened with extinction if trade is not strictly regulated and controlled;

APPENDIX III—in which nations may designate species subject to regulations within their borders to prevent or restrict exploitation.

A complex system of export and import permits and licenses was established under the convention. It should be noted, however, that the convention directly covers only international trade, not other, often more serious, threats to wildlife, such as expansion of agricultural development.

The culmination of all of these efforts to protect wildlife was the 1973 act, the comprehensive federal law. It required that all federal agencies utilize "all methods and procedures which are necessary to bring any endangered species or threatened species to the point at which [they are no longer threatened]."

The act is so sweeping that it defines wildlife as "any member of the animal kingdom."[92] Borrowing from the Convention and the Marine Mammal Protection Act, "endangered" and "threatened" categories are established with different degrees of protective action. There is a complex listing procedure to be applied by the secretary of the interior (or the secretary of commerce for some species).

Once a species is listed as "endangered," no person subject to United States' jurisdiction may "take" an animal. "Taking" is exhaustively defined to include "harass, harm, pursue, hunt, shoot, wound, kill, trap, capture or collect." Trade and possession are prohibited except in furtherance of very limited purposes consistent with the act.

For "threatened" species, "necessary and advisable" restrictions are to be established for protection.[93] Substantial criminal and civil penalties are established. For example, a willful violator is subject to a year's imprisonment and a $20,000 fine.

Not only does the act provide for review of all federal programs so that they are consistent with preservation purposes, it also contains broad authority for citizen suits "to enjoin any person including the United States and any other government instrumentality or agency" from violating it.[94]

This last provision has been widely used by citizen and environmental groups. For example, in *National Wildlife Federation v. Coleman*,[95] the Transportation Department had to act to relocate an interchange and eliminate a "borrow pit" in accordance with Interior Department directives to preserve the Mississippi sand hill crane.

The most significant endangered species case was *Tennessee Valley Authority v. Hill*,[96] the famed "snail darter" case. The Tellico Dam and Reservoir Project was begun in 1967 on the Little Tennessee River a short distance from where it joined the Big Tennessee. The dam project was to create a lake covering 16,500 acres of productive farmland and to change the free-flowing river's lower thirty-three miles into "a deep reservoir."

Obviously, many farmers and environmental groups were outraged by the proposed dam, which like so many similar projects, was designed to bring about the highly questionable benefits of "shoreline development," and "flatwater recreation and flood control," as well as to "heat 20,100 homes" and "improve economic conditions." In the eyes of critics, this was another project designed to turn a peaceful farming valley with a clear trout-filled river into a tacky, unnecessary resort region.

A variety of lawsuits and proceedings including resort to NEPA had failed to prevent the near completion of the dam project, but at the last moment a University of Tennessee ichthyologist discovered a three-inch-long tan colored fish numbering about ten to fifteen thousand and named *Peiceria* (Imostoma) *Tanasi*, or the snail darter. The finding of this previously unknown species did not persuade the district court to apply the Endangered Species Act retroactively and prevent completion of the multimillion dollar project. The Supreme Court disagreed.

The chief justice's opinion appeared to disparage the importance of the snail darter, noting that it was only one of 130 species of perch (with more being discovered all of the time). Nevertheless, the Court acknowledged the recognition by the secretary of the interior that the snail darter was a true species and that impoundment of water behind "Tellico Dam would result in total destruction of snail darter habitat." Thus, under section 7 of the act, all federal agencies were required to prevent its destruction. The Court therefore had no choice but to agree with the Court of Appeals[97] that a permanent injunction would have to issue halting all activities that "may destroy or modify the critical habitat."

It has been suggested that the majority decision in the *Hill* case, which plainly recognized the absurdity of eliminating a virtually completed dam merely to preserve the snail darter, was an obvious attempt to shift to Congress the responsibility for modifying and clarifying the Endangered Species Act. References to congressional concern for the preservation of the grizzly bear's habitat seem to point up the irony of applying extreme measures to the preservation of a barely distinguishable little fish. There is no direct evidence for this, but as the dissenters in the *Hill* case foresaw, Congress, in short order, modified the act to provide for a cabinet-level committee to resolve conflicts between endangered species protection and federal projects.[98]

Surprisingly, the committee ruled in 1979 that the snail darter's continued existence did indeed outweigh the value of Tellico Dam, particularly since there was so little justification for the dam on any grounds. An exasperated Congress then flatly exempted Tellico Dam from the Endangered Species Act in September 1979.

It is certainly clear that conflicts of this nature are inevitable. As Justice Powell pointed out in his dissent in *Hill*, there are literally hundreds of thousands of species of animals and plants that may be endangered or threatened. As of 1979, seventy-four species of animals were officially listed as endangered, ranging from the unarmored three-spine stickleback and the Santa Cruz long-toed salamander to the grizzly bear and the California condor.[99]

If there is a moral to the snail darter story, it is that the utilization of legislation in ways beyond the contemplation of Congress at the time of enactment are fraught with danger for environmentalists and preservationists, just as is the use of NEPA as a tool for delaying and frustrating development. The snail darter (which has apparently been found to have adapted to other habitats) was never the real issue for many opponents to Tellico Dam. The use of the ESA provision to attempt to derail the dam brought only temporary relief, while it gave lasting ammunition to development-minded enterprises and agencies who try to depict those concerned with the environment as tunnel-visioned fanatics unconcerned with economic and social needs beyond their own elitist and narrow priorities.

It is equally clear that, in the long run, unless Congress and a majority of the people become convinced that societal health and welfare requires that serious consideration be afforded to environmental quality, natural preservation, and parks and leisure needs, much of the hard-won legislative and administrative gains will be lost under the insistent pressures for economic resource development. Simply put, it is not yet certain that our society is willing to sacrifice in a substantial way for the kinds of values reflected in the parks and leisure services profession.

Nowhere is this evolving conflict more clearly demonstrated than in the legal battle to define and protect wilderness.

### Wilderness Preservation

Some of the most remarkable legislative enactments touching upon parks and recreation have resulted from the efforts by Congress to translate the philosophical concept of wilderness embodied in the writings of Leopold, Nash, and Marshall into working blueprints that will protect this elusive natural quality while recognizing competing and conflicting resource demands, including mining, logging, and mechanized or organized recreation.

The Wilderness Act of 1964[100] incorporated existing "wild" areas designated by the Forest Service into a National Wilderness Preservation System, initially some 9.1 million acres.

Furthermore, the Forest Service was to study an additional 5.4 million acres to determine whether they were suitable for designation as part of a wilderness system. In the Interior Department, long-term studies were required for roadless areas of more than 5000 acres in the National Park System and similar areas in the National Refuge Systems. Curiously the vast lands of the BLM were ignored.

The Wilderness Act contains an extraordinary legislative definition:

> A wilderness in contrast with those areas where man and his own works dominate the landscape, is hereby recognized as an area where the earth and its community are untrammeled by man, where man himself is a visitor who does not remain.

Furthermore, a wilderness would retain

> its primeval character and influence, without permanent improvement or human habitation which is protected and managed so as to preserve its natural conditions.

More precisely and narrowly, wilderness:

1. generally appears to have been affected primarily by the forces of nature, with the imprint of man's work substantially unnoticeable;

2. has outstanding opportunities for solitude or a primitive and unconfined type of recreation;

3. has at least five thousand acres of land or is of sufficient size as to make practicable its preservation and use in an unimpaired condition; and

4. may also contain ecological, geological, or other features of scientific, educational, scenic, or historic value.[101]

Despite this idyllic, even poetic, definition, the act provides for continued exploration to gather information about mineral and other resources and, until the end of 1983, continued mineral leasing, exploitation, and production. Furthermore, wilderness is subject to "existing private rights."

Although there have been conflicting judicial opinions over the extent to which Congress intended to eliminate incompatible uses,[102] there has been a substantial expansion of designated wilderness. By 1980, the National Wilderness Area System included more than 19 million acres (exclusive of nearly 60 million acres of Alaska wilderness). Even the BLM has designated a small number of "primitive areas."

By the end of 1980, the Sierra Club estimated that over 80 million acres would be preserved as wilderness, including the enormous (2,234,000 acres) River of No Return Wilderness in Idaho. The size of areas receiving wilderness designation is, of course, in large measure dependent upon their past isolation from population centers. Thus the Arctic Wildlife Refuge and the Wrangell-St. Elias Wilderness in Alaska each include over 8 million acres, while the Fire Island Wilderness Area in New York contains only 1,363 acres.

The determination of what forest lands were to be considered for wilderness status was made through two Roadless Area Review Evaluations (RARE). The first, RARE I, commencing in 1967 and concluded in 1972, was disappointing to most conservationists because it resulted in a designation of only 274 areas with a total of 12.3 million acres as suitable for serious wilderness consideration; this out of an original inventory of 1449 areas with 56 million acres. The resulting criticism caused the Forest Service to undertake a new evaluation in 1977 (RARE II), which was much more ambitious and covered 2918 areas with 62 million acres.

The complex RARE II procedures are discussed in detail in *California v. Bergland*,[103] in which a district court judge ruled that the EIS on the RARE II study violated NEPA.

This EIS, filed in 1979, identified specific allocations in one of three categories: wilderness, nonwilderness, and future planning. Nonwilderness designation meant that "the area was open to development without further consideration of wilderness," while "further planning" would "leave land use issues to the ordinary forest planning process." Thirty-six million acres were allocated for development, 10.8 million to further planning, and 15 million to be recommended to Congress for inclusion in the Wilderness Preservation System.

After an exhaustive review of the EIS processes, the court concluded that the Forest Service had failed to meet its obligations to administratively consider the lands it had surveyed for RARE II and therefore was enjoined from degrading the wilderness character of disputed areas. In reaching that conclusion Judge Carlton struggled to define and articulate in a legally comprehensible manner the concerns and conflicts over wilderness:

> Humankind has a deep and apparently abiding need for contact with nature. It may fairly be characterized as a profound spiritual longing that we ignore at our peril. It may arise from our need to be in contact with our roots, to replicate the history of the species, to test our ability to survive primitive conditions, and thus to stretch our ever more urbanized and accordingly constricted selves.
>
> Such needs, however, as profound as they may be, must be balanced against equally pressing concerns: our need for the resources of the land, and for employment in general, particularly in the rural areas where much of the RARE II land is located. Lack of employment in those areas will inevitably lead to future disruption of rural life, and still greater urbanization with all of its serious environmental consequences for the nation.
>
> The balancing of these concerns and the allocation of our limited resources to various compelling—but contradictory—goals are essentially political decisions.[104]

## Mining and Recreation

With the exception of those specially designated reserves, including national parks and wildlife preserves where Congress has specified the dominant purposes for federal lands, traditional land use law[105] appears to treat mineral resources as preeminent, and miners are subject to little restriction and regulation. In short, mining has been treated as an overriding use of land, not subject to consideration of multiple use balanced administration. It has only been since 1970 that the Forest Service has even claimed any authority to regulate mining in the national forests. Both the efficacy of Forest Service and other administrative regulations and the application of NEPA to mining activities remain unresolved controversies.

An interesting opinion by the Ninth Circuit Court of Appeal, *United States v. Curtis Nevada Mines, Co.*,[106] illustrates how the courts regard mining as clearly dominant. The case concerns the rights of owners of "unpatented" mining claims. Under section 26 of the Mining Law, those who locate a mine on federal land have "exclusive right of possession and enjoyment of all the surface included within the lines of their location." Curtis Nevada Mines (essentially a one-man operation) had filed 203 claims on 13 square miles of BLM lands in California and Nevada adjacent to Forest Service land. Although the plaintiff claimed that the properties contained "trillions" of dollars worth of minerals, little mining had actually taken place. Nevertheless Curtis attempted to exclude all recreational activities from its claims, even though they did not seem incompatible with the existing mining and prospecting operations. Before an actual "patent" or fee title to a mining claim may be issued, the claimant must prove that there are, in fact, valuable mineral assets which can be marketed at a profit.[107] If the court upheld Curtis' claim, an entrepreneur or opportunist could, by merely filing claims and making grandiose, unproven statements about their value, gain effective control of vast federal lands. Fortunately, the mining version of Multiple Use, the Surface Resources and Multiple Use Act of 1955, provided that "any such mining claim shall also be subject, prior to issuance of patent therefor, to the right of the United States, its permittees, and licensers, to use so much of the surface thereof as may be necessary [to manage other surface resources thereof] . . . or for access to adjacent land"[108] as long as mining or prospecting operations were not substantially threatened or hindered.

The circuit court discussed the abuses of mining law, particularly the practice of unscrupulous operators to seize large parcels of valuable timber and water resources under the guise of mining interests. Given this history, the court determined that recreational activities would be deemed a "surface resource" within the meaning of the statute and, further, that there was an implied license for recreational purposes such as camping, picknicking, hiking, and fishing, and therefore that formal licenses and permits are unnecessary. Thus the court held that the mere filing of a mining claim would not automatically eliminate recreation.

The result in Curtis Nevada Mines is not so extraordinary in itself. Rather, what is striking is that as late as 1980, it was still arguable (as the district court recognized) that a prospector could gain exclusive possession to public lands except for surface vegetation merely by filing a mining claim.[109] Regulations state that "any activity is permissible which is directly related to mining or prospecting."[110] Or, as another circuit court put it:

> A discovery of valuable minerals by a qualified locator upon unappropriated public land creates substantial rights. . . . [The prospector] has an exclusive right of possession to the extent of his claim as located with the right to extract the minerals . . . without even applying for a patent or seeking to obtain title to the fee.[111]

Even though Congress is now on record as declaring that the application of traditional mining laws "conflicts with the purposes" for which the National Park System was established, there is still sufficient discretionary language to permit a secretary of interior dedicated to full exploitation of mineral resources to reopen or continue to permit mineral exploration in vast areas critical to the preservation of America's wilderness heritage.[112]

### Other Federal Land Use Programs

Complementary to the parks and wilderness preservation programs discussed earlier are a number of innovative statutory schemes designed to protect a variety of unique land and water resources against the depradations of development, pollution, and neglect. We shall discuss a few that have particular significance to the parks and leisure services professional.

The Land and Water Conservation Fund (LWCF)[113] has been the prime financial tool in the recent expansion of federal, state, and local parkland. The LWCF is funded from the proceeds of such resources as outer-continental shelf mineral leases, the federal motorboat fuel tax, user fees, and the sale of surplus federal lands. The fund has grown to the point where its authorized level is $900 million a year through 1989. Statutorily, 40 percent of the first $225 million, 30 percent of the next $275 million, and 20 percent of all additional revenues are to be apportioned among the states by the secretary of the interior. In fact about 60 percent of the fund has been devoted to state and local recreation projects, and a high percentage of these funds ($2.5 billion since 1965) has gone into the planning and development of parks and recreation facilities under comprehensive outdoor recreation plans (SCORPs). The remainder of the fund is utilized for such federal recreation and park purposes as national parks and recreation areas, national forest recreation areas, and national wildlife refuge systems. The emphasis in the statute is clearly on acquisition of areas "primarily of value for outdoor recreation purposes."

Furthermore, with certain exceptions the statute emphasizes purchase and development of recreational lands in the eastern two-thirds of the country, which had previously had only limited federal recreational and park lands. Interestingly, in keeping with the new land use strategies, it is specifically provided that "less than fee interest" may be obtained where suitable.

Until recently the LWCF was administered by the Heritage Conservation and Recreation Service (HCRS) of the Interior Department, with a strong emphasis on capital planning and acquisition, which was in keeping with the statutory purposes. Demonstrating the substantial power of administrators to thwart or modify legislative intent, the Reagan administration has disbanded HCRS, frozen funds not actually appropriated, and indicated a strong desire to eliminate future grants to states and major federal land acquisitions for the National Parks and generally to utilize the LWCF for maintenance purposes.

The Wild and Scenic Rivers Act,[114] originally enacted in 1968, demonstrates a sophisticated understanding of the relationship between natural preservation and recreation. The statute recognizes that the national policy of river dam building and water resource management "needs to be complemented by a policy that would preserve other selected rivers or sections thereof in their free flowing condition." These should be water courses "which with their immediate environments possess outstandingly remarkable scenic, recreational, geologic, fish and wildlife, cultural, or other similar values . . . ."

The statute establishes three categories of rivers to be considered for inclusion in the system: wild, scenic, and recreational. Wild river areas "are free of impoundment and generally inaccessible except by trail, . . . essentially primitive and . . . unpolluted. These represent vestiges of primitive America." Scenic rivers are still largely undeveloped but may be "accessible in places by roads." Finally, recreational rivers "are readily accessible by road or railroad . . ., may have some development along their shorelines and . . . may have undergone some impoundment or diversion in the past."

The statute recognizes the need for cooperative efforts among federal and state officials to designate and protect rivers that meet the criteria for inclusion in the system. It assigns primary responsibility for protection and administration of each designated river to either the Interior or the Agriculture Department, depending upon which agency has major jurisdiction over federal lands in the areas through which the rivers flow. In addition to the rivers themselves, the act authorizes protection of river banks and bordering areas, including the elimination of dams, transmission lines, and other intrusive elements of modern society, although private mining rights are still generally preserved.

The names of the rivers designated for initial inclusion or recommended for inclusion upon the execution of appropriate agreements with state officials conjure up visions of an America of poets, painters, adventurers, and folk heroes: the Rogue, the Allagash, the Wolfe, the Lochsa, the Selway, the American, and the Missouri Breaks, among others.

Whether or not the vision and the ideal represented in the Wild and Scenic Rivers Act becomes a reality depends upon two interrelated factors. The first is whether state and federal officials have the dedication to persevere in developing the system against all of the special interest groups who will attempt to limit it (historically including the powerful Army Corps of Engineers). The second factor is whether Congress will make substantial amounts of public funding available for the purpose of preserving rivers in the face of continuing concern over inflation and government spending.

Another statutory plan that is even more ambitious in terms of its ultimate recreational goals than the Wild and Scenic River program is the National Trails System.[115] Although it was originally established in 1968 to protect the Appalachian Trail and the Pacific Crest Trail system, by 1978 the program included the Oregon National Historic Trail following the pioneer route from Independence, Missouri, to Portland, Oregon; the Mormon Pioneer National Historic Trail along the migration route of that historically persecuted people to their ultimate home in Utah; the Lewis and Clark National Historic Trail; the Continental Divide National Scenic Trail; and the Iditarod Trail (following the Alaskan gold rush from Seward to Nome). Several other similarly significant trails have been included or proposed for inclusion.

Obviously, it is impossible for all of the land within these trails to be included within federal parks ownership; thus the legislation envisioned a program that provides for cooperative federal, state, and local efforts. The plan allows the Interior Department to maintain portions of the trails outside of the boundaries of federal areas and permits judicious use of federal condemnation powers to acquire ownership of easements for critical portions of the trails in private ownership, funded, at least in part, by the Land and Water Conservation Fund.

Another example of the role of modern land use planning techniques and state and federal cooperation to achieve complementary recreational and conservation goals is the creation of the Pinelands National Reserve in southern New Jersey. Since this 2350 square mile chunk of swamp, woods, wildlife, and water has been the object of almost every kind of competing land use pressures, its recent history is worth relating in some detail.

Because of its unique geologic history, the New Jersey Pinelands holds the largest pure underground water reserve in the United States, approximately 17 trillion gallons. It also has almost limitless potential for hiking, canoeing, swimming, and camping. Pressed on all sides by expanding urban areas (New York to the north, Philadelphia to the west, Atlantic City and other Jersey shore communities to the south and east) and subject to increasing pollution and blight, the fragile ecosystem, with its variety of plant species and unique animal population (including the endangered timber rattler, southern gray tree frog, bog turtle, and eastern tiger salamander), may soon be lost forever. The consequences of the destruction of this great aquifer would be catastrophic for the many millions of people in the Northeast corridor whose clean water resources are already stretched to the breaking point.

After a long battle between conservation and development forces, intensified by the introduction of casino gambling to Atlantic City, the Reserve, the first of its kind in the United States, was created by the National Parks and Recreation Act of 1978.[116] This act protected 1,082,000 acres, almost a fourth of the state.

The statute authorized an initial expenditure of 26 million dollars: 3 million for planning and 23 million for land or property right acquisition. It prescribed a combination of "limited public acquisition and land use controls." The statute also directed the state to develop a master plan and established a Pinelands Commission with seven members named by the governor, one by each of the seven counties touching upon the Pinelands, and one by the Secretary of the Interior to oversee the plan.

After a number of intense political skirmishes, the New Jersey legislature enacted a Pinelands Protection Act recognizing the Reserve and providing implementation.[117] The Pinelands Commission drafted a comprehensive plan that was adopted by the state and formally accepted by the Secretary of the Interior, Cecil V. Andrus, only four days before the end of the Carter administration.

The plan is complex, but essentially it creates two principal zones, a "core preservation area" of 368,750 acres and a less rigorously controlled "protection area" of 564,950 acres. (The remainder of the Pinelands falls within the jurisdiction of authorities under the Federal Coastal Zone Management Act.)[118] In the preservation area, the plan provides for a combination of rigid land use controls, creative zoning techniques to preserve the value of agricultural land (largely planted in blueberries and cranberries), and judicious government purchases where there is no other constitutionally appropriate way to maintain the ecology. In the protection area, the emphasis is on intelligent and conservative land use planning to protect the water resource from pollution rather than an attempt to eliminate change altogether.

A five-year budgetary plan calls for total expenditures of over $100 million dollars, of which $81 million will be financed by the federal government largely through revenues from leases of the energy rich outer continental shelf. Of the initial $26 million, $12 million has already been appropriated.

Although these are large sums indeed, they are, in fact, very small amounts compared to what would have been required if total elimination of private ownership and complete government control had been the goal. The Pinelands Reserve plan, like the programs for wild and scenic rivers and national historic trails, recognizes that recreational and ecological goals may be met through a system of compatible private and public land ownership and use.

Of course, the success of such programs depends upon the ability of program managers to have adequate funds and political support to resist pressures to expand the private enterprise component when the basic goals of preservation are threatened. The Pinelands plan has been under constant attack since its conception, and if the resolve of its defenders slackens, it may be whittled away to the point where there is little worth salvaging. At this time there are doubts as to whether federal funds beyond the $12 million already appropriated for the Pinelands will become available. In short, there does not yet appear to be the kind of commitment to the sacrosanct nature of the property within reserves like the Pinelands which National Park status seems to engender. Unless there is universal recognition of the value and need for permanence of these new cooperative enterprises, their long-term promise for recreation and conservation may be illusory.

## PRESERVATION AND RECREATION: THE CONTINUING DILEMMA

A landmark 1970 report of the Public Land Law Review Commission entitled "One Third of a Nation" discussed the many conflicts over the uses of government property. With regard to recreational activities, the report recognized that states and local governments would have important responsibilities in providing active recreational opportunities, while the federal government, by the very fact that its park and forest lands contain "scenic areas, natural wonders, primitive areas, and historic sites of national significance," would have a great concern for preservation and enhancement of lands and waters themselves.

Thus a careful distinction must be made between property with significance because of what it is and that with significance because of the recreational activities that may take place there. Despite the increased involvement of the federal government in urban recreation over the past decade, its preservation-conservation function is still central and still controversial.

No one would suggest that the Liberty Bell in Independence National Historical Park should be used as a playground climber. Why then should the Colorado River as it flows through the Grand Canyon be reduced to the level of a spectacular, expensive amusement park water ride? Again, as with the Ruby Lake controversy, courts will try to discern a dominant purpose in the statutory background of a particular land use issue. Failing that, deference to administrative expertise and authority is likely to be crucial in a court's decision. Still the environmental/recreation-resource battle is so complex and so laden with emotion that traditional judicial conservatism and deference may be overcome in favor of an activist role in maintaining those values the court deems most significant.

Because of the volatile nature of the issues and the careful balancing required by multiple use concepts, it is apparent that even agencies that are quite conscious of their varied obligations are going to invite the wrath of one or more of the competing interest groups each time a significant administrative decision is made.

Consider, for example, the convoluted history of Walt Disney's Mineral King ski and recreation resort proposals. Mineral King is an isolated mountain valley in a national forest just south of Sequoia National Park. Pressures for a major ski area to serve the rapidly expanding recreation-minded population of Southern California have been growing since the 1940s. The Sierra Club initially favored the Mineral King site because it feared development of an even more primitive and sensitive area closer to Los Angeles. By the mid 1960s, when commercial developers became interested in Mineral King, a growing concern for the environmental devastation caused by new roads, high traffic volume, and the pollution and disruption of second-home communities provoked a bitter resistance by the Sierra Club and other conservation groups to the Forest Service's acquiescence in the rather grand Walt Disney Enterprises proposals.

The Supreme Court initially ruled that the Sierra Club did not have standing to sue the Agricultural Department over Mineral King[119] because it failed to allege that the project would actually affect the club's members. The concept of legal *standing* requires that the party bringing the lawsuit has a direct interest in its outcome. This interest does not have to be a financial one; it may relate to health, safety, constitutional rights, or other legally protected interests.

Despite this initial setback, the Mineral King decision provided a blueprint for environmental groups to ensure that the proper claims of injury were made on behalf of appropriate plaintiffs. Thus, allegations that organization members who used an area to hike or camp would be deleteriously affected by reduction in air quality or by some other aspect of environmental degradation would suffice for legal standing to sue.

When the final EIS on Mineral King was issued by the Forest Service, the "preferred alternative" supported the intensive Disney plan, which included eighteen ski lifts, other winter sports facilities, including ice rinks and a luge or bobsled run, and lodging for 4500 people, not to mention highway construction to permit attendance of 8000 people daily.

The Forest Service's decision provided substantial fodder for a series of costly legal actions debilitating to the project.[120] There were many complications. Stacked against the ambiguities of the multiple use concept was the valley's designation in 1926 as a federal game refuge, so it could be argued that protection of wildlife was its highest use.[121] The unique giant sequoia's shallow root system would be threatened by road building and disruption of drainage patterns. Fishing in the region's lakes and streams would be affected. In short, the disturbance of a complex ecosystem resulted in many factual disputes with legal consequences.

Eventually, the lawsuits, combined with inflation and a less optimistic investment climate, led the Disney people to abandon Mineral King. Since the Forest Service was merely Disney's handmaiden in proposing the project, that effectively brought the threat of development in Mineral King to at least a temporary end.

The battle over Mineral King is one which, in various forms and guises, has been and will continue to be fought and refought. We must create a legally and administratively sound program of investigation and mediation that can, within a reasonable time frame, consider the competing needs and arguments, provide an efficient mechanism for consideration of modifications and alternatives, and ultimately come forth with a total plan that will not be subject to piecemeal attack.

Specifically considering recreational aspects of federal land management, it is evident that there are not only real or potential conflicts with other uses, but also conflicts within the recreational use aspect itself. Many of these fall roughly within the categories of mechanized versus nonmechanized uses, or active versus passive leisure pursuits. Still other conflicts resist any easy categorization. There are such use conflicts as motorcycles versus horses, horses versus hikers, snowmobilers versus cross-country skiers, off-road vehicles versus backpackers, and so on. Even when there is general agreement on the desirability of certain recreational uses, subtle but significant distinctions in values and attitudes may result in administrative battles over such issues as the harmfulness of lugged hiking boots and creosoted boardwalks to delicate mountain environments.

The most difficult and intractible of these issues are manifested in the National Park System. The National Park Act specifically designates the National Park Service (NPS) to conserve and protect the parks and the wildlife and vegetation within them "to provide for the enjoyment of the same in such manner and by such means as will leave them unimpaired for future generations."[122] Thus, there is no question but that the Park Service's mandate to manage the parks must be read in the context of its conservation function.

Prior to World War II, the remoteness of most of the major parks and the lack of understanding of the extreme sensitivity of wildlife and wilderness to human intrusion meant that no real conflict was recognized between the NPS's functions. By removing the worst commercial eyesores from the parks and in eliminating vandalism, poaching, and other destructive practices, the service met the interest of enlightened tourists as well as the perceived requirements of the parks' environments.

Today, there are a number of almost impenetrable conflicts between the NPS's dual roles. Whether it is grizzly bear management in Glacier National Park, the removal of commercial attractions in the overcrowded and polluted Yosemite Valley,[123] or the battle between preservationists and homeowners in the Fire Island National Seashore in New York, the conflicts will inevitably find their way into the courts for resolution.

An instructive case is *Wilderness Public Rights Fund v. Kleppe*,[124] which considers the continuing controversy over the use of the Colorado River for commercial rafting and boating trips through the Grand Canyon.

By the early 1970s it had become clear that accomplishment of the once daring feat of navigating the Colorado had burgeoned to the point at which whitewater enthusiasts threatened the Grand Canyon ecosystem. The NPS concluded that the carrying capacity of the river was being exceeded. Therefore, it limited permits to the 1972 level of 96,600 user days annually, 92 percent of which were allocated to commercial concessioners, a substantial number of whom used motorized equipment.

*Wilderness Public Rights Fund* was a consolidation of actions brought to change the balance of permit allocations so that noncommercial recreational users could have substantially greater access. The court not only noted the preservation requirements of the National Park Act, but also observed that under the Concession Policy Act,[125] commercial development and concessions "shall be limited to those that are necessary and appropriate for public use and enjoyment of the national park area in which they are located." Nevertheless, it was noted that "the commercial operators as concessioners of the Service, undertake a public function to provide services that the NPS deems desirable for those visiting the area." Thus, the court held that the distribution of permits "if fairly done pursuant to appropriate standards . . . is well within the area of administrative discretion granted to the NPS."

It is extremely difficult to limit or eliminate commercial activities once they are established in a park. Not only will concessioners activate intense lobbying efforts in Congress, but there is also the inevitable evidence that these businesses contribute to increased accessibility, ease of travel, and comfort of visitors. When the NPS finally attempted to change the allocation system to expand noncommercial permits and restrict or eliminate motorized traffic altogether from the Grand Canyon, the cries of anguish were both loud and predictable. Elimination of motor trips would limit travel down the Colorado to those willing and able to spend more than two weeks on the river, an altogether different kind of experience than that provided by the relatively short and heavily equipped motorized journey.

Books like Sax's *Mountains Without Handrails* consider the philosophical reason for and the social and political consequences of different management approaches to the unique natural treasures found in the national parks. The point to be made here is that even where competing interests in timber, range, and mining are eliminated or minimized, serious legal and political disputes arise.

Under traditional administrative law principles of deference to an agency's expertise and political sensitivity, courts usually uphold the government's interpretation of law, but in extreme cases where it is clear that an agency decision conflicts with the mandate for preservation and protection, greater judicial activism may be anticipated. Once a judicial view develops that a particular agency, such as, hypothetically, a strongly development-oriented Interior Department, is not carrying out its mission in a balanced, responsible manner, courts have a way of finding errors and limiting actions while still utilizing the same language of administrative deference.

Today, with a substantial number of activist environmental and naturalist organizations lobbying and litigating on behalf of conservation against the background of idealistic preservationist language that Congress has incorporated in most of its natural resources and parks management legislation, the outcome of any particular legal battle over the utilization of natural resources is subject to doubt.

What is hardly in doubt is that in the long run, the demands for new energy resources and the proprietary attitude of the expanding population of water-poor western and southwestern states, with their burgeoning industrial and commercial development and increased political power, will lead to extremely intense pressures to maximize the exploitation of natural resources. Whether the legacy of legal recognition of the physical, spiritual, and intellectual value of recreation and preservation bequeathed to us by the thinkers and legislators of more optimistic times will prove to have been so deeply ingrained in the national psyche that the thrust toward total exploitation may be resisted is an open question.

## THE ENVIRONMENT

Environmental law is a highly technical and unwieldy subject. In fact, there is little agreement among experts as to what is included under the rubric "environmental" beyond air pollution, water pollution, hazardous wastes, and consideration of NEPA. The following review is therefore not intended to be definitive. It merely points out the principle federal pollution control statutes, the manner in which they are intended to operate, and some of the attendant problems.

The primary federal pollution control laws are popularly known as the Clean Air Act[126] and the Clean Water Act.[127] Another important environmental statute is the Toxic Substances Control Act.[128] These, along with a variety of other more specialized antipollution laws, are largely amalgams of statutes and amendments enacted over the last several decades, and they are certain to be modified in the future. These laws are extremely long, complex, and highly technical. As products of political, economic, and scientific compromise, they necessarily depend to an almost unprecedented extent on administrative interpretation and enforcement by the Environmental Protection Agency (EPA).

Rather than attempting to explain all of the provisions of these statutes, we shall concentrate on the conflicts they present and the general approach taken toward their resolution, particularly as it affects park and leisure interests.

There is, of course, an ideal that almost every rational human being may agree upon. That is that clean, healthy air, water, and land are desirable goals of a modern society. There is universal agreement that when pollution levels reach such extremes that health is immediately and unarguably affected to a serious degree, drastic measures must be taken to ameliorate the situation, regardless of the short-term economic consequences. Thus, when the rare combination of intense industrial pollution and extreme, prolonged air inversions have resulted in severe breathing problems, the closing down of industry and commerce is readily (if belatedly) accepted.

In Donora, Pennsylvania, a three-day period of critical pollution in 1948 left almost half the citizens ill and was directly blamed for 20 fatalities. In London in December 1952, a "killer fog" brought on by a temperature inversion caused an unprecedented concentration of industrial, transportation, and residential pollutants (most notably sulfur dioxide and sulfuric acid) that resulted in 4000 excess deaths over the two-week period when pollution was most intense. Similarly, outbreaks of disease attributed to water pollution, such as diphtheria or typhoid, will cause loud cries for immediate action.

Most pollution effects are not nearly so dramatic. Long-term health problems are manifested gradually and incrementally. Although pollution from automotive exhausts and stationary sources may be illustrated by the grey and yellow smog that hangs over the populated valleys of our industrial centers, much of the most dangerous pollution is invisible and its results are unpredictable. Other than the aged and infirm, the very young and sensitive, or those afflicted with severe allergies, most of us take ordinary pollution levels in stride, only occasionally remarking upon the unpleasant taste of our drinking water or the odor and lack of clarity of our air.

While individual subjective responses are important in determining the future of antipollution laws (for even the judges have to drink the water and breath the air), one area is more significant. There is a persistent lack of scientific data detailing specific pollution effects. Legislators and administrators need this data to set authoritative limits for various pollutants with confidence that the limits are both necessary and economically justifiable.

Controlled long-term studies on the deleterious nature of pollutants on humans, animals, and agriculture obviously present tremendous technical problems. Furthermore, until scientists are able to more directly relate causative environmental factors to such diseases as cancer, development-oriented mining and industrial interests will continue to argue that rigid pollution controls are unnecessary.

It is commonplace today that even the most ardent advocate of development will claim to be an environmentalist. His argument is that without proof of the effectiveness of strict limits on pollutants to enhance health, the productivity of industry should not be hampered or crippled. On the other hand, environmental activists take the position that since we know that pollution is generally unhealthful, the burden should be on industry to demonstrate the safety and healthfulness of its approach to pollution-control rather than forcing the proponents of a clean environment to prove harmfulness. They argue that statistically valid proof of injury from environmental pollution may not be available for several generations.

The Clean Air and Clean Water acts contain idealistic language reflecting ultimate environmental goals. The excruciatingly difficult task of setting concrete achievable standards has caused Congress to postpone or modify many of the original goals; nevertheless, surprising progress has been made, particularly in the control of water pollution.

At the time of this writing, the Clean Air Act is under congressional review. Even when the dust settles and the inevitable compromises have been struck and even when the still novel problems created by having pro-development, economically conservative appointees in such key positions of enforcement as EPA administrator have been sorted out, the basic questions will remain. They are surprisingly close to the kinds of questions that have always been central to the parks and recreation movement. Where is the balance to be drawn between material well-being and physical and emotional health? What kind of life do we want for ourselves? For our children?

## The Clean Air Act

The Clean Air Act currently requires the control of seven known environmental pollutants: sulfur dioxide, particulate matter, carbon monoxide, nitrogen oxides, hydrocarbons, ozone, and lead. Other substances may be added to the list of controlled pollutants upon the completion of specified administrative steps. National Ambient Air Quality Standards (NAAQS) are established for each of these pollutants.

Primary standards to be set by the EPA are those "requisite to protect the public health . . . allowing an adequate margin of safety." The agency is also required to promulgate secondary standards "requisite to protect the public welfare from any known or anticipated adverse effects."

Although both the primary and stricter secondary standards are to be set without direct reference to the cost of compliance, the cost of achieving the required emissions reductions to meet the standards may be considered in determining the most appropriate means to ensure ultimate compliance.

The statutory scheme calls for each state to submit a state implementation plan (SIP) demonstrating the methods by which the state proposes to implement these standards. Primary standards were to be achieved by 1982 and secondary standards within a "reasonable time" specified in the SIP. The SIPs were to include all manner of pollution control timetables and techniques and preconstruction review of new direct sources of air pollution.

New Source Performance Standards (NSPS) are set by EPA on an industry by industry basis. Among the most controversial of these have been auto-emission standards for new cars. Postponement of the most stringent and most technically difficult standards has become almost routine in the wake of industry pleas that requirements were both economically disastrous and scientifically unjustifiable.

Of all the provisions of the Clean Air Act, none demonstrates the link between parks and a healthy environment more dramatically than the requirements for classification within SIPs of air quality regions. There are three basic classifications. In Class I areas practically no significant increases in pollution levels are permitted. Most of the area within the United States falls within Class II. In Class II areas the Clean Air Act seeks a balance between economic development and preservation or improvement of current air quality. Class III designation is reserved by the Act for areas where significant industrial and commercial development are encouraged. Even in Class III areas pollution increases are permitted only up to the National Ambient Air Quality Standards.

As an example of the difference between classes, for sulfur dioxide in a Class I area the maximum increase is 2 micrograms per cubic meter of air on an annual mean basis, while in a Class III area, a 40 microgram per cubic meter increase is allowable.

The Clean Air Act specifies that:

(1) International parks

(2) National wilderness areas which exceed 5000 acres in size,

(3) National memorial parks which exceed 5000 acres in size and

(4) National parks which exceed six thousand acres in size, and which are in existence on the date of the enactment of the Clean Air Act Amendments of 1977 shall be Class I areas and may not be redesignated. All areas which were redesignated as Class I under regulations promulgated before such date of enactment shall be Class I areas which may not be redesignated.[129]

Section 164 of the statute provides that:

(1) an area which exceeds ten thousand acres in size and is a national monument, a national primitive area, a national preserve, a national recreation area, a national wild and scenic river, a national wildlife refuge, a national lakeshore or seashore, and

(2) a national park or national wilderness established after the date of enactment . . . [1977] which exceeds ten thousand acres in size . . . may be redesignated only as class I or II.

There have been numerous recommendations by the National Commission on Air Quality, which if adopted would in many cases weaken the current requirements. These include a drastic limitation of the Prevention of Significant Deterioration (PSD) principle to parks and wilderness areas. The result would be to permit deterioration of air quality under SIPs in the developing areas of the South and West to the minimum national health standard level.

Despite all of the problems, the Clean Air Act has definitely resulted in a significant improvement in much of the nation's air quality, particularly with regard to the industrial and power plant discharges of sulfur dioxide. Thre has also been substantial reduction in suspended particulates from steel mills, oil refineries, and cement and chemical plants. Much improvement has also been achieved in auto-emission levels, reducing carbon monoxide, nitrogen dioxide, and lead in the atmosphere.

At the same time, more radical solutions necessary for substantial improvements in urban air quality have either been watered down by statutory amendments or ignored by state and local administrators. The most prominent of these failures is the elimination of requirements for stringent Transportation Control Plans (TCPs).

A TCP might include such strategies as limitations on parking spaces, "preferential bus/car pool lanes," controls on parking garages and lots and promotion of mass transit generally.

Although the urban TCPs have been ineffectual because of the lack of funds for amelioration of commuting problems and a reluctance to add further economic burdens to already depressed urban centers,[130] there is promise for corresponding transportation plans to protect the national parks.

Under the National Park System Areas Public Transportation Program,[131] the need is recognized for funds for planning and activating transportation programs to

> minimize reliance on personal motor vehicles which . . . may diminish the natural and recreational value of such units by causing traffic congestion and environmental damage and by requiring the provision of roads, parking and other facilities in ever increasing numbers and density.

Although this statute is essentially a policy and planning statement, it would indeed be ironic if the national parks led the country in intelligent use of mass transit.

## The Clean Water Act

The Clean Water Act has, through its history, focused on the goal of cleaning up the nation's waterways to the point where they are "swimmable" and "fishable." Like the Clean Air Act, the statute has evolved since its origins in 1948 through its last major modification in 1977 from research and technical assistance through classification of the purposes of individual bodies of water by the states to a technology-forcing timetable for elimination of "point-sources" of pollution.

The most important provisions of the act call for the achievement by 1983 of "secondary" treatment of municipal wastes[132] under all circumstances, while keeping intact the goal of achieving "best practicable waste treatment technology." Massive federal assistance has been made available to municipalities in order to help them meet federal effluent limits.

The law contains complex requirements for the elimination of industrial sources of pollution. The effective date of these requirements has been postponed and will probably be delayed in the future.

The Clean Water Act is "technology-forcing" legislation and is designed to press for goals that may not be readily achievable. As long as the ultimate ends remain clear, their temporary postponement is regrettable but not disastrous. In the case of the Clean Water Act, the elimination of the discharge of all pollutants into navigable waterways in order to achieve "protection of public water supplies and the protection and propagation of shellfish, fish and wildlife, and to allow recreational activities, in and on the water," remains an uncompromised goal, although new requirements to consider "the reasonableness of the relationship between the costs of attaining a reduction in effluents and the effluent reduction benefits derived"[133] will undoubtedly push back the ultimate timetable beyond the decade of the eighties.

As with the Clean Air Act, there are complex technical regulations and limitations on such activities as oil spills and hazardous substances (§ 311), the dumping of dredged and fill materials (§ 404), and the disposal of sewage sludge (§ 405). New plants must meet specified New Source Performance Standards and the EPA has an ongoing program to develop guidelines for industries that utilize the waterways, ranging from seafood processing to pulp and paper manufacturing.

It should now be readily apparent that complex statutes like the Clean Air and Water Acts require dedicated and imaginative enforcement by the EPA and responsible state agencies.

Although direct participation in the enforcement of these and other environmental statutes by parks officials and leisure services professionals will be rather limited, the fact that much of the effectiveness of the laws is determined by assessing the increase in recreational value of crucial natural resources puts the profession in a unique position to provide dramatic and understandable evidence of whether the technical requirements are sufficient and whether enforcement is effective.

Testimony that the fish are biting, the mountains are visible, and the kids can swim in the river without being covered with slime will not only tell us much about the practical value of environmental statutes, but will also encourage further efforts for pollution control as the public begins to be aware of the immediate benefits and takes renewed pride in their natural environment. Human beings have always been more readily moved by the tangible evidence of their senses than by abstract statistics culled by computers from mortality tables and economic charts.

In K. Ross Toole's passionate account of the current battle for the lands of the West, *The Rape of the Great Plains*,[134] he recounts that a Crow Indian chief, Plenty Coups, dismissed the value of mirrors which were being offered by white traders for fur pelts. "How can you drink from a still pool and not see our face? The mirrors are fine, but they break very easily. The pools and lakes never break."

It is a sad but true thought that if the environmental laws fail, no one will drink from the pool, and though they may not break, the reflections of ourselves will be murky and ugly.

## NOTES

1. 42 U.S.C.A. §§ 4331 *et seq.*
2. Sec. 101(a), 42 U.S.C.A. § 4331(a).
3. Sec. 101(b), 42 U.S.C.A. §4331(b).
4. 42 U.S.C.A. § 4332(2) (C).
5. Mich. Comp. Laws Ann., §§ 691, 1201-1207.
6. See Camden County, N.J., Park Comm. resolution No. 12-74-73.
7. 42 U.S.C.A. §§ 4371-4374.
8. No. 15514.
9. *See* Moss, "Beyond Conflict—The Art of Environmental Mediation," *Sierra Club Bulletin,* Vol. 66, No. 2, at 40 (March-April 1981).
10. 40 Code of Federal Regulations (CFR), §§ 1500-1508 (published July 30, 1979).
11. 40 CFR, § 1501.5.
12. 40 CFR, § 1501.7.
13. 40 CFR, § 1503.4(b).
14. 40 CFR, §§ 1502.14, 1505.1(b) and (c).
15. 40 CFR, § 1502.7.
16. Sec. 102(2) (c).
17. 40 CFR, §1508.18(a).
18. 40 CFR, § 1508.17.
19. See 42 U.S.C.A. § 4332(2) (C).
20. *Scottsdale Mall v. Indiana,* 549 F.2d 484 (7th Cir. 1977), cert. den., 434 U.S. 1008 (1978).
21. *Hanly v. Kleindienst,* 471 F.2d 823, 830 (2d Cir. 1972), cert. den., 412 U.S. 908 (1973).

22. *Kisner v. Butz,* 350 F. Supp. 310, 323 (N.D. W. Va. 1972).
23. Alabama Forest Service, 11 *Env. Rptr* 2178 (N.D. Ala. 1981).
24. *Regenstein v. Anderson,* Civil No. 2-193-73 (D.D.C. 1974).
25. *Texas Comm. on Natural Resources v. United States,* 2 E.L.R. 20574 (W.D. Tex.) vacated as moot, 430 F.2d 1315, (5th Cir. 1970).
26. *Berkson v. Morton,* 2 E.L.R. 20659 (D. Md. 1971).
27. *Nat'l Forest Preservation Group v. Butz,* 485 F.2d 408 (9th Cir. 1973).
28. *Coalition for Canyon Preservation v. Bowers,* 11 *Env. Rptr.* 1035 (Oct. 9, 1980).
29. 40 CFR § 1508.27.
30. *Scientists Inst. for Pub. Info., Inc. v. Atomic Energy Com'n.,* 481 F.2d 1079, 1094 (D.C. Cir. 1973).
31. 40 CFR § 1508.23. See also § 1502.5.
32. *Strycker's Bay Neighborhood Council, Inc. v. Karlen,* 444 U.S. 223 (1980); *Cf., Vermont Yankee Nuclear Power Corp. v. NRDC,* 435 U.S. 519 (1978).
33. 427 U.S. 390 (1976).
34. 40 CFR § 1502.4(a).
35. See the discussion of this project in Joseph L. Sax, *Mountains without Handrails: Reflections on the National Parks* (Ann Arbor: University of Michigan Press, 1980), at 70-71.
36. 40 CFR § 1506-5(c).
37. 485 F.2d 460 (9th Cir. 1973), cert. den 416 U.S. 961 (1974).
38. See *Natural Resources Defense Council v. Morton,* 458 F.2d 827 (D.C. Cir. 1972); *Aberdeen & Rockfish R.R. v. SCRAP,* 422 U.S. 289 (1975); *Kleppe v. Sierra Club,* 427 U.S. 390 (1976). See Leventhal, Environmental Decision-making and the Role of the Courts, 122 *U. Pa. L. Rev.* 509, 514 (1974).
39. 401 U.S. 402 (1971).
40. 23 U.S.C.A. § 138.
41. 5 U.S.C.A. § 706.
42. 435 U.S. 519 (1978). *Cf., Kleppe v. Sierra Club,* 427 U.S. 390 (1976).
43. See *Short Haul Survival Comm. v. United States,* 572 F.2d 240, 249 (9th Cir. 1978); *Lathan v. Brinegar,* 506 F.2d 677, 693 (9th Cir. 1974).
44. *Environmental Defense Fund v. Corps of Eng., U.S. Army,* 470 F.2d 289, 300 (8th Cir. 1972) cert. den., 412 U.S. 931 (1973).
45. 40 CFR § 1500.2.
46. Leventhal, *supra* note 38, at 511.
47. For a succinct summary of land ownership in the United States, see Peter Meyer, "Land Rush—A Survey of America's Land," *Harper's Magazine,* January 1979, at 45-60.
48. Wolf, "New Voice in the Wilderness," *Rocky Mountain Magazine,* vol. 3, no. 2, at 29, 34 (March/April 1981).
49. See the espousal of this view in White, The Historical Roots of Our Economic Crisis, 155 *Science* 1203 (1967).
50. See Yi-Fu Tuan, Our Treatment of the Environment in Ideal and Actuality, 58 *American Scientist* 244 (1970).
51. An excavation site that fills with water creating a small lake or pond.

52. Joseph L. Sax, *Mountains Without Handrails: Reflections on the National Parks* Ann Arbor: University of Michigan Press, 1980.
53. 16 U.S.C.A. §§ 528-531. Early statutes structuring the national forest system were the Forest Reserve Act of 1891, 16 U.S.C.A. § 471 and the Organic Act of 1897, 16 U.S.C.A. §§ 473-478, 479-482. These were repealed in 1976.
54. See Harold W. Wood, Jr., "Pinchot and Mather—How the Forest Service and Park Service Got That Way," *Not Man Apart*, December 1976, reprinted in part in Coggins and Wilkinson, *Federal Public Land Resources Law* Mineola, N.Y.: Foundation Press, 1981.
55. *Id.*
56. 16 U.S.C.A. § 528.
57. 16 U.S.C.A. § 531.
58. 522 F.2d 945 (4th Cir. 1975).
59. 16 U.S.C.A. § 1600 *et seq.*
60. *Id.*
61. 43 U.S.C.A. § 315.
62. See *La Rue v. Udall*, 324 F.2d 428 (D.C. Cir. 1963).
63. 43 U.S.C.A. §§ 1701-1783. Specific reference to multiple use is found in § 1732.
64. See the discussion of multiple use in BLM, *Draft Plan for Managing the Public Rangelands* (1979).
65. 161 U.S. 519 (1896).
66. 441 U.S. 322 (1979).
67. 436 U.S. 371 (1978).
68. Tribe, *American Constitutional Law* 38-40 (1979 supp.).
69. 16 U.S.C.A. §§ 703-711, supplemented by the Migrating Bird Conservation Act of 1929.
70. 252 U.S. 416 (1920).
71. 18 U.S.C.A. §§ 42-44; 16 U.S.C.A. §§ 667e and 701 (1970).
72. A variety of statutes passed at various times attempted to solidify both the land and riverine bases for protection of migratory fowl. These include the Refuge Recreation Act of 1962; U.S.C.A. § 460k; the Refuge Revenue Sharing Act of 1964, 16 U.S.C.A. § 715s; the Migratory Bird Sanctuary Stamp Act of 1934; and the Water Banks Act of 1970, 16 U.S.C.A. §§ 1301-1311. See generally 16 U.S.C.A. §§ 661-668.
73. 16 U.S.C.A. § 668 *et seq.*
74. 11 E.R.C. 2098 (D.D.C. 1978) (Civ. No. 78-1210).
75. 16 U.S.C.A. § 715.
76. See 50 CFR § 25-11(b).
77. *Defenders of Wildlife v. Andrus*, 445 F. Supp. 446 (D.D.C. 1978) Cf., *National Wildlife Federation v. Morton*, 393 F. Supp. 1286 (D.D.C. 1975).
78. 426 U.S. 529 (1976).
79. 16 U.S.C.A. §§ 1331-1340.
80. Article IV, sec. 3, cl. 2.
81. 16 U.S.C.A. §§ 668-668d.

82. 16 U.S.C.A. § 757(b).
83. 16 U.S.C.A. §§ 661-667e.
84. 16 U.S.C.A. §§ 669-669i (1970) (originally enacted in 1937).
85. 16 U.S.C.A. §§ 777-777k.
86. 16 U.S.C.A. §§1361-1362, 137-184, 1401-1407.
87. 16 U.S.C.A. §§ 1531-1543.
88. Pub. L. No. 89-669 §§ 1-3, 80 Stat. 926 (repealed 1973).
89. 16 U.S.C.A. §§ 460L-1-460L-11.
90. Pub. L. No. 91-135, 83 Stat. 275.
91. 12 *Int'l Leg. Mtrs.* 1085 (1973).
92. 16 U.S.C.A. § 1532(5). Plants are equally broadly defined. *Id.* at § 1532(9).
93. 16 U.S.C.A. § 1533(d).
94. 16 U.S.C.A. § 1540(g).
95. 529 F.2d 359 (5th Cir. 1976), cert. den. 429 U.S. 979 (1976).
96. 437 U.S. 153 (1978).
97. 549 F.2d 1064 (6th Cir. 1977).
98. 16 U.S.C.A. § 1536(h).
99. 50 CFR § 17-11 (1979).
100. 16 U.S.C.A. §§ 1131-1136.
101. 16 U.S.C.A. §§ 1131(c).
102. See, e.g., *Izaak Walton League of America v. St. Clair,* 497 F.2d 849 (8th Cir. 1974), reversing 353 F. Supp. 698 (D. Minn. 173).
103. 483 F. Supp. 465 (E.D. Calif. 1980).
104. *Id.* at 501.
105. General Mining Law of 1872, 30 U.S.C.A. § 22 *et seq.*
106. 611 F.2d 1277 (9th Cir. 1980).
107. See *United States v. Coleman,* 390 U.S. 599 (1968).
108. 30 U.S.C.A. § 612(b).
109. *Id.* at §§ 611-612.
110. *United States v. Richardson,* 599 F. 2d 290, 294 (9th Cir. 1979).
111. *United States v. Zweifel,* 508 F.2d 1150, 1154 (1975), cert. den. 423 U.S. 829 (1975).
112. See Mining Activities Within National Park System Areas, 16 U.S.C.A. §§ 1901-1912.
113. 16 U.S.C.A. § 460L.
114. 16 U.S.C.A. § 1274 *et seq.*
115. 16 U.S.C.A. §§ 1241-1249. (See also the Archeological Resource Protection Act of 1979), 16 U.S.C.A. § 470aa *et seq.*
116. 16 U.S.C.A. § 46i *et seq.* (§ 502 of the statute).
117. N.J.S.A. 13:18A-1 *et seq.*
118. 16 U.S.C.A. §§ 1451-1464.
119. *Sierra Club v. Morton,* 405 U.S. 727 (1972).
120. *See* Commentary: Mineral King Goes Downhill, 5 *Ecology L.Q.* 585 (1976).
121. See 16 U.S.C.A. § 688.
122. 16 U.S.C.A. § 1.
123. See *Friends of Yosemite v. Frizzell,* 420 F. Supp. 390 (N.D. Calif. 1976).

124. 608 F.2d 1250 (9th Cir. 1979).
125. 16 U.S.C.A. § 20.
126. 42 U.S.C.A. § 7701 *et seq.*
127. 33 U.S.C.A. § 1251 *et seq.* This statute was primarily shaped by the Federal
     Water Pollution control Act of 1972 and was substantially amended in 1977.
128. 15 U.S.C.A. § 2601 *et seq.* (See also the Federal Insecticide, Fungicide, and
     Rodenticide Act, 7 U.S.C.A. §§ 135-136y.)
129. § 162(a).
130. Authority to promulgate TCPs was restricted and the use of such elements
     as parking surcharges was prohibited by § 110c(2) of the Clean Air Act, add-
     ed by a 1974 amendment. For a thoughtful discussion of TCPs see *South
     Terminal Corporation v. Environmental Protection Agency,* 504 F.2d 646
     (1st Cir. 1974).
131. 16 U.S.C.A. §§ 2301-2306.
132  § 301(i).
133. § 304(b) (4) (B).
134. K. Ross Toole, *The Rape of the Great Plains* (Boston: Little, Brown, 1976).

# 4

# Injuries to Visitors and Recipients of Leisure Services

## INTRODUCTION

### Concern over Liability

In the past, government agencies, charitable organizations, manufacturers and distributors of recreational equipment, and privately owned recreational enterprises had a number of traditional defenses protecting them against lawsuits for personal injury. Over the last several years, however, substantial limitations have been placed on these defenses. As a result, "law" and "liability" have become synonymous terrors to almost everyone in recreation, physical education, and related professions. Additional elements only indirectly related to traditional limits on liability suits also play a role in the increased concern for legal ramifications of recreation injury. Our consideration of a variety of these factors is necessary for a full understanding of the complex and volatile legal patterns now emerging.

The rapid demise of historic sovereign and municipal immunity in many states is certainly an important factor in the increase in liability. So too is the substitution of a "comparative negligence" standard for the former complete defense of "contributory negligence." Modification of the "voluntary assumption of risk" defense is particularly significant in adventurous leisure pursuits. Modification or elimination of the requirement of proof of fault has dramatically increased the number of successful lawsuits against enterprises that manufacture or supply equipment. These and other elements of the liability dilemma will be discussed in this chapter.

Before considering the legal elements of recreation injury compensation, we must give some attention to the incredible inflation in medical and rehabilitation costs over the last several years. Discussion with practitioners in recreation discloses that they are often more incensed by the amount of damage recoveries awarded unworthy plaintiffs in recreation suits than by the changes in law that permit suits to be maintained. Such litigants have been described as "overprotective parents, those who desire to get something for nothing, and greedy members of the legal profession."[1]

### The Costs of Liability

It is true that in our litigation-conscious society, there are numerous claims for a few hundred to a few thousand dollars involving vague and difficult-to-evaluate back injuries such as "whiplash" or exaggerated pain, suffering, and partial disability resulting from relatively minor trauma. Often these claims are settled by insurance carriers because the cost of litigating and defending against them may well be greater than the amount actually sought by the plaintiff.

The contingent fee system permits claimants to employ attorneys on a commission basis with no immediate outlay of fees. The general practice of American law requires each party to a lawsuit to bear its own legal costs in order to encourage the peaceful resolution of disputes by resort to the court system. Otherwise, early jurists reasoned, prospective plaintiffs would be so fearful of having to pay large legal expenses for defendants that they might resort to violence or other uncivilized methods for recovering their losses.

Exaggerated claims and the contingent fee system encourage the maintenance of questionable lawsuits. Furthermore, an irony of American law that largely bases the assessment of "pain and suffering" on the amount of actual medical costs encountered by the plaintiff prompts litigating plaintiffs and their attorneys to resort to the most expensive medical and therapeutic practices, even when they may be superfluous and unnecessary.

Having noted these improper and inflationary forces in our law, and recognizing the need for a reform of the system to eliminate such abuses, we must recognize that, contrary to myth, rumor, and gossip, massive awards through the litigation process are relatively rare. Furthermore, in the few negligence cases in which recoveries of hundreds of thousands or even millions of dollars are affirmed by higher courts, extremely serious and permanent injuries or death are always involved.

Quadriplegia, pariplegia, extreme neuro-psychiatric dysfunction, sensory impairment, and gross disfigurement resulting from burns are the kinds of injuries that result in large damage awards or settlements. There is rarely a windfall element in such cases.

To illustrate the point, consider the landmark *Sunday v. Stratton Corp.*[2] ski accident case in which Sunday, a novice skier, fell on some shrubbery and was rendered quadriplegic. The Vermont Supreme Court stated that up to the time of trial alone, $70,000 in medical bills had accumulated. The projected cost of just one required medication for the crippled youth was $94,000 over his lifetime. Future medical care, nursing, and hospitalization could total $2,500,000 without taking inflation into account. Even without considering the fact that Sunday's "efforts to complete his education are fraught with incredible difficulties; he can neither work nor father children and he has recurring fits of depression," it is obvious that the $1,500,000 recovery awarded him does not represent a windfall or "something for nothing"!

As those engaged in therapeutic recreation and other adjunctive therapies will readily understand, advances in rehabilitation and treatment of victims of crippling injuries are as costly as they are encouraging, and complex equipment and high-quality professional care necessary to achieve excellent rehabilitative results will continue to have a high price tag. Since no responsible recreation professional desires to return to an era when the severely impaired were put to bed or locked away until they died, the issue is not whether the costs should be paid, but rather, what is the most efficient, fairest system of paying them. Unless and until our society moves to a universal system of insurance and compensation, the litigation approach, despite its inadequacy, inefficiency, and abuses, will remain a major element in our injury compensation scheme.

Concomitant with advances in rehabilitative and medical technology has been a dramatic increase in the proportion of our population participating in active leisure pursuits. Nine-year-old gymnasts, forty-year-old marathoners, and seventy-year-old skiers would have been the topic of amazed conversations only a generation ago. Obviously, a significant increase in recreation and sports-related injuries accompanies this explosion in participation.

A recently emerging element in the activity/injury equation has been the pursuit of high-adventure recreation in programs such as Outward Bound by formerly unlikely stereotyped individuals: the tired executive, the harried housewife, or the bookish graduate student.

Certainly a price must be paid in occasional serious injury for this major change in recreational habits, but the price would appear to be almost insignificant in contrast to the physical, emotional, and spiritual degeneration resulting from lifelong sedentary pursuits.

Individuals rarely anticipate serious injury to themselves. Even if there is an intellectual appreciation of the dangers of physical participation, it is hard to translate that into personal terms. Sometimes this is unfortunate and foolish because precautions are simple and would not detract substantially from the value of the activity. The disdain for safety belts, motorcycle or bicycle helmets, or the use of spotters in gymnastics falls into this category. Yet in a larger sense, disdain and denial of risk is one of humankind's more ennobling characteristics. Those who dramatically visualize danger and disaster may be frozen into inaction.

Given the fact that the recreation and leisure service profession is dependent upon the willingness of people to take risks, it is hard to understand the often strong reaction against those who seek compensation for injuries suffered encountering those risks. Much of this reaction and resentment is based upon antiquated ideas concerning "fault." Indeed, the gulf between the legal and leisure service professions probably results in large part from the general movement by the law away from the proposition that the cost of inevitable injuries should be borne by the party "to blame" for them. Rather, the law has partially shifted to an economic basis for noncriminal injury compensation. This theory holds that costs are most efficiently allocated to those parties who are best equipped to meet the needs of compensation and distribute the losses to society as a whole. This may be done through insurance, adjustments in the price charged for goods and services, or changes in the tax structure.

### Comparison with Industrial Injuries

There is a close historical parallel to current attitudes and reactions to the problems of recreational injuries. Prior to the Industrial Revolution and before heavily mechanized farming, there were relatively few injuries in the workplace. The population was small, and disease usually cut life short. There was little medical treatment, and most crippled or injured individuals could be cared for within the confines of the family, the religious or charitable community, or by the local landowner who could find some tasks to provide for the needs of the debilitated until they died.

With the modern age, there came not only massive, dangerous machinery but also an almost total depersonalization of the work force. For most of the nineteenth and in the early part of the twentieth century, people in business, entrepreneurs, and the courts (which by and large reflected the interests of the wealthy new industrial barons) had an attitude of callous indifference to the economic and physical plight of injured workers. Not only was it extremely difficult for poorly paid and often illiterate laborers to find competent legal aid, but also a series of "defenses" made it virtually impossible for them to get reparation. Among these defenses were:

**Contributory Negligence.** If the worker were even minimally responsible for his or her own injury, there could be no recovery. Thus a ten-year-old girl who got drowsy and caught her hair in a textile machine after working for several hours could not recover because she was at least partly to blame for the accident.

**Voluntary Assumption of Risk.** Ignoring all economic realities, the courts held that a worker who knowingly went to work in a dangerous mine or operated a machine without a guard was a "volunteer" and could not complain if the predictable accident occurred.

**The "Fellow Servant" Rule.** This rule was a particularly insidious one. It held that not only did a worker assume the risk of injury by faulty equipment, but also, because the carelessness of co-workers could readily be anticipated, if an injury was caused by the actions of one of these "fellow servants," the employer was not responsible.

Eventually, revulsion against these kinds of rules led Germany, Great Britain, and ultimately the United States to the universal adoption of Worker's Compensation Systems that provide a degree of compensation for injured employees without regard to fault. More recently, as courts have gained a more sophisticated understanding of the economic realities of society, the absolute bar to recovery of contributory negligence and voluntary assumption of risk have been substantially modified in many areas of "tort" or personal injury law outside of the employment context. So, also, the requirement of proof of negligence or fault has been limited or eliminated in a number of states when injuries are caused by a defective commercial product or by a highly hazardous activity that no amount of caution can make safe.

These relatively recent developments in the law of personal injuries shall be discussed in the context of recreational accidents. Before this, however, we should put them in the appropriate philosophical context. Just as the nineteenth and early twentieth centuries regarded industrialization and commercialization as necessary for societal development, so in the latter part of this century is recreation coming to be considered a critical component of human existence. Inevitably, if participation in leisure activities is more than mere frivolity and is important to society's progress, the argument that participants in recreation must simply shoulder the costs of their own injuries comes to have the same callous, hollow ring as the nineteenth-century arguments that workers should bear their own burdens. The ultimate issue is not whether recreation injuries should be paid for by society as a whole, but rather, whether our current system of tort liability is adequate to allocate costs, and if not, how may it be improved upon?

In order to respond to this issue, let us consider the background and status of the law.

## THE LAW OF TORTS

### Historical Development

There is no simple definition of *tort*. Derived from the Latin and French, it is also found in Old English and in a broad sense is a synonym for *wrong*. In law, a "tort" is a civil wrong; that is, a noncriminal harm done to person or property. Torts may be intentional, as in *assault, battery,* or *false imprisonment*. Other torts are based on unintentional violations of societal standards, such as *negligence,* or violations of professional standards, including medical and legal "malpractice."

Some torts result from violations of property interests. As noted in Chapter 2, these include *trespass,* the interference with the rights of possession of property, and *private nuisance,* the interference with the use and enjoyment of property. These latter torts may have elements of both intentional and negligent conduct.

Not all torts are physical. Some are at least partially based on mental and emotional injuries. These include *libel* and *slander* (the written and spoken defamation of character and reputation through false statements), and the *intentional infliction of emotional harm* through harassment, mockery, and humiliation. Courts have more recently recognized the law of *negligent emotional harm* where direct physical injury may be minor or even nonexistent, but the related mental injuries are substantial.

In the last two decades a new tort has emerged. It is *strict liability for defective products*. This tort is not based on fault but as we have discussed, on an assessment of the relative costs and profits of enterprise, the economic impact of injury, and to some extent on a determination of which party has the greatest access to information about the cause and prevention of injuries.

Some intentional torts may also be crimes. For example, the victim of a beating may recover damages in civil law for an assault that placed her in fear of harm and the battery or actual physical attack upon her. At the same time, the criminal process may separately try and convict the perpetrator and sentence him or her to an appropriate fine and prison term to satisfy society's need to protect itself through the punishment and hopefully the rehabilitation of those who break its rules.

There would be little point here to detail the gradual emergence of tort law from the recesses of the Dark Ages. Suffice it to say that the first recognition of tort as separate and distinct from criminal law probably will be found in the thirteenth and fourteenth centuries in England. Trespassess or direct injuries to persons or property were seen as threats to the "king's peace." There was no distinction between intentional and negligent or careless injuries, or even as to whether there was fault at all. Rather, since the concern was initially with acts that could lead to violent reprisal, fines and, later, the payment of damages to the victim of the trespass or his or her family were assessed without proof of any real harm or injury.

A parallel action *on the case* or *trespass on the case* involving indirect injuries (injuries that did not follow immediately from the defendant's action) developed at a somewhat later date, because it did not carry the same threat of violence and reprisal. The following example illustrates the difference. If A threw a rock and struck B, A would be liable for damages whether or not B was actually injured and whether or not the striking was intentional or accidental. On the other hand, if the rock A threw fell to the ground in the middle of a path, and later B's carriage struck it and collapsed, injuring B, this action *on the case* could be maintained only upon proof of actual damage and either intent of A to cause harm, or negligence or carelessness by A resulting in harm.

Although distinctions based on *trespass* and *case* have long since largely disappeared, it is the essential quality of the action on the case that forms the basis of most modern tort law. Yet, just as in the ancient form of trespass, in most intentional injuries no proof of actual injury is needed in order for the victims to receive *punitive* or *exemplary damages*,[3] and as noted above, liability without proof of fault for injuries caused by dangerous products and hazardous activities is being revived.

## Intentional Torts and Agency Responsibility

The intentional torts are rarely of major concern to the parks and leisure services profession. Obviously, if a park official assaults a visitor, the official would be liable for damages, both actual and punitive. The broader issue is whether the employer, be it a parks department or private recreation agency, will be liable as well.

There is a general rule in law of *respondeat superior*, literally, "the master is responsible," which holds that when an employee negligently injures someone in the course of his or her employment, the employee is acting for the business, and thus the employer should pay for the damages caused. There are a number of justifications for this rule. Employers operate their businesses or activities through employees who may have insufficient resources to pay the cost of injuries they cause. Furthermore, it is argued that the employer has the "deeper pocket" and can usually spread the cost of injury through insurance, prices, or taxes.

In theory, employers who are without fault themselves may seek *indemnification*, repayment from the employee who is the actual wrongdoer. In practice, this seldom occurs. Both employer and employee may be covered by the same insurance carrier. The employee is often *judgment proof;* that is, financially unable to meet the costs of injuries. Thus an action against the employee would not only be damaging to employer-employee relations but would probably be futile as well. Some state statutes specifically require that employees be "held harmless" or indemnified by the government entities which employ them if they are negligent in carrying out their duties. The United States Supreme Court has ruled that where the federal government pays damages under the Federal Tort Claims Act, it may not seek indemnity from the employee who was directly responsible for the compensated injury.[4]

In short, fears by individual parks and leisure services employees that they will have to bear some substantial share of damage judgments against their employers are exaggerated, if not entirely groundless. Disciplinary action and discharge are more likely to result from an employee's work-related torts than being saddled with a large judgment is.

Intentional torts have been an exception to the *respondeat superior* rules, and even today where there is a personally motivated or unprovoked assault by an employee on a visitor or client, the employee, not the employer, will generally be held responsible. Nevertheless, the employer may be held liable for negligence in the selection or training of violent employees. Furthermore, in cases where the enterprise has complete control of the visitor, such as, for example, during a senior citizen bus trip, the duty of the agency to protect may be held to be *nondelegable*. Moreover, there has been a trend toward holding the agency liable when the intentional tort directly arises from the employment situation, such as where a guard at a sporting event may intentionally shove a ticket holder in order to close a gate behind him or when a playground supervisor slaps an unruly child.

Improper detention and restraint are the most likely intentional torts involving recreational enterprises. One of the more famous cases arose when a patron at a baseball game found himself hemmed in by a crowd when the main entrance to the ball park had been intentionally closed.[5] The actual injury suffered by the plaintiff was a minimal affront to his dignity. The only damages the court awarded were a nominal punitive amount for the technically intentional tort.

Consider, on the other hand, the 1980 tragedy in Cincinnati where several young rock-and-roll fans were crushed to death and a great many more were injured as a result of inadequate access to the nonreserved seating in the auditorium. Although the incident contains elements of negligence, it is not inconceivable that it might also be characterized as the intentional tort of false imprisonment, subjecting the promoters and other management enterprises to punitive damages. It should be noted at this point that both the Federal Tort Claims Act[6] and numerous state statutes have specific exemptions for certain intentional torts. These statutes are discussed in more detail below.

Attempts by park employees or officials of recreational enterprises to restrain individuals on suspicion that a crime has been committed present some of the thorniest legal problems likely to be confronted, particularly since there is rarely time to seek an attorney's advice prior to taking action. This is among those predictable situations in which it would be helpful for all employees to be carefully instructed in the manner in which they should act. In general, the power of non-law enforcement employees to restrain or arrest is severely restricted. Without specific statutory authority, it is only when a criminal act is committed in one's presence that immediate forceful action may be taken. Mere suspicion or acting on information received from another person would not justify a restraint if the individual held is, in fact, innocent.

Of course, the amount of damages in such a case will depend upon the degree of physical force used or threatened, the length of time the visitor is restrained, the exposure of the arrest to others, and the degree of humiliation suffered. It may not even be necessary to physically restrain an individual for false arrest or imprisonment to be claimed. The seizure of valuable property such as a wallet, or the taking of a bicycle, may be sufficient to cause an individual to remain against her will.

An immediate report to the police with the fullest particulars, including, if possible, the names and addresses of both suspects and witnesses, is certainly the most prudent response to the cry on the playground or park of "He stole my bike ... baseball glove ... etc."

Greater leeway for investigation and detention may be afforded when there is an *in loco parentis* (in place of the parent) situation such as a resident camp or a school. In most jurisdictions briefly and nonforceably detaining an individual to ascertain names and addresses or to contact the police where there is no actual restraint or defamatory accusation would probably be regarded as appropriate behavior not subjecting the park employee to any real threat of a lawsuit. However, it should be noted that although a number of states have enacted laws permitting brief detention of suspected shoplifters, these statutes would not be applicable to the typical parks and leisure services situation.[7]

## Nonintentional Torts

By far the most significant aspects of tort law relating to the leisure services field are the nonintentional torts, negligence and strict liability, and the hybrid torts of nuisance and trespass, the land use aspects of which were considered in Chapter 2.

Inextricably tied to the elements of the torts discussed in this section are the twin phenomena related to the expansion of agency liability: the decline of governmental immunity and the limitation of traditional tort defenses, particularly contributory negligence and voluntary assumption of risk.

## Negligence in General

Although there had been a slow development of the concept of fault prior to the nineteenth century, it was not until the Industrial Revolution that negligence became recognized as a separate and distinct tort. Some legal historians argue that proof of negligence or fault became crucial in the law in order to protect the growth of industry. Without the requirement of fault, lawsuits would have crippled the development of commerce, particularly since early railroads were as much infernal machines of destruction as they were boons to transportation.

Whatever the validity of this theory, the negligence concept quickly took hold in this country, most notably in a Massachusetts case, *Brown v. Kendall*,[8] in which it was held that there was no liability when the defendant, while trying to stop a dogfight, accidentally struck another man with a stick. Chief Justice Shaw of the Massachusetts Supreme Judicial Court, a leading jurist of the time, stated:

> The plaintiff must come prepared with evidence to show either that the *intention* was unlawful, or that the defendant was *in fault;* for if the injury was unavoidable, and the conduct of the defendant was free of blame, he will not be liable.

The judge went on to state that in determining fault, the conduct of the defendant was to be measured by a test of *ordinary care:*

> What constitutes ordinary care will vary with circumstances of cases. In general, it means that kind and degree of care, which prudent and cautious men would use, such as is required by the exigency of the case, and such as is necessary to guard against probable danger. A man who should have occasion to discharge a gun, on an open and extensive marsh, or in a forest, would be required to use less circumspection and

care, than if he were to do the same thing in an inhabited town, village or city.

As it has evolved, the general rule of determination of negligence has remained true to the essence of Justice Shaw's reasoning. A person is negligent when he or she fails to act as a reasonably prudent person under the circumstances.[9]

Ignorance or stupidity are no excuses for dangerous and inappropriate behavior, at least in adults. In a classic English case, a slow-witted farmer had improperly stacked hay with resulting spontaneous combustion and the destruction of his neighbor's property. The defendant argued that he should be excused from responsibility if "he acted *bona fide* [in good faith] to the best of his judgment."[10]

The court recognized that to have a subjective rule of conduct that varied from person to person would result in a societal disaster. Thus, ignorance of the facts of daily life, or common knowledge of the community, or an inability to respond in the manner of an ordinary person will not be recognized excuses for negligent conduct.

There are two groups of particular significance to recreation and leisure services for whom at least limited exception to the general rule of reasonable conduct may apply: children and the disabled.

**Children.**    Unless they are engaged in adult activities (such as driving a car), children are expected to meet only a standard of conduct compatible with other children of similar age, experience, and development. It might be said that this is a compromise between a purely objective and subjective standard.

This reduced standard of care for children can be the deciding factor in many claims arising from recreational injuries. For example, in a recent case, the New Jersey Supreme Court held that a novice teenager skier who went off course and injured two people standing at the door to the base lodge was not engaged in an adult activity and therefore could escape liability since he had not breached the standard of conduct required of young inexperienced skiers.[11]

The rationale for this differential standard is obvious. Young people must learn to live in society. During their developing years, they cannot be expected to act as mature, experienced adults. Thus, the risk that children will behave in a less careful way has been placed on the victims of injuries rather than on the children causing them.

Actually, the reduced standard of care for children is more likely to emerge in cases where they have been injured themselves and it is argued that they should be barred from recovery because they have contributed to their injury. Thus, when a twelve-year-old on a bicycle collided with and was injured by a car driven by a sixteen-year-old, the younger child was not barred from recovery by contributory negligence, while the older one was held to an adult standard.[12]

As this case illustrates, adult activities are more likely to cause injury than are children's activities and games. Thus, the balance of judgment may shift to favor the victim rather than the youth who causes the harm. With regard to recreational activities, there is certainly judicial disagreement concerning what "adult" activities are. Generally, operation of powered vehicles such as power boats[13] and motorcycles[14] are likely to result in operators being held to adult standards, and even an eleven-year-old golfer whose ball struck another was required by one court to meet an adult standard on the grounds that to do otherwise would expose players to an unreasonable risk of injury.[15] Older youths acting as counselors and instructors may well be held to adult standards since they have undertaken supervisory and teaching responsibilities.

In practical terms, what the parks, recreation, and leisure services professionals should bear in mind is that, in the context of lawsuits for recreation injuries, children will often be the plaintiffs and the application of the reduced standard of care may make it extremely difficult to utilize their own carelessness to excuse negligent conduct toward them. Ironically, if teenagers are used as employees and counselors, their greater likelihood of being negligent will not afford greater protection to the agency, because they may be held to an adult standard. In addition, the agency may be found independently negligent for employing or inadequately supervising a careless young person.

The number of negligence actions against children is relatively few. One of the reasons for this is that, contrary to widespread public belief, parents are generally not liable at common law for the torts of their children. Parents may be held liable for negligently entrusting dangerous instrumentalities (such as fireworks or weapons) to children or when, because of past misconduct by the child, parents are held independently negligent for failure to supervise and control their offspring. Yet in the absence of proof of a child's propensity for dangerous conduct, the child's torts are his or her own.[16]

There is one general exception to this rule. Utilizing a fiction called the "family purpose doctrine," a number of states have held that the parent-owner of a vehicle is responsible when a child driver causes negligent injury. Other states reach the same result by statutes making owners of vehicles liable for all damages, or requiring insurance to cover all drivers.

A number of states have enacted statutes making parents liable for certain wrongful acts of children, but most of these involve only intentional or willful conduct and limit recovery to property damage or a nominal amount.[17] Louisiana[18] and Texas[19] have statutes permitting substantial recoveries against parents for the negligence of children. Perhaps this is indicative of a trend.

Since children rarely have substantial resources, many possible actions are simply abandoned because the cost of litigation will often outweigh the possibility that at some dim future date a substantial amount may actually be recovered.

**The Disabled.**   The other group of special concern to leisure services for whom standards of care are somewhat specialized are the physically, mentally, or emotionally disabled. Obviously they are of particular interest to those engaged in therapeutic recreation programs.

With regard to physical impairment, the courts have largely adopted the attitude that the reasonably prudent person must act in consideration of his or her own physical defects or limitations. On the other hand, if a disabled person is injured through the negligence of a recreation agency or its employee, the fact that the injuries suffered may be more severe than those which would have been suffered by a vigorous or unimpaired person under like circumstances will be deemed irrelevent. The world contains people with a variety of physical and mental conditions. The wrongdoer or *tort feasor* is as responsible in terms of compensation for injury to the *eggshell plaintiff* as to anyone else.

As eloquently stated by a great law professor, Jacobus Ten Broeck, who happened to be blind, the handicapped have a "right to live in the world,"[20] and those knowing of their handicaps, or who may anticipate their presence, must take reasonable precautions to protect them. Thus a city excavating on a park pathway frequented by the blind could not merely put up a "danger" sign.[21] Similarly, precautions should be taken to warn the blind of curb cuts created to aid those in wheelchairs. In the latter case, moving the curb cut away from the center of the normal crosswalk or installing small metal plates to provide an audible warning would be among the ways of reasonably meeting the foreseeable risks. These are merely illustrative. The greater the known disabilities, the greater the precautions that must be taken. This applies both to the disabled individual and to the agencies dealing with them. It would obviously be negligent for a blind person to drive a car, while it would ordinarily be reasonable for the same person to walk with a seeing-eye dog even if there is a somewhat greater risk of collision than a sighted person would have. Similarly, one confined to a wheelchair could be negligent in attempting to negotiate a steep set of steps when, albeit with some inconvenience, a ramp is available. A person who knows that she has coronary disease may be negligent in engaging in an active pastime such as mountain climbing when an attack might be dangerous to others. On the other hand, sudden unforeseen physical or emotional breakdowns would not ordinarily result in liability.

The other side of the rule noted earlier, that the law doesn't recognize stupidity, foolishness, or unexcused ignorance as defenses in negligence, teaches that persons engaged in routine activities of life will not be held to a higher standard merely because they might be brighter, quicker, or better educated than the average person. Thus a race car driver who gets involved in a traffic accident on the highway will not be required by the courts to have displayed extraordinary reflexes and skill, although if the accident were on the racetrack the driver would be held to the higher level one might expect of a professional under the circumstances.

There are very few cases involving individuals who suffer severe mental impairment or are insane. It has been suggested that in cases of extremely impaired mental capacity, the individual should be treated in the same manner as are very young children; that is, since they are incapable of reasoning, they cannot be expected to meet any standard of care based upon reasonableness. Historically, tort law has rejected such suggestions,[22] but the relatively few cases involving mentally deficient plaintiffs indicate that their handicap should be considered in determining whether they have exercised reasonable care for their own safety.[23] In fact, Dean William Prosser, the greatest modern torts expert, concluded that in virtually all such cases contributory negligence would be discounted, or as put in one case, a mentally retarded person should exercise care for himself "based upon the capacity of the claimant and his perception of danger considering the degree of his illness."[24]

What emerges from this discussion is that leisure service agencies dealing with children or people who are disabled must take their limitations into consideration. What would be reasonable care in dealing with ordinary adults may fall well short of required conduct toward individuals with known limitations, and, although the law will impose an obligation on all individuals beyond infancy to act with some care, it will not require children or the disabled to meet the same level of skill and ability as a physically unimpaired ordinary adult.

**Evidence of Negligent Conduct.**    The mythological reasonably prudent person is not perfect. The law recognizes that people will take risks in their lives. Thus, as stated in one famous case, the reasonable person "is not necessarily a supercautious individual devoid of human frailties and constantly pre-occupied with the idea that danger may be lurking in every direction about him at any time."[25] On the other hand, unlike any real person, the mythological reasonably prudent one is *always* careful. An individual or agency cannot excuse an act of carelessness on the ground that ninety-nine times out of a hundred, proper care would be taken.

It is one thing to require reasonable care, but to define and apply the standard is a complex matter. First, with regard to leisure services, as with any professional activity, the standard of care will be determined by reference to appropriate professional practices. Just as a doctor, airplane pilot, and plumber cannot defend themselves against charges of negligent performances by arguing that they did as well as the ordinary untrained individual would have, so too the park manager, the coach, or the recreation therapist must adhere to the reasonable standards of their particular profession.

Courts derive information on how professionals are expected to act from a variety of sources including laws, regulations, and codes of professional conduct and standards of behavior. Statutes, ordinances, building codes, governmentally sanctioned standards, and guidelines are reflective of the considered judgment of a democratic society and are extremely important sources of standards of reasonable conduct. If a legislative body has adopted these rules in statutory form, and if the rules are intended to prevent the kind of harm that actually occurred, then evidence of their violation may be virtually conclusive. Under the Federal Consumer Product Safety Act knowing violation of rules or orders of the Consumer Product Safety Commission may result in liability and damages including attorney's fees over and above common law remedies.[26] Less formal governmental guidelines, municipal ordinances and codes, or the published standards of professional organizations may still be persuasive evidence of negligence unless an affirmative defense is presented that demonstrates valid reasons for nonadherence.

Customary practices may be evidence of proper or due care, just as deviation from recognized standards may demonstrate negligence. The testimony of fellow professionals or experts in the field may be useful as well. On the other hand, where the activity in question is a common one, a court may determine that professional expertise is superfluous.

Two examples derived from actual cases may serve to illustrate these points.

1. An eighteen-year-old diver plunged from a newly installed aluminum spring board and struck his head on the bottom of the pool at a depth of eight feet. In order to determine whether the construction and location of the board was reasonable, reference was made to the National Swimming Pool Institute Standards of Design and Construction. The local building code was examined to determine whether the board's

specifications were in compliance. A number of diving experts, including Olympic coaches, were called to testify concerning the practices of the profession and the installation's conformity to them. When it was determined that the installation did not comply with industry standards, that the board was constructed of different material, and that there were several other deviations from the plans approved under the local construction code, and finally, when nationally recognized coaches testified that the installation was inappropriate for an unsupervised motel pool, a substantial judgment for the crippled young diver was affirmed.[27]

2. A physical education class was meeting on a rainy day. With the regular boys' instructor absent, the girls' instructor attempted to teach golf to sixty boys and girls on the gym floor with only the aid of an untrained substitute teacher. One boy who had never had a golf lesson before was struck in the head and killed by another boy. With sixty boys and girls age ten or eleven all swinging clubs in a confined space at "wiffle" balls, the dangers are so apparent that little more than proof of the facts stated was necessary for a jury to reach the conclusion that the conduct of the teacher was negligent. The testimony of experts is not required when a jury may reach a conclusion based on common knowledge and understanding.[28]

In addition to evidence of practice and custom, and expert opinion where appropriate, the typical trial of a negligence action may contain evidence of the facts of the case, whether in dispute or not and, most critically in a practical sense, evidence of the nature and degree of physical and emotional injury as well as property damage. The burden of proof by a "fair preponderance of the evidence" is on the plaintiff. That is, if a jury or court finds the factual evidence equally convincing for both sides, the defendant should win. Nevertheless, unlike criminal cases, where the state must meet a very heavy burden of proof "beyond a reasonable doubt," in tort actions, if the trier of fact (jury or judge) is somewhat more convinced by the plaintiff in the material elements of the dispute, there is no requirement that all doubts be resolved in his or her favor.

The negligence issue is central to all determinations. Some judges and commentators have even attempted to reduce "negligence" to a formula. The aptly named Judge Learned Hand suggested that conduct is negligent when the burden (B) of taking precautions is less than the probability that injury would result without precautions (P) multiplied by the gravity of the resulting injury (L), or $B < PL$.[29]

Although not always applicable and somewhat misleading, this formula is useful in focusing on some principal elements of the determination of reasonableness. For example, in the swimming pool injury cases, one could say that if there is insufficient depth under a springboard, the probability of injury is high and the seriousness or gravity of the resulting injury (possible paralysis) is very great. Therefore, in the formula B < PL, the burden on a pool owner of eliminating the hazard (lowering or eliminating the diving board, restructuring the pool to provide greater depth) would have to be very substantial before it would outweigh the combined risk and seriousness of injury. Similarly, the negligence of such practices as issuing a cracked football helmet to a high school player[30] or permitting a large group of youngsters to swim in a pool rendered "murky and almost opaque" by an excessive release of purifying chemicals[31] is made readily apparent by the use of the Hand formula.

Sometimes, of course, a risk is worth taking. There may be an important objective of such value that even though there may be some possibility of injury, the action is reasonable.[32] For example, rope courses in modern playground equipment present an element of risk to the user. Yet our society may well determine that the values in confidence, agility, physical coordination, and familiarity with the natural world which the use of innovative equipment may encourage outweight the risk.[33]

Of course, it may be argued that as safer equipment that may have similar recreational, if not spiritual, benefits comes into general use at lower cost, the professional must alter his or her standards. Certainly yesterday's "reasonably safe" monkey bars set in concrete are no longer reasonable in the light of standards and guidelines developed by the Consumer Product Safety Commission, the NRPA, the American National Standards Institute, the American Society for Testing and Materials, and the National Bureau of Standards as reflected in the availability of climbers with fall-free design and resilient playground surfaces.[34]

Part of the determination of whether conduct is reasonable involves the element of *foreseeability* of injury. That is, an individual or an agency is not expected to guard against hazards that are not known or that would not be known through the exercise of reasonable foresight. By and large, we are not absolute insurers of the safety of others. Thus, in a lawsuit arising from a tragic occurrence in which a swimmer was attacked by a shark at a municipally operated beach, it was held that there was no duty to guard or warn against shark attacks since there had been no attack on record and no prior evidence of shark activities.[35] Obviously, if shark attacks in the area became more frequent, the time would soon arrive when attacks were foreseeable, and reasonable prudence would dictate precautions and safety measures commensurate with the risk.

In another case, where a ten-year-old boy crawled through a hole in a playground fence and was injured by a train on adjacent railroad tracks, it was held that even though there was no proof of prior accidents, worn paths leading to both sides of the fence openings should have alerted the recreation supervisors to the need for precautionary repairs.[36]

**Other Elements of Negligence.**   In discussing negligence to this point, we have largely confined ourselves to the issue of the standard of care and its violation. However, there are other elements of the negligence tort that must be present before a defendant may be held liable.

*Duty.*   If there is no legal duty owed to the injured plaintiff, there may be no recovery regardless of the unreasonableness of the defendant's conduct. For example, a rule of Anglo-American law, as opposed to civil law, is that unless there are specific statutes to the contrary, no duty is owned to aid or rescue a stranger in distress.

Thus a passerby could callously watch a floundering swimmer drown in a pool, even though he might have thrown a life preserver at no risk to himself. This is an instance where a moral duty does not have a legal counterpart.[37]

Various elements of duty will be considered below. For now, it is sufficient to say that the trend of the law is clearly toward the enlargement of the duty of reasonable care in contrast to the restriction of that duty prevalent in the nineteenth and early twentieth centuries.

*Causation.*   Another element is that there must be proof of *legal causation.* Often referred to as "proximate cause," this principle requires that there be a reasonably close or proximate causal connection between the act of the defendant and the injury of the plaintiff. In most recreational injuries, the causal relationship is clear and immediate, although one can always imagine bizarre situations to illustrate the rule.

A pragmatic application of the causality requirement may be found in a 1976 North Carolina case in which the court dismissed a wrongful death negligence action against a football coach. The death resulted from a collision between two players, one of whom was ineligible to play. The court held that although the coach violated league rules by using the disqualified player, there was no legal causal relation between the violation and the injury. It was not the kind of occurrence foreseeable from using such a player in the game, nor was there a "risk" of such an injury resulting from the rule infraction.[38] But what if the player in question had been barred because he had been involved in a number of flagrant, violent rules violations? In such a case, the element of foreseeability, the fact that the injury is within the "zone of risk" created by the coach's conduct, might be a sufficiently cognizable causal connection!

*Injury.* Another element necessary to the negligence action is a requirement of actual harm and damage. Unlike intentional torts, where punitive damages are assessed because an act is closely related to unlawful or criminal conduct, in nonintentional torts a plaintiff must prove injury in order to be awarded compensatory damages based on ordinary negligence. At one time only physical harm was recognized. Later, mental and emotional damage that accompanied or followed physical harm were compensated, along with substantial amounts for the pain and suffering involved in serious injuries.

Varying degrees of physical manifestation of emotional harm have been required by the courts over the years, largely to prevent fraud. As there has come to be a greater understanding of the interrelationship between the physical and the emotional, courts have moved to a requirement of only minimal physical impact and, finally, in a number of states to the abandonment of a requirement of physical impact altogether. A key case in this development arose out of a recreation incident.

A nine-year-old girl was placed in a chairlift at the state-operated Belleayre Mountain Ski Center in New York. The attendant failed to secure the guardrail properly and the girl became hysterical and suffered subsequent fear of heights and of the dark, headaches, and assorted other emotional ailments. The court held that despite the risk of fraud in cases of purely emotional injury, a deserving plaintiff should not be denied recovery when there is substantial medical evidence of the reality of her injuries.[39]

Several states, most notably California, Hawaii, New Jersey, Rhode Island, and Massachusetts, have gone even further and permitted recovery for serious physical manifestations of emotional injury when a parent, child, or other close relative is a direct witness to a negligent injury or comes on the scene immediately after the accident.[40] In *Nazaroff v. Superior Court,*[41] a mother who was searching for her infant son heard a scream. She ran to a neighbor's yard and saw the boy, near death, being pulled from the swimming pool. It was held that if she could prove physical manifestations of her emotional shock she could recover for her own injuries as well as for the death of the child.

Most courts have not yet followed the California lead, fearing the impossibility of drawing meaningful distinctions between observed injuries to close relatives as opposed to the shock of hearing about rather than observing the actual injury. Courts are also concerned about the arbitrariness of distinguishing between close relatives, friends, or even strangers, for that matter,[42] since it is certainly foreseeable that an individual would suffer emotional harm from witnessing violent injury, even without close family ties to the victim.

Should the reasoning of cases like *Nazaroff* prove persuasive, the implications for the parks and leisure services field are substantial. Not only may there be liability for negligently causing injuries to children, but also for the shock and emotional upset suffered by their parents observing nearby.

Despite the expansion of liability described above and elsewhere in this chapter, the reader should not lose sight of a paramount reality. That is, that although the cases in which liability is found are more dramatic and more likely to be noticed, there are many instances in which, despite suffering serious injuries, parks and leisure services visitors and clients do not bring actions, they settle claims out of court for relatively minor amounts, or they are unsuccessful if they do prosecute a claim.

**Defenses to Liability**

*Due Care.*   There are several specific defenses available, but the best defense is always the absence of negligence. Meeting recognized professional standards of conduct, conforming to applicable safety codes, recognizing the increased responsibility of supervising and caring for young children, the ill, and the physically or developmentally disabled are all indicia of reasonable prudence. Most importantly, being aware of the true nature of the risks inherent in a particular activity and taking appropriate action to limit or eliminate them is the best insurance against unnecessary injuries and the liability that results from a finding of negligent lack of care. In some cases, this may mean substituting a less hazardous activity while preserving the same programmatic goals. Bear in mind also that, as one court put it in ruling against a plaintiff who was injured in a high school gym accident, a teacher or programmer is not an insurer of the participant's safety. Except for the very young or the totally dependent, an agency is "not required to provide such continuous supervision that it controls the movements of all of the students [or visitors] at all times."[43]

*Affirmative Defenses.*   We have previously introduced the related concepts of contributory negligence (failure to take due care to avoid injury to oneself) and *voluntary assumption of risk* (knowingly undertaking a dangerous activity or encountering a hazard). Although these defenses have not been eliminated in negligence law as they have in worker's compensation, in recent years they have been substantially modified by statute and judicial decision so that plaintiffs have a greater chance of winning lawsuits. Perhaps of greatest significance is that, with the weakening of traditional defenses, judges are increasingly reluctant to summarily dismiss claims, which leaves a correspondingly greater number of issues to the unpredictable vagaries of juries. As a result, defendants' attorneys, particularly those representing insurance carriers, are much more likely to settle cases through compromise, even if the defense is potentially strong.

*The Development of "Last Clear Chance" and Comparative Negligence.* The harsh rule that any degree of contributory fault or negligence on the part of the plaintiff would completely bar all recovery, regardless of the relatively lesser culpability of the plaintiff as compared to the defendant, has given rise over the years to all sorts of exceptions as courts have sought to avoid unjust results. Thus if a defendant's conduct was "willful" or "wanton" or "gross" some courts would hold that the mere ordinary contributory negligence of a plaintiff would not be a bar to recovery.

Similarly, a doctrine of *last clear chance* was evolved. A hypothetical illustration of this would be:

> A kayaker carelessly, but unknowingly, paddles to a dangerous falls in the river. A guard charged with lowering a gate to cut off access to the falls sees the kayaker but negligently fails to drop the gate in time, and the kayak goes over the falls.

Since the guard had the last clear chance of avoiding the injury, his negligent act would be the *proximate cause* and the contributory negligence of the paddler would be excused as too remote.

In recent years there has been a trend away from these obviously strained efforts to soften the harsh effects of the absolute bar of contributory negligence. By 1979, over half the states had adopted a *comparative negligence* rule, and the trend is continuing. Most states have done this by statute, although a few, including California, have acted, at least in part, through judicial decision.

*Problems in Application of Comparative Negligence.* Comparative negligence decisions can become rather complex, particularly when there are more than two parties involved in a case (a chain collision, for example), because the court or jury will have to express the degree of fault of each on a percentage basis.

In some states, a plaintiff will be able to recover only if her fault is less than defendant's (no more than 49 percent to 51 percent). In other states, a plaintiff may recover as long as his contribution is no greater than the defendant's (50 percent to 50 percent). This seemingly miniscule distinction may be important, since given the artificiality of attempting to pinpoint a precise percentage of fault, juries will often decide that blame is shared equally or 50 percent to 50 percent. Other states have adopted a "pure" form of comparative negligence derived in part from maritime law, in which an injured plaintiff who suffers substantially greater harm than the defendant may still recover even if the defendant is less responsible for the injury. An illustration will point up the problems and procedures.

Tom, a baseball player using improper technique, slides head first into a poorly buckled base in the county park and is injured when the metal fastener breaks loose and strikes his head.

It is determined that Tom is 25 percent responsible and the county park is 75 percent responsible. Tom's medical costs total $10,000. Under the traditional contributory negligence rules, Tom would recover nothing. Under the comparative negligence rules adopted in most states, Tom's recovery would be reduced by his 25 percent contributory negligence to $7,500 dollars.

If Tom were found to be 75 percent responsible for his own injuries and the county park only 25 percent responsible, Tom would recover nothing in most states, but in the "pure" comparative negligence states like California, he would still recover $2,500 ($10,000 reduced by his 75 percent responsibility). As you can see, the addition of other potentially responsible individuals (the other team, the volunteer umpire who failed to adjust the base, etc.) could result in a complex mathematical problem. Furthermore, states differ on whether the percentage of fault of different defendants may be lumped together to reach a percentage greater than the plaintiff's. Also, where plaintiff and defendant are both injured in a "pure" state or where a jury finds them equally responsible in a state permitting recovery if plaintiff's fault is "no greater than" defendant's, the amount of recovery will be determined by "setting off" their respective damages. For example, suppose that Tom collided with the third baseman, Bill, and they were each 50 percent at fault. Tom's injuries were less severe and his damages were $10,000, but the other player's more serious damages amounted to $20,000. Since each was 50 percent responsible for his own injuries, Tom would be entitled to recover $5,000 and Bill, $10,000, or half their damages. These would be *set off* against one another, and Bill would actually receive $5,000 from Tom, and Tom would get nothing.

These complexities may be left to the lawyers. What is most significant about the whole trend to comparative negligence from the perspective of parks and leisure services agencies is that many more cases are likely to be sent to a jury for evaluation and judgment rather than being dismissed because the judge concludes that there has undoubtedly been some degree of contributory negligence. Because they are afraid of exorbitant jury verdicts, the attorneys for the defendants and their insurance carriers will often succumb to the irresistible temptation to agree to substantial settlements rather than fight the plaintiff's charges.

Lawyers generally believe that public or private agencies that have contributed to the injury of an individual may not expect much sympathy at the hands of a jury, especially since the likelihood of insurance coverage is widely understood. Probably one should not be too cynical in this regard. What little is known of juries would tend to indicate that they are generally conscientious and will not blatantly ignore the facts. Nevertheless, given the difficulties of arriving at a fair apportionment of fault, the possibility of recovery by the sympathy-provoking plaintiff has greatly increased, even in the face of her own substantial carelessness.

*Voluntary Assumption of Risk.*    The classic defense to injuries arising from adult recreation activities, particularly those that involve an element of danger, risk, or high adventure, is that of *voluntary assumption of risk,* or v.a.r.

There has been much debate among legal scholars as to whether voluntary assumption of risk is nothing more than a form of contributory negligence. The New Jersey Supreme Court went so far as to abolish the separate v.a.r. defense altogether. This basically occurred in a case in which a patron of an ice skating rink fell on allegedly overhard and slippery ice. The court held that the v.a.r. defense was superfluous. If the ice rink managers had behaved reasonably, there was no breach of duty and no negligence and no need to consider v.a.r. On the other hand, if there were negligence in preparation of the rink surface and the plaintiff had been careless of her own safety, a clear contributory-comparative negligence determination was presented.[44] Still, courts and commentators such as Dean Prosser have argued that, although there is considerable overlap, there are times when assumption of risk is neither contributorily negligent nor indicative of an absence of duty.

The dispute might be considered esoteric if it were not for the advent of comparative negligence. Several courts have chosen to limit the defense's application to the same degree as comparative fault.[45] Other courts still regard v.a.r. as a separate and therefore total defense.[46]

Whatever the exact nature of the v.a.r. defense, many of the same limitations that apply to contributory negligence will also be pertinent. Children have decreased capacity to fully comprehend a risk and the defense may not be utilized at all against the very young. Presumably the same limits would apply to the mentally disturbed or developmentally disabled.[47] On the other hand, obvious ordinary risks such as the slippery nature of an icy pavement (or an ice rink) will be assumed even if a plaintiff claims a lack of appreciation of the nature of the risk. There is, however, some greater room for explanation and a subjective denial of assumption of risk because of the "knowing" and "voluntary" requirements.

There have been several cases in which plaintiffs claimed they did not understand the risks involved in attending a hockey game. Whether or not a court will accept such a claim will depend on the general level of community knowledge of hockey and on an independent evaluation of the plaintiff's claim. In one case in Nebraska where plaintiff proved that he knew nothing about hockey and had never seen a game, the defense of v.a.r. was defeated,[48] but in Minnesota, where hockey knowledge is widespread, application of v.a.r. to bar recovery was upheld.[49]

Obviously, the more universal the knowledge of an activity, the less credence would be placed in a plea of ignorance of the risk. Even the relatively young may be conditioned by experience to a point at which it may be held that they comprehend and assume the risk. In one case an experienced teenage trampoline performer was held to have assumed the risks involved in practicing when his coach's attention was diverted elsewhere.[50]

In general, since a growing number of states are treating v.a.r. as a comparative defense rather than a complete one, some of the traditional impact upon plaintiffs is diminished. Probably more important is a subtle but accelerating shift in attitude toward risk-taking activities and their promotion.

In one of the most famous cases, *Murphy v. Steeplechase Amusement Co.,*[51] the great judge Benjamin Cardozo wrote an opinion holding that a young man who was injured on an amusement park ride called the "Flopper" was barred from recovering by assumption of risk.

The "Flopper" was basically a moving belt that ran up an inclined plane. Participants in the ride tried to keep their balance and place on the belt, but inevitably fell and tumbled into one another. The plaintiff, Murphy, claimed he was thrown down by a sudden jerking of the belt.

Judge Cardozo wrote:

> A fall was foreseen as one of the risks of the adventure. There would have been no point to the whole thing, no adventure about it, if the risk had not been there. The very name above the gate, the Flopper, was warning to the timid. . . .
>
> *Volenti non fit injuria.* [The volunteer may not complain of injury.] One who takes part in such a sport accepts the dangers that inhere in it so far as they are obvious and necessary just as a fencer accepts the risk of a thrust by his antagonist or a spectator at a ball game, the chance of

contact with the ball. . . . The plaintiff was not seeking a retreat for meditation. Visitors were tumbling about the belt to the merriment of onlookers when he made his choice to join them. He took the chance of a like fate, with whatever damage to his body might ensue from such a fall. *The timorous may stay at home.* [emphasis added]

*The Stratton Mountain Case and V.A.R. in Skiing.*  Compare Judge Cardozo's view of the relative responsibilities of the participant and the enterprise in *Murphy* with that of the Vermont Supreme Court in the *Stratton Mountain* case.[52] There the court ruled that Mr. Sunday, the novice skier who was crippled, did not assume the risk. The ski area promoted skiing as a sport for people of all ages and abilities. It advertised its careful grooming and its ability to convert its slippery slopes to a near carpetlike consistency. The court decided that "the timorous no longer need stay at home" because "there is concerted effort to attract their patronage and to provide novice trails suitable for their use."

The *Stratton Mountain* case was somewhat unusual in that Sunday's injury in falling over some partially concealed shrubbery was the kind of incident and hazard even a novice skier might expect to encounter. A critical factor was that Stratton Mountain made extraordinary claims about their slope preparation that lulled the unwary.

On the other hand, in *LaVine v. Clear Creek Skiing Corp.*[53] the court stated: "The jury in a ski slope case tends to view the entire skiing scene as one involving a high degree of risk by merely taking to the slopes. This is an attitude which tends to be persuasive in injuries which involve participation in sports."

*Statutory V.A.R. in Ski Injuries.*  It is clear that many legislatures share the view that skiers have voluntarily accepted the risks of participation in a dangerous activity and therefore should shoulder the burden of meeting the costs of injuries that result from accidents on the slopes.

In fact, in what is an unprecedented response to the publicity resulting from the *Stratton Mountain* case, virtually every legislature in states that have downhill ski areas (including such outposts of the ski world as North Dakota, Tennessee, and Virginia) has enacted a statute designed to limit ski area operators' liability to mechanical failures and injuries resulting from improper or inadequate signs and markings.

Whether these statutes will be effective in limiting ski area liability to the point at which insurance rates will decrease is far from established at this time. Courts are historically reluctant to allow legislatures to dictate strict limitations on common-law remedies. Furthermore, although the ski liability statutes vary considerably, they generally contain enough qualifying language to permit interpreting courts to uphold liability judgments where, in their opinions, justice requires it. Nevertheless, enactment of these statutes is certainly reflective of a rare phenomenon in which public opinion and perceptions coincided and supported an extraordinary lobbying effort by a recreational industry.

One of the most thorough of these statutes was enacted by the Colorado legislature in 1979.[54] This statute defines the duties of ski area operators in signing ski trails and in operation of ski lifts. The law also specifically sets forth codes of conduct for skiers both on the slopes and on the lifts. The statute states that violations of their respective obligations will be considered to constitute negligence on the part of skiers and operators. Nevertheless, although the statute appears to place the burden of proof of responsibility for downhill injuries heavily upon the injured skier, the loopholes remain.

For example:

It is presumed, unless shown to the contrary by a preponderance of the evidence, that the responsibility for collisions by skiers with any person, natural object, or man-made structure marked in accordance with . . . [this statute] is solely that of the skier or skiers involved and not that of the ski area operator.

*V.A.R. and High Adventure Programming.* There are, despite *LaVine* and *Murphy* and the attitudes expressed in the ski liability laws, numerous cases where the defense of v.a.r. in sports and recreation has been defeated by finding that the injury that occurred was not the one which should have been anticipated. One of the ironies of the defense of v.a.r. is that where risks are general and nonspecific, such as those encountered in wild or undeveloped country, participants will likely be held to have assumed even the extraordinary risks. On the other hand, where activities take place at a carefully prepared site, participants will not be held to assume the risk of hidden or undiscovered hazards. Thus, where a plaintiff fell in a hole on a prepared softball field, the v.a.r. defense was rejected.[55]

As a result of this phenomenon, there have been few cases involving adults injured in activities conducted in back-country settings. Participants in mountain climbing, kayaking, backpacking in the wilderness, and similar recreation activities must be prepared for the unexpected.

Despite the foregoing conclusion, as more and more individuals who are not really conditioned by age, experience, or ability are lured into rugged outdoor activities, we may anticipate that the number of injuries and lawsuits will increase, while the viability of the assumption of risk doctrine diminishes. Particularly vulnerable are camps and organizations that provide wilderness and backcountry experiences to teenagers, especially such enterprises as Outward Bound or the National Outdoor Leadership School, which promise the development of wilderness and survival skills. Not only may it be argued that a novice in the wilderness will not fully comprehend the dangers, but whenever an enterprise represents itself as offering expert teaching, coaching, or guidance, it must exercise an intense degree of care and supervision.

The compulsion to do what the leader demands is very powerful. For example, when a young woman in an amateur opera production was instructed by the director to make a "haughty" exit from the stage, she protested that she would fall if required to negotiate the twenty-inch drop without looking. Nevertheless, she proceeded to make the attempt, with the predictable injurious result. The court ruled that she did not act unreasonably:

> We must give consideration to the relationship existing between the [defendant] and the plaintiff. One was the instructor, the other the student. . . . To all intents and purposes he was her superior whose orders she was obliged to follow.[56]

At the time of this writing, several suits are pending against various high adventure recreation enterprises. In one, Sonya Ross, a twenty-year old ballerina, died when a falling rock allegedly struck her while she was descending from a mountain climb. According to an article in *Outside* magazine, Sonya had written her parents that she was "in over her head" and was "the weakest in the patrol."

Another suit that was recently settled concerned three Southwest Outward Bound students who drowned when their kayaks were swamped during a storm in the Gulf of California. The families of two of the students, David Schwimmer and Tim Breidegan, received $200,000. Furthermore, Outward Bound revised its policies to require the presence and supervision of its expert teachers during the "final or solo stages of the courses." They also specified that finals would be eliminated if "terrain and weather characteristics" so indicate.[57]

This settlement and others that will undoubtedly follow dramatize the conflict between the thirst for challenge and the common law's demand for socially responsible behavior. Not only private enterprises, but also government parks, recreation, leisure service, and therapeutic agencies must ponder the conflicting demands upon them. By increasing access to hazardous recreation and remote facilities, the risk of liability increases while the usefulness of the voluntary assumption of risk defense decreases.

*Releases and Express Assumption of Risk.* One of the ways in which leisure service agencies have traditionally tried to protect themselves from liability is to require that participants, or in the case of children, their parents, agree in writing to assume all risks and release the agency from all liability in case of injury. We shall examine the validity and effectiveness of such agreements.

First, let us consider their application to adults. Releases are generally regarded as *contracts of adhesion.* That is, rather than being the result of bargaining between parties, the agency with superior power and knowledge prepares the agreement and the prospective participant can either *adhere* and agree or forgo the activity.

Because the courts appreciate the realities of the situation—the lack of any real bargaining—they will tend to construe the release strictly against the preparer and liberally in favor of the participant. Thus, where a release is written in fine print on the back of a ticket, or hidden in the depths of a long contract, the courts may refuse to enforce it as a matter of public policy. Also, if the release has a loophole, a court may well permit the participant to escape through it. In the *Rosen* ski injury case the plaintiff, a season pass holder, had been required to sign "rules and regulations" of the ski area at the time of his purchase. These stated:

> I understand that skiing is a hazardous sport and that hazardous obstructions, some unmarked, exist in any ski area. I accept the existence of such dangers and that injuries may result.[58]

The court held that the ski area was negligent in erecting a steel sign post set in concrete on a ski trail, and that since the stipulation did not specifically state that the ski area would not be responsible for its own negligence, it was invalid and the waiver of liability had no effect.

Where the releases from liability from negligence are clearly and specifically stated the courts may uphold them (although not if they go so far as to try to limit liability for intentional harm or gross negligence). Nevertheless, public utilities, providers of essential services, and, in some instances, operators of parking garages have had great difficulty convincing courts to honor general releases of liability since their patrons are virtually forced to deal with them. Similarly, releases required by landlords and employers will generally not be enforced.

Historically, since recreational activities have not been regarded as necessities of life, properly executed adult releases have had some validity.

In *Ciofalo v. Vic Tanney Gyms, Inc.,*[59] the plaintiff's membership contract specifically provided that she would assume full responsibility for "any claims for personal injuries resulting from or arising out of the negligence" of the defendant. Thus, when she fell on a slippery pool deck the court dismissed plaintiff's suit characterizing her as a volunteer who applied for membership and agreed to the terms.[60]

Since the time of the *Ciofalo* case, New York state has enacted a statute that declares "void as against public policy and wholly unenforceable" agreements eliminating negligence in contracts, applications, and tickets of admission for any fee-based "pool, gymnasium, place of amusement or recreation . . . ."[61]

With regard to children, there is a general rule that, except for certain necessities of life, they may not be bound to contracts. Those under the age of eighteen (twenty-one in some states) do not have the legal capacity to contractually release recreation enterprises, camps, sports teams, and so on, from liability. Nor may the parents of minor children contract away the nonemancipated child's rights to recovery by signing a release on his or her behalf. It is, in short, very doubtful that any kind of exculpatory contract or release concerning a child's legal rights would be enforced by the courts. However, this does not mean that the requirement of having parents (and children if they are of reasoning age) sign a form acknowledging the risks of participation is without value.

*Activities Information and Permission Forms.*   An appropriate form would set forth all of the activities that could reasonably be anticipated to take place. Thus, prospective field trips, use of equipment, which equipment and clothing would be supplied by the recreation agency and which by participant, strenuous exercise, physical contact, or risk-bearing activities should all be brought to the attention of parents and children through a clearly worded form requiring acknowledgment. The form should detail the level of skill required for participation and any particular risks not readily apparent from the program description.

A signed certification as to the health of the child and his ability to withstand strenuous exercise and activities should be required where appropriate. (Similar acknowledgments should obviously be required of adults about to engage in recreational activities.)

Most importantly, the form should provide a prominent place for listing any physical or other condition that might affect the ability of the participant to successfuly undertake the activity or that might be crucial in case of injury (such as intolerance for certain drugs or allergies to bee stings). If there are any doubts about fitness for participation, an agency should not hesitate to require a physician's certification and to reject participants if doubts persist. A sample activity participation form is included in Appendix C. Obviously, the appropriate form must be varied according to the nature of the activity and the legal decisions of the particular state, but, by and large, a full explanatory form will serve a recreation agency better than a self-serving broadly worded release of liability.

*The Value of Signed Forms.*  Even if invalid as releases, such signed acknowledgments are useful in demonstrating voluntary assumption of risk, in proving that the agency acted reasonably and in refuting claims by parents and participants that they were unaware of the physical demands and conditions of an activity.

In a very significant California case, a teenage boy was seriously injured in a motorcycle race. The court held that, while a parental consent form would not sustain a defense of voluntary assumption of risk, if the promotor of the race could show that the boy's parents acted unreasonably in permitting him to participate in a race beyond his capabilities, they would have to contribute to the recovery the boy had won against the promotor. Such a result is possible because California, like many other states, now permits lawsuits between parent and child.[62]

Cases often arise where it is claimed that a recreation program ignored evidence of a child's physical limitations or ailments. For example, in *Summeir v. Milwaukee Union High School District*,[63] it was held that a school was liable for a student's injuries from gymnastics. The student had a history of back problems, and the school negligently failed to record information that the boy's doctor had attempted to provide to them. The use of an appropriate form could have eliminated this failure. Conversely, a signed form that did not reveal the back condition could have provided the school with a strong defense if the parents tried to claim that they had attempted to inform the school and were ignored.

**Liability and Visitor Services.**  In dealing with injuries caused by conditions of property, the issue of liability often turns on the degree of care or duty owed to the specific class of visitor to which the injured plaintiff belongs. Although we owe a general duty of reasonable care to the world at large, the responsibility owed to individuals with limited rights to be on our property may be substantially reduced.

Our first concern is with adult visitors. Perhaps because land was considered unique, and its possession and ownership a matter of prime importance in the development of Western civilization, the law has often given extraordinary protection to landowners.

People who enter upon the land may be divided into three distinct classes: business and public invitees, licensees, and trespassers.

*Invitees.*  At one time, there was a distinction between a business visitor or paying guest and one who enters a museum, auditorium, or developed park or recreational area without paying a fee for the purposes of engaging in the activities offered there. Today there is little, if any, difference left between these categories. They are both considered *invitees*. The duty of the land possessor (whether under ownership or lease) is to make reasonable inspections of the premises to discover dangerous conditions that exist and to either repair them or to properly warn visitors of their existence if they are not obvious. There is a fairly rigorous duty of care involved here. Patrons and participants in organized recreational and physical education activities in public parks, voluntary agencies, or private facilities are invitees. Where the individual is a guest in a hotel or resort, the duty owed may be even more rigorous since the law historically has imposed a very high duty of care on innkeepers and others serving the traveling public.

In any event, ignorance of the concealed hole in the ball field, the sharp edge in the water fountain, or the protruding bolt on the playground swing will not be excused if regular inspection would have revealed these conditions. On the other hand, the recreation enterprise is not a complete insurer. If the dangerous condition was not created by the land possessor, and if there was not sufficient time for it to be discovered by reasonable inspection, there will be no liability. (For example, there have been several cases involving food stores where responsibility for a patron's fall on a banana peel was determined by evidence of the condition of the peel at the time of the fall. A black, dried-out peel would indicate that it had been there long enough to be discovered and removed.)

*Licensees.* Those whose entry onto the premises was merely permitted, and who were not there to engage in business, have been called *licensees*. Someone who received permission to fix his car on your driveway or to hunt and fish on your farm would fit into this category.

In the case of licensees, the duty of the land possessor is limited to acting with ordinary care and to warn of dangerous concealed conditions of which the possessor is aware. There is no independent duty to inspect the premises or to warn of obvious dangers. Surprisingly, social guests have historically been treated as mere licensees.

In recent years the courts have had increasing difficulty classifying visitors to determine what standard of care is owed. How would you expect them to classify people who stroll through shopping malls? People who use public telephones? People who are visiting a hospital patient? Because of this difficulty, there is a tendency to blur the distinctions between invitees and licensees, particularly with the emergence of the public invitee category. Influenced by this trend and by the universal availability of homeowner's insurance, a number of courts have placed social guests into the invitee category.[64]

*Trespassers.* The lowest duty of care is owed to *trespassers,* those who are illegally on the land. Other than a duty not to intentionally harm a trespasser or to set up dangerous traps, there is no duty to avoid dangerous activities or warn of hazards. However, once the trespasser's presence is known, the same reasonable care would be due as is afforded licensees.

Because of the historic rigidity of the classifications, the courts have established a number of exceptions. The most important exception is that if a land possessor knows that trespassers frequently utilize a portion of the property (such as a worn path indicating a much-used shortcut), then they must take reasonable care to prevent injuries and give appropriate warnings.

*Elimination of Classifications.* In the last few years there has been a trend away from the complexities of the tort law of land possession. The California Supreme Court abandoned this "semantic morass" and simply applied the general test of *reasonable care under the circumstances.* The status of the injured plaintiff as trespasser, licensee, or invitee might "have some bearing on the question of liability" but would not be determinative.[65] New York quickly followed the California lead.[66] A number of other states have also adopted this approach, although some have retained a special "child trespasser" category.

This movement toward the substitution of the general duty of care, along with the merging of public and business invitees with licensees, will inevitably lead to greater liability, since more cases will go to the jury to determine "reasonableness" of conduct rather than having the judge rule as a matter of law that the obligations of land possessors were specifically limited.

*Child Trespassers.* Natural curiosity and lack of caution are among the traits most widely associated with children. In fact, there is a good deal of admiration for adventurous youths in our culture. The midwesterner sneaking into the farmer's field at midnight to sample the watermelon crop (none ever tasted sweeter!) or the city kid climbing over a high locked fence to gain access to the schoolyard basketball court are fixtures of our sentimental appreciation of the healthy mischievousness of children.

In some part, the law reflects this tolerance of child trespassers. As one New York court put it, the age of an injured trespasser is a significant factor in light of the "well known propensity of children to climb about and play."[67]

At one time this susceptibility of children to the temptation to trespass was recognized in the *attractive nuisance* or *turntable doctrine,* so named because some early cases involved injuries to children playing on railroad turntables used in the switching of engines.[68] A problem with this doctrine was that it required the child to be lured onto the land by some irresistible apparatus or attraction. Thus when a child was injured because of a poisoned pool, which he had discovered only *after* he had trespassed, it was held there could be no recovery.[69]

Criticism of that case, as well as attacks on the logic of *attractive nuisance,* led to modifications such as the *playground doctrine.* This provides for liability for dangerous conditions when children are permitted to trespass over a substantial period of time without objection or attempts by the owner to prevent their entry.[70] Ultimately *attractive nuisance* fell into disfavor and only a few courts still refer to it.

The more modern rationale for protecting child trespassers is largely based on foreseeability of the trespass. As set forth in Section 339 of the Restatement (2d) of Torts, landholders may be liable for injuries to children who trespass if there is or should be knowledge of the likelihood of such trespasses and where conditions exist that are dangerous and that children do not recognize as dangerous because of their immaturity. If such requirements are met, the relative considerations of the extent of the danger, the cost of repair, and the value of maintaining the condition must be weighed to determine the reasonableness of the land possessor's actions. Child trespassers are not always successful in their legal actions. For example, in a District of Columbia case the court held that a nine-year-old boy who was seriously injured while trying to "hop" a freight train could not recover because he "unquestionably understood and appreciated the risk."[71]

Whether or not the California or the Restatement approach is utilized, the fact remains that in dealing with children there is minimal protection given to land possessors based on the impropriety of the presence of the injured individual. Certainly in many recreation situations it can readily be anticipated that children may be present and will be likely to encounter a threat of injury posed by dangerous conditions. Thus, in a Utah case the Utah Supreme Court ruled that where the owner of a swimming pool had left a gate improperly mounted so it would not lock correctly, it was a jury question whether there was liability when plaintiff's three-year-old wandered in and drowned.[72]

*Diminished Capacity.*    Just as in other areas of tort law, courts tend to be liberal in their attitude toward people who are mentally retarded when they are injured on another's premises.

As one court stated in permitting a retarded eighteen-year-old to sue when he was injured on an electric pole that had a printed warning:

> Appellant . . . had the mental development of a child not more than six years of age. He was in fact a child, without judgment or discretion, and as such should be held to that degree of care as children of his mental capacity and judgment are reasonably chargeable.[73]

*Recreational Landowners Liability Acts.*    In contrast to the growth of potential liability in the common law for all classes of visitors upon property, over forty states have enacted statutes that supply some degree of protection to private (and, in some instances, public) landowners who permit their property to be used by the public for recreational purposes.[74] Many of these statutes are directly aimed at rural property holders who may voluntarily open their lands for hunters, fishermen, dirtbikers, hikers, and the like.[75]

The protection afforded varies. For example, the California statute does not protect landowners if there is "willful or malicious failure to guard or warn against" a dangerous condition. Furthermore, the statute does not protect where a charge was made for entry or where visitors were "expressly invited" rather than merely permitted to come upon the premises.[76]

Some courts may seek to limit the protection provided by these statutes in cases where the court determines that liability is warranted by the facts. For example, in *Harrison v. Middlesex Water Co.,*[77] the New Jersey Supreme Court reversed a lower court decision and held that the Landowner's Liability Statute[78] was not applicable in the case of a drowning of an individual who ventured out on a reservoir to attempt to rescue two teenagers who fell through the ice while skating. Despite the fact that skating was among the activities specified in the statute, the court held that a rescue effort was not within the protection given to landowners. Furthermore, it was held that the act contemplated rural lands where there would be great difficulty in acting to prevent intrusions. Since this tragedy took place in a developing suburban area where there was a substantial population, despite the statute, the burden of guarding against dangerous ice skating by the property owner was outweighed by the foreseeable risks.

A Wisconsin decision held that the state's recreation sightseer statute "is obvious" in limiting its scope to private individuals and does not protect a municipality.[79] By contrast, a Nevada statute was held applicable to the federal government in preventing liability where a sightseer was hurt while exploring a deserted mine on federal lands adjacent to a highway.[80]

Montana's Recreation Liability Act[81] includes typical exceptions:

Nothing . . . [in the statute] limits in any way any liability which otherwise exists (1) for willful or malicious failure to guard or warn against a dangerous condition, use, structure or activity, or (2) for injury suffered in any case where the owner of land charges the person or persons who enter or go on the land.

The North Carolina statute specifically exempts "the doctrine of attractive nuisance" from its protection, thus leaving open the possibility of liability to children.[82] In Rhode Island, before the protection of liability limitations are available, a landowner must file a formal letter of permission with the state director of environmental management setting forth a number of facts, including: "A statement of the specific recreational purposes for which such permission is granted or that such permission extends to all recreational purposes contemplated by this chapter."[83]

The proffered property is subject to inspection and acceptance or rejection. Presumably, if dangerous conditions are found and the land is rejected, the landowner would be at risk in opening the property to the public.

These kinds of quirks and exceptions are typical of landowner liability acts. Furthermore, there haven't been many appellate decisions that interpret the language of the acts and that adds to uncertainty about their coverage.

A conservative evaluation at this time would conclude that some statutes may yield a substantial degree of protection to private landowners and are very useful in shielding organizations such as the Nature Conservancy in their protection of rural recreational and scenic property. Nevertheless, the specific wording of each statute must be carefully considered by landowners before they open their properties for recreational use. We may anticipate that at least some judges will be hostile to the intent of the statutes and will seek to limit their effect because they are intrusions on common-law liability. In any event, most landowner liability acts afford little or no protection to urban recreation agencies, commercial leisure services, or other organized park and recreation programs.

## Governmental and Charitable Immunities

*Charitable Immunity.*   As noted at the outset of this chapter, charitable and public organizations were once generally protected against lawsuits of all kinds. The historical justification for protecting charities and voluntary agencies was that their donated funds constituted a trust that could not be diverted from the charitable purposes for which it was intended.[84] Other theories included one suggesting that the recipient of charity waived the right to recover for damages suffered at the hands of his or her benefactor. At the time the doctrine was established there was fear that liability would have the effect of discouraging charitable endeavors.

All of these rationales have been swept away by modern decisions.[85] Today there is a greater sense that individuals using the services of nonprofit agencies such as hospitals, churches, or recreational agencies like the Y's or the Scouts should not be unprotected against negligence. Because of the availability of insurance, there is less fear that useful charitable services would be destroyed by exposure to damages. As a result of these attitudinal changes, the demise of charitable immunity is virtually universal, although there may be some statutory limits on the amount of recoveries.

*Governmental Immunity.* Governmental immunity from tort actions presents a far more complex picture. Historically, the federal government and the states were immune from suit, because as sovereigns they could not be sued in their own courts. Whether historically accurate or not, the motto "the king can do no wrong" became the theme of American courts[86] despite criticism that blanket immunity "rests on medievalisms about monarchs."[87]

Local governmental units—cities, towns, counties, and so on—did not have the attributes of sovereignty, so there was a possibility that they could be sued. The first case to hold that they also were not subject to liability for torts was *Russell v. Men of Devon.*[88] The decision in this case was based on the absence of a specific fund from which a judgment could be paid (Devon was an unincorporated county) and, more importantly, that "it is better that an individual should sustain an injury than that the public should suffer inconvenience."

Despite the fact that most local governmental units in the United States are incorporated and there are funds from which judgments may be paid, the reasoning of *Men of Devon* became the general rule in this country. Nevertheless, immunity was never complete.

While there was immunity with regard to *governmental acts,* there could be liability arising out of *proprietary* operations. The theory was that where activities had no equivalent in private life, it would be inappropriate to utilize private common law to hold governments liable, but where government engaged in the same activities as a private enterprise (a proprietary operation) it should not have an advantage. Thus, police and fire protection and enforcement of law and regulations by officers, administrators, and courts could not be the subjects of liability.

Obviously the line between governmental and proprietary functions is far from clear. Recreational activities and programs are particularly susceptible to being termed either governmental or proprietary, depending upon how the courts view the necessity and appropriateness of governmentally sponsored recreation, sports, and leisure services.

As stated in the leading case of *Muskopf v. Corning Hospital District,*[89]

> some who are injured by governmental agencies can recover, others cannot, one injured while attending a community theater in a public park may recover . . . , but one injured in a children's playground may not . . . . *The rule of governmental immunity for tort is an anachronism, without rational basis, and has existed only by force of inertia.* [emphasis added]

In state after state, courts reached similar conclusions, and governmental immunity was substantially reduced or eliminated. Today a majority of the states through judicial or legislative action have permitted a broad range of both contractual and tort actions against government, both state and local. However, unlike the general demise of charitable immunity, legislatures in many of the states, fearful of too great an extension of liability, have at least partially reinstituted some forms of immunity or protection for states and municipalities. This immunity generally extends to law enforcement, fire protection, and natural property conditions, as well as *discretionary* administrative acts in keeping with federal tort policy, which is discussed below.[90] Furthermore, the governmental-proprietary distinction still has validity in some states. For example, a North Carolina court recently held that provision of foster care was an immune governmental function.[91]

Despite the setbacks to broader governmental liability, the general judicial trend toward elimination of immunity continues. The Delaware Supreme Court put it simply: "Sovereign immunity is an unjust concept."[92]

In New Jersey, abolition of the sovereign immunity doctrine came about in a parks and recreation case. A three-year-old child suffered a traumatic amputation of her arm as she attempted to feed sugar to an inadequately caged bear in a state wild animal exhibit.[93] In dismantling sovereign immunity, the court stated: "It is plainly unjust to refuse relief to persons injured by the wrongful conduct of the State. No one seems to defend that refusal as fair." Shortly thereafter, New Jersey, as have so many other states, enacted a state Tort Claims Act[94] largely modeled on federal legislation.

*The Federal Tort Claims Act.* As noted above, the most significant legislation limiting the defense of sovereign immunity, and the model for many of the state statutes, was enacted by Congress in 1946.

Its passage was prompted by two primary factors. First, there was a determination by Congress that it should provide a mechanism for compensating individuals who had been negligently injured in the ever-expanding activities of the federal government. Second, the preexisting system of compensation through the introduction of private claim bills in Congress was cumbersome, inefficient, and subject to political considerations. This system basically required individuals to petition their congressman to introduce legislation to appropriate funds to compensate them for their injuries. In fact, in each of the several sessions of Congress preceeding the enactment of the Tort Claims Act, between 1600 and 2300 such bills were introduced, of which approximately 20 percent were approved.

The basic mandate of the Federal Tort Claims Act is that the United States is to be held liable in each state "in the same manner and to the same extent as a private individual under like circumstances."[95] Despite this broad statement, the legal history of the act has largely been concerned with arguments and discussions about exceptions to coverage. Many of these exceptions (such as those relating to military personnel and federal prisoners) are beyond the scope of this book. Other statutory exceptions for such intentional torts as assault, battery, false imprisonment, libel, and misrepresenation have little direct impact on federal recreation and leisure services activities. However, it should be noted that in response to a series of abusive activities by federal narcotics agents, Congress amended the act in 1974 to permit suits based on intentional torts and abuses of power by federal officers "empowered . . . to execute searches, to seize evidence, or to make arrests." This change would clearly apply to certain National Parks, Forest Service, and Fish and Wildlife Service rangers, wardens, and agents.

The most significant exceptions to coverage are found in Section 2680 of the act. First, claims may not be based on injuries arising from the careful execution of statutes or regulations. That is to say, even if a governmental activity is harmful, if it is authorized or directed by law, no claim shall be recognized under the Tort Claims Act, although other constitutional or civil rights remedies may be available.

Second, the most important exception, and the one which has caused the most litigation, excuses negligence "based upon the exercise or performance or the failure to exercise or perform *a discretionary function* or duty on the part of a federal agency or an employee of the Government, *whether or not the discretion involved be abused"* (emphasis added).

Almost from the beginning, controversy has swirled around the question of what is or what is not *discretionary.* The issue also arises in the context of similar state tort claims acts. The original purpose of the exemption was to insulate high-level decision makers from fear of litigation over difficult policy decisions, and not to protect low-level *operational* or *ministerial* activities, even when they might involve some basic local decision making. From the first, the courts have had trouble in drawing the line. In one of the earliest and still most important decisions under the act, *Dalehite v. United States,*[96] a bitterly divided court ruled that the government was not liable for some 200 million dollars in claims arising from a terrible disaster in Texas City, Texas. In this case, ships loaded with volatile government-produced ammonium nitrate fertilizer blew up in the harbor, leveling much of the city and taking over five hundred lives. A majority of the court ruled that decisons at every step of the way, from the initial determination to help rebuild Europe's war-torn agriculture down to the procedures used to buy and store the fertilizer, were all discretionary acts since each decision was "part of a plan developed at high level under a direct delegation of plan-making authority from the apex of the Executive Department."

Given the penchant of government bureaucrats to codify and formalize even the most minute details into rules and regulations, a continued literal interpretation of *Dalehite* would have limited government liability to the kind of negligent accident in which no thought or conscious choices were involved, such as losing control of a vehicle and driving into a group of tourists or omitting to place a bolt in a swing so that it would collapse under a child's weight.

Fortunately, the courts have retreated somehwat from *Dalehite,* particularly in refusing to give immunity merely because an activity appears uniquely governmental. Today, most low-level determinations not involving significant decisions on resource allocation have been deemed operational.

An excellent example of the problems arising under the Tort Claims Act may be found in a recent case arising in Illinois. Here a young man was tragically crippled when he struck his head on a submerged stump as he dove into an Army Corps of Engineers reservoir, Lake Shelbyville, in Eagle Creek State Park.

The Department of the Army specified that the trees above the water level had to "be removed to a height not exceeding six (6) inches above the ground surface . . . ." They had no requirement, however, regarding the clearing of submerged timber, and they made no attempt to clear the stumps to create a safe diving area. Nevertheless, the Corps and its contractors maintained a swimming area, despite their knowledge of the hazards and in the face of a contrary state policy prohibiting swimming.

There were no signs posted indicating that diving was forbidden, nor were there warnings of the hidden tree stumps. Nevertheless, the court held that the decision not to clear the submerged timber was a protected "discretionary" one because the

> Corps' Office of the Chief of Engineers was engaged in a planning function involving some considerations of public policy. . . . The Corps weighed cost and engineering factors and arrived at a design decision that applied to all . . . clearing projects at this time, *not just Lake Shelbyville*. This decision appears to be clearly within *Dalehite's* bounds of discretion which is entitled to immunity.[97] [emphasis added]

Despite its conclusion on the basic decision not to remove the stumps, the court held that the plaintiff did have a cause of action based on

> failure to prohibit diving by all persons in all swimming areas of Lake Shelbyville which contained submerged tree stumps; and failure to warn plaintiff of the existence of the hidden danger . . . . Neither of these facts or omissions are incident to the decision to leave stumps in the lake . . . . The government cannot avoid its duty to warn by assimilating . . . [it] into another decision protected by the discretionary function exception.

The lesson to be drawn from this case is that where decisions affecting recreational use are made on a general basis, as part of an overall plan of resource allocation, the courts may well determine that they are discretionary. The closer one comes to an individual decision, the more likely it will be considered operational. Furthermore, the relative formality or spontaneity of a decision may also be a factor.

Given all of the ambiguities of language in the law and the decisions, very minor differences in fact may dictate contradictory results. For example, in *Martin v. United States*,[98] the discretionary exception protected the Park Service from the plaintiff's claim of negligence stemming from a bear attack in Yellowstone. Martin had essentially challenged the overall bear management plan.

Conversely, in *Claypool v. United States*,[99] the court held that failure to warn of the threat of bear attacks would result in liability. The rangers knew that bears had been in the vicinity of the campground where the plaintiffs were located, but still assured them of their safety. (See further discussion in the sample memorandum in Appendix B). In the Claypool case, it was not the bear management policy but the individual and local failure to warn that became the focus of the court's attention.

*Government Liability Today.* Summing up the issue of government liability, we can say that some states still provide substantial scope to avoid liability for governmental operations. Where there are established tort claim procedures, exceptions such as the discretionary/operational distinction have been legislatively enacted. Nevertheless, reliance by parks and leisure services agencies on these exceptions to liability would be misplaced.

Most recreation injuries arise at what is, at least arguably, the operational level. Courts are very reluctant to exclude deserving plaintiffs from the protection of tort law, and they may have little sympathy for negligent government agencies or employees. Given the imprecise nature of the exceptions, the value of governmental immunity as a predictable protection is minimal in all but the highest level of planning and decision making.

Individual government employees are protected in their good-faith actions from liability suits through a variety of statutory and judicially created privileges and immunities.[100] Thus the possibility of government liability should not result in timidity or dangerous indecision on the part of officials entrusted with responsibilities. Even if the amount paid out by government in tort claims damages is substantial in individual cases, the overall total is small compared to the mind-boggling expenditures for the military, public safety, education, welfare, and the entire spectrum of government-supported programs. Certainly to attempt to justify a continued refusal to compensate the innocent victims of official negligence on the historic rationales for sovereign immunity or the philosophy of *Men of Devon* would be both intellectually indefensible and morally repugnant.

**Strict Liability.** As must be clear by this point, most major developments in tort law over the last generation have resulted in a shift of the burden of costs of major injuries from the shoulders of the injured individual to the persons or enterprises responsible for the injury, even where the relative merits of the case or the comparative degree of fault may not be entirely clear. Certainly a recognition of the availability of insurance and the ability of enterprises to distribute costs of injuries incurred in their products and services has played a major role in the policy underlying the movement of the law from protection of defendants to concern for plaintiffs.

In no area of tort law has social and economic policy played such a significant part as in the rapid development of what is known as *strict products liability*. The courts have frankly concluded that enterprises are better able to withstand costs and distribute losses than consumers. As a result, the traditional view that liability must be designated on the basis of fault or wrongdoing has been substantially eroded, but not eradicated.

Recreational and sports products have been a major focus of this recent development. The law reporters are replete with cases involving football helmets, snowmobiles, dune buggies, toys, games, and gadgets. These products are designed to be used by children and fun-seeking adults who may suspend their sense of caution while relaxing. Additionally, there is an unfortunate tendency of some recreational product manufacturers to operate low-budget enterprises with poor product planning and production methods that exacerbate the likelihood of injuries. Sharp points, rubber bands, projectiles of all sorts, unguarded drive belts and chains, and the general shoddiness of "throw-away" recreational products result in many recurring types of injuries and lend support to the notion that predictable injuries should be treated as a cost of doing business.

*Historical Development of Strict Liability.*   Before we deal with what has been characterized as the products liability revolution, let us examine some background on the historic development of strict liability. From the earliest days of the evolution of tort law, the courts have recognized that certain activities and enterprises are inherently dangerous and cannot be made completely safe even if carried on carefully.

Perhaps the earliest cases of liability without fault (at least since the very idea of "fault" developed) involved animals. Wild animals, as one commentator noted, "are notoriously unreliable, even when they are raised in captivity and display none of the viciousness of their kind."[101]

The rule of strict liability for injuries caused by wild animals remains applicable in situations involving zoos, wild animal exhibits, commercial wildlife parks, and the keeping of wildlife as pets,[102] although government maintenance of parks as wildlife sanctuaries may be treated differently given statutory mandates to maintain and preserve wild species.[103] Similarly, there is a general rule of liability for damage done by escaping livestock.

These rules were analogized to escaping noxious or "unnatural" substances from one landowner's property to that of a neighbor in the landmark case of *Rylands v. Fletcher*,[104] which was discussed in detail in Chapter 2.

Today, exterminators, explosives manufacturing and transportation, demolition and excavation operations, quarries, rocket manufacture, and a host of other enterprises that result in excess vibration, escaping dust, rocks, and liquids may all be subject to liability for damages without proof of fault whether under the *Rylands* rationale, strict liability for ultrahazardous activities, or under a "nuisance" category that will be considered below.

In any event, the basis for liability is essentially similar. Those engaged in dangerous or destructive activities are usually well rewarded for their risks. It is only fair that they should shoulder the economic burden of predictable injuries.

Application of this kind of strict liability to the parks and recreation field is rather limited, although problems arising from the damming of streams to create swimming pools or, more likely, injuries to persons or property from windblown or waterborne insecticides, fertilizers, or defoliants obviously could involve park management in strict liability situations.

Other historically significant areas of the law that might have application to leisure services involve such activities as food service and the operation of hotels, inns, and sightseeing tours. The vulnerability of consumers to danger from improperly prepared food and drink (and in all probability the fact that judges eat out a good deal), caused the courts to hold restaurateurs and sellers of prepared food strictly liable either under a tort or an *implied warranty of fitness* theory. In the case of innkeepers and common carriers and conveyers (railroads, buses, airplanes, etc.), the fact that the traveler totally entrusted her person and possessions to the care of such enterprises impressed the English courts at an early date, and, although their liability was not "absolute," the degree of care required was and remains so high that it borders on strict liability.

*Development of Products Liability Law.* The modern law of products liability really has two starting points. As in many other areas of tort law, courts in heavily populated and consumer-oriented states, including New York, California, and New Jersey, played an instrumental role in the development.

In 1916 in the famous case of *MacPherson v. Buick Motor Co.*,[105] Judge Cardozo sharply limited the application of a principle of law known as *privity of contract.* Developed as a protection for industry and commerce during the Industrial Revolution, privity required that before a manufacturer or seller of goods could be held liable for a product's defects, a direct contractual relationship would have to exist between the enterprise and the injured consumer or bystander. Otherwise, the courts reasoned, liability would extend far beyond the bargained-for obligations and considerations.

Although the privity of contract requirement might have had some justification when most business was conducted directly between the consumer and the local blacksmith, farmer, or carpenter, when applied to the modern commercial marketing system, it often left an injured user of goods with no real remedy. The article might not have been purchased by the person injured. Even if a local retailer could be sued, he might have specific contractual defenses whose technicalities may have been appropriate in commercial transactions but were disastrous for unknowing consumers. furthermore, the retailer would often have limited resources and be effectively judgment-proof.

In the *MacPherson* case, Cardozo brilliantly manipulated the limited precedent to modify the law. The case involved an automobile that proved defective and caused injury to a retail purchaser. The judge bluntly pointed out that under the prevailing privity requirement the only one who could maintain an action against the manufacturer would be the retailer, who would be unlikely to have actually used the car.

To avoid an unjust result, Judge Cardozo expanded the exceptions to the privity rule from such *inherently dangerous* products such as drugs and firearms to any product that would be dangerous if negligently made. Since the manufacturer knew that vehicles would ultimately be used by the public, it would certainly be foreseeable that if manufactured negligently they would cause harm to consumers and those with whom they came into contact.

From the time of *MacPherson*, the Cardozo approach was adopted in state after state and became universally acknowledged by midcentury.

Despite *MacPherson*, two major difficulties remained as obstacles to the general public seeking protection from defective and dangerous products. One was the limitation on liability that a manufacturer or seller might attach to a product, usually in the form of an ostensible *warranty*. Although advertised and presented as guarantees that manufacturers stand behind their products, the terms of these *express warranties* usually severely restricted remedies so that even if repair or replacement might be provided for a certain time, liability for physical injuries to product users would be disavowed.

The other principle difficulty centered on problems of proof of negligence. If the injury suffered was one that would not ordinarily take place without negligence, and where the person injured had not been an active participant in the activity, the principle of *res ipsa loquitur* (which means "the thing speaks for itself") might shift the burden of presenting evidence from the plaintiff to the defendant. Thus, when a baseball came crashing through a window or a grandstand collapsed on a spectator, the injured plaintiff would only have to prove what injured him, not how it occurred. Unfortunately, *res ipsa loquitur* was often of little use in cases involving injuries by manufactured products. Usually the injured plaintiff had been actively involved in events leading up to the accident. In many instances it would be extremely difficult for an injured consumer to find witnesses or evidence demonstrating an actual deviation from the reasonable standard of care demanded in negligence cases. Time, distance, expense, and the hostility of those who had actual knowledge of the manufacturing process were major burdens. Very often, the product itself had been so damaged at the time of the injury that no amount of examination could conclusively show the cause of an accident.

A combination of both the warranty limitation and evidence factors emerged in the first major decision that began the overthrow of what has been called a "citadel" of protection for manufacturers,[106] *Henningsen v. Bloomfield Motors, Inc.*[107] In that case, Mrs. Henningsen was injured while driving a new car a few days after her husband had purchased it. With no prior warning, she heard a loud noise and felt the steering wheel spin. The car veered off the road at a ninety-degree angle and was demolished when it struck a wall. The exact cause of the crash could not be determined, although there was evidence that some mechanical failure was to blame.

Rejecting all of the limitations on liability set forth in the "warranty" provision of the sale contract as a "sad commentary upon the automobile manufacturer's marketing practices" and reflecting "the gross inequality of bargaining position occupied by the consumer," the court imposed an *implied warranty* that *manufactured products were reasonably suitable or fit for their expected users.*

By emphasizing implied contractual obligations and eliminating vestiges of privity, the court was able to hold the auto manufacturers liable without the necessity of proof of negligence.

A couple of years after *Henningsen,* the California Supreme Court in *Greenman v. Yuba Power Products, Inc.,*[108] a case involving injuries stemming from the use of a home power tool, expanded on some earlier views. Justice Traynor wrote that contractual remedies were unnecessary, since "a manufacturer is strictly liable in tort when an article he places on the market . . . proves to have a defect that causes injury to a human being." Furthermore,

the purpose of such liability is to insure that costs of injuries resulting from defective products are borne by the manufacturers that put such products on the market rather than by the injured persons who are powerless to protect themselves.

*Strict Liability Today.*    The reasoning of cases like *Henningsen* and *Greenman* has been widely adopted in other states. Today the application of strict liability in tort is practically universal. Not only consumers but also bystanders are protected. Some problems still remain, however. The application of strict liability to wholesalers who merely pass products on through without doing anything to them is a subject of controversy. The availability to manufacturers of tort defenses such as contributory negligence or comparative negligence is a subject of considerable disagreement among the courts. It is clear that misuse of a product and voluntary encountering of known risks are defenses in most product liability cases, although there is some disagreement about safety devices in industrial applications.

More ominously for consumers, there are legislative rumblings promoted by manufacturers and their insurance companies that the courts have gone too far in the area of products liability and that corrective statutes alleviating some of the costs of protection are required. Several states have already passed such legislation and a federal statute (under the commerce power of the Constitution) may eventually be forthcoming.

Typically such statutes restrict liability to a limited period of years from the time of product manufacture and sale and provide for presumptions in favor of manufacturers who conform to recognized standards or the "state of the art" in their product designs.[109]

Whatever the ultimate shape of products liability law, it is clear that no amount of pressure is going to put the liability genie back into the bottle. Nevertheless, strict liability should not be confused with absolute liability. Although courts disagree on whether a "defective" product must be "unreasonably dangerous," as suggested by the Restatement of Torts,[110] or whether a defect may stand alone without the negligence connotations of "unreasonably dangerous," there is universal agreement that some flaw or defect must be shown.

A defect may be either the result of an unintended error in manufacture or assembly (for example, an improperly fastened bolt on a bicycle that causes a wheel to fall off) or it may be the result of a conscious design choice (for example, an unguarded snowmobile chain that causes injury to a passenger's foot).

There is little difficulty in succeeding in the former kinds of cases, since the product obviously did not fulfill the manufacturer's intentions. There is much greater difficulty in the design defect area, since here the same considerations as in negligence come into play. The reasonableness of the design choice, the standards and customs of the industry, the expense and availability of superior designs, and the predictable degree of danger are all elements of concern in determining whether a design is defective. There is also continuing controversy and disagreement over whether and to what extent designs of vehicles must anticipate accidents and be crashworthy.

*Strict Liability for Recreational Products.*   The most significant and, in terms of effect upon the entire field, the most potentially costly products liability cases in the recreation/sports field revolve around issues of design. Among the most controversial are football helmet disputes, since not only do many injuries result from head contacts in football, but helmets are also held out as safety gear. Because of this helmets come under particularly close scrutiny by the courts. For example, in *Burns v. Riddell, Inc.,*[111] the court in finding the defendant manufacturer liable considered the following matters:

1. The usefulness and desirability of the product.
2. The availability of other, safer designs to meet the same needs.
3. The likelihood and probable seriousness of injury.
4. Common knowledge and public expectation.
5. The ability of the user to avoid danger by proper use of the product.
6. The ability to eliminate the danger without seriously affecting its usefulness or making it unduly expensive.

The court concluded that the cost of making a safer helmet was not so great as to outweigh the benefits the manufacturer secured from the profitable business of making and merchandising helmets.

One of the ironies of the revolution in the development of recreation products is that lightweight, convenient, attractive, and easily maintained equipment (be it biking gear, skis, football helmets, etc.) has made difficult or dangerous leisure activities more accessible and ostensibly safer. At the same time, they have also undoubtedly emboldened those pursuing adventurous recreation to take even greater risks. Thus, although the exact nature of injuries may change, the numbers and seriousness may not diminish. For example, in football the use of lightweight helmets and protective face guards has promoted greatly increased use of the head in blocking and tackling, and as one official of a helmet manufacturer put it, "All we are doing is turning head injuries into neck injuries."[112]

Not all product liability cases result in judgments for the plaintiff.

For example, in *Heldman v. Uniroyal, Inc.,*[113] a professional tennis player was held to have assumed the risk of injury when she fell on an obvious bubble in a synthetic court surface. On the other hand, some recreational products are so clearly hazardous that whether under strict liability or a warranty theory liability seems a foregone conclusion.

In one particularly egregious example a thirteen-year-old boy was seriously injured while playing with a Christmas present, the "Golfing Gizmo," which was labeled, "Completely Safe—Ball Will Not Harm Player." The Gizmo consisted of a regulation golf ball attached to a twenty-one-foot cotton cord affixed to an elastic band looped around two stakes. When struck by the player, the return angle of the ball was to indicate whether the user was hooking, slicing, or hitting straight. The thirteen-year-old caught the cotton cord and the ball on his club, and as he followed through, the ball struck him in the temple.

Since the "Gizmo" was to be used by learners and "duffers" who rarely strike a ball cleanly, the court agreed with a safety expert who labeled it a "major safety hazard."[114]

Courts are reluctant to make sweeping conclusions of design defectiveness with regard to major mass-produced products such as automobiles. Since recreation products are not viewed as having particularly high social or economic utility, the courts are somewhat bolder in reaching decisions that may appear to require substantial design changes. Furthermore, particularly because of the variety of uses of recreation products, the courts are also less likely to find misuse or assumption of risk. As one court put it in refusing such a defense in a case where a shard from a rock hammer entered a child's eye while his father attempted to shatter a rock, the manufacturer "well knew that the hammer was purchased and used by hobbyists and could not assume that the purchasers would be aware of the distinction between chipping and breaking."[115]

As noted earlier in the discussion of negligence, evidence of violation of design and manufacture standards may be conclusive on the question of whether a recreational product is defective. The Consumer Product Safety Commission has thus far only formulated formal design standards for swimming pool slides and bicycles along with banning such obviously dangerous toys as baby rattles with loose wires or attachments. However, the commission has cooperated in the development of voluntary standards for a wide variety of recreational products and equipment. Of course these voluntary standards are generated with considerable industry input and may be expected to be somewhat less stringent than formal government requirements. On the other hand, the promulgated standards have, at times, seemed overly rigid. For example, the swimming pool slide standard is admittedly less than satisfactory and clearly contributed to driving all but one manufacturer out of the business.[116]

In conclusion, the profound effect that the strict product liability movement has had on the manner in which society apportions responsibility for injuries has resulted in substantial costs to recreational equipment manufacturers. At the same time, this common-law development, along with the activities and promulgation of standards by agencies such as the Federal Consumer Product Safety Commission and the American Safety Standards Institute, will continue to cause greater care and more concern for safety in the design and marketing of leisure products, although as inflation continues, pressures on legislatures and courts to relieve businesses of some degree of responsibility for the costs of injuries will undoubtedly increase.

**Nuisance and Trespass.**   Related to the issues of strict liability are the torts of nuisance and trespass. The land use aspects of these torts were discussed in Chapter 2.

To briefly recapitulate, trespass is an intentional tort concerned with an interference with or invasion of a property holder's title or interest in land, while a nuisance is an act that interferes with the use and enjoyment of property.

Nuisance is much more likely than trespass to affect parks and leisure services. Nuisance may be intentional or negligent or may have elements of both. It may be "private" or it may be "public," affecting the community in the general use of water, air, and resources. Some nuisances are both. For example, a noxious chemical that is improperly dumped may pollute a well on someone's property, resulting in a private nuisance (or a strict liability claim under *Rylands v. Fletcher* for ultrahazardous activities). It may also result in pollution of public waterways, affecting the use of streams and rivers for swimming, boating, and fishing.

Theoretically, unless an individual can show damages distinctly different from the public in general (such as a professional fisherman's loss of employment) a public nuisance may be remedied only by action of a government agency or community organization. In fact, nuisance is a loosely used term, applied by courts and litigants to a wide variety of negligent and intentional torts.

*Nuisance and Recreation.*   Nuisance actions related to parks and leisure services are most likely when there is a claim of continuing or recurring interference with the living conditions of park neighbors. Examples of typical recreational nuisance situations include: a playground that is utilized late in the evening by noisy adolescents; the parking problems caused by a community theater; or the ball park located so close to housing that balls are perpetually breaking windows or bombarding residents (this may also be a physical trespass). The Kalispell Pee Wee Baseball controversy discussed in Chapter 2 is a case in point.[117]

Although proof of nuisance should result in an injunction against continuance of the disturbing activity, courts are reluctant to absolutely prohibit socially valuable programs. Thus, limitations on hours of operation, requirements for protective fences or barriers, elimination of use of loudspeakers, or other compromise solutions will either be ordered by the courts or arrived at through negotiation so that a reasonable accommodation between competing users may be reached.

One final note on nuisance and trespass: Although it was clear at one time that a trespass had to involve a direct physical invasion of property and courts worried about distinctions in the remedies for noise, light, and vibration on the one hand and the intrusion of rocks, soot, and other finite physical particles on the other, such distinctions have been minimized today. The remedies available, whether injunctive relief or compensatory and punitive damages, will be molded to the kind of activity and its harmfulness rather than to a particular legal definition.

## CONCLUSION

In the preceding sections we have discussed a variety of legal actions falling within the general category of tort law. We have not discussed particular methods of avoiding liability. Parks and leisure services professionals do not need instruction from lawyers on reasonable ways to act in order to minimize injuries in preparation for, during, and if an accident should occur, after a recreational activity. Adherence to professional standards and codes of conduct, awareness and utilization of the best methods and equipment, and use of competent caring personnel, along with the maintenance of relevant records and forms, will minimize injuries, litigation, and liability. There is no legal formula to gain immunity for suit, nor should the profession become timid and narrow in its approach to programs and services out of unreasoning fear of liability.

Certainly over the last several years, courts have become more sympathetic to the plight of the injured in our society and less protective of industry, commerce, and government. At this time of economic upheaval and retrenchment, we may see some retreat from the liberality of the last two decades. In the long run, however, it seems clear that nothing short of a cataclysm will reverse the trend toward greater awareness of the social responsibilities of business and government enterprise to compensate victims of injury. Ultimately, the increased burden of responsibility of the parks and leisure services profession (along with medicine, law, commerce, manufacturing, and government in general) may lead to a transformation of common-law torts into a kind of social insurance not unlike social security or worker's compensation. In the meantime, individual cases of liability will continue to be resolved on the historic rationales and distinctions made by tort law.

## NOTES

1. John P. Jesse, Hazards in Recreational Sports and Physical Fitness Programs, 32 *California Parks and Recreation,* August/September 1976, at 30.
2. 136 Vt. 293, 390 A.2d 398 (1978).
3. A recent exception is in the law of defamation, where, because of the constitutional protection afforded free speech and freedom of the press, the Supreme Court has ruled that, absent proof of knowing falsehood or reckless disregard of the truth, fault and actual injury must be proven! See *Gertz v. Robert Welch, Inc.,* 418 U.S. 323 (1974).
4. *United States v. Gilman,* 347 U.S. 507 (1954).
5. *Talcott v. National Exhibition Co.,* 128 N.Y.S. 1059 (App. Div. 1911).
6. 28 U.S.C.A. §§ 1346(b), 2671-2680.
7. See, e.g., New York General Business Law § 218.
8. 60 Mass. 292 (1850).
9. See Restatement (Second) of Torts § 283.
10. *Vaughan v. Menlove,* 132 Eng. Rep. 490 (1837).
11. *Goss v. Allen,* 70 N.J. 442, 360 A.2d 388 (1976).
12. *Baxter v. Fugett,* 425 P.2d 462 (Okla. 1967).
13. See *Dellwo v. Pearson,* 259 Minn. 452, 107 N.W. 2d 859 (1961) (twelve-year-old held to adults' standard).
14. See *Fishel v. Givens,* 47 Ill. App. 3d 512, 362 N.E.2d 97 (1977) (fourteen-year-old minibike rider held contributorily negligent).
15. *Neumann v. Shlansky,* 63 Misc.2d 587, 312 N.Y.S.2d 951 (1970).
16. See *Patterson v. Weatherspoon,* 29 N. Car. App. 711, 225 S.E.2d 634 (1976) (not foreseeable that a child would use a golf putter in a manner likely to cause injury).
17. See *Crum v. Groce,* 556 P.2d 1223 (Colo. 1976).
18. La. Civ. Code § 2318.
19. Tex. Fam. Code § 33.01.
20. Jacobus Ten Broeck, The Right to Live in the World: The Disabled in the Law of Torts, 54 *Calif. L. Rev.* 841 (1966).
21. *Cf. Fletcher v. City of Aberdeen,* 54 Wash. 174, 338 P.2d 743 (1959).
22. See Restatement (Second) of Torts § 464 and § 283B.
23. See *DeMartini v. Alexander Sanitarium, Inc.,* 192 Cal. App. 2d 442, 13 Cal. Rptr. 564 (1961).
24. *Horton v. Niagara Falls Memorial Medical Center,* 380 N.Y.S.2d 116, 121

(App. Div. 1975). See W. L. Prosser, *The Law of Torts,* 4th ed. (St. Paul: West Publishing Co., 1971). See also *Miller v. Trinity Medical Center,* 260 N.W.2d 4 (N. Dak. 1977).

25. *Heaven v. Pender,* 11 Q.B.D. 503 at 507 (1883).
26. 15 U.S.C.A. § 2072.
27. See *Hooks v. Washington Sheraton Corp.,* 578 F.2d 313 (D.C. Cir. 1977), in which a record judgment of over $4,500,000 to a quadriplegic Eagle Scout and his family was affirmed.
28. See *Brohatcek v. Millard School Dist.* (Nebr. Douglas Cty—D. Ct. Docket G78, at 371, Aug. 1, 1977).
29. See *United States v. Carroll Towing Co.,* 159 F.2d 169 (2d Cir. 1947).
30. See *Carroll v. Whittier Union High School Dist.* (L.A. Cty. Super. Ct. C-61522, Aug. 4, 1978).
31. See *Honeycutt v. City of Monroe,* 253 So.2d 597 (La. App. 1971).
32. See H. Terry, Negligence, 29 *Harv. L. Rev.* 40 (1915).
33. See Karl Rohnke, *Cowstails and Cobras* (Hamilton, Mass: Project Adventure, 1977).
34. See, e.g., the 1981 *Miracle Recreation Equipment Catalog.* See generally, the Consumer Products Safety Act, 15 U.S.C.A. §§ 2047-2084.
35. See *Wamser v. St. Petersburg,* 339 So.2d 244 (Fla. App. 1976).
36. *Lukasiewicz v. Buffalo,* 390 N.Y.S.2d 341 (App. Div. 1976).
37. Parenthetically, once a volunteer comes to the aid of someone in distress, the duty of reasonable care is applicable. Furthermore, if the bystander's actions discourage other would-be rescuers, or if there is some familial or supervisory relationship between the parties, a legal duty may well exist.
38. *Barrett v. Phillips,* 223 S.E.2d 571 (N.C. App. 1976).
39. *Battala v. State of New York,* 10 N.Y.2d 237, 219 N.Y.S.2d 34, 176 N.E.2d 729 (1961). The reader may conclude that the plaintiff overreacted to the absence of the safety bar (particularly since many Western ski areas don't have them at all), but remember the rule of the "eggshell" plaintiff—that is, within the realm of the foreseeable, a tort-feasor takes the frailties of the injured as they exist.
40. See *Dillon v. Legg,* 68 Cal.2d 728, 441 P.2d 912 (1968); *Archibald v. Braverman,* 275 Cal. App. 2d 263, 79 Cal. Rptr. 723 (1969).
41. 80 Cal. App. 3d 553, 145 Cal. Rptr. 657 (1978).
42. See, e.g., *Tobin v. Grossman,* 24 N.Y.2d 609, 249 N.E.2d 419, 301 N.Y.S.2d 554 (1969).
43. *Passafaro v. Bd. of Ed. of City of New York,* 43 App. Div. 918, 353 N.Y.S. 178 (1974).
44. *Meistrich v. Casino Arena Attractions, Inc.,* 31 N.J. 44, 155 A.2d 90 (1959).
45. See, e.g., *McConville v. State Farm Mutual Ins.,* 15 Wis.2d 374, 113 N.W.2d 14 (1962); *Farley v. M & M Cattle Co.,* 529 S.W.2d 751 (Tex. 1975).
46. See, e.g., *Roberts v. King,* 102 La. App. 518, 116 S.E.2d 85 (1960). But see Maine's agreement with New Jersey in *Wilson v. Gordon,* 354 A.2d 398 (Me. 1976).
47. See *Brevard County v. Jacks,* 238 So.2d 156 (Fla. 1970).

48. *Tite v. Omaha Coliseum Co.*, 144 Neb. 22, 12 N.W.2d 90 (1943).
49. *Modec v. City of Eveleth*, 224 Minn. 556, 29 N.W.2d 453 (1947).
50. *Chapman v. State*, 6 Wash. App. 316, 492 P.2d 607 (1972).
51. 250 N.Y. 479, 166 N.E. 173 (1929).
52. 390 A.2d 398 (Vt. 1978), *supra* note 2.
53. 557 F.2d 730 (10th Cir. 1977). See, *contra*, *Rosen v. LTV Recreational Development, Inc.*, 569 F.2d 1117 (10th Cir. 1978), where a skier was held not to assume the risk of running into a metal pole in the middle of a slope. See also *Blair v. Mt. Hood Meadows Devel. Corp.*, 48 Or. App. 109, 616 P.2d 535 (1980).
54. Colo. Rev. Stat. 33-44-101 to 111.
55. *Garafano v. Neshobe Beach Club, Inc.*, 126 Vt. 566, 238 A.2d 70 (1967).
56. *Verduce v. Board of Higher Education*, 192 N.Y.S.2d 913 (1959) (dissenting opinion) affirmed on appeal, 8 N.Y.2d 928, 168 N.E.2d 838, 204 N.Y.S.2d 168 (1960).
57. These cases are discussed in the April/May 1980 and August/September 1981 issues of *Outside* magazine.
58. *Supra* note 53.
59. 10 N.Y.2d 294, 177 N.E.2d 925, 220 N.Y.S.2d 962 (1961).
60. See also *LaFrenz v. Lake County Fair Board*, 360 N.E.2d 605 (Ind. App. 1977) (releases to enter the pit area at a demolition derby held valid!).
61. N.Y. General Obligations Law § 5-326. See also Cal. Civ. Code § 1668.
62. *American Motorcycle Ass'n v. Superior Court*, 20 Cal.3d 578, 578 P.2d 899, 146 Cal. Rptr. 182 (1978).
63. 481 P.2d 369 (Or. App. 1971).
64. See, e.g., *Ferguson v. Bretton*, 375 A.2d 225 (Me. 1977).
65. *Rowland v. Christian*, 69 Cal.2d 1081 443 P.2d 561 (1968).
66. *Basso v. Miller*, 40 N.Y.2d 233, 352 N.E.2d 868, 386 N.Y.S.2d 564 (1976).
67. *Scurti v. City of New York*, 40 N.Y.2d 433, 354 N.E.2d 794, 387 N.Y.S.2d 55 (1976).
68. See *Sioux City and Pac. R.R. Co. v. Stout*, 84 U.S. 657 (1873).
69. *United Zinc and Chemical Co. v. Britt*, 258 U.S. 268 (1922).
70. See *Altenbach v. Lehigh Valley R. Co.*, 349 Pa. 272, 37 A.2d 429 (1944).
71. *Alston v. Baltimore and Ohio R.R. Co.*, 433 F. Supp. 553 (D.D.C. 1977).
72. *Butler v. Sports Haven International*, 563 P. 2d 1245 (Utah 1977). *Cf, Colavaturo v. Passaic*, 124 N.J. Super 361 (App. Div. 1973).
73. *Harris v. Indiana General Service Co.*, 206 Ind. 351, 189 N.E. 410 (1934).
74. See John C. Barrett, Good Sports and Bad Lands: The Application of Washington's Recreational Use Statute Limiting Landowners Liability, 53 *Wash. L. Rev.* 1, 2 (1977) listing state statutes. Also, the American Motorcyclist Association lists statutes of forty-four states in a 1978 pamphlet entitled "Landowner Liability Laws."
75. See *English v. Morin Municipal Water Dist.*, 66 Cal. App. 3d 729, 136 Cal. Rptr. 224 (1977).
76. Cal. Civil Code § 846.
77. 80 N.J. 391, 403 A.2d 910 (1979).

78. N.J.S.A. 2A:42A-2.
79. *Goodson v. Racine,* 61 Wis.2d 554, 213 N.W.2d 16 (1973).
80. *Gard v. United States,* 594 F.2d 1230 (9th Cir. 1979) citing Nev. Rev. Stat., § 41.510.
81. Mont. Rev. Codes Ann. §§ 37-1001-1008.
82. N.C. Gen. Stat. § 113-120-5.
83. R.I. Gen. Laws § 32-6-7.
84. See *McDonald v. Massachusetts General Hosp.,* 120 Mass. 432 (1876).
85. See *Bing v. Thunig,* 2 N.Y.2d 656, 143 N.E.2d 3, 163 N.Y.S.2d 3 (1957).
86. See Edwin M. Borchard, Governmental Responsibility in Tort, 34 *Yale L.J.* 1 (1924).
87. Kenneth Culp Davis, Sovereign Immunity Must Go, 22 *Administrative L. Rev.* 383, 393 (1970).
88. 100 Eng. Rep. 359 (1798).
89. 55 Cal.2d 211, 359 P.2d 457. 11 Cal. Rptr. 89 (1961).
90. See, e.g., the discussion of the Illinois experience in Comment: Illinois Tort Claims Act, 61 *Nev. L. Rev.* 265 (1961).
91. *Vaughn v. County of Durham,* 34 N.C. App. 416, 240 S.E.2d 456 (1977).
92. *City of Wilmington v. Spencer,* 391 A.2d 199 (Del. 1978).
93. *Willis v. Dept. of Cons. & Ec. Devl,* 55 N.J. 535, 264 A.2d 34 (1970).
94. N.J.S.A. 59:1-1 et seq.
95. 28 U.S.C.A. § 2674.
96. 346 U.S. 15 (1953).
97. *Stephens v. United States,* 472 F. Supp. 998 (D. Ill. 1979).
98. 546 F.2d 1355 (9th Cir. 1977).
99. 98 F. Supp. 702 (S.D. Cal. 1951).
100. See *Barr v. Matteo,* 360 U.S. 564 (1959).
101. C. Morris and C. R. Morris, *Morris on Torts,* 2d ed. (Mineola, N.Y.: Foundation Press, 1980) at 226.
102. See e.g., *Cowden v. Bear Country, Inc.,* 382 F. Supp. 1321 (S. Dak. 1974).
103. See the discussion in *Ashley v. United States,* 215 F. Supp. 39 (D. Neb. 1963). Of course natural wildlife habitat must be distinguished from zoos or other artificial settings.
104. L.R.3 H.L. 330 (1868) affirming L.R.1 Ex.265 (1866).
105. 217 N.Y. 382, 111 N.E. 1050 (1916).
106. See W. L. Prosser, The Fall of the Citadel, 50 *Minn. L. Rev.* 791 (1966).
107. 32 N.J. 358, 161 A.2d 69 (1960).
108. 59 Cal.2d 57, 377 P.2d 897, 27 Cal. Rptr. 697 (1963).
109. See, e.g., Kentucky Rev. Stat. §§ 411.300-411.340.
110. Rest. (2d) § 402A.
111. 113 Ariz. 264, 550 P.2d 1065 (1975).
112. *Monahan v. Wilson Sporting Goods Co.,* U.S. Dist. Ct., D. Mass. No. CA74-55 20-6 (1978).
113. 53 Ohio App. 2d 21, 371 N.E.2d 557 (1977).
114. *Hauter v. Zogarts,* 14 Cal.3d 104, 534 P.2d 377, 120 Cal. Rptr. 681 (1975).

115. *Singer v. Walker,* 331 N.Y.S.2d 823 (App. Div. 1972), aff'd. 32 N.Y.2d 786, 298 N.E.2d 681, 345 N.Y.S.2d 542 (1973).
116. See 9 *Prod. Safety and Liability Reporter* (PSLR) 529 (1981).
117. See *Kasala v. Kalispell PeeWee Baseball League,* 151 Mont. 109, 439 P.2d 65, 32 A.L.R.3d 1120 (1968), and Note, Children's Playground as Nuisance, 32 A.L.R.3d 1127.

## REFERENCES

In addition to the cases and materials cited in the footnotes, the following works were generally referred to in the preparation of this chapter.

Dooley, J. *Modern Tort Law,* Callaghan & Co., Chicago, 1977.

Franklin, M. *Tort Law and Alternatives,* 2nd ed., Foundation Press, Mineola, N.Y., 1979.

Morris, C. and Morris, C. R. *Morris on Torts,* 2nd ed., Foundation Press, Mineola, N.Y. 1980.

Prosser, W. L., *The Law of Torts,* 4th ed., West Publishing Co., St. Paul, Minn., 1971.

The principal work on the subject of recreational injuries is:

VanDer Smissen, B., *Legal Liability of Cities and Schools for Injuries in Recreation and Parks,* W. H. Anderson Company, Cincinnati, Ohio, 1968 (Supplement 1975).

# 5
# Parks and the Constitution: Civil Liberties and Civil Rights

## INTRODUCTION

Parks and public gathering places have often been the geographic focal points for the expression of dissident views and protests. They have also been the location for more conventional political speeches and patriotic rallies. Consider the scenes of some of the dramatic events of history: the meadow at Runnymede where the Magna Charta was signed; Speaker's Corner in Hyde Park, London; the village greens of colonial New England; the crowded turf of Grant Park, Chicago, during the tumult and violence of the 1968 Democratic convention; and the Mall, the Ellipse, and Lafayette Park in our nation's capital during the recent decades of civil rights, antiwar, and environmental activism.

Beyond the realm of speech and demonstration, park activities are often an index of growth and change in societal attitudes and mores. What happens in leisure settings is a measure of how well we have met the challenge of integration and acceptance, both racial and sexual, and how well we have responded to the legitimate demands of those with disabilities to enjoy a full measure of the rights and privileges of citizenship.

This chapter is divided into two principal sections with distinct but related constitutional bases. Civil liberties are firmly rooted in the First Amendment, civil rights are largely derived from the due process clause of the Fifth Amendment, the equal protection clause of the Fourteenth Amendment, and particularly with regard to private discrimination against racial minorities, in the overall intent of the Thirteenth Amendment.

Other areas with constitutional and civil rights implications, such as employment discrimination, criminal law, and the taking and regulation of property used for parks purposes, are dealt with in the appropriate chapters throughout this book.

## CIVIL LIBERTIES

Particularly today when large corporate and governmental entities control the means of mass communication, parks must be used as public forums if we are to preserve even a modicum of the values of participatory democracy. Ironically, dissenters and supporters of minority viewpoints often depend upon dramatic presentations and confrontations in the parks to gain the attention of the media, which might ignore the traditional methods of letter writing, handbills, and soap-box oratory.

Efforts of officials to repress or eliminate dissent in the parks have been sporadic but recurring in our modern history, particularly when a despised or antagonistic group seeks to promulgate its views. Very often parks managers find themselves caught between their constitutional duty as defined by the courts and a hostile majority community. Many Americans simply cannot equate providing space and facilities for the American Legion, the Republican or Democratic party, the AFL-CIO, or a production of Hamlet, on the one hand, with providing similar accommodations to the American Nazi party, the Ku Klux Klan, the Yippies, or controversial, sexually explicit works of art, on the other.

Groups that seek to use the parks for religious activities, proselytizing, and worship often engender popular ambivalence or antagonism. Protection of their constitutional rights and of the public at large raises substantial challenges for leisure services professionals.

In order to understand the specific constitutional problems as they affect parks and leisure services, we must understand the main themes of constitutional history.

### Background

The First Amendment specifies that:

> Congress shall make no law respecting an establishment of religion, or prohibiting the free exercise thereof; or abridging the freedom of speech, or of the press; or of the right of the people peaceably to assemble and to petition the Government for a redress of grievances.

Just from a brief perusal of these words, the libertarian principles of the framers of the Bill of Rights becomes clear. Individual freedom is a corrective to the perpetual threat of repression lurking in all strong central governments. Nevertheless, the absolute nature of the commands of the First Amendment and the breadth of its coverage inevitably will cause disagreement over interpretation and application. A few examples will suffice.

What is meant by "no law respecting an establishment of religion?" Does it simply bar a national or government religion, or does it mean that religion in general may not be aided or enhanced?

Does the clause prohibiting interference with "free exercise" of religion mean that unusual or dangerous religious practices, such as snake handling, polygamy, or the use of hallucinogenic drugs, must be tolerated by law-enforcement officials? Do the clauses pertaining to freedom of speech and of the press require that society tolerate all publications no matter how obscene, libelous, or provocative they may be? Surely speech utilized to exhort criminal conduct must be subject to some limitation? Is the right to assemble to be read only in conjunction with petitions to the government? Must public property, including parks, be made available to all groups seeking to assemble? Do protest marchers have the right to block traffic or to invade recreational areas?

The courts have wrestled with these and other equally vexing questions from the beginning of our constitutional history, and disputes will undoubtedly continue as each generation reinterprets the Constitution within its own unique social and political framework. However, certain principles of interpretation have become firmly established over the years, although details and forms of application may be modified.

Almost from the very first it became clear that in the absence of continual vigilance by the public and the courts, the legislative and executive branches could not be relied upon to fulfill the strict mandates of the First Amendment.

The judicial responses to attacks on constitutional rights have been mixed. This ambivalence is understandable. If some alien philosophy threatens the American way of life, why should the courts afford it the protection of those very precepts that it mocks and undermines?

On the other hand, didn't the First Amendment envision a "marketplace of ideas" as advocated in the writings of John Milton and John Stuart Mill, as well as Jefferson and Madison? Must we not have faith that an informed public in its collective wisdom would reject obnoxious political creeds and philosophies?

The first major constitutional test of these central issues did not arise in the Supreme Court until World War I, with the passage of the Espionage Act of 1917 and the Sedition Act of 1918. In *Schenck v. United States*,[1] an antiwar activist had mailed leaflets opposing the draft to several men who were eligible for military service. The government charged that this violated the Espionage Act, which forbade the obstruction of recruiting.

Although there was no evidence that Schenck's activities were effective, Justice Oliver Wendell Holmes emphasized the circumstances of the war with Germany:

> The most stringent protection of free speech would not protect a man in falsely shouting fire in a theater and causing a panic. . . . The question in every case is whether the words used are used in such circumstances and are of such a nature as to create a *clear and present danger* that they will bring about the substantive evil that Congress has a right to prevent. It is a question of proximity and degree. [emphasis added]

Although Holmes was the father of the "clear and present danger" test, it soon became evident that the majority of the Court took a far more restrictive view of the right of free speech than Holmes had intended, regardless of the test used.

The country embarked upon a great "Red" hunt in the post-World War I era, which culminated in the "Palmer raids," a massive effort, led by the opportunistic Attorney General A. Mitchell Palmer, to repress and prosecute Communists, radicals, and the unorthodox. The Supreme Court acquiesced,[2] but Justice Holmes, joined by Justice Louis Brandeis, used the "clear and present danger" test to attack the Court majority's ready acceptance of suppression of dissent. Finally in 1937 in *Herndon v. Lowry*,[3] in a 5-4 opinion by Justice Roberts, the "clear and present danger" test was utilized to reverse a conviction for violation of a Georgia law prohibiting attempts to incite insurrection. Contemporaneously, in *DeJonge v. Oregon*,[4] Chief Justice Hughes wrote an opinion overturning a conviction for organizing a peaceful Communist party meeting. The Court reasoned that "peaceable assembly for lawful discussion cannot be made a crime."

With the ebb and flow of political sentiment and concern over internal and external threats to American security, judicial opinions have made it clear that no "test" including "clear and present danger" would always protect the exercise of fundamental rights.

Without reciting all of the recent history of First Amendment litigation, we may make a principal point. That is, during the long tenure of Chief Justice Earl Warren, from 1954 to 1969, the use of the "clear and present danger" test was strengthened. The state could justify suppression and criminal sanctions against speech only where there was a likelihood of "imminent lawless action." Despite an increasing number of more conservative justices since the ascendancy of Chief Justice Warren

E. Burger in 1969, this basic recognition of the importance of protection for political speech has continued to evolve.

Before discussing particular park and leisure services related constitutional concerns, a few general observations are required.

**Incorporation.**  As noted in Chapter 1, the First Amendment speaks in terms of "Congress" and was originally intended to prevent restrictions on the rights of the people and the states by the federal government. The Supreme Court ultimately accepted the premise that the Fourteenth Amendment provisions forbidding a state to deprive "any person of life, liberty or property, without *due process* of law" or to deny "any person within its jurisdiction the *equal protection* of the laws" are to be interpreted as *incorporating* the provisions of the First Amendment, along with most of the other individual protections of the Bill of Rights, against intrusions by state and local governments. Lawsuits alleging violations of basic constitutional and civil rights by state and local governments and their officials "under color of" law will, therefore, generally set forth as a basis for the legal action both the specific Bill of Rights provision and the Fourteenth Amendment. These are directly applied through 42 U.S.C.A. § 1983, which is the specific statutory vehicle for legal actions of this nature.

There has been considerable judicial and scholarly debate concerning the historical validity of the "incorporation" theory. These arguments will never be conclusively settled, since the Constitution is a fluid instrument which must respond to the changing needs of our society. The principle debates over "incorporation" today center upon the question of whether due process of law mandates identical application of First Amendment principles to federal, state, and local government actions. Some justices believe that a general application of the fundamental principles of the American concept of liberty will meet the needs of "due process."[5]

Justices adhering to the latter view are likely to permit differentiations among the states in their protection of fundamental rights. They will also allow greater state restriction and control over expressions of marginal societal value such as sexually explicit literature and films or defamatory falsehoods.

**Strict Scrutiny.**  A related principle of great practical importance concerns the strictness and degree of judicial scrutiny that will be applied to official actions impinging upon individual constitutionally protected rights.

Normally, courts presume that laws and governmental actions are constitutionally valid. There is a correspondingly heavy burden on individuals challenging official acts to overcome such presumptions. In fact, in most matters of economic regulation, an individual must demonstrate that the law is totally irrational before a court will find the rule or action unconstitutional. Obviously, successful challenges under this standard are extremely rare.

In civil liberties matters, the Supreme Court has often taken a radically different approach. In a footnote to an 1938 economics regulation case that applied the "rational basis" standard,[6] Justice Stone indicated that where government actions impinged upon *fundamental rights* guaranteed by the Constitution or upon *historically disadvantaged "discrete and insular" minority groups* who might not be adequately represented before or within our legislative bodies, a narrower presumption of constitutionality might be afforded legislation; and government action would be subject to "more exacting judicial scrutiny."

As with every important judicial departure, Justice Stone's suggestion has been the subject of considerable controversy; nevertheless, a "preferred position" for First Amendment rights and a judicially protective attitude toward racial and religious minorities has generally prevailed. This is often expressed in certain key words or phrases that have great legal import. Thus, when a legislative or administrative action directly impinges upon free speech or assembly, or upon the free exercise of religion, *"strict"* or *"close scrutiny"* will be afforded by the court reviewing the action. This entails a "compelling" or "substantial" government justification along with a requirement for demonstrating that narrower or "less intrusive" means are not available to meet the government's legitimate goals. Similar tests are applied to racially discriminatory legislation. Other protective principles may also be applied depending upon the nature of the restriction.

**Overbreadth.** The "overbreadth" doctrine teaches that if the sweep of a statute or regulation includes protected as well as unprotected activities within its coverage, then the entire provision may be struck down because of its "chilling" or inhibiting effect upon legitimate activities,[7] even if a narrower restriction on the conduct in question might be constitutional.

**Void for Vagueness.** Related but not identical to the "overbreadth" doctrine is the "void for vagueness" doctrine, which bars the enforcement of laws or regulations that are so vague that they do not offer guidance as to what is or is not prohibited, fostering an excessive reliance on the often prejudiced interpretations of administrative and law enforcement officials.[8]

**Current Developments.** Despite the protections afforded to the exercise of individual rights, one must exercise caution when predicting the outcome of civil-liberty-related controversies. Through the 1960s and into the 1970s the opinions of the courts reflected a greater sense of security in the American people, in both the political and economic spheres, along with an increased sophistication concerning literature, religion, and morals in general. These developments led to a substantial broadening of judicial tolerance for all forms of dissent and difference that not even the tensions and excesses of the domestic reaction to the Vietnam war could seriously impede.

With the growing doubts and concerns of society in the late 1970s and early 1980s has come an increasing ambivalence and inconsistency on the part of the judiciary in ruling on constitutional matters. While the Supreme Court under Chief Justice Burger has greatly increased the scope of protection for privacy and for commercial speech, it has narrowed and limited the Warren Court's jurisprudential liberalism in such matters as obscenity, defamation by the press, and the rights of criminal defendants.

No one can confidently chart the future course of constitutional and civil rights laws. Leisure services administrators should be aware of the volatile nature of the First Amendment's protections within a framework of broad civil liberties principles.

### Parks as a Public Forum

**Hague v. C.I.O.** Probably the clearest enunciation of the principle that a park is an appropriate place for public political discussions and activities and for the exercise of constitutional rights generally is to be found in the opinion of Justice Roberts in the 1939 case of *Hague v. C.I.O.*[9] In *Hague* the Court struck down a Jersey City ordinance forbidding the leasing or use of any city facility for a public meeting without a permit from the chief of police.

The ordinance included many vague and overbroad provisions. One mandated the denial of a permit for a meeting "at which a speaker shall advocate obstruction of the Government of the United States or a state . . . ." The CIO, a major labor union (at the time, considerably more militant than the AFL with which it ultimately merged), was denied a permit to hold meetings and distribute leaflets and materials. Its members were improperly searched, arrested, and generally harassed when they attempted to organize meetings.

The Jersey City government under the dictatorial rule of the legendary "Boss" Frank Hague contended that the city's ownership of its streets and parks *"is as absolute as one's ownership of his home, with consequent power altogether to exclude citizens from the use thereof..."* (emphasis added). The Court responded:

> Wherever the title of streets and parks may rest, they have immemorially been held in trust for the use of the public and time out of mind have been used for the purpose of assembly, communicating thought between citizens and discussing public questions.
>
> Such use of the streets and public places has, from ancient times, been a part of the privileges, immunities, rights, and liberties of citizens. The privilege of a Citizen of the United States to use the streets and parks for communication of views on national question may be regulated in the interest of all; it is not an absolute, but relative, and must be exercised in subordination to the general comfort and convenience, and in consonance with peace and good order, but it must not in the guise of regulation be abridged or denied.

**Time, Place, and Manner Restrictions.**  This right of individuals and groups to utilize the parks for the communication of ideas and information does not leave officials powerless in their attempts to impose limits and restrictions. It does mean that any regulations must be confined to those necessary to protect significant governmental interests. The legal shorthand for such appropriate limitation is *"time, place, and manner"* regulation[10] applicable as part of the police power in the interests of health, safety, morals, and welfare.

When are restrictions appropriate? A few general examples demonstrate the kinds of legitimate concerns that parks and public safety authorities may consider in controlling and restricting First Amendment activities:

1.  A reasonable flow of traffic should be permitted.
2.  Park officials should structure the use of park property to afford a reasonable share of availability to competing or mutually exclusive uses (e.g., ball playing, concerts, political rallies, etc.).
3.  Residents in the vicinity of a park should be permitted to live in relative tranquility, particularly in the late evening or early morning or at other times when the need for peace and quiet is paramount.
4.  Overcrowded conditions with attendant risks of fire, heat exhaustion, and so on, must be avoided.

5. The health and safety of children should be given high priority.

6. When there is an imminent danger of violence, beyond sincere efforts of control, law enforcement officials should be able to take restrictive action.

*Time, place, and manner* regulations must be narrowly drawn to meet the *least restrictive means* test and to avoid overbreadth and vagueness. Furthermore, laws must clearly limit the discretion given to administrators to avoid favoritism or prejudice. In other words, restrictions must be *content neutral;* that is, their application must not depend on the character, political ideology, or theme of the speakers or demonstrators but must focus on the specific health, safety, and welfare matters that are legitimate objects of concern.

Even where official fears of potential for disturbance and increased costs for providing protection may be justified, undue restriction upon First Amendment activities will be struck down by the courts.

For example, in *Gregory v. City of Chicago*[11] police broke up a march by civil rights demonstrators to the late Mayor Daley's home in a hostile white neighborhood after the marchers refused to disperse. The convictions of the demonstrators for disorderly conduct offenses were reversed by the Supreme Court despite the police's contention that the arrests were necessary because of the threat of violence caused by the confrontation between the marchers and the onlookers. "Petitioner's march, if peaceful and orderly, falls well within the sphere of conduct protected by the First Amendment."

On the other hand, the Court has recognized that there is a point at which there is such a threat of a violent response to a constitutionally protected speaker that the speech may legitimately be silenced to maintain the public peace.[12]

If the cases are somewhat contradictory in result, it is at least clear that nothing short of a "clear and present danger" of violence will justify even temporary suppression of a speaker threatened by a hostile audience. This principle is applied even when the speaker's utterances are generally offensive to community standards—as when foul language is an integral part of a demonstrator's vocabulary.[13]

Consider the dramatic series of incidents in the heavily Jewish Chicago suburb of Skokie, Illinois, in which officials were unsuccessful in prohibiting a march by members of the Hitler-worshipping National Socialist Party of America. After some prodding by the United States Supreme Court, Illinois state courts rejected attempts to eliminate the display of Nazi paraphernalia, including the Swastika, even though "survivors of the Nazi persecutions, tormented by their recollections, may have strong feelings regarding its display."[14] Simultaneously, federal courts struck down a set of comprehensive parade and public assembly ordinances that, among other criteria, required that groups of fifty or more would need to secure $350,000 in liability insurance before they would be issued demonstration permits.[15]

**Fees and Permits.**  Generally, small fee requirements that are clearly neutral in intent and application have been upheld when they are directly related to the actual costs of administering and policing parks and public places. In fact, in the 1941 case of *Cox v. New Hampshire*[16] a parade permit scheme was upheld that provided for a fee schedule up to a maximum of $300. On the other hand, the Court has invalidated convictions of a number of Jehovah's Witnesses who failed to pay a licensing tax before they sold religious books and pamphlets because the sales were merely incidental "to the principal purpose of disseminating their religious beliefs."[17] Lower courts have reached contradictory results in cases requiring small permit fees for the use of sound-amplification equipment.[18]

Although the ultimate validity of the imposition of substantial fees and charges on First Amendment activities that engender law enforcement and administrative costs remains an open question, a fee that would have a prohibitory effect upon a person or group's right of expression will not be tolerated. In any event, given the requirements of *content neutrality* and *equal protection of the laws,* attempts to impose fees and charges upon disfavored groups such as the Nazi or Communist parties appear doomed to failure since it is rare that similar exactions are sought from more preferred organizations.

**Conflicting Uses.**  Park managers are not in the position of some other government officials who may argue that their facilities are dedicated to competing and incompatible uses. As examples, the Supreme Court has concluded that a jail courtyard,[19] a courthouse,[20] and a military reservation[21] may be restricted to their primary purposes so long as the prohibitions are uniformly applied. Unlike parks, such facilities perform their primary functions all of the time, so their managers may claim that demonstrations would interfere with normal functioning. This is not to say that a request to hold a political meeting must take precedence over a scheduled softball game, but it is the rare park that is used exclusively and constantly for recreational purposes.

In *Collin v. Chicago Park District,*[22] a circuit court rejected the authorities' attempt to deny a permit for a demonstration in Marquette Park to the leader of the Nazi party. Park officials had claimed that the park was normally used as a family picnic area on Sundays in warm weather. They had referred the plaintiff to "four free forum areas within the Park District." The court recognized that three of the four areas were in predominantly black neighborhoods and the fourth was several miles from Nazi headquarters. Furthermore, the area for which the permit was sought was not used exclusively for picnics and, in fact, had previously been the site for rallies and demonstrations. Past violence that had accompanied Nazi gatherings would be relevant only if "extremely closely related in time and character to the permit for which plaintiff applies." Finally, the court held that even a five-day delay in acting upon the permit application was not justifiable in the absence of procedures for prompt review.

In the event that there is a legitimate use conflict for the time at which a permit for a speech or demonstration is sought, a suitable alternative site or time must be made available.

As indicated in the *Collin* case, common sense will usually dictate whether restrictions and alternatives will be found constitutionally acceptable. The park commission should not meet a request for a permit to hold a demonstration in a park across from city hall at noon on a weekday with an offer to permit a demonstration in a neighborhood park at ten o'clock on Sunday morning.

A number of cases involving attempted limitations on demonstrations in the park areas surrounding the White House and the Capitol illustrate some of the subtleties and problems involved in fair and sensible accommodation for free-speech activities in relation to other interests.[23] Certainly, intense congestion in the area of a proposed demonstration is a legitimate consideration,[24] and as the *Collin* court put it, the preservation of a "tranquil" park area is an appropriate concern as long as it is not maintained at the expense of effective communication.[25]

Although the more subtle distinctions may be left to the lawyers, it is important for park professionals to impress upon their political or community supervisors and employers the importance of having a well-reasoned and neutrally applied permit policy. Too often, community pressure will mandate an ad-hoc unjustifiable response to demands for space and time by an unpopular group. In fact, there are times when denials of permits are simply the result of pettiness. In one county park system with which we are familiar, the desire of a Republican group to hold a political picnic was met by the Democratically controlled park commission with orders to its professionals to draft regulations banning all political activities, even picnics, from the parks!

Dealing with such machinations falls more in the realm of psychology and public relations than law. Nevertheless the grosser manifestations of political ignorance may be avoided if the professional staff anticipates and prepares a policy for carrying out its constitutional obligations in a manner least disruptive of other park functions.

**Nonpolitical Free Speech.**   If the event under consideration is within the realm of literature, the arts, or popular entertainment, First Amendment protections still apply, although in some instances the courts may allow greater discretion in regulating the manner and place of presentation. Thus the Supreme Court has upheld a Detroit ordinance that severely restricts the location of "adult" theaters presenting sex-laden motion pictures, even if their offerings are not obscene.[26] Furthermore, the Court has held that where children are subject to exposure to sexual materials, the determination of whether material is obscene *for children* may, to some degree, turn on their more sensitive and less mature responses.[27] In fact, in a case involving the broadcast of a comic monologue, "Filthy Words," by George Carlin, the Court upheld time restrictions by the Federal Communications Commission (FCC) partly on the basis that society has a "right to protect its children from speech generally agreed to be inappropriate for their years . . . ."[28]

Despite these cases, a broad limitation or prohibition on performances and activities based on the rationale that children must be protected may not withstand judicial scrutiny if the result is to substantially restrict what adults or even older children can see and hear. Thus when the City of Jacksonville, Florida, attempted to justify an ordinance prohibiting the showing of nudity in films exhibited in drive-in theaters with screens visible from the streets or parks, the Court noted that minors as well as adults were "entitled to a significant measure of First Amendment protection" and that nonobscene nude depictions "cannot be suppressed solely to protect the young from ideas or images that a legislative body thinks unsuitable for them."[29]

The case that best illustrates the point that parks and other government officials may not set themselves up as arbiters of moral or artistic values and must remain within narrow boundaries in censorship of sexual material is *Southeastern Productions, Ltd. v. Conrad.*[30] In that case the directors of Chattanooga's municipal theaters refused to lease a theater to the producers of the rock musical *Hair* for a week of performances despite the fact that there were no conflicting engagements scheduled.

The rejection was ostensibly "in the best interests of the community" because the directors understood from "outside reports" that the play involved sex and nudity. In condemning this *prior restraint* (censorship of speech or writing before performance or publication), the Court used unusually strong language. It was obliged to condemn systems in which the exercise of such authority was not bounded by precise and clear standards. The reasoning has been, simply, that the dangers of censorship and of abridgement of our precious First Amendment freedoms is too great where officials have unbridled discretion over a forum's use. Our distaste for censorship—reflecting the natural distaste of a free people—is deep written in our law.

As discussed earlier, restraints based upon actual experience with violence are much more likely to be upheld than when officials act on the basis of preconceived fears. Thus a federal court dismissed a suit by the promoters of a series of rock concerts against the Chicago Park District, which had canceled the remainder of the concerts after the first one had erupted in violence and riot. In light of the considerable property damage, the court rejected claims of violation of free speech and equal protection of the laws.[31] On the other hand, cancellation of a concert by activist folk singer Pete Seeger was held to be an unconstitutional prior restraint.[32] Most recently, the courts ordered officials to permit rugby football games involving a touring South African team despite threats of civil rights demonstrations.

Despite some inconsistencies, the sum of these cases makes it clear that a narrow interpretation of what is protected speech and a limited or grudging acquiescence in the use of parks as vehicles for expression will *not* meet constitutional requirements. Restrictions must be no broader than necessary to meet legitimate protective goals, and drastic remedies such as restraints or arrests and prosecution may be justified only where there is a clear and convincing demonstration of their necessity.

## The Religion Clauses and the Parks

**Introduction.** The Constitution's approach to religion is certainly not a hostile one. The *free exercise* clause of the First Amendment forbids interference with religious beliefs. And, as with free speech and expression, religious practices may be limited and controlled only when government demonstrates *compelling* health, safety, and welfare justifications. This protection for individual religious beliefs and activities reflects the experience of the Founding Fathers, some of whom, as we all learned in grade school, were descended from refugees from religious persecution in Europe.

At the same time, the other religion clause, which prohibits laws "respecting an *establishment* of religion," reflects the distrust that constitutional delegates had of the potential for the new federal government to impose a national religion on the states. Madison's "Memorial and Remonstrance" to the Virginia legislature in 1785 remains the key historical document in understanding the fears that ultimately resulted in the adoption of the principle of separation of church and state.

The ambivalence and tension generated by the sometimes competing requirements of the *free exercise* and *establishment* clauses have resulted in an extremely complex and often seemingly quite illogical series of judicial decisions. The courts have struggled to distinguish between those government activities that serve the health, safety, and welfare needs of persons engaged in religious practices and those activities that would involve the government in an active sponsorship or "establishment" of religion.

Obviously there are times when a certain degree of government cooperation is necessary to permit the "free exercise" of religion, but there is a very delicate balance that may easily be tipped in favor of one religion over another or religion over atheism or agnosticism. Another complicating factor is that, very often, religious activities, particularly proselytizing for converts or seeking donations, will involve other First Amendment rights, including freedom of speech and assembly.

The crazy quilt of decisions results in the following governmental prohibitions and strictures, among others. The state may pay to transport school children to parochial and other religious schools if payment is on a nondiscriminatory basis as a public safety measure,[33] but it may not provide buses for field trips for religious schools because that would be considered a direct subsidy for religious education.[34] Ministers may not come into the public schools during regular school hours to teach religion classes,[35] but students may be released early from public school to attend religious instruction at their church.[36] A law requiring all children to remain in school until the age of sixteen is found unconstitutional as applied to children of members of the Amish sect because their religion rejects formal education beyond the "three R's,"[37] while the conviction of the guardian of a nine-year-old is upheld because the child sold religious pamphlets in violation of state laws aimed at preventing public solicitation by minors. The grounds for affirming the conviction were that "the state has a wide range of power for limiting parental freedom and authority in things affecting the child's welfare; . . . [including] matters of conscience and religious conviction."[38]

This tightrope walking act by the courts obviously has its counterpart in the way park administrators must deal with religion. The Supreme Court has provided us with a basic test for determining the constitutionality of governmental actions with respect to the religion clauses:

First, the statute [or ordinance or administrative regulation] must have a secular [nonreligious] purpose; second, the principal or primary effect must be one that neither advances nor inhibits religion . . . ; finally, the statute must not foster an *excessive governmental entanglement with religion.*[39] [emphasis added]

Even this test must be read in the context of a judicial recognition that religion plays a large role in our national life, or as Justice Douglas once put it:

We are a religious people whose institutions presuppose a Supreme Being . . . . Government may not finance religious groups nor undertake religious instruction . . . . But we find no constitutional requirement which makes it necessary for government to be hostile to religion and to throw its weight against efforts to widen the effective scope of religious influence . . . . The problem, like many problems in constitutional law, is one of degree.[40]

**The Establishment Clause.**  The problem of degree to which Justice Douglas referred is a sensitive one to which the Supreme Court has given few precise answers. For example, the placing of religious symbols in the parks, such as crosses at Easter or creches (manger scenes) at Christmas, has been met with contradictory judicial opinions,[41] with some courts finding minimal religious depictions are like "In God We Trust" on the coinage; that is, they represent a ceremonial cultural heritage and not an organized religious effort by government.[42] On the other hand, when there was fairly substantial federal involvement in a Christmas pageant involving religious scenes in a Washington, D.C., park, including planning and financing, the government's participation was held unconstitutional because of the "entanglement" with religion.[43]

Whenever possible, courts will try to avoid ruling on matters involving religion because of the emotion and controversy religious disputes invariably cause. The opening of legislative sessions with a prayer or the holding of a sunrise Easter service in a park will usually escape judicial scrutiny on the grounds that they are *de minimis* (of such slight significance that judicial intervention is not warranted).

Sometimes courts will avoid ruling on religious questions by finding that the persons complaining lack standing to sue; that is, they have no real stake in the outcome of litigation. This is a complex subject beyond the scope of this work. To give a graphic example, however, consider a recent Colorado case.

A federal district court ruled that a nativity scene displayed at

Christmas at Denver City Hall was in violation of the establishment clause of the First Amendment because it encouraged divisiveness among the citizenry and evidenced substantial government involvement in religious matters. On appeal, the Tenth Circuit Court of Appeals avoided a ruling by finding that the group that had brought the suit had not demonstrated sufficient involvement as taxpayers or citizens of Denver to justify their maintenance of the suit. The case was remanded for further findings.[44] Thus the controversy was avoided for one Christmas, and officials had time to reassess their participation in the religious depictions before another Christmas.

On the other hand, the California Supreme Court held that the display of a cross in lights on the Los Angeles City Hall Tower during Christmas and Easter seasons violated the establishment clause of the California Constitution. Chief Justice Rose Bird found that the display also violated the First Amendment: "The city hall is not an immense bulletin board whereon symbols of all faiths could be thumbtacked."[45]

If any generalizations may be made about "establishment" of religion and the parks, they would probably be twofold.

First, nondiscriminatory, short-term, or temporary use of park property by religious organizations is normally constitutional, particularly if similar accommodations are afforded other religious as well as nonreligious groups; however, it is critical that there is no substantial government involvement in planning, funding, or supervising religious activities.

Second, neutrality in dealing with religious organizations does not require complete isolation from religious activities, but at the point at which there is an appearance of sponsorship of religion by government or when benevolent neutrality merges into permanent support, the establishment clause presents a formidable barrier.

For example, if a religious group wishes to hold an Easter sunrise service in a park, there is no constitutional barrier to providing facilities in the same manner and for the same consideration as there would be for a service club or other community organization. There would be a secular purpose—the provision of a facility for a community activity; the primary effect would, arguably, not involve substantial government enhancement of religion, and most importantly, there would not be an excessive administrative entanglement that might lead to community strife.

Of course, it could be argued that religion is indeed enhanced by even the one-time provision of facilities for services, but it is unlikely that a court, bearing in mind the strictures of Justice Douglas, would take so literal a view of the establishment clause.

Perhaps the most significant guidance in this troublesome area came from Chief Justice Burger in *Waltz v. Tax Commission*,[46] in which tax exemptions for religious property were held constitutional:

> The general principle deducible from the 1st Amendment and all that has been said by the Court is this: that we will not tolerate either governmentally established religion or governmental interference with religion. Short of those expressly proscribed governmental acts there is room for play in the joints productive of a *benevolent neutrality which will permit religious exercise to exist without sponsorship and without interference*. [emphasis added]

The benevolent neutrality described above may justify the provision of property for religious services in national parks or remote state parks just as the provision of chaplains in the military service is justified. Because of the inaccessibility of religious services in such areas, government may facilitate their provision.

Other than in the military, where the issues are still open,[47] governmental provision of facilities would appear to require the most neutral type of buildings. If a park building used for religious services were to have substantial permanent facilities clearly identified with any one religion, it would offend the establishment clause.

The question of what constitutes temporary or emergency use of government facilities in aid of "benevolent neutrality" is also open to question. The New Jersey Supreme Court recently upheld "temporary" use of public school facilities on a weekly basis by several religious groups. Facilities had been used for several years while young congregations raised money for permanent churches and synagogues. Furthermore, religious artifacts were stored in the public school during the regular school week. The New Jersey Court also held that commercial rates need not be charged the church groups but they would be required to reimburse the Board of Education for actual operating expenses.[48]

By analogy it would seem clear that if a religious or parochial school wished to use a park athletic facility for a ball game, the park authorities could certainly grant permission for such use without offending the Constitution, providing the fee charged was comparable to that charged other community groups. The establishment clause would be violated if the particular field was used on an *exclusive* and regular basis over a lengthy period so that, in effect, the public park system was providing the parochial school's athletic and physical education facilities.

There is always a strong temptation on the part of politicians to cater to the desires of the majority who may not always recognize the wisdom of the Bill of Rights. This is particularly true in the area of religion, since in many communities religious and civic activities are intertwined. The extent to which a park administrator will be able to resist pressures for improper religious use of public facilities will depend upon a combination of his or her own professionalism, support from responsible officials and community leaders, including the clergy, and public education to recognize the distinctions between government responsibility and community sentiment.

**Free Exercise of Religion.** If the establishment clause requires resistance to public pressures to permit increased religious use of the parks, the free exercise clause, ironically, often requires the parks to provide a platform for the expression of unpopular religious views and practices. This is particularly true when minority sects utilize the parks to proselytize. Not only are they exercising their religious rights, but they are also protected by First Amendment prohibitions against government interference with free speech and the right of assembly.

This is not to say that park officials must sit idly by and tolerate any and all activities that are arguably religious. Historically, "free exercise" protects the right to believe in any doctrine regardless of how bizarre it might appear to the majority of Americans. Furthermore, government may not challenge the truthfulness of anyone's religious beliefs.[49] The courts may not entertain theological disputes or conduct heresy trials. Conversely, if a religiously inspired activity creates a substantial danger to society, then government may intervene under its police power. Thus polygamy,[50] snake handling,[51] and the sale of religious tracts by young children[52] have all been held within the purview of state criminal laws.

Similarly, courts have been able to examine the sincerity of those professing religious justification for their activities. Thus the Florida Supreme Court recently gave short shrift to the argument by a group known as the "Ethiopian Zion Coptic Church" that their use and distribution of marijuana was protected by the free exercise clause. "Easy access to Cannabis for a child who had absolutely no interest in learning the religion, coupled with the indiscriminate use of the drug by members . . . clearly warrants intervention by the state."[53]

In recent years it has become more difficult for government to justify interference with religious activities other than those that plainly threaten the public welfare. Officials must have a "substantial" or "compelling" reason for interfering with practices central to the beliefs of a particular sect. The "least intrusive or restrictive means" must be utilized to satisfy the government's legitimate interests.

Under this stricter standard, a Seventh Day Adventist could not be denied unemployment compensation because she had refused to work on Saturdays and therefore lost her job in a textile mill. As noted earlier, school authorities could not force the children of members of the Amish community to remain in school until the age of sixteen.[54]

Given this heightened sensitivity to the rights of free exercise, and the concomitant free speech and assembly elements in such religious activities, it should come as no surprise that efforts to substantially limit the proselytizing activities of religious sects in the parks and other public places have usually been rejected by the courts.

In recent years controversy over public proselytizing and solicitation has centered on members of the International Society for Krishna Consciousness, whose practice of "Sankirtan" requires constant proselytizing activities. Most of the cases involving this group have focused on their activities in airports, but they have also been active at state fairs. Typical of futile attempts to limit Krishna activities is *Bowen v. Int'l Society for Krishna Consciousness*,[55] a circuit court case in which Indiana fair officials confined religious societies to booths and did not permit them to wander around the fairgrounds. The court held that the state could not justify such severe restrictions despite its professed interest in preventing fraud, protecting the business of concessionaires, and preventing the disturbance of fair-goers.

In a recent case involving similar activities at the Maryland State Fair, another circuit court noted:

> The state has little right to regulate the exercise of 1st Amendment rights in a public place, since persons present are fully capable of refusing any solicitations and continuing on their way.[56]

Some restriction on the actions of religious groups is possible. There may be substantial evidence that religious solicitors are interfering with other activities or that they are provoking disturbances of the peace by seeking donations of large-denomination bills and then resisting or refusing to give change (an accusation frequently made against Krishna solicitors). Some time, place, and manner restrictions may be upheld if they clearly are limited to a response to these or other specific complaints or problems.

In a significant recent opinion, *Heffron v. International Society for Krishna Consciousness*,[57] the Supreme Court upheld a Minnesota State Fair rule that prohibited the sale or distribution of merchandise except from a licensed booth. This prevented the Krishna devotees from dispensing their religious tracts through the fairgrounds, but it did permit them to speak and proselytize in a face-to-face manner. The Court stressed the nondiscriminatory manner in which the rule was applied; however, the opinion did substantially limit the claims of religious groups to greater First Amendment rights than other organizations. The Court stressed that religious organizations do not

> enjoy rights to communicate, distribute, and solicit on the fairgrounds superior to those of other organizations having social, political, or other ideological messages to proselytize. These nonreligious organizations seeking support for their activities are entitled to rights equal to those of religious groups to enter a public forum and spread their views, whether by soliciting funds or by distributing literature.

Certainly, parks and leisure services managers may forbid solicitations on a football field during a game or in a concert audience while the orchestra is playing. Rather, the problem with most restrictions has been that they are overbroad and not enforced equitably against all groups.

For example, a District of Columbia court dismissed the prosecution of a Krishna sect member who was charged with unlawful solicitation and distribution of religious literature inside the Kennedy Center in Washington.[58] The court noted that, despite protestations concerning the need for tranquility in the center, the government "permitted commercial sale of souvenir programs and other commemorative items" as well as the hawking of beverages and refreshments before performances and during intermissions. Although stricter time, place, and manner regulations would be appropriate because of the right of patrons to be free from interruptions and intrusions while enjoying performances, nevertheless these particular restrictions were overly broad.

The lesson to be drawn from these cases is not only that restrictions on religious solicitation must be narrowly drawn, keeping in mind the function of the parks as appropriate places for the expression of both religious and secular opinion, but also that equal protection of the laws requires neutral enforcement. A park board cannot eliminate Krishna solications without also banning Girl Scout cookie sales.

### Private Recreational Facilities and the First Amendment

The strictures of the First Amendment and the due process clause of the Fourteenth Amendment apply only to "state action." In other words, private enterprises are not bound to afford the same access and protection for fundamental liberties as the government must.

There has been considerable historical debate concerning the degree of government involvement necessary to impress constitutional obligations upon private enterprises. Much of this centers upon civil rights and the access of minority groups to services and property rights. With regard to the First Amendment, it appeared for a time that large-scale privately owned shopping centers and, by inference, major private recreational projects would be considered by the courts to be the functional equivalents of public gathering places and therefore subject to the same constitutional obligations.

This trend began with the case of *Marsh v. Alabama*,[59] which involved a "company town" owned by a shipbuilding corporation. Since the "town" performed all essential municipal services and was to all appearances functioning as a municipality, the Supreme Court ruled that First Amendment rights applied there. Otherwise, the opportunity for the exercise of such rights would be lost in a practical sense to the workers and residents.

In a 1968 case,[60] a majority of the Court equated a private shopping center with a traditional commercial main street. The justices found that because the shopping center was generally open to the public, which was encouraged to think of it as a community center, the state's trespass laws could not be utilized to prevent members of the public from exercising rights of free expression.

In a sharp reversal of position, the Supreme Court first limited this opinion[61] and then expressly overruled it in *Hudgens v. N.L.R.B.*[62] Obviously, the current Supreme Court majority is not ready to impress the constitutional obligation of the First Amendment upon private enterprises even if they are the "functional equivalent" of a business district in a company town.

Despite the Supreme Court's actions in limiting First Amendment rights to public places, the California Supreme Court recently held that the California State Constitution guaranteed access to private shopping centers for the exercise of free speech and assembly. Thus the owners of the Prune Yard Center, a sophisticated multipurpose mall near San Jose, could not evict a group of high school students soliciting signatures on a petition deploring United Nations resolutions against Zionism.

The case was appealed to the United States Supreme Court, which held that the states were free to expand and extend civil liberties to private property as long as there was no direct "taking" of the property and no serious interference with the economic well-being of the enterprise.[63]

The *Prune Yard* case may be very significant for major private or commercial recreation enterprises that may function as the equivalent of a community center or focal point. Indeed, the line between an entertainment-shopping-dining center like the Prune Yard and a recreation center is hardly a clear one. Liberal state courts now appear to have been given a green light to expand the coverage of state constitutional rights without substantial threat of federal judicial intervention.

## CIVIL RIGHTS

### De Jure Segregation

Most Americans are probably somewhat familiar with the landmark case of *Brown v. Board of Education.*[64] In this case the Supreme Court addressed the issue of whether intentionally (*de jure*) racially segregated public schools and, by implication, other segregated public facilities were inherently unequal and therefore in violation of the equal protection clause of the Fourteenth Amendment.[65]

The principle that *de jure* segregation or discrimination on the basis of race, creed, or color is unconstitutional has become deeply embedded in our law and widely accepted in our society over the last quarter-century. Therefore, there would be little point in closely examining the painful and tedious judicial process by which official segregation was first sanctioned and later dismantled by the courts. We shall limit our consideration to the application of civil rights laws to the parks and leisure services field, with historical references only to those elements of the law relevant to current problems and controversies.

The examination in this chapter is restricted to provision of services and accommodations. Employment discrimination is considered in Chapter 6.

**Racial Segregation and the Fourteenth Amendment.** It became obvious at a very early date that official segregation would not be tolerated in the parks any more than it would be in the schools. When the city of Memphis sought to delay desegregation of its parks and recreation facilities by claiming that gradual and slow action was necessary to overcome public resistance, the Supreme Court responded sharply:

> The claims of the city to further delay in affording the petitioners that to which they are clearly and unquestionably entitled cannot be upheld except upon the most convincing and impressive demonstration by the city that such delay is manifestly compelled by constitutionally cognizable circumstances . . . . In short, the city must sustain an extremely heavy burden of proof.[66]

A Macon, Georgia, park was theoretically in the hands of "private" trustees who had taken over from the city in order to try to meet the desires of the benefactor, who had left the park for the use of whites only. The Supreme Court ruled that black people could not be excluded. Justice Douglas wrote:

> This conclusion is buttressed by the nature of the service rendered the community by a park. The service rendered even by a private park of this character is municipal in nature. It is open to every white person, there being no selective element other than race. Golf clubs, social centers, luncheon clubs ... and other like organizations in the private sector are often racially oriented. A park, on the other hand, is more like a fire department or police department that traditionally serves the community. Mass recreation through the use of parks is plainly in the public domain .... Like the streets of the company town in *Marsh v. Alabama* .... the predominant character and purpose of this park are municipal.[67]

The parkland was originally a bequest from Senator Augustus Bacon, who specified that it would be available "for members of the white race only." Despite Justice Douglas's stirring words, when the Georgia Supreme Court reexamined the case on remand, it ruled that since Senator Bacon's will had specified the segregated nature of the park, the inability of Macon to operate it in that manner meant that the bequest was void under Georgia law. Therefore the property reverted to the heirs of the senator to dispose of as they pleased. On appeal, the United States Supreme Court held that since the reversion did not involve any discriminatory action by Georgia authorities, in that the park would cease to exist for whites as well as blacks, it would not interfere with termination of the trust.[68] A Pyrrhic victory for desegregation!

Another questionable opinion of the Supreme Court dealing with the desegregation of recreation facilities is *Palmer v. Thompson.*[69] This 1971 decision has been subject to much criticism and is of doubtful validity today. In *Palmer,* the Court upheld the closing of several municipal pools in Jackson, Mississippi, effectively eliminating the opportunity for most black residents to swim under sanitary and economically feasible conditions. Noting that other municipal facilities had been integrated, the Court refused to look behind the professed justification of the city council that the integrated pools could not be operated on a safe and economically sufficient basis. A dissenting opinion strongly attacked the refusal of the majority to examine the motives of the city council in closing the pools.

More recently, in *Washington v. Davis*,[70] a case concerning the validity of qualifying tests for police officers, the Court appeared to limit the importance of *Palmer* and stated that "invidious discriminatory purpose may often be inferred from the totality of the relevant facts." We should also note that the Supreme Court did invalidate the closure of a school system when the closure was accompanied by grants to white children attending private academies.[71]

Despite the occasional wavering illustrated above, there is no question that any serious attempts to maintain segregated public recreation facilities or to thwart the integration of such facilities by subterfuge will encounter stiff judicial resistance.

Even the use of public parks by racially restricted groups is subject to constitutional challenge. In *Gilmore v. City of Montgomery*[72] the Supreme Court held that exclusive use of public recreational facilities by a private white school was unconstitutional because it "significantly enhanced the attractiveness of segregated private schools . . . by enabling them to offer complete athletic programs." The Court further indicated that even nonexclusive use of recreation facilities could be barred if such use had a significant impact on public school desegregation

**"Private" Racial Discrimination.**    While it may be almost universally acknowledged that racial segregation in public facilities is unconstitutional, it still comes as a surprise to some that most private discrimination is also barred by a combination of constitutional and statutory law dating back to 1865.

Unlike the Fourteenth Amendment, which has historically been limited in application to "state action," the Thirteenth Amendment, which eliminated slavery and involuntary servitude, has been interpreted as affording Congress broad powers to eliminate "badges and incidents of slavery," whether privately or publicly maintained.[73]

Among the statutes enacted to eliminate the lingering evils of slavery were the Civil Rights Acts of 1866, 1870, and 1871. Portions of these acts are encompassed within modern civil and criminal law. Most significantly, 42 U.S.C.A. § 1981 declares that all persons shall have the same right to make and enforce contracts "as is enjoyed by white citizens," and 42 U.S.C.A. § 1982 provides that "all citizens of the United States shall have the same right . . . as is enjoyed by white citizens . . . to inherit, purchase, lease, sell, hold and convey real and personal property." Section 1985 of the same statute permits damage suits against private individuals who conspire to deny civil rights, and there are also criminal provisions under 18 U.S.C.A. § 241.

It should again be noted that these statutory provisions are in addition to those directed against interference with civil rights on the part of government employees, agencies, municipalities and others "acting under color of . . . law . . . ."[74]

In 1968 in the landmark case of *Jones v. Alfred H. Mayer Co.*, the Supreme Court ruled that Section 1982 prohibited "all discrimination against Negroes in the sale or rental of property—discrimination by private owners as well as discrimination by public authorities." The following year in *Sullivan v. Little Hunting Park, Inc.*,[76] the Court was confronted with the refusal of a private community park and playground to admit a black family to membership despite the fact that they were renting a home in the area that the park served. The Court rejected the argument that Little Hunting Park was a private social club because "there was no plan or purpose of exclusiveness. It is open to every white person with the geographic area . . . ."

It was further held that the plaintiffs had a remedy under 42 U.S.C.A. § 1982 for injunctive relief as well as for damages under federal and state law because of the denial of their real and personal property rights.

A major addition to the post-Civil War statutes is found in the various provisions of the Civil Rights Act of 1964. This law was enacted by Congress under the prodding of President Johnson in the wake of the assassination of John F. Kennedy. It was followed by the Civil Rights Act of 1968, which applies to housing.

These acts set up comprehensive statutory and administrative schemes intended to eliminate discrimination in most phases of American life. Their principle provisions are as follows.

Forty-two U.S.C.A. § 2000 (Title II) prohibits discrimination on the grounds of race, color, religion, or national origin in most places of public accommodation, including hotels, restaurants, theaters, sports arenas, and most certainly parks and playing facilities open to the public. The principle exception to the statute is found in Section 2000a(e), which states that it "shall not apply to a *private club* or other establishment not in fact open to the public" except to the extent that the facilities are made available to nonmember customers of the hotels, inns, and so on, in which the club is located. Section 2000d (Title VI) prohibits discrimination in any federally assisted program. Section 2000e (Title VII) prohibits discrimination on the basis of race, color, religion, national origin, or sex in employment, the principal exemption again being a "bona fide membership club" and the federal government, which is covered by executive order of the President. This section is discussed in some detail in Chapter 6. The 1968 statute (42 U.S.C.A. § 3601 (Title VIII) makes it unlawful to discriminate on the basis of race, color, religion, sex, or national origin in the sale or rental of most dwellings.

The complexities of administrative enforcement of these statutes and their interrelationship with state civil rights laws are largely beyond the scope of our examination. What is most significant here is the fact that in the *Alfred H. Mayer* case the Supreme Court rejected the contention that the enactment of the fair housing sections (Title VIII) of the 1968 act had any effect on the continued viability of Section 1982.

In *Sullivan v. Little Hunting Park,* the Court avoided the question of whether the private club exemption in the 1964 act (Title II) applied because it found that the recreational facilities were clearly not private. The issue was presented again in *Tillman v. Wheaton-Haven Recreation Association.*[77]

Wheaton-Haven was a nonprofit association that organized and raised funds to build a swimming pool. Membership was limited to 325 families, and those residing in the geographic area of the pool received preference. Unlike Little Hunting Park, Wheaton-Haven required that formal approval by vote of the board of directors of the club be obtained by prospective members. Nevertheless, considering the totality of the circumstances the Court found that "Wheaton-Haven is not a private club" and refused to consider whether any implied limitation on Section 1982 existed because of the "private club" exemptions to the 1964 and 1968 acts. The Court has not directly considered the question since.

There has been considerable litigation on the private club exemption in Title II suits. Although some courts have found defendants to fall within the private club category,[78] most Title II litigation has resulted in findings that most recreational facilities calling themselves private clubs are actually public accommodations because there is no selectivity in membership or membership control over operations and because there is a profit motive and advertising.[79] Certainly the number of truly selective member owned and controlled nonprofit recreational facilities will continue to decline in the face of inflation, personal mobility, and changing lifestyles.

The Supreme Court has gone so far as to declare that Section 1981 prohibitions against the refusal to contract with nonwhites outlaws discrimination in admissions by private schools and, by implication, in private sports academies, camps, and recreational enterprises even when they are generally selective in admission. Parental claims of "constitutionally protected rights of free association and privacy, or a parent's right to direct the education of his children" have been rejected thus far.[80]

**The Demise of De Jure Segregation.**    Enforcement of civil rights laws relating to leisure services involves a complex combination of state civil rights agencies and federal agencies such as the Department of Housing and Urban Development, suits by the Attorney General of the United States, and private damages and injunctive actions. In many areas of the country, free legal services are available to the victims of discrimination. Courts have been particularly sensitive in dealing with meritorious civil rights complaints and have demonstrated imagination and flexibility in fashioning appropriate remedies to ensure meaningful long-term integration.[81]

The result of all of the administrative and judicial enforcement of antidiscrimination legislation is that, at least with regard to activities, facilities, and accommodations, there is virtually no room in the recreation and parks field for exclusion based on race, creed, or color. Even the limited exceptions for private clubs and religious organizations are narrowly construed. Continued vigilance and aggressive enforcement may remain necessary, but in this area of concern, the civil rights revolution has been won.

## De Facto Discrimination

The elimination of official discrimination hardly means that blacks and other racial or ethnic minorities have the same recreational opportunities as many whites. Differences in employment and economic status, housing patterns, *de facto* segregation resulting from historically established racial distinctions, and a variety of social, political, and psychological factors as complex as the nation itself have conspired to limit and exclude minorities from participation in many programs. On the whole, the courts have been extremely reluctant to consider people who are linked by economic or social status as comprising judicially recognizable classes. In the most significant case on this issue, *San Antonio Ind. School Dist. v. Rodriguez*,[82] the Supreme Court overruled a district court finding that the Texas system of funding local school districts violated equal protection because it allocated funds on the basis of local property taxes, resulting in a wide disparity in per-pupil expenditures in rich and poor districts. The Court found that it could not sufficiently identify a category of "poor" people as a distinct class and "at least where wealth is involved, the Equal Protection Clause does not require absolute equality or precisely equal advantages."

Some state courts have accepted arguments that funding differentials violate basic precepts of constitutional law.[83] Nevertheless, it is clear that inequities that result from economic differences are unlikely to be remedied through judicial action without a clear governmental discriminatory motive, even if there is a significant racial or ethnic component. Thus, for the foreseeable future the substantial differences between recreational resources available in the largely white suburbs and the inferior facilities offered in the largely black inner cities will remain beyond the reach of legal remedy.

### Sex Discrimination*

Although overt racial discrimination in the provision of leisure services is largely a thing of the past, sex discrimination and differential treatment is still very much with us. There are many reasons for this.

It has only been recently that substantial numbers of women (and men) have articulated the themes enunciated by pioneer feminists like the Pankhursts, Elizabeth Cady Stanton, and Susan B. Anthony that the subordinate roles afforded women in our society are oppressive and not ordained by nature. Judges as well as legislators generally reflect society's biases. Thus, to this day most courts reject arguments that historic civil rights laws enacted in response to discrimination and oppression directed against black people should also apply to women. Furthermore, a good deal of sexually differential treatment has been paternalistically justified as protective of the special status of females in our social structure.

Certainly, fear that statutory and constitutional changes to ensure equality would have a damaging effect on traditional values has not only led to resistance to an Equal Rights Amendment but also to a marked reluctance on the part of the courts to alter the status of women in society.

**Judicial Attitudes.**  The Supreme Court's position has been somewhat ambivalent. Where legislation clearly discriminates against women economically or reflects old societal stereotypes, the Court has often placed a very heavy burden of justification on government. Among the discriminatory laws that have been struck down are the following:

1. A legislative preference for males to be the administrators of the estates of deceased family members.[84]
2. A federal statute that permitted male armed services members to automatically receive dependency benefits for their wives, while female soldiers had to prove dependency on the part of their husbands.[85]

---

*Sex-related employment discrimination is considered specifically in Chapter 6.

3. A similar statute that denied social security benefits on the earnings of a deceased wife to a surviving husband.[86]

4. An Oklahoma statute prohibiting the sale of "3.2" beer to males under the age of twenty-one while permitting its sale to females down to age eighteen.[87]

On the other hand, where the Court has seen the legislative distinctions as being favorable to women's economic interests, there has been a tendency to uphold them. Thus in *Califano v. Webster*[88] the Court permitted women to have the benefit of more favorable Social Security calculations than men, and in *Kahn v. Shevin*[89] a Florida law that granted property tax exemptions to widows but not to widowers was upheld. In the *Kahn* case, the Court found a "fair and substantial relation to an object of the legislation" in that it recognized the general substantial disparity in economic status between men and women.

Obviously, the Court has not been completely consistent in its sex discrimination decisions. Nor has a majority been able to settle upon an appropriate constitutional test for legislative and administrative actions that make gender-related distinctions.

At one point the Court came close to putting sex in the same category as race.[90] If sexual classifications were "suspect" and subject to "strict scrutiny," any institution with substantial government funding would have to meet an extremely high degree of justification for gender distinctions. The Court stopped short of this for a variety of reasons. Some members of the Court favored retention of the traditional "rational basis" test, but even they seemed inclined to subject gender distinctions in law to a more searching inquiry than would normally be the case under such a test.

At this time a majority of the Court appears to have agreed upon a mid-level test, the "fair and substantial relation" test used in the *Kahn* case, or as stated in more detail:

the classification must be reasonable, not arbitrary, and must rest upon some ground of difference having a fair and substantial relation to the object of the legislation, so that all persons similarly circumstanced should be treated alike.[91]

Nonlawyers may wonder how minor differences such as the distinction between the "strict scrutiny-compelling reason" wording in race cases and the "fair and substantial" language used above can result in major differences in the case result. The answer is that the language becomes a shorthand code for a whole series of judicial actions at every level of litigation. The words themselves are not so important for their dictionary meaning but rather for the kinds of results their use has engendered in cases over the years. In short, "strict scrutiny" almost always results in the governmental agency losing, "fair and substantial" means that the result may go either way, and "rational basis" will usually justify the government's actions.

Perhaps the most striking example of the effect of judicial refusal to consider sex a suspect classification is found in *Vorcheimer v. School Board of Philadelphia,*[92] in which an equally divided court affirmed a circuit court's rejection of a female high school student's petition to be admitted to Philadelphia Central High, an academically superior boys' school. The grounds for the rejection were that a superior school for girls, Girls High, was available.

Despite Vorcheimer's claims that Central offered superior science and other facilities, the circuit court found that since the Supreme Court had not characterized sex as "suspect" there were "differences between the sexes which may, in limited circumstances, justify disparity in law." This kind of thinking obviously has serious implications for parks and leisure services programs that provide separate and questionably equivalent services and facilities to men and women.

**Statutory and Constitutional Remedies.**    There is very limited application of federal law to gender-related cases involving denial of access to recreational facilities and sports that are privately funded and operated. Sections 1981, 1982, and 1985 of the Civil Rights Act have generally been interpreted as not applying to sex discrimination, although a few judges have been persuaded that women are a historically discriminated against group in our society and should be protected. The statutes measure the contract and property rights to which all persons are entitled by those enjoyed by "white citizens." Since all women, including "whites," were a disenfranchised and legally inferior class at the time of the Civil War and the passage of the Thirteenth and Fourteenth Amendments, a strong argument may be made that race or ethnic background should not be the only criteria for coverage under the statute. Nevertheless, most courts have relied on both the references to race and the overriding concern of the Congress at the time for the newly freed slaves to limit coverage of these important acts.

Private sex discrimination in housing is barred under Title VIII of the Civil Rights Act of 1968.[93] This statute permits discrimination victims to seek redress through "immediate suit in federal district court, or a simple inexpensive, informal conciliation procedure [through HUD or state agencies] to be followed by litigation should conciliation efforts fail."[94] Sex discrimination in facilities that are related to or dependent upon one's dwelling place, such as a health spa that is part of an apartment complex or a swim club featured as an inducement to purchase in a real estate development, would be subject to the same legal prohibitions as would racial restrictions. Many states have similar laws. Sexual discrimination in privately owned "public accommodations" and facilities not related to housing must be attacked under state law, since efforts to apply Title II of the 1964 Civil Rights Act to sex discrimination have failed.[95]

A number of state laws not only prohibit discrimination in places of public accommodation on the basis of sex but also have a very liberal interpretation of the scope of facilities covered and strict limitations on any private club exemptions.[96] There are, of course, disagreements about what constitutes sex discrimination under state laws as well as federal, but at least one court has gone so far as to hold that a "ladies' night" promotion at a ball game violated the law.[97]

Although peripheral to our considerations here, it is obvious that access to many recreational opportunities is dependent upon money and the availability of credit and financing. Many women have been victims of discrimination in these areas. The federal Equal Credit Opportunity Act[98] and related state statutes attempt to rectify some of these problems.

A substantial amount of litigation revolves around state action and government involvement in sex discrimination. One of the most significant sex discrimination cases involving recreation is *Fortin v. Darlington Little League*,[99] in which ten-year-old Allison "Pookie" Fortin contested her rejection by a Little League in Pawtucket, Rhode Island. "Pookie" and her family brought the action under Section 1983 (applying to "state action"), and the equal protection clause of the Fourteenth Amendment. While the case was pending, Congress amended the federal charter of Little League Baseball, Inc., to allow girls to participate on an equal basis with boys. Nevertheless, the Darlington Little League "refused to give assurance of a change of heart." The court then decided that the necessary significant government involvement was demonstrated by the following facts:

1. Little League diamonds were laid out and maintained by the city to the specifications and for the primary benefit of the league.
2. The general public was "often precluded from utilizing the facilities."
3. Because of the interest and involvement of the city and the sym-

pathetic relationship it had with the league, a government function was effectively being carried on by a quasi-private organization (much like the company town rationale of *Marsh v. Alabama).*

The *Fortin* court also examined the justification for maintaining a sexually separate baseball program:

> A sex based classification denies equal protection in the constitutional sense unless shown to rest on a convincing factual rationale going beyond "archaic and overbroad generalizations" about the different roles of men and women.

After a detailed inquiry into the alleged strength and ability distinctions between preteen boys and girls, the court concluded that not only was there "meager" evidence that girls were weaker and more injury prone, but also that, "should girls find Little League Baseball too demanding, the problem would seem self-regulating in that the girls would withdraw." Furthermore, although all girls were rejected regardless of individual strength and prowess, even those boys who were physically weak, awkward, or disabled found places on the teams, a distinct denial of equal protection.

The result of *Fortin* has been echoed in several other cases.[100] Of course, utilizing the same criteria as the First Circuit Court did in *Fortin,* a court could find that in those sports that put heavy emphasis on physical strength or violent body contact, such as high school football, a substantial basis for sexual distinctions exists. Most cases involving such sports as hockey, boxing, wrestling, and even basketball have upheld exclusive boys' programs as long as comparable sports programs exist for females. Nevertheless, a Pennsylvania court has held that the state's Equal Rights Amendment was violated by rules barring girls from competing or practicing with boys even in wrestling and football,[101] and a Washington state court ruled that a "qualified" female could not be denied the opportunity to play high school football.[102]

Challenges have been most successful where no comparable teams exist for girls and when the sports are of the noncontact variety, such as tennis, golf, cross-country skiing, or running.[103] Ironically, one of the best discussions of the problems of sexual integration of athletic teams is found in *Gomes v. Rhode Island Interscholastic League,*[104] in which a male high school student sought to participate in interscholastic volleyball, a sport heretofore limited, in Rhode Island, to girls. The court was troubled by testimony that males would have an unfair height and strength advantage and found that "separate but equal volleyball teams do appear the most advantageous athletic approach." Nevertheless, it held that when "opportunities for males have been severely limited" an exclusively female team could not be justified; furthermore, the judge doubted that there would be a "sudden male influx or domination of Rhode Island Interscholastic Volleyball."

As a practical matter, once past the early teenage years, physical differences between males and females would substantially limit the numbers of women who would be successful in direct team and individual competition with males in those sports in which height, weight, and upper body strength are important. It is therefore more important that the law afford females substantial recreational and athletic opportunities in their own right than that occasionally the courts order a competitive girl to be admitted to a boys' basketball, tennis, or track team.

Since the equal protection clause of the Fourteenth Amendment has, thus far, not been a consistently effective vehicle to remedy gender discrimination, the principal tool for assuring equality of opportunity for women in sports and athletics has been Title IX of the Educational Amendment of 1972.[105] Title IX requires that there shall be no sexual discrimination, denial of benefits, or exclusion from participation in any *"educational program or activity receiving Federal financial assistance."* Obviously, this statute does not apply to the entire leisure services field. The requirements that an *educational* program or activity that receives federal financial assistance be the source of discriminatory conduct have thus far limited Title IX recreation cases to school and university sports and recreation programs, although at least one court has applied Title IX to a prison education program.[106] Furthermore, there are certain exceptions to the statute that preserve traditional sex distinction policies of historic all-female and all-male colleges, military academies, and certain religious institutions.

A major limitation that is the subject of continuing judicial controversy is the extent and relationship of the necessary federal aid to the particular program required to trigger application of Title IX. As interpreted and applied by the Department of Education (formerly HEW), a school or program "benefits" from indirect federal assistance such as a general student loan program. Certainly public schools that receive federal impact aid because of the presence of federal installations in the area are subject to coverage under Title IX. On the other hand, federal district courts in Michigan and Texas recently ruled that unless there is direct federal involvement in the particular athletic program under consideration, Title IX would not apply,[107] and in *Dodson v. Arkansas Activities Assn.,*[108] a federal court held that, although the use of half-court basketball rules for girls violated equal protection, Title IX coverage was not available because of the absence of federal assistance. A federal district court in Pennsylvania disagreed with these decisions and held that Title IX was applicable to athletic programs as long as a university received some substantial federal funding, even if the support was in other academic areas.[109] Clearly, challenges to the breadth of Title IX will continue until the Supreme Court decides the issue or Congress clarifies the statute.

The Supreme Court *has* resolved one important question concerning available legal remedies under Title IX. In *Cannon v. University of Chicago*,[110] the court upheld the right of individuals to base private causes of action on violations of the statute. Heretofore, the principal means of forcing compliance was a cut-off of federal funds, including federally secured student loans.[111]

A full review of the administrative interpretations of Title IX by the Department of Education would require volumes. Furthermore, political changes in government are likely to result in modifications of the regulations relaxing strict requirements. At present, the basic thrust of the Title IX rules is to bring about proportionate equality, on the basis of participation, in funding male and female athletics on an intercollegiate, club, or intramural level.

The theme of equality of athletic opportunity is sounded over and over again in the regulations. Provisions for coaching, scheduling, travel and expenses, lockers, training, housing, dining facilities, and publicity to "effectively accommodate the interests and abilities of members of both sexes" are factors to be considered in determining whether equal opportunity exists. Recruitment and support services such as academic tutoring will also be subject to judicial scrutiny. Identical benefits and treatment are not required as long as the overall results of athletic and other educational recreation programs are essentially equal. Even in the absence of equality, schools may be in compliance if they can demonstrate that unique aspects of certain sports require increased funding. Thus a school may justify spending more money on football because of the expense involved in crowd management and the cost of equipment and training.

There is no general requirement to integrate teams, but if a team is established for one sex only, a school may be required to permit members of the opposite sex to compete for a position. A full-fledged team would only have to be sponsored for noncontact sports

if (I) opportunities for members of the excluded sex have been historically limited and (II) there is sufficient interest and ability to sustain a viable team and a reasonable expectation of intercollegiate competition; and (III) members of the excluded sex do not possess sufficient skill to be selected for an integrated team or to compete actively if selected.[112]

The same requirements apply for contact sports, with the exception of (III).[113]

Although the most recent guidelines may suffer from ambiguity and confusion, the thrust toward a pragmatic equality in educationally related sports and recreation is clear. Whether government officials will enforce the law vigorously and expansively is open to conjecture.

**The Half-Court Basketball Example.**  Perhaps the most graphic example of the courts struggling with these complex questions is found in the consideration of the female game of half-court basketball. Unlike the male game, and the female game played at colleges and many high schools today, traditional girls' half-court basketball has six girls to a side, three of whom play the offensive half of the court and three the defensive. Since colleges and universities play a full-court game, even the most talented female half-court players find themselves at a distinct disadvantage in competing for athletic scholarships and places on college teams. At least two courts dismissed challenges to the continued use of differential rules as either of minimal concern or simply not reaching constitutional proportions.[114]

As noted above, in the *Dodson* case an Arkansas federal court took a different view. The court examined the justifications for continuing the half-court game. For example, it permits more girls to play, it allows girls to develop agility and skill in moving, and it achieves higher-scoring games with more shooting. The court found that these objectives could not be justified under equal protection criteria in that they were supported only by tradition and not on scientific or factual basis. Furthermore, if the objectives were justifiable and rationally related to the rules, then they should be equally applicable to boys as well as girls.[115]

Therefore, half-court girls' basketball will undoubtedly soon disappear as the result of social changes if not judicial pressures. The general prospect for sexual equality in all aspects of recreation, sports, and leisure services will continue to depend upon the aggressive application of Title IX by federal administrators and of equal protection under the Fourteenth Amendment by federal and state trial courts. This, in turn, depends upon the evolving attitude of the Supreme Court toward gender discrimination.

## Leisure Services Rights of the Disabled

**Constitutional Rights.**  As we have seen, there is very strong constitutional and statutory support for equality and integration on a racial basis. Constitutional and statutory backing for sexual equality is somewhat less insistent, and certainly limited in scope.

Individuals who have physical, emotional, or mental disabilities have only the most limited constitutional basis for their demands for fair and equitable access to leisure and rehabilitative recreational services. Furthermore, the disabled have not been determined to be an historically discriminated against "suspect" class, despite eloquent pleas to the contrary.[116]

There is, of course, some state legislation aimed primarily at the educational needs of disabled children,[117] and to a limited degree, Fourteenth Amendment due process and equal protection requirements have been judicially applied to protect the rights of the handicapped. In fact, one federal court held that children with learning disabilities are close to being a suspect class, invoking a "midlevel" scrutiny. This led to a requirement for special education classes in Pennsylvania.[118] The North Dakota Supreme Court found that disabled children were a "suspect classification" under the state constitution and required equal educational opportunity for them.[119] Nevertheless, until the United States Supreme Court recognizes that the disabled are a class requiring special consideration, a mere "rationality" or "reasonableness" test will be applied by most courts to governmental actions affecting them. Therefore, the most significant legal support for the disabled comes from statutory rather than constitutional law.

The principle sources for rights to service for people who are disabled are Section 504 of the Rehabilitation Act of 1973,[120] the Education of All Handicapped Children Act of 1975,[121] and the Developmentally Disabled Assistance and Bill of Rights Act.[122] (Section 503 of the Rehabilitation Act relating to federal contractors and the employment aspects of Section 504 are discussed in Chapter 6.)

The statutory reach of Section 504 is very broad. It states:

> No otherwise qualified handicapped individual in the United States . . . shall, solely by reason of his handicap be excluded from the participation in, be denied the benefits of, or be subjected to discrimination under any program or activity receiving Federal financial assistance.

HEW promulgated a complex series of regulations (at C.F.R. § 84) to ensure equality of opportunity to the handicapped in all programs and institutions receiving federal assistance from the department; these include grants, loans, contracts for assistance, property, and the services of federal personnel.

Those covered under the statute include all who suffer from physical or mental impairments that "substantially limit one or more of the major life functions." Alcoholics and drug addicts are included within the coverage.

By its very nature, the primary emphasis in application of Section 504 has been on educational institutions, yet it is clear that recreational and leisure services programs that benefit from federal assistance are also covered. The regulations do not require that absolute equivalent opportunities must be afforded to all disabled persons in all programs. All buildings or parts of buildings used in an assisted program need not be totally accessible, as long as the program itself is reasonably accessible or equivalent alternatives are afforded. For example, if a state park benefits from federal grants it would not have to build barrier-free wheelchair trails through all of a natural wildlife area, but it might be required to create a nature trail or observation area that would afford access to a wildlife or wilderness experience. Relocation of nature talks or outdoor education classes from remote areas to those accessible to the disabled might be considered. Essentially, the law does not require the impossible. The regulations seek cooperation and common sense along with the maximum practical utilization of ever more sophisticated rehabilitative equipment and techniques.

The courts have thus far not provided a great deal of guidance in the application of Section 504; however, the liberal interpretation that HEW gave to the statute received a significant setback when the Supreme Court narrowly construed the statute in *Southeastern Community College v. Davis.*[123]

In the *Davis* case, a nursing school rejected a severely hearing impaired applicant on the grounds that her disability would render her unable to meet the essential obligations of a nurse. The Supreme Court agreed, holding that in order for a handicapped person to be considered "otherwise qualified" under Section 504, he or she would have to meet program requirements "in spite of [the] handicap," and that different selection criteria for handicapped applicants could not be compelled.

At the time of this writing the Supreme Court has granted certiorari to review a circuit court decision requiring a university to hire an interpreter to assist deaf students. The court had concluded that it was only if an applicant's handicap precluded ever achieving his or her vocational goals that exclusion from a program would be appropriate.[124]

In addition to the regulations of HEW (currently the Department of Education and the Department of Health and Human Services), other federal agencies have issued regulations implementing Section 504. The Department of Transportation, the Architectural and Transportation

Barriers Compliance Board, and the General Services Administration are all developing accessibility standards. It is clear that as part of a general movement to reduce government regulation, the trend through the early 1980s will be against federal imposition of particular requirements to aid the disabled.

Obviously, those who are involved in specialized leisure service programs and therapeutic recreation must pay close attention to developments in administrative law and regulation so they may meet their obligations to the disabled. Similarly, leisure services programs for the general population must make appropriate adjustments and expenditures so the disabled may have a reasonable opportunity for participation. Nevertheless, it is likely that the degree of commitment to services for the disabled on the part of sensitive professionals and a corresponding willingness to expend a substantial proportion of limited funds to accommodate their needs will be more significant in a practical sense than will the promulgation of rules and regulations under broad statutory mandates such as Section 504.

Most recently, the Supreme Court has delivered a severe blow to the hopes of those who looked to federal law as a major force to reform state attitudes and actions with regard to the mentally and emotionally retarded. In *Pennhurst State School v. Halderman*[125] the Court considered conditions at Pennsylvania's Pennhurst State School, a large and admittedly inadequate institution that housed 1200 residents, 75 percent of whom were severely or profoundly retarded with IQs under 35. Many had multiple disabilities.

The plaintiffs sought to have Pennhurst closed and to require that most of its residents be placed in appropriate "community living arrangements." Both district and circuit courts had held that there was a basic right to "appropriate treatment, services, and habilitation" in "the setting that is least restrictive of . . . personal liberty." Although the courts referred to the Eighth Amendment's prohibition against "cruel and unusual punishment" and to the state's mental health laws and the federal Rehabilitation Act, they relied primarily on the Developmentally Disabled Assistance and Bill of Rights Act. Most particularly the court referred to Section 6010, which sets forth a patient's rights to "appropriate treatment, services, and habilitation."

In an extremely narrow reading of the statute, the Court, led by the conservative Justice Rehnquist, rejected the lower courts' interpretations and held that the "Bill of Rights" was only meant "to encourage, rather than mandate the provision of better services to the developmentally disabled." The act merely indicates a general policy and some funding incentives, nothing more. Obviously this decision has profound negative implications for the short-term likelihood that adequate therapeutic and other recreational services will be provided to the developmentally disabled.

### Rights of the Incarcerated to Recreation

A slightly less negative Supreme Court approach has been taken with regard to the recreational needs of incarcerated persons. In *Rhodes v. Chapman*,[126] a majority of the Supreme Court rejected lower court rulings that "double celling" of prisoners in sixty-three square feet of cell space was cruel and unusual punishment that violated the Eighth Amendment and the Civil Rights Act.[127] The decision written by Justice Powell permitted two prisoners to be housed in extremely confined circumstances. However, the Court did not totally reject the pioneering efforts by such federal judges as Frank Johnson of Alabama to utilize the Eighth Amendment's strictures to force states to provide "meaningful vocational, educational, *recreation* or work programs"[128] (emphasis added) in their prisons. In fact, the Supreme Court in the *Rhodes* case continually emphasized the availability of recreation as being a factor that ameliorated conditions in the Ohio prison." It has gymnasiums, workshops, school rooms . . . . Outdoors . . . [it] has a recreation field." Day rooms attached to the small cells "are designed to furnish that type of recreation or occupation which an ordinary citizen would seek in his living room or den," including card tables and television.

Although the Eighth Amendment is concerned with "unquestioned and serious deprivation of basic human needs," these are found in "the evolving standards of decency that mark the progress of a maturing society." The opinion makes clear that some degree of "exercise and recreation, educational and rehabilitative programming" are required. Thus, this decision, although harsh on its face, should encourage those involved in rehabilitative and therapeutic recreation to continue to press penal officials to provide meaningful recreational opportunities to the inmate population.

### CONCLUSION

These recent developments reemphasize that in all but the most basic matters, modification of existing recreational facilities and programs and the adoption of new and innovative techniques to involve the disabled, disadvantaged, or incarcerated may be given only general impetus by the law. In fact, we may reach similar conclusions with regard to most legal and constitutional requirements for the protection of civil rights and liberties.

Even where the demands of the law are clear-cut, relatively few people are both aware of their rights and aggressive enough to insist upon them. The leisure services profession has the burden and challenge of demonstrating adherence to the principles of civil rights, equal opportunity laws, and constitutional requirements by providing high-quality leisure and recreation opportunities for all. Rather than viewing civil rights laws and regulations as examples of red tape and bureaucratic excess, park managers should view them as honest if occasionally awkward efforts to articulate democratic goals and objectives. If the Battle of Waterloo was won on the playing fields of Eton, as the Duke of Wellington said, the battle for a fair and just society may at least be encouraged in the playgrounds of our parks and the gymnasiums of our institutions.

## NOTES

1. 249 U.S. 47 (1919).
2. *Abrams v. United States*, 250 U.S. 616 (1919).
3. 301 U.S. 242 (1937).
4. 299 U.S. 353 (1937).
5. See the debate between Justices Black and Frankfurter in *Adamson v. California*, 332 U.S. 46 (1947).
6. *United States v. Carolene Products Co.*, 304 U.S. 144 (1938).
7. See, for example, *Kunz v. New York*, 340 U.S. 290 (1951), reversing the conviction of a minister who violated an ordinance prohibiting the holding of a religious meeting in the streets without a permit.
8. See *Keyishian v. Board of Regents*, 385 U.S. 589 (1967).
9. 307 U.S. 496 (1939).
10. See *Poulos v. New Hampshire*, 345 U.S. 395, 398 (1953), and *Cox v. Louisiana*, 379 U.S. 559 (1965).
11. 394 U.S. 111 (1969).
12. *Feiner v. New York*, 340 U.S. 315 (1951).
13. See, for example, *State v. Rosenfeld*, 62 N.J. 594, 303 A.2d 889 (1973), where a speaker at a public meeting was found to have been improperly silenced despite the fact that he punctuated all of his fiery oratory with liberal use of Anglo-Saxon expletives. See also *Cohen v. California*, 403 U.S. 15 (1971), in which the defendant wore a jacket with the words "Fuck the Draft" on the back in the halls of the Los Angeles County Courthouse. This "expression" was protected by the First Amendment despite the presence of women and children.
14. *Village of Skokie v. National Socialist Party*, 69 Ill.2d 605, 373 N.E.2d 21 (1978). The Supreme Court had earlier reversed a refusal to stay on injunction prohibiting the wearing and display of Nazi symbols, 432 U.S. 43 (1977).

15. See *Collin v. Smith,* 447 F. Supp. 676 (N.D. Ill. 1978), aff'd, 578 F.2d 1197 (7th Cir. 1978), cert. den., 439 U.S. 916 (1978).
16. 312 U.S. 569 (1941).
17. *Murdock v. Pennsylvania,* 319 U.S. 105 (1943).
18. Compare *United States Labor Party v. Codd,* 391 F. Supp. 920 (E.D. N.Y. 1975) ($5.00 daily permit fee struck down), with *Faria v. Violette,* 32 F. Supp. 239 (D. Mass. 1940) ($3.00 fee upheld as reasonably related to cost of administration).
19. *Adderley v. Florida,* 385 U.S. 39 (1966).
20. *Cox v. Louisiana,* 379 U.S. 559 (1965).
21. *Greer v. Spock,* 424 U.S. 828 (1976).
22. 460 F.2d 746 (7th Cir. 1972). Cf. *Kunz v. New York,* 340 U.S. 290 (1951).
23. See, for example, *Women Strike for Peace v. Hickel,* 420 F.2d 597 (D.C. Cir. 1969), and *Women Strike for Peace v. Morton,* 472 F.2d 1273 (D.C. Cir. 1972), upholding the right to demonstrate on the Ellipse and in the White House vicinity; but see, on the other hand, *Viet Nam Veterans Against the War v. Morton,* 506 F.2d 53 (D.C. Cir. 1974) where an attempt to establish an overnight campsite vigil was rejected as constitutionally unprotected.
24. See *Blasecki v. Durham,* 456 F.2d 87 (4th Cir. 1972), which upheld a limit of fifty demonstrators in a small downtown park.
25. *Supra* note 22.
26. *Young v. American Mini Theatres,* 427 U.S. 50 (1976).
27. See *Ginsberg v. New York,* 390 U.S. 629 (1968), upholding a New York criminal statute aimed at preventing distribution of sexual material to minors.
28. *FCC v. Pacifica Foundation,* 438 U.S. 726 (1978), concurring opinion of Mr. Justice Powell.
29. *Erznoznick v. City of Jacksonville,* 422 U.S. 205 (1975).
30. 420 U.S. 546 (1975).
31. *Contemporary Music Group v. Chicago Park District,* 343 F. Supp. 505 (N.D. Ill. 1972).
32. *East Meadow Community Concerts v. Board of Education,* 18 N.Y.2d 129, 219 N.E.2d 172, 272 N.Y.S.2d 341 (1967), aff'd. 19 N.Y.2d 605, 224 N.E.2d 888, 278 N.Y.S.2d 393 (1967).
33. *Everson v. Board of Education,* 330 U.S. 1 (1947).
34. *Wolman v. Walter,* 433 U.S. 229 (1977).
35. *McCollum v. Board of Education,* 333 U.S. 203 (1948).
36. *Zorach v. Clauson,* 343 U.S. 306 (1952).
37. *Wisconsin v. Yoder,* 406 U.S. 205 (1972).
38. *Prince v. Massachusetts,* 321 U.S. 158 (1944).
39. *Lemon v. Kurtzman,* 403 U.S. 602 (1971).
40. *Supra* note 36 at 312-314.
41. See, for example, *Paul v. Dade County,* 202 So.2d 883 (Fla. 1967), cert. denied, 207 So.2d 690 (Fla. 1967), finding the placement of a cross on public property constitutional, while a contrary result was reached in *Lowe v. City of Eugene,* 254 Or. 518, 459 P.2d 222 (1969), cert. den., 397 U.S. 1042 (1970).

42. *Curran v. Lee,* 484 F.2d 1348 (2d Cir. 1973).
43. *Allen v. Morton,* 495 F.2d 65 (D.C. Cir. 1973).
44. *Citizens Concerned for Separation of Church and State v. City and County of Denver,* 481 F. Supp. 522 (D. Colo. 1980), remanded, 628 F.2d 1289 (10th Cir. 1980).
45. *Fox v. City of Los Angeles,* 22 C.3d 792, 587 P.2d 663 (1978).
46. 397 U.S. 664 (1970).
47. Compulsory chapel requirements at the military service academies were held unconstitutional, *Anderson v. Laird,* 466 F.2d 283 (D.C. Cir. 1972), cert. denied 409 U.S. 1076 (1972), but the broader issues of military chaplains have been avoided through the use of the requirement for "standing" to sue. See, on the issue of federal taxpayer suits in establishment clause controversy, *Flast v. Cohen,* 392 U.S. 83 (1968).
48. *Resnick v. East Brunswick Tp. Bd. of Educ.,* 77 N.J. 88, 389 A.2d 944 (1978).
49. See *United States v. Ballard,* 322 U.S. 78 (1944).
50. *Reynolds v. United States,* 98 U.S. 145 (1878).
51. *Hill v. State,* 38 Ala. App. 404, 88 So.2d 880 (1956) cert. denied 264 Ala. 697, 88 So.2d 887 (1956); *State ex rel. Swann v. Pack,* 527 S.W.2d 99 (Tenn. 1975).
52. *Prince v. Massachusetts,* 321 U.S. 158 (1944).
53. *Town v. State ex rel. Reno,* 377 So.2d 648 (Fla. 1979).
54. *Sherbert v. Verner,* 374 U.S. 398 (1963); and *Wisconsin v. Yoder, supra* note 37.
55. 600 F.2d 666 (7th Cir. 1979).
56. *Edwards v. Maryland State Fair and Agricultural Society, Inc.,* 628 F.2d 282 (4th Cir. 1980).
57. 101 S.Ct. 2599 (1981).
58. *United States v. Boeswetter,* 463 F. Supp. 370 (DDC 1978).
59. 326 U.S. 501 (1946).
60. *Amalgamated Food Employees Local 590 v. Logan Valley Plaza, Inc.,* 391 U.S. 308 (1968).
61. *Lloyd v. Tanner,* 407 U.S. 551 (1972), limited *Logan Valley's* application to picketing and demonstrations relevant to businesses which had facilities at the mall. (*Logan Valley* involved a labor dispute).
62. 424 U.S. 507 (1976).
63. *Prune Yard Shopping Center v. Robbins,* 447 U.S. 74 (1980).
64. 347 U.S. 483 (1954).
65. Since the Fourteenth Amendment did not apply to the federal government, the Supreme Court ruled that the due process clause of the Fifth Amendment had the same effect on federal actions as did the equal protection clause of the Fourteenth on the states. See *Bolling v. Sharpe,* 347 U.S. 497 (1954), although there might be some differences in application. See *Hampton v. Mow Sun Wong,* 426 U.S. 88 (1976).
66. *Watson v. Memphis,* 373 U.S. 526 (1963).
67. *Evans v. Newton,* 382 U.S. 296 (1966).
68. *Evans v. Abney,* 396 U.S. 435 (1970).
69. 403 U.S. 217 (1971).

70. 426 U.S. 229 (1976).
71. *Griffin v. County School Board of Prince Edward County,* 377 U.S. 218 (1964).
72. 417 U.S. 556 (1974).
73. *The Civil Rights Cases,* 109 U.S. 3 (1883).
74. See 42 U.S.C.A. § 1983 and 18 U.S.C.A. § 242. Until recently local governments had substantial immunity from civil rights suits, but that has been largely eliminated. See *Monel v. Department of Social Services,* 436 U.S. 658 (1978), and *Owen v. Independence,* 445 U.S. 622 (1980).
75. 392 U.S. 409 (1968).
76. 396 U.S. 229 (1969).
77. 410 U.S. 431 (1973).
78. See, for example, *Solomon v. Miami Woman's Club,* 359 F. Supp. 41 (S.D. Fla. 1973); *Cornelius v. B.P.O.E.,* 382 F. Supp. 1182 (D. Conn. 1974). See also *Wright v. Salisbury Club,* 479 F. Supp. 378 (E.D. Va. 1979), applying a private club exception to § 1981.
79. See, for example, *Olzman v. Lake Hills Swim Club,* 495 F.2d 1333 (2d Cir. 1974); *Bell v. Kenwood Golf and Country Club,* 312 F. Supp. 753 (D. Md. 1970); *Wright v. Cork Club,* 315 F. Supp. 1143 (S.D. Tex. 1970). In *United States v. Trustees of Fraternal Order of Eagles,* 472 F. Supp. 1174, (E.D. Wis. 1979), the court rejected arguments that the Eagles were a private club. Some of these cases not only recognize the right to injunctive relief and attorney's fees under Title II, but also private damage actions under Sections 1981-1982.
80. *Runyon v. McCrary,* 427 U.S. 160 (1976).
81. See, for example, *Katz v. Massachusetts Comm. Against Discrimination,* 365 Mass. 357, 312 N.E.2d 182 (1974).
82. 411 U.S. 1 (1973).
83. See *Serrano v. Priest,* 5 Cal.3d 584, 487 P.2d 1241, 96 Cal. Rptr. 601 (1971); *Robinson v. Cahill,* 62 N.J. 473, 303 A.2d 273 (1973).
84. *Reed v. Reed,* 404 U.S. 71 (1971).
85. *Frontiero v. Richardson,* 411 U.S. 677 (1973).
86. *Weinberger v. Wiesenfeld,* 420 U.S. 636 (1975).
87. *Craig v. Boren,* 429 U.S. 190 (1976).
88. 430 U.S. 313 (1977).
89. 416 U.S. 351 (1974).
90. *Frontiero v. Richardson, supra* note 85.
91. *Craig v. Boren, supra* note 87, at 197.
92. 430 U.S. 703 (1977) affirming 532 F.2d 880 (3d Cir. 1976).
93. 42 U.S.C.A. § 3601 et seq. (as amended 1974).
94. *Gladstone Realtors v. Village of Bellwood,* 441 U.S. 91 (1979).
95. See *Seidenberg v. McSorleys' Old Ale House, Inc.,* 317 F. Supp. 593 (S.D. N.Y. 1970).
96. See, for example, *National Organization for Women v. Little League Baseball, Inc.,* 127 N.J. Super. 522, 318 A.2d 33, aff'd 67 N.J. 320, 338 A.2d 198 (1974). Cf. *Commonwealth Human Relations Comm. v. Loyal Order of*

*Moose,* 448 Pa. 451, 294 A.2d 594 (1972), appeal dismissed, 409 U.S. 1052 (1972). See generally, Note; Discrimination in Access to Public Places: A Survey of State and Federal Public Accommodations Law, 7 *N.Y.U. Rev. of L. and Soc. Change* 215 (1978).

97. *McLean v. First Northwest Industries of America,* 600 P.2d 1027 (Wash. App. 1979).

98. 15 U.S.C.A. § 1691 et seq. See also the Housing and Community Development Act of 1974, 42 U.S.C.A. §§ 5301 et. seq. requiring lending institution to count a wife's income in determining whether to grant financing for housing.

99. 514 F.2d 344 (1st Cir. 1975).

100. See, for example, *Brenden v. Independent School Dist.,* 477 F.2d 1292 (8th Cir. 1973); *Lavin v. Illinois High School Asso.,* 527 F.2d 58 (7th Cir. 1975); *Gilpin v. Kansas State High School Activities Assn.,* 377 F. Supp. 1233 (D. Kans. 1974).

101. *Commonwealth v. Pennsylvania Interscholastic Athletic Ass'n,* 18 Pa. Comm. Ct. 267, 334 A.2d 839 (1975).

102. *Darrin v. Gould,* 85 Wash. 2d 859, 540 P.2d 882 (1975). See, to the same effect, *Leffel v. Wisc. Interscholastic Athletic Assn.,* 444 F. Supp. 1117 (E.D. Wisc. 1978).

103. See the discussion of the application of equal protection in *Dodson v. Arkansas Activities Association,* 468 F. Supp. 394 (E.D. Ark. 1979).

104. 469 F. Supp. 659 (D.R.I. 1979); vacated as moot (no longer a case or controversy), 604 F.2d 733 (1st Cir. 1980). This case considered equal protection and Title IX (see below).

105. 20 U.S.C.A. § 1681 et seq. See the *HEW* interpretation at 46 C.F.R. § 86 (1978). See also the Federal Aid to Vocational Education Act, 20 U.S.C.A. § 2305(a)(17).

106. See *Glover v. Johnson,* 478 F. Supp. 1075 (E.D. Mich. 1979).

107. *Othen v. Ann Arbor School Board,* 507 F. Supp. 1376, (E.D. Mich. 1981); Cf. *Bennett v. West Texas State University,* 525 F. Supp. 77 (N.D. Tex. 1981); see also the broad interpretation in 44 Fed. Reg. 71414 (1979).

108. *Supra* note 103.

109. *Haffer v. Temple University,* 524 F. Supp. 531 (E.D. Pa. 1981).

110. 441 U.S. 677 (1979). See *North Haven Board of Education v. Hufstedler,* 629 F.2d 773 (2d Cir. 1980) cert. granted, 101 S. Ct 1345 on the scope of application of Title IX regulations.

111. 20 U.S.C.A. § 1682, 44 Fed. Reg. 71413 et. seq. (1979) interpreting 45 C.F.R. § 86 41(h).

112. 44 Fed. Reg. 7148.

113. For a full description of the regulations as of 1980, see Gaal, DiLorenzo, and Evans, HEW's Final "Policy Interpretation" of Title IX and Intercollegiate Athletics, 6 *J. Coll. and Univ. L.* 345 (1979-80).

114. *Cape v. Tennessee Secondary School Athletic Ass'n,* 563 F.2d 793 (6th Cir. 1977); *Jones v. Oklahoma Secondary School Activities Ass'n,* 453 F. Supp. 150 (W.D. Okla. 1977).

115. See the extended discussion in Comment, Half Court Girls' Basketball Rules: An Application of the Equal Protection Clause and Title IX, 65 *Iowa L. Rev.* 766 (1980).
116. See, for example, Symposium on the Rights of the Handicapped, 50 *Temple L. Q.* 941 (1977); Ten Broek, The Right to Live in the World, 54 *Calif. L. Rev.* 841 (1966).
117. See Cal. Educ. Code §§ 6750-6948-6.
118. *Frederich L. v. Thomas,* 408 F. Supp. 832 (E.D. Pa. 1976), aff'd 557 F.2d 373 (3d Cir. 1977).
119. *In re G. H.* 218 N.W.2d 441 (N.D. 1974).
120. 29 U.S.C.A. § 794, as amended by the Rehabilitative, Comprehensive Services and Development Disabilities Amendments of 1978 (amending 29 U.S.C.A. §§ 701-796).
121. 20 U.S.C.A. § 1401 et. seq.
122. 42 U.S.C.A. § 6000 et. seq.
123. 442 U.S. 397 (1979).
124. *Camenisch v. Univ. of Texas,* 616 F.2d 127 (5th Cir. 1980), cert. granted 449 U.S. 950 (1980).
125. 101 S. Ct. 1531 (1981).
126. 101 S. Ct. 2392 (1981).
127. 42 U.S.C.A. § 1983.
128. See *Pugh v. Locke,* 406 F. Supp. 318 (M.D. Ala. 1976), aff'd as modified, sub nom. *Newman v. Alabama,* 559 F.2d 283 (5th Cir. 1977), rev'd in part on other grounds, sub nom. *Alabama v. Pugh,* 438 U.S. 781 (1978).

## REFERENCES

In addition to the cases and materials cited in the footnotes the following works were generally referred to in preparation of this chapter.

N. Dorsen, P. Bender, B. Neuborne, and S. Law, *Political and Civil Rights in the United States,* Vol. 1 (1976), Vol. 2 (1979), Little, Brown and Co., Boston.

J. Nowak, R. Rotunda, and J. N. Young, *Handbook on Constitutional Law,* West Pub. Co., St. Paul, 1978.

L. Tribe, *American Constitutional Law,* Foundation Press, Mineola, N.Y., 1978.

# 6

# Legal Aspects Related to Employment

## INTRODUCTION

This chapter deals with a variety of laws, judicial decisions, and administrative regulations concerning the employment relationship as it relates to the parks and leisure services field. This is a rapidly changing area of the law, particularly with regard to equal opportunity and affirmative action. Although it is impossible to discuss in detail all aspects of employment relations law, we have attempted to touch upon the major areas. The chapter goes from a general introduction to labor-management law to specific individual employment problems, including workers' compensation and unemployment.

## LABOR RELATIONS IN PARKS AND RECREATION

A large body of statutes, cases, and administrative procedures regulates, directs, and protects management and workers in all aspects of the employment relationship. In all likelihood, parks and recreation administrators, whether they are in the private, voluntary, or public sectors of the field, will be involved with some aspects of labor law. While we cover the major concerns in this section, it is important for the leisure services administrator to communicate promptly with the agency attorney whenever there are employee requests for union representation, threats of strikes, slowdowns, substantial grievances, or demands for arbitration of disagreements. The employer-employee relationship is under pressure from a variety of sources, and under the best circumstances, it requires constant tending and the skills of good personnel management. When individual employees are devoting their energies to concerns about take-home wages, working conditions, overtime, and benefits, they may not be giving their best efforts toward the job itself. At the same time, an administrator whose only focus is profit-and-loss schedules, increased attendance, production programs, and client satisfaction may shortly find that an unhappy, demoralized, work force will not permit him to attain or maintain programmatic excellence.

## Historical Framework

Labor law has a fascinating and extensive history, which has been chronicled in a number of classic works.[1] Most sources agree that the roots of modern labor law go back as far as 1348, when the plague called Black Death ravaged the population of England. With the resultant worker shortage, noblemen tried to entice away the servants of their friends; wages soared, and crops went unharvested in the fields. The Ordinances of Laborers[2] was enacted to fix wages, to compel workers to accept employment, and to regulate the terms of the labor contract.

Labor codes enacted over the succeeding four hundred years continually emphasized that the labor contract was different from other contracts and made it illegal for workers to join together to attempt to bargain with employers. When journeymen tailors banded together in 1721 and refused to work for less than a set wage, they were found guilty of criminal conspiracy.[3] The essence of their crime was their joining together, not their individual decisions to refuse to work for low wages. The courts utilized this conspiracy theory in England up to 1906 and in the United States until 1842.[4]

**Union Organization.** Early unions were usually made up of skilled craftspeople. The union members would establish a set price for their services and agree among themselves not to work for less. There were few efforts to enter into bargaining with employers. The organizations were generally located in urban areas. They formed to address a particular problem and tended to disband whenever that problem was solved or when economic depression forced the individual members to accept whatever work they could get. Printers, comb-makers, tailors, carpenters, weavers, coopers, and cordwainers (shoemakers) were among the various groups to organize into unions.

The short-lived National Trade Union, established in 1834, was the first attempt to unite all unions. This was followed by a series of national craft unions, but the financial panic of 1837 wiped out nearly all of these early efforts.

After the Civil War, the radical Knights of Labor formed. This organization differed from its predecessors in that it admitted both skilled and unskilled workers without regard to race, creed, nationality, or sex. The Knights succeeded in winning several strikes, but their involvement in the bloody Haymarket Riot in Chicago in 1886 discredited the union, and they were ineffective thereafter.

In spite of the fact that the courts were uniformly hostile to labor and often were instrumental in limiting union activities, the extremely poor working conditions in most industries promoted continued labor organization. Most importantly, the American Federation of Labor (AFL) was founded in 1886 as a loose federation of skilled craft unions.

For many years the AFL fought for workers' rights without any support in the law for union rights. During this time employers frequently required job applicants to sign agreements that as a condition of employment they would not become or remain a member of the union. These "yellow dog" contracts were upheld by the Supreme Court in a number of decisions.[5]

**Legislation.**    Finally, in 1926, Congress passed the Railway Labor Act,[6] which expressly forbade the use of "yellow dog" contracts or other limitations "upon freedom of association among employees" or upon "the right of employees to join a labor organization" within the railway industry. The scope of this sentiment was expanded to other industries in 1932 with the Norris-LaGuardia Act,[7] which provided that federal courts could not be used to enforce contracts in which employees agreed not to join a labor union.

In 1935 Congress passed the original National Labor Relations Act,[8] which is commonly known as the Wagner Act. The primary purpose of this legislation was to equalize the bargaining power between the employer and the employee. The Wagner Act guaranteed to employees the right to organize and bargain collectively through their own elected representatives. Furthermore, it indicated that this right could not be violated through certain employer actions known as *unfair labor practices.* Among these were: discrimination on the basis of union affiliation; interference with the employees' right to organize; refusal to bargain collectively; and other acts of retaliation or recalcitrance to deal with organized employees. The Supreme Court found the Wagner Act to be constitutional in *N.L.R.B. v. Jones & Laughlin Steel Corporation.*[9]

To administer the Wagner Act, Congress established an independent quasi-judicial agency known as the National Labor Relations Board (NLRB). This board, through a system of regional offices, is empowered to initiate an action against any party engaging in unfair labor practices and to make the appropriate rules and regulations to carry out the provisions of the act.

As the face of American industry changed, philosophical differences developed within the AFL. The structure of the union, an amalgamation of numerous craft organizations, did not lend itself to the mass-production industries that developed after World War I. In 1938 the Congress of Industrial Organizations (CIO) was born out of these differences to meet industrial union needs. In 1955 these two organizations came back together to merge into the AFL-CIO, which at the time brought 85 percent of all union membership in the United States under one parent organization.

The passage of the Labor Management Relations Act of 1947, commonly known as the Taft-Hartley Act, was an attempt by Congress to address some objections to the Wagner Act. The most frequent criticism was that the restrictions relating to unfair labor practices were one-sided; the proscribed activities were those of the employer, not the labor union. The Taft-Hartley Act attempted to balance the power between labor and management and stated the congressional policy as follows:

It is hereby declared to be the policy of the United States to eliminate the causes of certain substantial obstruction to the free flow of commerce and to mitigate and eliminate these obstructions when they have occurred by encouraging the practice and procedure of collective bargaining and by protecting the exercise by workers of full freedom of association, self-organization, and designation of representatives of their own choosing, for the purpose of negotiating the terms and conditions of their employment or other mutual aid or protection.

The Taft-Hartley Act further established the Federal Mediation and Conciliation service (FMCS) and procedures for presidential intervention and injunctions against strikes that threaten or imperil national health, safety, or welfare.

During the formative stages of labor law, the legislation related only to private sector employment, not to public employees. As the American work force slowly moved from an industrial and agricultural base toward a service-oriented one, more and more people were employed by the government. As government employment became more central to our economy, traditional patronage and spoils systems, with the accompanying evils of bribery, incompetence, and insecurity, were no longer acceptable. The first great reform was the introduction of federal and state civil service.

Civil service systems have been adopted by 95 percent of cities with populations over 100,000 and by 27 states, and they are the primary personnel administration systems in government. Although they eliminated or modified many of the evils of the patronage system, many people felt that the civil service systems were not adequately protecting the interests of the public employee. Jerry Wurf, president of the American Federation of State, County and Municipal Employees (AFSCME) stated:

> In my view, civil service is nothing more—and not much less than management's personnel system. Viewed as such, it fills an important role in government, as a tool of management . . . . The employee's rights and benefits are best protected through some form or other of negotiation and collective bargaining between his representative agency—preferably a trade union—on the one hand, and the representative of governmental management, which is often called Civil Service, on the other hand.[10]

In the early 1960s President John F. Kennedy formed a task force to study labor-management relations in the federal government. He stated:

> The right of all employees of the Federal Government to join and participate in the activities of employee organizations, and to seek to improve working conditions and the resolution of grievances should be recognized by management officials at all departments and agencies. The participation of Federal employees in the formulation and implementation of employee policies and procedures affecting them contributes to the effective conduct of public business . . . . We need to improve practices which will assure the rights and obligations of employees, employee organizations and the Executive Branch in pursuing the objective of effective labor-management cooperation in the public service.[11]

The work of the task force led to the development of Executive Order 10988, which established a program of labor-management relations in the federal government and gave rise to the rapid growth of unionism in all levels of public employment. In an article discussing the "widespread erosion" in industrial union membership and power, the author notes that "the most conspicuous increases in union membership have occurred in the civil service."[12] Certainly AFSCME and other government employee unions such as the American Federation of Teachers have grown dramatically.

Federal employee-management relations improved as a result of Executive Order 10988, and the basic principles remained unchanged, even though Executive Order 11491, signed by President Nixon in 1969, made substantial modifications in the program.

## State Statutes Relating to Public Sector Labor Relations

The first law recognizing the rights of municipal employees to bargain was passed in Wisconsin in 1959.[13] Since that time a majority of the states have enacted legislation relating to the bargaining rights of state and local employees.

As of January 1980, more than forty states had enacted legislation governing public employees' rights in labor actions.[14] These laws vary widely; some require or authorize the parties to bargain collectively, while others specify that the parties should "meet and confer." A "meet and confer" statutory scheme is normally a greater departure from the private sector collective bargaining system—it usually involves the retention of more managerial discretion. In a few states the statutory language is sufficiently vague so as to blur the distinctions between "meet and confer" and collective bargaining.

Some state statutes cover all public employees, while others specify classes of employees who are either covered or exempted (e.g., teachers, police and fire personnel, state employees, local government employees, school administrators, etc.).

Most states expressly prohibit strikes by public employees, although a few, like Minnesota and Pennsylvania, have recently granted nonessential employees the right to strike upon certain conditions. At least twenty states have legislated arbitration, while others make provisions for voluntary arbitration.

Despite prohibitions on striking and substantial statutory or judicially imposed penalties, increasingly militant employees are likely to strike whenever labor-management problems reach the stage of impasse. Massive fines and incarceration for strike leaders have not often been effective in bringing an end to public employee strikes. In some instances these tactics have solidified workers' resolve. Sometimes harsh penalties have been eliminated as part of the ultimate price for a labor settlement.

## Collective Bargaining

The phrase "collective bargaining" is a shorthand way of indicating a complex system of almost ritualistic rules and statutes governing an employee-management negotiation process. Collective bargaining is defined in the National Labor Relations Act as follows:

> To bargain collectively is the performance of the mutual obligation of the employer and the representative of the employees to meet at reasonable times and confer in good faith with respect to wages, hours, and other terms and conditions of employment, or the negotiation of an agreement,

or any question arising thereunder, and the execution of a written contract incorporating any agreement reached if requested by either party, but such obligation does not compel either party to agree to a proposal or require the making of a concession.[15]

This definition, and particularly the requirement that negotiations be conducted "in good faith," has been the source of thousands of NLRB and court decisions. Good-faith bargaining has itself been further defined by the courts. The Ninth Circuit Court of Appeals held that the duty to bargain in good faith is "an obligation . . . to participate actively in the deliberations so as to indicate a present intention to find a basis for agreement . . . ."[16]

In addition to the National Labor Relations Act, many states have legislation that imposes separate requirements upon the parties in a collective bargaining setting. While these statutes often parallel the federal legislation, in states where public employees have bargaining rights the applicable state statutes may vary significantly from those governing the private sector. Some state statutes mandate bargaining timetables, compulsory fact finding, or compulsory arbitration.[17] Needless to say, the attorney representing a parks and recreation agency should be thoroughly familiar with the applicable laws prior to representing a client at the bargaining table.

Examples of "bad-faith" bargaining include such infractions as undermining the bargaining representative by communicating directly with the employees,[18] unilaterally taking away a benefit that the employees had prior to bargaining,[19] the use of delaying tactics by management,[20] withdrawing previously agreed upon items,[21] and the employer's failure to make concessions.[22]

As a practical matter, the leisure services administrator should be very careful during the period in which a new contract is being negotiated. A change in working conditions or a reprimand, a casual comment or joking threat at the water cooler, could all be interpreted as counterindicative of "intention to find a basis for agreement."

**The Bargaining Process.**    Let us assume in a hypothetical case that Central City Public Employees Union has just given management the required sixty days' notice (prior to the expiration date of their existing contract) that they desire to modify the agreement. They offer to meet with the city administration for the purpose of negotiating a new contract. Approximately one-third of the city employees work in Central City's extensive park system, so the city manager asks the director of parks and recreation to serve as a member of management's negotiating team. The chief negotiator for management expects that the director will have a thorough understanding of the park laborers' working conditions and specific job requirements and will be able to help determine the cost and hidden problems of proposals that come across the bargaining table.

Prior to the opening bargaining meeting, the management team will meet together to establish ground rules and alternative strategies. Generally there is only one official spokesperson for each side; this avoids confusion and the embarrassing situation where two people from a side respond simultaneously and differently to a query. During the course of the negotiations the chief negotiator will often solicit the views and opinions of the other members of the team. Sometimes this is done at the table, but more often it occurs during a caucus when the members of the team meet out of earshot of the other team to discuss the nuances of various proposals. Little bargaining will occur at the opening meeting—generally this is when proposals are exchanged and reviewed, one point at a time. Following this, and during the succeeding bargaining sessions, various proposals and counterproposals are exchanged, discussed, modified, and hopefully agreed upon. As each item reaches a tentative agreement the parties will generally initial or "sign off" that item.

What subjects would you expect to cover in the collective bargaining sessions? The various subjects over which bargaining can occur have been classified by the NLRB into three categories: mandatory subjects, permissive subjects, and illegal subjects.

A mandatory subject is one over which the parties must bargain, and a refusal by one side constitutes a violation of the duty to bargain in good faith. Most subjects that will come onto the table are mandatory—wages, vacations, holidays, pension and benefit plans, discipline and work rules, even the price of employer-provided meals. In short, the terms and conditions of employment are to be negotiated.

A variety of subjects that management may deem within its prerogatives will be considered mandatory. For example, suppose Central City Parks and Recreation had decided that the tree trimming that had, in the past, been done by park laborers could be done more efficiently and at a lower cost by "contracting out" or giving the work to an outside agency. The union would probably want this subcontracting of bargaining unit work to be on the list of subjects under discussion, as it is a change in the terms and conditions of employment.[23]

A permissive subject is one over which the parties may negotiate and which, if an agreement is reached, may be a part of the contract. However, if no agreement is reached the parties may not bargain to impasse. *Impasse* has a technical legal meaning, and marks the point at which the duty to continue bargaining ceases. When each team has bargained to a position where they are "irreconcilably fixed"[24] and when further discussions would be futile, then impasse has been reached.

Examples of permissive subjects include the presence of an official reporter at negotiations, the procedures under which unions vote on contracts or conduct internal affairs, or even the scope of the bargaining unit.

Illegal subjects are those whose inclusion in the agreement would be improper and unenforceable. A clause sanctioning or permitting racial discrimination or contract language that violates federal or state statutes would fall into this category.

What variables could you expect to affect the bargaining process? At least for the decade of the 1980s, it is probably safe to say that there will be a continual fiscal crisis in the public sector. The so-called taxpayers' revolt has assured spending limitations on governmental services and, at least in California, has caused the bargaining process to focus on non-salary issues.[25] Concerns about layoffs, retrenchment, safety, subcontracting, department or jurisdictional consolidations, changes in merit increases, and increased workloads have surfaced at the bargaining table.

It is important to remember that not all concerns are subject to bargaining; a *bona fide* fiscal crisis may be justification for unilateral action on the part of management. This generally falls under the rubric of "management prerogatives." Certainly one of the most difficult situations that can face labor and management is a confrontation with the reality that there may be no way to meet legitimate employee concerns within the fiscal limitations imposed by circumstances beyond the employer's control.

Another variable with regard to public sector employees is the presence or absence of state or local "sunshine laws." "Sunshine" legislation requires that deliberations and decisions be made in the bright light of public scrutiny. This open-meeting policy has generally, although not always, been found to be a detriment to productive good-faith bargaining. There is, apparently, a tendency on the part of both sides to grandstand or make speeches for the benefit of the reporters or outsiders present; these speeches often cause one side or the other to become militant and uncompromising so it doesn't lose face.

Obviously the political environment in which the negotiations are taking place will have a bearing on the outcome. Whether public opinion is aligned with the union or management, whether the employer or the union can most afford a strike, whether the union's membership is backing the negotiating team, and even daily time pressures are all variables that cause one side or the other to make concessions. The sum total of these compromises generally yields a contract. When the process breaks down there are frequently "job actions," employee work stoppages, employer lockouts, and a series of escalating confrontations that make it very difficult to return to commonsense good-faith bargaining.

### Employee Work Stoppages

One of the best examples of the basic dilemma presented by job actions in parks and leisure services, as opposed to the more normal business world setting, is a New York case—*Byrne v. Long Island State Park Commission.*[26] The lifeguards at Jones Beach State Park, under the jurisdiction of the Long Island State Park Commission, were customarily reemployed at the beginning of each summer. Before the start of the 1971 season, however, the commission announced that it would pay the lifeguards less than they had received in 1970. The guards, who were members of a union, refused to apply for employment at a reduced salary and engaged in a labor dispute in which they picketed the beach, carrying placards and disseminating information. The commission petitioned the court, asking for an injunction to stop the lifeguards' activity.

In noting that the lifeguards were seasonal employees, and therefore not within the coverage of a statute prohibiting strikes by public employees, the court ruled that peaceable demonstrations were protected "unless there is something special about Jones Beach which removes it from the scope of the Labor Law."

The court then scrutinized the nature of Jones Beach to see if the environment there was so fragile as to justify serious limitations upon First Amendment freedoms. This examination relied heavily on testimony from former Commissioner Robert Moses during a trial that took place in 1941.[27] The decision from the early case quotes Commissioner Moses as he extolled the virtues and purposes of outdoor recreation. He referred to the "assumption that people had to get away from cities to repair some of the damage and shock to their nerves caused by city life . . ." and of the need for these park visitors to be free from noise, advertising, and parading.

Judge Harnett of the New York Supreme Court summarized the problem confronting the court as follows:

> We have poised before us the clash of competing social principles. On the one hand, there is the desire, indeed the necessity, of people to seek leisure and quiet in a natural environment free from the pressures of everyday living. What was true 30 years ago of the need for the individual to seek sustenance in [a] natural setting is even more applicable today . . . .

On the other hand, there is the competing drive for civil liberties and for appropriate expression in labor matters. The past 30 years have also seen marked development in the social conception of the rights of man. It is diminished solace for man to have comfortable physical surroundings if the conditions of his life in that environment are not tolerable. And so, we have our conflict at Jones Beach.[28]

In the end, the court tried to balance the social utilities involved. It concurred with the union that if the lifeguards could not picket at Jones Beach then they were restrained from effectively picketing at all. Judge Harnett wrote that, while the public was entitled to peace at the beach, it was, in fact, the work place of the lifeguards. As such, a total preclusion was unacceptable. He went on to outline the limitations that would apply. These restrictions specified the allowable locations, limited the number of pickets at any one location, limited the size of the placards, prohibited artificial sound amplification and the distribution of leaflets ("because of their litter potential"), and generally attempted to ensure a peaceable assembly.

Judges who are experienced in dealing with governmental labor disputes often take this kind of moderate approach. Indeed, some engage directly in mediation. These judges recognize that the heavy-handed application of laws limiting the rights of public employees often leads to contempt for the courts and a worsening of labor tensions.

The strike is not the only type of work stoppage that both public and private sector employees might utilize. Other job actions that are being used with increasing frequency include:

Work slowdowns—deliberate actions by employees to reduce their output.

"Sick-outs"—where employees call in sick and refuse to come to work (called the "blue flu" when applied to police officers).

Rulebook slowdown—where employees adhere strictly to the letter of regulations and assume that operations will become inefficient.

Refusal to accept any overtime work.

Wildcat strikes—short, spontaneously organized strikes usually triggered by a specific incident on the job.

Sympathy strikes—showings of support for other workers who are specifically involved in a primary labor dispute.

Safety strikes—refusal to work because of abnormally dangerous conditions that represent significantly increased dangers.

Boycotts, secondary strikes, and informational pickets.

One important distinction that the student should understand is the difference between the right to strike and the power to strike. As noted earlier, with few exceptions, the "right" to strike is virtually nonexistent for public employees. On the other hand, as managers in the public sector have discovered, the power to strike or to conduct alternative job actions exists in many governmental settings. Therefore, it is essential for the parks and recreation administrator to anticipate job actions and to have carefully thought out contingency plans. Political and tactical considerations, as well as the more pragmatic concerns of keeping the agency functioning, will be important. In our experience, the threat of a job action is almost always timed so that it coincides with some major special event, and under these circumstances it is easy to understand how an administrator could lose her composure and take unwarranted reprisals. This will do little to mitigate the bitter feelings that usually accompany the end of the job action, particularly if the workers did not achieve their goals. An astute administrator will take appropriate steps to effectuate the healing process.

**Third-Party Intervention.**    Often the way agreements that have reached impasse finally get settled is through a neutral third-party intervention. This can be the courts, as in the lifeguard example, or through a variety of other techniques. These include a "factfinder" or fact-finding panel who examines the dispute in a quasi-judicial hearing and then issues a report that explains the circumstances and generally makes recommendations for a settlement. While the recommendations are not usually binding, the publicity accompanying the report is an added inducement to the parties to settle.

Mediation represents another form of third-party intervention in a labor dispute. Mediation has been called the "most successful impasse resolution process."[29] It involves an individual, the mediator, who meets with each party separately, defines the scope of the dispute, seeks concessions, and looks for alternatives that might lead to a settlement. In many states mediation is voluntary, but in some participation is a mandatory step in the bargaining process. In all situations the recommendations made by a mediator are not binding unless both parties agree.

Several types of arbitration are also used to settle labor disputes. Arbitration can be binding or advisory; voluntary or compulsory. With arbitration both parties submit their cases to a neutral, mutually agreed upon third party in a hearing-type setting. Labor arbitrators are most frequently drawn from one of two national sources, the American Arbitration Association or the Federal Mediation and Conciliation Service.[30]

## Other Labor-Management Regulations

Although the majority of this section is concerned with the steps necessary to reach a workable employee-employer agreement, there are a number of other employment-related laws with which the administrator should at least be familiar. While we cannot cover them in detail in this volume, they include laws like the Employee Retirement Income Security Act (ERISA),[31] which established regulations for nongovernmental employees' pension and welfare benefit plans, and the Fair Labor Standards Act (FLSA),[32] which established employment requirements relating to minimum wage, overtime compensation, child labor, and equal pay for both sexes.* Another law that affects parks and recreation managers, as it applies to an estimated 5 million work places and over 70 million employees, is the Occupational Safety and Health Act (OSHA).[33] The purpose of this act is to "assure so far as possible every working man and woman in the nation safe and healthful working conditions to preserve our human resources." The law imposes duties on the employer to furnish a place of employment free from recognizable hazards that are likely to cause death or serious physical harm to employees. OSHA has been particularly controversial because its enforcement seems to impinge upon traditional management rights and, more importantly, because its safety regulations are often very specific and complex.

As a matter of fact, all of these laws concerned with the employment relation are accompanied by a wealth of standards, regulations, and rules for enforcing compliance. Their enforcement is largely the province of highly specialized attorneys, accountants, and administrators. The most important functions that the parks and leisure services administrator may perform with regard to these laws is to furnish appropriate information to the specialists and to be responsive to the procedures and changes required by the laws.

## EQUAL OPPORTUNITY AND AFFIRMATIVE ACTION IN EMPLOYMENT

### Summary of Laws

We have previously discussed the problems of discrimination in the provision of leisure services. Our focus in this section is on the various legal tools and strategies utilized to promote equal opportunity and eliminate discrimination in parks and leisure services employment.

---

*See the discussion of the Equal Pay Act in the next section of this chapter.

**Title VII.**    Title VII of the Civil Rights Act of 1964,[34] as amended by the
Equal Opportunity Act of 1972 and the Pregnancy Discrimination Act of
1978, is the single most important federal law protecting civil rights in
employment. We shall focus most of our attention on it. Title VII prohibits discrimination against employees and applicants for jobs in all
aspects of the employment relationship, on the basis of race, color,
religion, sex, or national origin.

Very few public or private enterprises are exempted from the
coverage of Title VII under the Supreme Court's expansive view of
federal power over commerce. The only specific exemptions for private
employment are for businesses that for most of the year have fewer than
fifteen employees and for *bona fide* tax exempt private membership
clubs. The courts have consistently given a narrow definition to private
club exceptions to civil rights laws. State and local governments fall
within the coverage of Title VII. Although the federal government is exempted from the statute's definition of "employer,"[35] Section 717 of the
act does specifically forbid discrimination in the executive branch of
government (with certain exceptions) and in those segments of the
judicial and legislative branches subject to civil service competition.
Ironically, congressional employment is not covered by Title VII.
The only other important exemption is for religious institutions and
corporations, which are permitted to consider religion as a factor in
employment.[36]

The principal enforcement machinery for Title VII is the Equal
Employment Opportunity Commission (EEOC), a five-member presiden-
tially appointed panel with a substantial bureaucracy behind it. The
EEOC investigates, conciliates, and litigates employment discrimination
cases, both through its own initiatives and procedures and by interven-
ing in private lawsuits. The EEOC attempts to ensure compliance with
the spirit as well as the letter of Title VII through regulations and
guidelines as well as through record-keeping procedures that it imposes
upon employers.

**The Civil Rights Act of 1871 (Section 1983).**    This general civil rights act,
which is applicable to all denials of constitutional and other civil rights
"under color of any statute, ordinance, regulation, custom, or usage, of
any State . . ." (or local governmental unit), has been the vehicle for a
wide variety of antidiscrimination suits against government agencies in
the employment field. These range from First Amendment complaints
over dismissal based on political activities, to Fourteenth Amendment
allegations of religious, racial, or sexual discrimination. Since the
Supreme Court has expanded the scope of Section 1983 to apply both to

municipalities and individual government employees and officers, Section 1983 will usually be cited in civil rights actions as a general basis for jurisdiction, often in combination with other statutes. It does not apply to nongovernmental or private activities.

The rights of government employees generally to continued employment, notice, hearings, and other procedural safeguards whether under Section 1983, tenure laws, or contract are too varied and complex to be considered here. However, as a basic guideline, government employers should understand that even when an employee has no right or privilege to continued employment, he may not be dismissed or denied promotion for a reason which would violate a constitutional right enforceable through Section 1983. Thus, if a parks maintenance person were dismissed because she wrote a letter to a local newspaper suggesting that the park commission was politically motivated and should be replaced, that could not be used as a reason for dismissal, even if the employee could have been dismissed for no reason at all!

**The Civil Rights Act of 1870 (Section 1981).**[37]    This historic statute gives all persons the same rights as "white citizens" to make and enforce contracts. Section 1981 has been interpreted to prohibit racial discrimination in all employment.[38] It has also been held to bar discrimination on the basis of alienage (noncitizenship),[39] although that, as well as its application to national origin or ethnic discrimination, is still open to question. Courts have generally not applied Section 1981 to sex discrimination, despite strong arguments that the "white citizens" referred to in the statute meant only males.

Although a Section 1981 complaint may parallel Title VII, the Supreme Court has held that Section 1981 is not limited by Title VII's definitional and procedural requirements.[40] Therefore, under certain circumstances, this simple law may provide a more effective remedy, including compensatory and punitive damages, than the modern complex civil rights statutes. In any event, many civil rights attorneys will file a Section 1981 action independent of the commencement of Title VII proceedings, despite procedural complications. Section 1981 has been applied to state and local employment,[41] but not to federal employment.[42]

**The Civil Rights Act of 1871.**[43]    Section 1985 of this act, commonly known as the Ku Klux Klan Act, has been applied by the courts to private conspiracies. Thus, if employment discrimination results from "class-based discriminatory animus,"[44] a damages action including punitive penalties may be based upon Section 1985. Theoretically at least, Section 1985 may provide a civil remedy for nonracial minority groups such as aliens or women in employment fields from which they have been excluded. As of this time only a few courts have been willing to consider such actions.[45]

**The Vocational Rehabilitation Act of 1973.** This statute prohibits discrimination on the basis of mental and physical handicaps by a variety of federally related agencies and enterprises. Section 501[46] requires federal agencies to implement affirmative action plans for the handicapped. Section 503[47] requires that employers holding federal contracts take "affirmative action" to employ and promote qualified individuals. Section 504[48] generally applies to any program that receives federal financial aid, including training programs and virtually all educational institutions. Section 504 is currently enforced by the Department of Education or by granting agencies. Section 503's implementation is the responsibility of the Department of Labor's Office of Federal Contract Compliance Programs (OFCCP).

Both Sections 503 and 504 limit their application to "qualified handicapped individuals," but there are substantial differences. Section 503 requires that affirmative action clauses be included in all government contracts over $2,500. Where the contract is worth more than $50,000 and there are more than fifty employees, an affirmative action program must be incorporated. Section 503 further requires the review of mental and physical job qualifications to "insure they are job related and necessary for efficient operation of the employer's business." By contrast, Section 504 merely requires that recipients of government funds refrain from discrimination solely by reason of handicap, and that "reasonable accommodation" for handicapped persons in employment should be provided by funding recipients. No affirmative action plan is required under Section 504, and the inability of an applicant to perform an essential element of the job because of a handicap would be legitimate grounds for disqualification.

In the key Supreme Court case, *Southeastern Community College v. Davis*,[49] the Court interpreted Section 504 as permitting consideration of the handicapping condition itself in determining whether an applicant was qualified. The Court upheld the rejection of a deaf applicant to nursing school without requiring the school to consider her other qualifications or to provide facilities to permit the applicant to overcome her disability. Nevertheless, the Court acknowledged that if the case had arisen under Section 503, the affirmative action obligation might require substantial modifications and reasonable accommodations to a job candidate who was handicapped. Hopefully, future cases will further develop this requirement.

**The Vietnam Era Veterans' Readjustment Assistance Act of 1974.**[50] This act contains provisions prohibiting discrimination against disabled veterans. It requires affirmative action by federal contractors, and it is enforced by Department of Labor regulations similar to those under Section 503 of the Rehabilitation Act.

**The Age Discrimination in Employment Act of 1967 (ADEA) (as amended).**[51] This statute has many similarities to Title VII. Since 1979 it has been interpreted and enforced by the EEOC. In its simplest terms, ADEA prohibits discrimination in employment against persons from age forty to age seventy. The act applies to private employers with twenty or more employees (for twenty calendar weeks during the current or preceding year). Since 1974, state and local government has also been covered. The federal government is exempted from the enforcement provisions of the statute, although employers in the executive branch and the military are forbidden to engage in age discrimination in their personnel actions.[52]

The ADEA, like Title VII, contains a limited exception for *bona fide occupational qualifications* (BFOQ). The BFOQ permits employers to make hiring decisions with reference to age when there are substantial nondiscriminatory reasons to do so. We discuss this exception in greater detail below.

Most employers understand that the ADEA does not permit them to prefer younger workers to older ones, except in limited union-management apprenticeship programs. They may not be aware that ADEA also protects workers in the lower ranges of the 40-70 age bracket. For example, if two applicants for the Central City Park directorship have essentially similar qualifications except that one is 55 and the other 41, the Park Board could not choose the 55-year-old on the basis of age, yet both the 55-year-old and the 41-year-old could be preferred to applicants who were 38 and 72 since the latter individuals are outside of the scope of ADEA's protection.

**The Equal Pay Act of 1973.**[53] This statutory provision, as amended, is a part of the Fair Labor Standards Act (FLSA). Until recently it was enforced through the Department of Labor, but as of 1979 the Equal Pay Act has become the responsibility of the EEOC.

Coverage of the Equal Pay Act for private employers is even broader than under Title VII. All businesses engaged in commerce with annual sales in excess of $362,500 are included. State and local government and public agencies also fall within the province of the Equal Pay Act. There are some limited exceptions to the FLSA generally involving certain seasonal enterprises. On the other hand, schools and hospitals are covered without regard to their size or number of employees.

The key provision of the Equal Pay Act prohibits discrimination in the payment of wages on the basis of sex "for equal work on jobs, the performance of which requires equal skill, effort, and responsibility, and which are performed under similar working conditions . . . ." The act contains exceptions for nonsexual distinctions based on seniority, merit, or productivity.

Those charged with enforcement of the Equal Pay Act have had some difficulty determining when tasks and working conditions were equal. For example, if male and female district supervisors within the Central City Recreation Department have distinctly different duties, the fact that they have the same job title does not necessarily entitle the female to the same pay as the male.

Suppose the female is in charge of an area that contains no recreation centers in its parks or no major facilities other than golf and tennis. The male supervisor, on the other hand, has been given responsibility for several community centers with substantial evening programs and accompanying security problems. The issue under the Equal Pay Act will be whether the differences in duties are so significant that a court would properly conclude that they are unequal and therefore not properly comparable for pay rates.

Generally, the courts have been unsympathetic to claims by employers that male employees are entitled to higher rates of pay than females in the same category of work because the males may be called upon to perform tasks requiring greater physical strength or exposing them to increased danger of injury.[54] Recreation managers should be particularly wary of pay differentials when the distinctions in tasks assigned are more reflective of historic sexual stereotypes than they are of real differences in skill or responsibility. For example, a park superintendent would have difficulty in justifying pay differentials between female and male laborers because the males were assigned to such tasks as tree removal, dredging, and mowing, while the females worked in the horticultural center, tended flower beds, and cared for small shrubbery.

A ruling that is potentially very significant in the equal pay area was issued at the end of the Supreme Court's 1980-81 term in *County of Washington v. Gunther.*[55] This case concerned pay differentials for male and female prison guards, and it was brought under Title VII's general prohibition of sex discrimination rather than under the Equal Pay Act. In a closely split decision, the Court ruled that although Title VII contained a provision permitting differences in pay if authorized by the

Equal Pay Act,[56] that provision related to the specific exemptions for seniority, merit, promotion, and the like. A Title VII action for sex-based wage discrimination could be maintained even if "equal work" could not be demonstrated. The majority was very cautious in its opinion, and it seems unlikely that they were inviting suits based upon differing pay scales for secretaries versus mechanics, but at least where the skills and responsibilities of positions are roughly comparable, the requirement of equality in responsibility should not be as burdensome for underpaid women in future legal actions.

**Executive Order 11246 (1965).**[57]  This order, initially issued by President Lyndon Johnson, bars discrimination by federal contractors on the basis of race, color, religion, sex, and national origin. There are different requirements placed upon construction and nonconstruction contractors. The rules under Executive Order 11246 are enforced by the Office of Federal Contract Compliance Programs (OFCCP) through regional Labor Department offices. The order applies to all domestic contracts over $10,000 in value.

The order requires that all contracts specify "equal opportunity." Most importantly, "affirmative action" is mandated on behalf of women and specified minority groups (blacks, Hispanics, American Indians, native Alaskans, Asians, and Pacific Islanders). To enforce the order, the Secretary of Labor has issued a comprehensive set of rules and guidelines covering everything from recruitment and testing to maintenance of records and promotion procedures. At the time of this writing, it appears that these requirements will soon be simplified and made less stringent.

Although there are many parallels between Title VII and Executive Order 11246, the requirements for reporting, compliance procedures, and enforcement differ substantially. There is no provision for individual lawsuits based upon violation of the order. Thus, a president who was less committed to an aggressive civil rights policy could readily change procedures, and, of course, the order could be withdrawn completely (although this would appear politically unlikely for even the most conservative administration).

As Executive Order 11246 has been applied up until now, its requirements are even more demanding than those of Title VII, particularly with regard to affirmative action. Leisure service agencies participating in federal programs may not be required to have specific minority quotas; nevertheless, goals, timetables, audits, and reports coupled with "good-faith" requirements enforced by federal officials have a strong motivating, if not coercive, effect on professional parks and recreation managers.

**Title IX of the Education Amendments of 1972.**[58]   As noted in Chapter 5, these provisions prohibit sex discrimination in programs and activities of educational institutions receiving federal funding. Only religious institutions and military academies are generally exempt, although private undergraduate schools and traditional single-sex public colleges have exemptions with regard to their admissions policy.

The great controversies under Title IX have centered around the requirements for expanding sports and recreation activities for women. To the extent that the Department of Education's Title IX regulations mandate an increase in emphasis on female sports, it is obvious that there will be a corresponding increase in coaching and athletic and recreation administration opportunities for women. Nevertheless, Title IX does not specifically refer to employment.

At the time of this writing, the majority of courts that have considered the question have ruled that Title IX does not apply to employment discrimination per se,[59] but the Second Circuit Court of Appeals disagreed and ruled that Title IX provided a cause of action independent of Title VII and the Equal Pay Act.[60] The United States Supreme Court has agreed to decide the question, and an authoritative decision should be forthcoming by the end of 1982.

**State Civil Rights Laws.**   Although the major civil rights focus is upon federal legislation, there are some forty states with broad civil rights statutes, several of which fill gaps in coverage in federal legislation (such as forbidding discrimination based on marital status) and provide for state and local enforcement machinery that may be more convenient and quicker than federal action.[61]

Although it seems unlikely that a federal equal rights amendment will be ratified in the foreseeable future, several states have enacted equal rights provisions in their own constitutions.[62] For example, Pennsylvania's Constitution provides: "Equality of rights under the law shall not be denied or abridged . . . because of the sex of the individual."[63] This has been interpreted as forbidding most classifications based on sex.

**Veteran's Preference Laws.**   The most significant officially sanctioned discriminatory actions undertaken by government result from veteran's preference statutes, which in one form or another may be found in all of the states as well as in federal law. Title VII specifically exempts veteran's preference laws from its nondiscrimination coverage.[64] Ironically, these laws were not intended to injure women in the job market but were designed by legislatures to provide both a reward and a form of compensatory treatment to those who have spent substantial amounts of time in active military service.

Most of the schemes give a veteran a point advantage on civil service examinations and have time limits, but a few give absolute preferences to veterans over nonveterans whenever the veteran applicant meets minimal job qualifications. Since the percentage of women in the armed forces has always been severely restricted by regulations, exclusion from the draft and combat, as well as by social mores, most women competing for classified government positions are at a distinct disadvantage.

In a case challenging the Massachusetts veteran's preference statute,[65] one of the most stringent in the nation, the Supreme Court ruled that even though the statute "operated overwhelmingly to the advantage of males" it was constitutional. The reason was that the law was not based on an invidiously discriminatory purpose and was "neutral" on the matter of gender.

## The Application of Equal Opportunity Legislation

Most parks and leisure services professionals strongly agree that the elimination of discrimination on the basis of race, religion, sex, age, national origin, and disability is a worthy goal. Indeed, after the turbulence of the civil rights struggle that engulfed the nation from the 1950s through the early 1970s, the most blatant forms of racial discrimination have largely been eliminated in the employment field. Although sex discrimination is deeply ingrained in the fabric of our society, women have made great progress over the last twenty years in their efforts to eliminate officially sanctioned differential treatment and opportunities. In fact, as our summary of laws demonstrates, most of the recognized kinds of employment discrimination are forbidden or limited by at least one, if not several, overlapping laws.

Of course there are still some legal gaps where a majority of society is not yet convinced of the validity or worth of a group's claim to equal rights. Although homosexuals have occasionally won some judicial protection for employment rights under due process and equal protection or, in California, under state constitutional interpretations,[66] they are generally excluded from the protection of federal antidiscrimination legislation and most state and local coverage as well. The rights of the disabled are just beginning to receive serious legal attention. And private social discrimination and discrimination based on economic status are ever-present conditions of the American lifestyle.

The elimination of legal employment discrimination has obviously not obliterated real job prejudice in a variety of forms. Unconscious or subconscious prejudices that build during our growth and socialization spill over into our work life. Employers and managers tend to hire people with whom they are comfortable, particularly when they will be working closely with them. Thus most leisure services administrators must make a conscious effort to employ and promote those who are different for positions that may lead to leadership and management opportunities.

Related to this is the tendency to stereotype people in job categories. Why are there so few black professional football quarterbacks? Why are there so many women playground leaders and special population programmers and so few women in park planning and maintenance? It is not just employers who reflect unconscious choices. School officials, guidance counselors, parents, peers, and, in general, an individual's cultural background and expectations may create a pattern of behavior that results in missed opportunities and wasted talents.

Even if employers overcome prejudices in their individual employment and promotion activities, related sets of problems interfere with the attainment of a fully integrated work force. Members of minority groups as well as women, in those fields from which they have historically been excluded, may be at a distinct disadvantage when trying to compete on an equal nondiscriminatory basis. White males hold the overwhelming majority of upper-level management positions. Quite often, white men have the advantage of superior education and training. Their connections and the comfortableness of their relationships with other white males in similar or superior positions at work, socially, and in sports and recreation afford them access to information about job opportunities, awards, educational benefits, and the like. These will not only aid them in current or prospective employment, but also will over time provide superior credentials and experience, so that when the white male candidate is competing with a female or minority, he may well have a legitimately preferable record, even though his underlying abilities and potential may be equal or less.

Of course, there is a counterargument that runs against legal actions to correct the imbalance created by the societal realities discussed above. Individual white males can hardly be held responsible for overall historical behavior patterns. If a white male with superior experience and credentials applies for a position, he will feel strongly resentful if he is rejected, not on his merits, but because of a need to establish racial and sexual balance.

The argument over "affirmative action," or "reverse discrimination," as its detractors refer to it, continues in political circles. In the meantime, antidiscrimination agencies like the EEOC and OFCCP and the courts have struggled to interpret and apply the requirements for fair employment practices in a manner that will effectuate the purpose of integrating the work force while avoiding new forms of government-imposed discrimination. For example, one area of increasing concern to the courts is sexual harassment. It is now clear that blatant sexual misconduct in the workplace not only creates potential liability under a variety of statutory and common law remedies, but also under EEOC regulations. An employer who condones a sexually oriented and uncomfortable work environment may be subject to Title VII sanctions.

Rather than bury the reader under the deluge of regulations, guidelines, and interpretations issued by the various civil rights agencies and subject to constant revision, we shall focus on the EEOC's basic approach to enforcement as it applies to the leisure services field.

**Nondiscrimination and Affirmative Action under Title VII.** Section 703(j) of Title VII specifically states that it *does not*

> require any employer . . . to grant preferential treatment to any individual or to any group because of race, color, religion, sex or national origin . . . on account of any imbalance . . . with respect to the total number or percentage of persons employed . . . in comparison with the total number or percentage of persons of such race, color, religion, sex or national origin . . . in the available work force . . . .

In addition to this statutory prohibition against required affirmative action, the Supreme Court in the case of *McDonald v. Santa Fe Trail Transportation Co.* [67] ruled that whites were protected by Title VII as well as blacks, and therefore could maintain a lawsuit if they suffered differential employment treatment. (In the *McDonald* case, a white employee suffered harsher discipline than a black who was guilty of the same offense.)

Despite Section 703(j) and the *McDonald* case, the Supreme Court has upheld voluntary affirmative actions programs favoring previously underutilized black workers. In *United Steelworkers of America v. Weber,* [68] Kaiser Aluminum Corporation and its skilled trade unions had agreed to a plan in which 50 percent of positions in apprenticeship training programs would be filled by blacks until the proportion of black workers approximated their representation in the local labor force.

Justice Brennan's opinion for the Court recognized that the argument that the voluntary plan violated Title VII had some force; nevertheless, he found it more persuasive that the historic impetus for the passage of Title VII had been the continued exclusion and underutilization of blacks in the work force. As long as the plan was a voluntary one, not imposed by the government, and was intended to "break down old patterns of racial segregation and hierarchy," it was within the spirit of Title VII. The Court emphasized that the plan didn't require that any white worker be discharged and replaced with a black. It was a temporary measure, and because it still kept half of the positions open for whites, it did not create an absolute bar to white advancement.

Although affirmative action programs are voluntary under Title VII, the EEOC has promulgated "Guidelines for Affirmative Action" for voluntary action and for employers with federal government contracts who are required to have an affirmative action plan under Executive Order 11246.[69] There are also basic sex discrimination guidelines[70] issued by EEOC that are a useful tool in meeting Title VII responsibilities.

Despite the potential for conflict with employers who are bound by both the executive order requiring affirmative action and Title VII's general ban on discriminatory treatment, recreation agencies that make a good-faith effort to follow EEOC guidelines are probably safe from the potential threat of private lawsuits alleging either direct or reverse discrimination.

Whether or not an affirmative action plan is voluntarily adopted by an agency, Title VII does give courts broad power to remedy intentional discrimination by mandatory affirmative action,[71] including required minority hiring ratios.[72] State courts may provide similar remedies under state antidiscrimination laws. As noted in the summary above, Section 503 of the Rehabilitation Act mandates affirmative action requirements for government contractors similar to Executive Order 11246, but does not require specified goals and timetables.

It should be clear to the reader that some form of affirmative action will be required of most public employers and many private employers as well. More importantly, even if the law does not directly impose an affirmative action policy on a recreation or leisure services agency, administrators are well advised to institute such programs and to carefully maintain records of their actions not only to ensure compliance with Title VII and other antidiscrimination laws but also as a defense against unwarranted charges of bias.

Complaints of discriminatory intent and action are very common both in government and private enterprise. They are easy to make and often difficult to disprove. Furthermore the availability of free or low-cost investigative and legal services for the processing of such complaints by state and federal agencies may encourage disgruntled applicants for jobs or promotions to file such charges.

Perhaps the best way to describe a typical nondiscriminatory employment policy that meets EEOC guidelines would be to follow the employment steps in a hypothetical situation.

## The Central City District Recreation Supervisor Case

Central City operates a Parks and Recreation Department under the general direction of the Park Board. On the recreation and leisure services side of the organization (as opposed to the parks, facilities planning, and maintenance side), there are an assistant director for visitor services, four district supervisors, twenty center directors and playground supervisors, and numerous part-time leisure program employees. Assume that one of the four district supervisor positions is open. Assume further that the department does not have a formal affirmative action plan.

**Position Description.** The position should be carefully and concisely defined and described. The essential functions should be set forth with particular attention to special or unusual duties and conditions. An example of a position description follows:

*District Supervisor—Recreation Division*

Salary Range: $22,000 to $26,000 annually

Position Description: Under the direction of the Director, the employee will be responsible for supervision of all recreation and leisure programs in an area of Central City currently containing one major regional park, several neighborhood playgrounds, and three community centers. Duties include participation in hiring, promotion, evaluation, and supervision of program personnel, coordination with park maintenance and central administration in facilities planning, and primary program planning and community relations within the area.

Additional duties: The employee will be responsible for staffing, evaluating, and general program supervision for Central City Family Camp in coordination with the resident director. This responsibility entails considerable travel and limited periods of residence in connection with the camping season.

**Qualifications.** This is a critical aspect of the process. The requirements of the position should closely fit its needs. The more stringent the requirements, the harder it will be to find qualified applicants from an already limited minority pool. If there are minimum requirements that cannot rationally be demonstrated to have a legitimate relationship to the real requirements, a suspicion of discriminatory purpose is invited by the department. In our hypothetical situation we find the following:

*Minimum Qualifications*

The candidate must have a bachelor's degree in recreation or a closely related field; a minimum of three years full-time experience in recreation with at least one year in a supervisory capacity. Supervisory experience in camping preferable, but not required.

A fair balance between professional quality and a realistic appraisal of the potential candidate pool should suffice to avoid charges of discrimination with regard to qualifications. Requirements of formal education and degrees may present a problem where the number of minority candidates having such credentials is very limited and the need for degrees versus direct field experience is open to question. In this situation with a position calling for a high level of skill and responsibility, the degree requirement is certainly justifiable.

At this stage, the department should not limit the candidate pool by adding a number of qualifications relating to strength, physical abilities, family circumstances, or any other attributes that would have a substantially negative impact on female, minority, handicapped, or older applicants. For example, just because the position requires considerable travel, there should not be a flat requirement that the candidate be a licensed driver, or provide his or her own vehicle. This might exclude the visually handicapped or have a harsher impact on poor minority applicants. Of course, the candidate's ability to get around and supervise the activities at the various parks and the camp is an important consideration, but the department should provide potential candidates who don't drive an opportunity to demonstrate that they may meet the transportation requirements in other ways. Similarly, a flat restriction of the position to single people, or elimination of consideration of pregnant women because of the nature of accommodations at the camp, would be inappropriate and would open the door to charges of discrimination. There are limited *bona fide* occupational qualifications (BFOQ's) that may be included in some job descriptions despite their exclusionary effect under Title VII and other laws. These are discussed below.

**Announcement and Advertisement of the Position.** Both under affirmative action and nondiscrimination guidelines, Central City's goal should be to circulate information about the position of district recreation supervisor to such an extent and in such a manner that a substantial pool of potential candidates will emerge. This pool should be composed of representatives of all groups within the relevant labor force.

Fair employment practices require a commonsense balancing of the nature of the position, the prospective applicant pool, and the prior history of employment both within the agency generally and with regard to the class of position in particular.

To reach the general candidate pool for a position such as the one described here, it would not ordinarily be necessary to place ads in the help-wanted pages of the newspaper, nor would Central City have to advertise in specialized women's or minority-oriented publications. Because of the supervisory nature of the position, Central City could meet its obligations (assuming no special civil service requirements) by: (a) posting the announcement within the department where it would be seen by qualified lower-ranking professional personnel, and (b) announcing the position in widely circulated professional publications such as the state parks and recreation association journal and placement bulletins of related professions. Obviously, the higher the level of the position, and the smaller and more homogeneous the local pool, the greater the impetus on Central City to advertise in national publications such as the NRPA Job Placement Bulletin.

Employment applications should be restricted to pertinent information related to the qualifications for the position. Questions as to age, marital status, number of children, height, weight, and so on, even if innocently intended, may raise questions about possible discriminatory effects. Under certain circumstances preemployment inquiries may seek affirmative action information regarding sex, race, and so on. The personnel officer should consult the EEOC Guidelines with regard to this delicate matter.

**Special Problems.** Up to this point, we have been describing a process that is essentially no more than good management practice. What if there are complicating factors? Suppose, for example, that there is a distinct disparity between females and males at the upper management levels of Central City's Parks and Recreation Department, and, as a matter of fact, the three remaining district supervisors are all male. Whether or not Central City is bound by affirmative action requirements under Executive Order 11246 or other direct legal mandates, the various methods outlined in EEOC and OFCCP publications provide practical guidance and the basis for a record to refute discrimination charges.

Among the strategies that the department might utilize could be direct contact with female professional recreation administrators asking them to aid in the location of qualified female candidates. Direct recruitment of female applicants through professional associations and publications might be advisable. Although it would not be necessary for a recreation supervisor's position, in other areas of the profession, such as landscape architecture or park planning, where there is a scarcity of females at the entry level, Central City could use a variety of strategies to make students aware of career possibilities. Participation in job fairs, educational programs at institutions with high female enrollment, and contact with national and local women's groups like the YWCA are ways to increase awareness of potential candidates. Obviously, similar efforts may be undertaken to increase minority entry into the field. Equally important is the use of minority and female professionals in the recruiting process whenever feasible.

**The Evaluation Process.** Assuming that recruitment efforts have resulted in a number of candidates reasonably approximating the racial and sexual composition of the potential applicant pool, the next question confronting the Central City department is how to evaluate these candidates on an unbiased and objective basis.

In some cases, state or federal civil service laws and regulations will prescribe specific tests and standards and may present a limited group of qualified candidates. In any event, whether mandated by civil service or created by Central City, tests and evaluation procedures must be nondiscriminatory.

Title VII specifically provides that *it is not*

> an unlawful employment practice for an employer to give and act upon the results of any professionally developed ability test provided that such test, its administration or action upon the results is not designed, intended or used to discriminate . . . .[73]

There have been two key cases decided by the Supreme Court concerning job testing. In the first, *Griggs v. Duke Power Co.*,[74] the Court found that the tests applied were not saved by the preceding section since they had an adverse effect on black applicants and had not been proved by the employer to be job related. In the second case, *Washington v. Davis*,[75] the Court declared that at least in situations where Title VII was not applicable, the mere fact that an employer used a test that had a negative racially disproportionate impact on minority applicants was not sufficient grounds to hold the test unconstitutionally discriminatory.

It is not yet clear whether the limitations of the *Davis* case will be applied to public employers under Title VII. In *Davis*, the court noted that under Title VII where "hiring and promotion practices" disqualified "substantially disproportionate numbers of blacks" they would have to be validated by the employer,

> in terms of job performance . . . perhaps by ascertaining the minimum skill, ability or potential necessary for the position at issue, and deter-

mining whether the qualifying tests are appropriate for the selection of qualified applicants for the job in question.

The EEOC has issued Uniform Guidelines on Employment Selection Procedures,[76] which are based on complex criteria developed by the American Psychological Association.

Whatever the method of validation, as a general principle, where adequate alternative testing procedures have a less discriminatory impact, they should be used. Cutoffs and numerical rankings based on test scores should have some demonstrable correlation to the skills needed and performance level expected. On the whole, the courts have become increasingly tolerant of management decisions concerning the use of testing and have put the burden on the unsuccessful candidate to demonstrate discriminatory purpose and impact. Thus the use of a test for skills and knowledge in connection with the district recreation supervisor's position should not present a major obstacle to Central City.

**The BFOQ.**    Title VII contains a provision permitting employers to consider "religion, sex, or national origin" as employment criteria but only if they are "bona fide occupational qualification[s] necessary to the normal operation of that particular business or enterprise."[77]

This is in addition to the religious criterion for employment which sectarian institutions may employ. As noted in the summary, the ADEA contains a BFOQ for age[78] and regulations under Executive Order 11246 have a BFOQ for sex similar to Title VII. The reader should note that race *cannot* be a BFOQ under any circumstances.

A recreational employer's scope for claiming a BFOQ based on sex, age, religion, or national origin is extremely limited. It may not be based on historic stereotypes or gross generalization. In the legislative history of Title VII and the ADEA, the BFOQ was characterized as applicable to "rare situations" and in very "limited circumstances."

The fact that many older persons could not meet the physical demands of a positon as a mountain climbing guide, for example, does not permit a blanket rejection of all applicants over the age of fifty. Each applicant should be judged on the basis of objective tests of condition and stamina.[79] It is only when an employer can demonstrate that elimination of a maximum hiring age would have a substantial safety detriment on the public that a general age BFOQ will be upheld.[80]

Sex would not be a valid BFOQ because a park director viewed a park superintendent's job as requiring an ability to work with heavy equipment and to control a rough crew of park laborers. The public preference for members of one sex over another, or one nationality over another, is not sufficient reason for a BFOQ. Stewardesses and hostesses may not be given preference over stewards and hosts.[81]

As with most rules, there are exceptions. If sex, religion, or national origin are necessary aspects for authenticity, EEOC regulations may countenance a BFOQ. The most obvious examples are positions in which employees will actually play male or female roles in dramatic works or pageants. Disneyland does not have to consider a male to portray Snow White!

The prime candidates for BFOQ exemptions involve sexual privacy and safety. Thus there may be a requirement for female attendants in women's restrooms or bath houses, or male bunk counselors at a boys' camp. The Supreme Court has upheld the exclusion of women guards from direct contact positions in male penitentiaries because of the reasonable expectation of an increased number of violent sexual assaults, although the Court cautioned that the BFOQ "was in fact meant to be . . . extremely narrow."[82]

Obviously, in our Central City district supervisor hypothetical situation, a BFOQ exception could not be justified. Of course, social, sexual, and ethnic factors often play a role in determining which candidates for a position have stronger qualifications and experience. It would be unusual to find a highly qualified female candidate for the positon of football line coach or a male with the background to be highly qualified in field hockey.

Although *pregnancy* is now included under the general category of "sex" in Title VII, employers do have greater leeway in considering pregnancy as a temporary disqualification from strenuous physically demanding employment.[83]

**Height, Weight, and Strength.**    Related to the BFOQ are physical requirements that may disqualify many women. Height and weight minimums, in particular, bear a heavy burden of justification since it is rare that they are directly related to physical ability. On the other hand, agility and strength tests may be valid if they are reasonably linked to occupational necessity. Again, a commonsense rule should be followed. Are there ways other than through brute strength that the demands of the position can be met? Clearly, for the district recreation supervisor post, strength, height, or weight requirements are not justifiable.

**Other Considerations and Exceptions.**    The various fair employment laws do not eliminate most management prerogatives. Seniority, merit, the quality or quantity of production, and differences in geographical and physical conditions may all justify differences in salary, benefits, and promotion.[84] Age is a valid criterion for entrance into joint union management apprenticeship programs, and employee benefits may be reduced based on actual cost differentials for older workers.

## Conclusion—The Meaning of Nondiscrimination and Affirmation Action in Hiring and Promotion

Let us suppose that Central City has purged its employment practices of all discrimination. Questions that might be utilized for improper motives have been eliminated from employment applications; discriminatory testing procedures and exclusionary requirements have been eliminated or reformed, and the applicant pool has been extended to include a substantial number of females and minority group members.

The most important question still remains. If there are qualified minority, female, and white male (nonminority) candidates for the district recreation supervisor position, must Central City offer the job to either a minority or female (depending upon which group is most critically underrepresented in the relevant work force)? The answer is a qualified "no."

A judicial order requiring certain minority or female quotas in hiring and promotion may result from a finding of discriminatory practices. Central City, as a federal contractor, may not have met its specific hiring goals under Executive Order 11246 and may, therefore, be compelled to employ a minority candidate. Ordinarily, however, even under an affirmative action plan, Central City would not be required to employ a female or minority as long as the preference for the white male candidate is not based on an improperly discriminatory motive. Of course, as a practical matter, a continued pattern of selection of white male applicants over qualified females, blacks, and other minority candidates may not only serve as evidence of discrimination, but may also engender pressure from federal and state fair employment officials that would be difficult to resist.

It is obvious that the higher the level of a professional position, the harder it is for a manager to articulate the reasons for preferring one candidate over another when both possess similar credentials. Recently the Supreme Court has apparently made the employer's task substantially less burdensome. In *Texas Department of Community Affairs v. Burdine*,[85] the Court considered the case of a female who had been employed by the defendant agency in its "Careers Division." She had had several years experience in the field at the time of her hiring, and was rapidly promoted and given additional responsibilities when her supervisor resigned. Nevertheless, the supervisory position that she had applied for remained vacant for months. Finally, a male from another division was brought in to fill the upgraded position, and the plaintiff was discharged, leaving only a male professional in the division. The court of appeals[86] held that since Burdine had demonstrated a *prima facie* case of gender discrimination, the defendant agency had the responsibility of "proving . . . the existence of legitimate non-discriminatory reasons for the employment action" and to "prove . . . that those hired or promoted were better qualified than plaintiff."

The Supreme Court disagreed.[87] Even if an inference of unlawful discrimination may be drawn, all that the defendent agency must do is to produce evidence "that the plaintiff was rejected, or someone else was preferred, for a legitimate non-discriminatory reason." The plaintiff retains the burden of proving that the reason was only a pretext and that the real intent was to discriminate. Obviously, this will be very difficult for plaintiffs to do.

Furthermore, the Court held that the defendant did not have "to show that the plaintiff's objective qualification was inferior to the person selected."

> Title VII does not obligate an employer to accord this preference. Rather the employer has discretion to choose among equally qualified candidates, provided the decision is not based upon unlawful criteria.

This is not an open invitation to discriminate. The legal as well as moral obligation on Central City's Parks and Recreation Department, or any leisure service agency, remains as firm as ever. Rather, once the agency takes the steps to provide full employment opportunities, always remaining on guard against subtle and unconscious as well as overt job prejudice, the best person should be selected for a position regardless of race, religion, national origin, ethnic background, or gender.

## WORKERS' COMPENSATION AND LEISURE SERVICES

Another area of concern to managers and administrators involves workers' compensation statutes. Since the first modern American compensation act was passed in New York in 1910, every state and territory and all of the Canadian provinces have enacted comprehensive legislation protecting employees from the financial burdens of occupational injuries. There are also several federal compensation statutes, most notably the Federal Employees Compensation Act,[88] covering government workers, and the Longshoremen's and Harbor Workers Compensation Act,[89] protecting privately employed workers engaged in interstate and international maritime commerce.

The essence of workers' compensation is exquisitely simple. Disabilities, temporary and permanent, and death that occur as the result of an injury "arising out of and in the course of" employment will be compensated on the basis of a percentage of the worker's salary up to a statutory maximum.

A typical maximum today would be two-thirds of the average income of all workers covered by unemployment insurance within a state, or the state's average weekly wage. The District of Columbia is currently the most generous jurisdiction, permitting weekly compensation for lost wages up to 200 percent of the national average. In 1981 this maximum was $456.24 a week. At the other extreme were Mississippi with a maximum of $98 and Florida and Georgia with $110 weekly maximums. Most states also have statutory minimum amounts.

We must emphasize that these maximum weekly benefits are intended to ensure only that a disabled worker receives enough compensation to maintain a modest living. An employee who had earned $1000 per week will still receive only the statutory maximum plus whatever personal insurance and social security benefits she may be entitled to.

In addition to partial compensation for lost salaries, workers' compensation provides for reimbursement of the medical costs resulting from an injury and for rehabilitation expenses. These vary widely from state to state, but they are generally quite liberal, since a primary goal of workers' compensation is to return an individual to a productive role in society.

Although the basic structure of workers' compensation may be simple, the details are very complex. There are, for example, several different kinds of compensation payments.

Perhaps the easiest way to understand the system is to follow an imaginary employee through the process. We shall use New Jersey[90] as our model, not only because we are familiar with it, but also because it is among the most developed and progressive of the state systems.

### The Swamptown Fourth of July Example

Mary Doe is a recreation supervisor employed by the Swamptown, New Jersey, Recreation and Parks Department. On July 4, 1981, she was injured by an exploding firecracker at a Fourth of July celebration that she was supervising. Putting aside her own insurance or other insurance supplied by her employer, and assuming no disputes as to eligibility, here is how the compensation system would work.

First, notice is given to Swamptown, Mary's employer. This must be given within fourteen days, but failure may be excused up to ninety days. Special-notice provisions apply to occupational diseases whose effects might not be realized until years after exposure. On the other hand, very short notice is required of such injuries as a hernia where there might be fraud and proof problems.

After a seven-day waiting period, Mary Doe should begin to receive temporary total compensation (assuming her salary has been cut off) for as long as she is being treated and is recuperating and unable to work, up to a maximum of 400 weeks.

The requirement of a waiting period is to discourage use of the workers' compensation machinery for minor short-term disabilities. If the disability continues for a certain time (two to four weeks in most states) the initial waiting period is waived and compensation is paid for the full period. Many states, including New Jersey, found that the effect of a waiting period was to prompt workers to file claims for minor permanent injuries because they felt cheated at not being compensated for their temporary injuries. Thus the retroactive period has been shortened or eliminated in several states. In New Jersey, Mary Doe would receive full temporary disability compensation, including the first seven days, after only eight days off the job.

Most minor claims are settled between employer and employee, subject to approval of the agency administering the law, in this case, the New Jersey Division of Worker's Compensation. If there is a dispute, it will be submitted to an administrative judge who is an expert in workers' compensation. Appeals are ultimately heard through the normal appellate judicial system.

Now things begin to get complicated. If workers' compensation were purely a device for replacing lost income, it would seem appropriate that Mary Doe's payments would cease as soon as she returned to work. However, all legislatures, including New Jersey's, have determined that there should be some compensation for permanent injuries even if they have no bearing on actual income.

A partial justification is that even if a substantial injury doesn't affect current employment, it may have negative implications for future promotion or getting or qualifying for other positions. Thus, if Mary has permanent burns, in most states she would receive a degree of compensation called permanent partial. Sometimes judicial attempts to justify such awards on the basis of relationship to employment verge on the ludicrous. For example, a Delaware minister was compensated for a work-related injury in which he was burned on the back.[91] The court acknowledged that the scars would normally be invisible, but nevertheless concluded that the minister might have to change ceremonial vestments in front of others or to don a bathing suit to perform a baptism; therefore, compensation was justified. It is certainly far more intellectually honest to acknowledge, as many courts now do, that permanent injuries may be compensated even where there is no potential dimunition of earnings.

Although payments for generalized permanent injuries may be based, in some states, on a percentage of the difference between wages earned before and after the injury, New Jersey and other states compensate on the basis of a percentage of total disability. Therefore, if Mary Doe suffered a permanent back injury causing her difficulty in bending as well as permanent burns, she might receive a benefit of 25 percent of *permanent total disability* based on a rough estimate of potential loss of future employment and general life problems. This would be based upon a 450-week compensation period (in addition to the time period during which Mary was temporarily totally disabled). Some jurisdictions also provide for *temporary partial disability.*

If Mary was permanently totally disabled and rehabilitation failed to improve her condition to the point where she could rejoin the work force on a regular basis, that 450-week period could be extended for life, with the proviso that if Mary found employment from time to time, the amount of compensation would be reduced during those periods.

Again, each state has its own system for limiting or extending permanent total compensation, and many are less liberal than New Jersey's.

Legislatures were not content to let courts or workers' compensation agencies make all of the determinations of the amount of compensation for permanent partial injuries. In all states except Florida and Nevada, there is a "schedule of benefits" for specific injuries. These have no direct relation to actual wage loss, and, in fact, appear to the casual observer to be a rather ghoulish attempt to put a dollar value on various parts of the body. For example, in New Jersey, if Mary Doe had her hand amputated as a result of the fireworks accident, she would currently receive $29,255 in permanent compensation. If she lost only her third finger, the amount would be a mere $1,833. Loss of use of a limb without amputation would be reflected in a reduced amount of compensation. There are all manner of combinations and percentages of schedule injuries depending upon the degree of loss. Because the schedule amounts are not tied directly to loss of employment, they may often be paid in a lump sum, even though calculated on a percentage of total disability. (Thus in New Jersey, under a complicated formula with rates changing to reflect the seriousness of injuries, loss of a thumb gets 75 weeks of compensation, and loss of a leg is compensated for 315 weeks.)

When someone is permanently and totally disabled, the courts frown upon reducing their award to a lump sum. Since workers' compensation is viewed as replacement income in this context, there is fear that if it is all paid at once, it may be squandered, leaving the injured worker to the mercy of public charity or welfare. Assume that Mary Doe grew up in an urban area and had spent her working life on the playground. If she were totally disabled, the court would probably paternalistically refuse her plea to give her all of her compensation at once so she could invest in a chicken farm.

An additional complication should be mentioned. Suppose Mary's injuries, although serious, do not totally physically disable her in the ordinary sense of that term, but because of her lifelong involvement in recreation programming, the loss of her hand and other injuries make it impossible for her to find regular employment in her chosen field, and she is not readily able to move into another area of endeavor. In many states Mary would be considered an "odd lot," and because of the combination of physical injuries, the economics of the labor market, and, to some degree, her emotional and psychological state she would be held to be permanently totally disabled.

Obviously the "odd lot" doctrine is readily subject to abuse. In fact, the New Jersey legislature recently became so aroused by what it considered an excessive number of individuals with relatively minor impairment who were found permanently disabled by the courts that it amended the workers' compensation law to provide that:

> Factors other than physical and neuropsychiatric impairment may be considered in the determination of permanent total disability where such physical and neuropsychiatric impairment constitutes at least 75% or higher of total disability.[92]

## Second Injury Funds

One of the more constructive aspects of workers' compensation law is the prevalence of "second injury funds." These are special programs designed to encourage employers to hire and retain partially disabled workers by relieving the employers of the additional burdens of compensating for cumulative injuries caused by more than one accident. If Mary Doe had previously lost a hand in an unrelated accident, an employer might be disinclined to hire her for fear that if she were injured in the future, the combination of injuries might cause permanent total disability. The second injury funds, which are derived from assessments against insurance carriers or from special state appropriations, pay the difference between the loss directly caused by an accident in current employment and the total disability which is the combination of past and current disabilities. In order to be able to take advantage of such funds, it is very important that the employer have a full, documented history of an employee's health at the time of employment.

## The "Course of Employment" Requirement and Extent of Coverage

In addition to coverage and death benefits for the results of work-place accidents, modern workers' compensation statutes provide coverage for occupational diseases, either through a schedule or a general statement of coverage.

Difficulties often arise in attempting to link a disease with a specific risk of employment. Although it is clear that black lung disease is linked to mining and brown lung to the textile industry, could Mary Doe claim she caught the flu because of her contact with children on the playground? What about chicken pox? Most courts reject tenuous connections between illness and work, particularly if the disease is a common risk of life. As a general rule, the more common the disease, the greater the proof must be of causation by special conditions of the work.

Perhaps the most vexing problem of coverage of workers' compensation today revolves around heart attacks, strokes, and related circulatory problems. Is a heart attack a disease or an "accident"? Does the fact that the stresses of work over a period of years contribute to a degenerating heart condition justify compensation? Should the fact that an employee like Mary Doe was under unusual strain in supervising the Fourth of July festivities, or that she had been engaging in unusual physical exertion during the fireworks program when she suffered a heart attack render the attack compensible? These are intractable problems in which courts try to balance the desire to liberally compensate work-related injuries with the fear that workers' compensation may get out of hand, forcing the employer to become a general insurer of the health and safety of all employees.

Most problems of coverage revolve around the "arising out of and in the course of employment" language which is standard in compensation laws. Today, most injuries that are even marginally work related will be compensated. Injuries occurring during "horseplay," work breaks, and even, in the most liberal jurisdictions, lunch breaks off the premises will be compensated even when general work rules are being violated. The courts reason that the employee is not a machine; the employer hires a total person complete with human weaknesses. It is only when deviations are so extreme that it can be said that there has been an abandonment of work that most courts will reject a compensation claim.

Of particular interest to leisure service professionals is the attitude of courts toward injuries that take place during employer-sponsored recreation programs. Mixed business and pleasure trips such as excursions to a football game with a client or company picnics will fall within compensation coverage, particularly where the employer has some formal involvement in sponsorship and financing of the activity. The same may be said for company-sponsored employee participation in sports.

Courts justify these holdings on the basis that company-sponsored recreation provides physical benefits and promotes loyalty and high morale, which increase productivity and are, therefore, a value to the employer. In fact the New Jersey courts went so far in permitting compensation for injuries received in informal recreational activities[93] that the legislature responded by decreeing that compensation would not be applicable "unless . . . recreational or social activities are a regular incident of employment and produce a benefit to the employer beyond improvement in employee health and morale . . . ."[94]

It will be interesting to see if other states follow suit. Those involved in industrial recreation should pay particularly close attention to compensation trends in their state, since an employer's willingness to sponsor recreational activities may, in part, be dependent upon what they perceive to be the potential for compensation liability.

There is a general rule that employees are not protected by workers' compensation while going to or coming from work; however, the rule is riddled with exceptions. Among the most significant to parks and leisure services is the rule that if an employee is traveling between work assignments, he is in the course of employment. A recreation supervisor who leaves home and heads directly for a park or recreation site before checking into the office or who is on the way to or returning from a special activity such as a teen dance or a night ball game would probably be covered. In short, where time and destination vary, and where an employee is not on a fixed routine, compensation for injury is likely. Furthermore, when the employer furnishes transportation or compensates for expenses, a good argument can be made that the worker is within the scope of employment.

When a recreation employee is required by the nature of the work to reside temporarily or permanently at a work site, particularly if on call (as would be the case with a camp counselor, a park ranger, or a recreation therapist residing at an institution), a good deal of the ordinary activities of life will be considered within the ambit of employment for compensation purposes. For example, in one notorious case, a state game warden who patrolled a large area was found dead of carbon monoxide poisoning on an isolated stretch of road. The interior of the warden's car had been made up into a bed, and lying next to him in an unclad state was the body of a young lady named Chelsea Miami. Compensation to the warden's dependents was affirmed because the nature of his job sometimes required him to spend the night in the woods and there were no rules forbidding him to have company while on duty.[95]

A unique but significant case that takes on increased importance in the current controversy over the professionalization of college athletics is *University of Denver v. Nemeth.*[96] The claimant, a football player, was injured during spring practice. He was dropped from the squad and lost all financial aid, including his "job" of keeping litter off the tennis courts. The court ruled that since the employment was conditioned on young Nemeth (not to be confused with Joe Namath) playing football, his injury was compensable.

This example, although extraordinary, indicates the general liberality with which courts regard workers' compensation. It is remedial legislation intended to meet a major social problem. Funded by private insurance, state funds or, in the case of some large employers and government agencies, self-insurance, workers' compensation replaces the traditional tort liability-adversary system for a substantial proportion of injuries. Because claims are processed through specialized agencies and cooperation is encouraged, the compensation procedure is often, but not always, less costly and time-consuming than traditional litigation.

Since fault is not normally a factor in workers' compensation and an employee's own negligence will not affect his recovery, what does the employer gain from participating in the system? Conversely, what does the employee give up?

First, an employee covered by compensation may not sue the employer or a co-worker in negligence even if the injury would ordinarily produce a much higher recovery in a liability action. At least until very recently, when maximum compensation has been somewhat liberalized, compensation awards were much lower than tort judgments. Secondly, if a third party or independent contractor is found even partly responsible for the injury, most states permit the employer to be indemnified, that is, reimbursed for compensation payments even if the employer might have been at fault.

## Exemptions

Who is covered by compensation? Participation is compulsory for most private occupations in virtually all states. In the few states where it is theoretically voluntary, the procedures and legal disabilities related to rejection of compensation render the voluntary nature effectively mandatory. There are a few states, mostly in the South, that permit small-scale employers (of up to three to five workers) to avoid the system. Many states exclude most agricultural and domestic workers from coverage. Some exempt corporate officers and employees of charitable or religious organizations.

With regard to governmental employees, the pattern is a bit more complex. Some states exclude elected officials. Others have specific provisions covering or exempting trainees in state and federal training programs and handicapped workers in state operated sheltered workshops.

Part-time recreational workers are usually covered, even if their compensation is limited to expenses and meals. For example, in an Oregon case, *Buckner v. Kennedy's Riding Academy*,[97] a teenage girl was injured by a horse while she was doing chores around the stable. The petitioner was one of several girls who spent time around the stable, only one of whom would be paid on any particular day. Nevertheless, the fact that Buckner was given a free lunch, "free use of the horses for riding and an occasional payment of a couple of dollars . . . is sufficient as remuneration." The court found that her injuries were compensable and took into consideration the fact that the chores that she did were an integral part of the operation of the stable, and that the owner exercised control and direction over her work efforts.

The largest category of those who perform work but are exempt from workers' compensation coverage are those considered to be *independent contractors*. These are individuals who have a distinct and separate profession or occupation, often unrelated to the employer's regular business, who are not directly subject to the employer's control and instruction and who normally have the trappings of independent businesspeople (i.e., insurance, advertising, separate office, etc.). Even if the injured worker appears to be independent, in a number of states, if the work she was engaged upon was integral to the functioning of the employer's business and if there was no real economic independence, workers' compensation coverage would be required.

As an example, let us suppose that Central City wishes to offer a summer tennis instruction program. If the Central City Recreation Department contracts with an independently incorporated or established tennis school to conduct its operation, or if it merely leases court space to tennis professionals who will supply their own equipment and charge and retain their own fees, Central City may escape compensation responsibility if there is an injury to an instructor. On the other hand, if Central City provides the instructors with racquets and balls for use in the program, if it pays an hourly or weekly salary rather than an overall percentage of receipts or a flat fee, if it instructs the tennis teachers or exercises control over the details of their work, they may be considered employees. This would be particularly likely under the "relative nature of the work" test, which would find tennis instruction integral to Central City's recreation department's activities.

Most of the remaining intricacies of workers' compensation may be left to the insurers and the lawyers, but a couple of points significant to the leisure services field bear comment.

Although many recreation positions are part-time or seasonal in nature, that does not mean that the injured employee will receive only a percentage of his part-time wage. Most states have statutory minimums. More importantly, many jurisdictions attempt to translate part-time earnings into a full-time or potential full-time equivalent through one formula or another. Thus in a 1972 Michigan decision,[98] the decedent died while officiating at a football game for which he was being paid $15. The court divided his previous year's earnings as a referee by the number of days he had actually worked and ascertained that $15 was an appropriate daily figure. They then multiplied the $15 by five to reflect an ordinary work week and reached a figure of $75 per week as the basis for compensation.

Although workers' compensation laws generally exempt "casual" employments, as *Buckner v. Kennedy's Riding Academy* demonstrates, the exemption doesn't usually apply if the work being performed is within the normal course of business of the employer. Thus even a very brief period of employment, say as an aide in a one-week tiny tots class or as an extra guard at a rock concert, would probably be considered to fall within compensation protection. On the other hand, a pure volunteer such as the manager of a Little League team[99] would not be considered an employee.

## Conclusion

Let us briefly address the questions of what the leisure services professional should do to ensure that the compensation system works fairly and effectively.

Obviously, in a system that is so liberal in granting recoveries, fraud is a major problem. Employers should establish procedures and forms for prompt notice of injuries by workers to supervisors. Of course, there must also be immediate medical attention to injuries, with a full report of the nature, extent, and circumstances surrounding the accident.

At the other end of the spectrum, professionals should emphasize the rehabilitative aspects of workers' compensation. The real value of the system is in returning employees to their functions as productive individuals with a sense of self-worth and dignity. Certainly the leisure service profession has a major role to play in this aspect of compensation.

## UNEMPLOYMENT COMPENSATION

Unemployment compensation is a form of social security that protects workers against loss of income when they are involuntarily unemployed.

With unemployment in the United States consistently running at an annual rate of 5 to 8 percent or higher, the availability of income security is of great importance. This is particularly the case in leisure services. Private recreation feels the pinch of loss of discretionary income, high energy costs, and the generally increased costs of doing business; voluntary agencies notice the general reduction in financial support; and public recreation and park services are cut in efforts to limit the cost of government. Furthermore, the seasonal nature of much of recreation results in many workers in the field being underemployed.

We shall attempt to give only a brief outline of the unemployment system and its peculiar problems. Each state has its own unemployment compensation law and there is great variation within a general framework prescribed by federal statute. In fact, unemployment compensation is a unique blend of coercive federal taxation and state administrative machinery.

Fundamental to the scheme is a federal tax[100] imposed on employers at a basic rate of 3.2 percent (3.4 percent in certain high unemployment situations) of the first $6000 of wages paid to each employee, but the employer is allowed a credit against that tax of 90 percent of taxes paid into a state unemployment fund up to a certain maximum. A state is forced to have an unemployment compensation plan because benefits are paid only under state, not federal, law. Therefore, without a state plan the employer and employee would receive no benefit from the federal tax.

There are major variations in tax rates paid by employers based on "experience ratings." Thus employers have an interest in ensuring continuity of employment. From a litigation standpoint, experience rating also means that employers will sometimes resist unemployment claims. The employer will argue that a worker left voluntarily or was dismissed for some disqualifying cause such as misconduct, which would prevent the worker, at least temporarily, from being eligible for benefits.

Although states are permitted substantial discretion in creating or modifying unemployment schemes, the federal government requires that monies collected under a state plan be deposited in a special fund in the

United States Treasury.[101] Federal authorities may appropriate federal funds to be used by the states in administering their unemployment programs. Therefore, the United States Labor Department retains considerable power to influence state actions. One of the federal requirements is that each state must have an employment service and that there must be a state plan for job promotion, development, counseling, and placement of handicapped workers.[102]

Since 1972, Congress has expanded requirements for unemployment coverage to include a number of state institutions and nonprofit organizations.

Major exceptions are similar to those discussed under workers' compensation. Independent contractors, domestic workers, "casual" workers, and many agricultural workers are generally exempted from unemployment compensation coverage.

### Requirements

Although state schemes vary, there are two general areas of requirements for unemployment compensation. The first is eligibility. A worker must be unemployed; he must have filed for benefits; he must be available for work, able to work, and have made reasonable efforts to obtain work in the region. Most importantly, he must have been employed for a certain time period prior to becoming unemployed. Those who were never employed or who are chronically underemployed will probably not benefit from unemployment compensation, or will cease to receive benefits after a fairly lengthy period of unemployment.

Secondly, and of greatest concern to the employer-employee relationship, applicants must not have been disqualified for benefits by reason of the nature of their leaving their employment, although in some states disqualification may only be temporary, and workers who are unemployed long enough will receive benefits if they are otherwise entitled to them. Let us expand upon some of these requirements. An unemployed worker must do more than merely register at a state employment office. She must "make an independent, diligent search for work in ... [the] locality."[103] Although an unemployed person may not be forced to submit to work in a separate field for which she is not qualified, refusal to accept a comparable though somewhat different position may result in loss of unemployment compensation. Thus a recreation therapist who loses his job at a nursing home for geriatrics may not be able to reject a position as a recreation therapist at a center for rehabilitating accident victims even if the pay scales, assignments, and conditions of work are somewhat different.

Retired people, those who are severely impaired, or physically ill persons may not qualify because they are not really a part of the labor market. In sum, the more unrealistic and inflexible a person's demands are and the more serious their limitations, the greater the likelihood that their eligibility for continued unemployment compensation will be challenged.

Misconduct and fraud will disqualify a worker, at least temporarily, from unemployment eligibility.[104] A number of states disqualify workers who voluntarily leave their employment "without good cause." Some states require that the "good cause" be attributable to the employer, not related to personal reasons such as a family move.

Because of the important social purposes of unemployment compensation, most courts require disqualifying "misconduct" to have an element of culpability or willfulness beyond the ordinary failures and dissatisfaction of employment. Thus, for example, if a park maintenance person were discharged when she overwatered the grass or forgot to fertilize some delicate plants, that in itself would probably be insufficient to be disqualifying misconduct.

Typically, state laws disqualify workers who are unemployed because of participation in a strike or labor dispute, although a growing number of jurisdictions will not disqualify workers who have not struck but have been "locked out" by employers during a dispute.[105]

### Benefits

Each state's laws differ with regard to the benefits to be received, but the general pattern is that a qualified worker who has earnings over several immediately past quarters will receive a benefit based upon average earnings up to a typical maximum of twenty-six weeks with provisions to extend that maximum during periods of chronic unemployment. These benefits will be charged in varying proportions to the accounts of employers for whom the worker labored during the base earnings period.

Professional athletes whose activities are seasonal are generally disqualified, as are those employed by educational institutions during summer recesses, periods between semesters, and the like.

To illustrate how unemployment compensation currently operates, let us briefly consider the Pennsylvania law.[106] Here, in order to qualify for benefits, an individual must have been employed for at least eighteen "credit" weeks during a "base" year. A "credit" week is defined as one in which there was at least $50 in wages and the "base" year is four of the last five calendar quarters prior to filing for compensation.

Once benefits begin, the qualified individual is eligible for payments of from $35 up to $162 per week during the "benefit year," with the weekly maximum adjusted annually to reflect the average wage in the state. The maximum benefits for the year may ordinarily not exceed thirty weeks, but Pennsylvania law has a provision for extended benefits when, under a complicated definition, there is relatively high local or national unemployment.

## Conclusion

Unemployment compensation is subject to considerable criticism from all sides of the political spectrum. On the one hand, many state systems are subject to fraud and abuse, rewarding individuals who appear to be avoiding rather than seeking work. On the other hand, compensation is too little and too short-lived to really aid the hard-core unemployed or chronically underemployed. Yet, more radical solutions such as massive governmentally funded retraining and employment programs, negative income tax, or a guaranteed annual wage do not command substantial popular or political support in this country. Thus, for the foreseeable future, unemployemt compensation will continue to provide an unsatisfactory answer to a chronic problem.

## NOTES

1. See, for example, Charles O. Gregory, *Labor and the Law* (New York: W. W. Norton, 1946); Archibald Cox, *Law and the National Labor Policy* (Los Angeles: University of California Institute of Industrial Relations, 1960); and Morris O. Forkosch, *A Treatise in Labor Law* (Indianapolis: Bobbs-Merrill, 1953).
2. 23 Edw. III, cc. 1,2 (1349).
3. *Rex v. Journeymen Tailors of Cambridge*, 8 Mod. 10 (1721).
4. *Commonwealth v. Hunt*, 4 Metcalf, III (Mass. 1842).
5. See *Coppage v. Kansas*, 236 U.S. 1 (1915), *Hitchman Coal & Coke Co. v. Mitchell*, 245 U.S. 229 (1917), and *Eagle Glass and Mfg. Co. v. Rowe*, 245 U.S. 275 (1917).
6. 45 U.S.C.A. § 152.
7. 29 U.S.C.A. §§ 101-115.
8. 29 U.S.C.A. §§ 151-168, as amended by the Taft-Hartley Act (29 U.S.C.A. § 141 et. seq.).
9. 301 U.S. 1 (1937).
10. Address by Jerry Wurf, Federal Bar Association, March 28, 1968, as quoted in Marvin Levine and Eugene Hagburg, *Labor Relations in the Public Sector* (Salt Lake City: Brighton, 1979).
11. Quoted in Levine and Hagburg, *supra* note 10, at 70.

12. A. H. Raskin, "The Big Squeeze on Labor Unions," *Atlantic Monthly*, October, 1978, at 41.
13. Wisc. Stat. Ann. § 111.70-71.
14. Stuart Linnick in *Public Sector Labor Relations* (Practising Law Institute, 1980).
15. 29 U.S.C.A. § 158(d).
16. *N.L.R.B. v. Montgomery Ward and Company*, 133 F.2d 676, 686 (9th Cir. 1943).
17. For a listing of state statutes relating to public sector labor-management relations see, Joyce M. Najita, *Guide to Statutory Provisions in Public Sector Collective Bargaining* (Honolulu: University of Hawaii, Industrial Relations Center, 1978).
18. *Safeway Trails, Inc.*, 233 NLRB No. 171 (1977).
20. *General Motors Acceptance Corporation v. N.L.R.B.*, 476 F.2d 850 (1st Cir. 1973).
21. *N.L.R.B. v. Industrial Wire Products Corporation*, 455 F.2d 673 (9th Cir. 1972).
22. *N.L.R.B. v. General Electric Company*, 418 F.2d 736 (2d Cir. 1969). G.E.'s chief negotiator, Lemuel Boulware, used a bargaining strategy in which his first offer was also his final offer. This tactic, later called "Boulwarism," was frowned upon by the NLRB and the courts.
23. See *Fibreboard Corp. v. N.L.R.B.*, 379 U.S. 203 (1964).
24. *Bio-Science Laboratories*, 209 N.L.R.B. 796 (1974).
25. See J. Nicholas Counter III, "Impact of Fiscal Limitations upon the Bargaining Process—The California Experience," *Public Sector Labor Relations 1980* (Practising Law Institute, 1980).
26. 66 Misc. 2d 1070, 323 N.Y.S.2d 442, (Sup. Ct. Sp. Term, 1971).
27. *People v. Richards*, 177 Misc. 912, 31 N.Y.S.2d 457 (Nassau Cty. D.C., 1941).
28. *Supra* note 26 at 1079.
29. Wesley M. Wilson, *Labor Law Handbook* (Indianapolis: Bobbs-Merrill, 1963).
30. See "Voluntary Labor Arbitration Rules" (New York: American Arbitration Association, 1975).
31. 29 U.S.C.A. § 1001 et. seq.
32. 29 U.S.C.A. §§ 201-219.
33. 29 U.S.C.A. § 651 et. seq.
34. 42 U.S.C.A. § 2000e et. seq.
35. § 701(b).
36. § 702.
37. 42 U.S.C.A. § 1981.
38. See *McDonald v. Santa Fe Trail Transportation Co.*, 427 U.S. 273 (1976).
39. *Guerra v. Manchester Terminal Corp.*, 498 F.2d 641 (5th Cir. 1974).
40. *Johnson v. Railway Express Agency, Inc.*, 421 U.S. 454 (1975).
41. *Sethy v. Alameda County Water Dist.*, 545 F.2d 1157 (9th Cir., 1976).
42. *Brown v. General Services Adm'n.*, 425 U.S. 820 (1976).

43. 42 U.S.C.A. § 1985.
44. *Griffin v. Breckenridge*, 403 U.S. 88 (1971).
45. See *Life Ins. Co. of North America v. Reichardt*, 591 F.2d 499 (9th Cir. 1979).
46. 29 U.S.C.A. § 791.
47. 29 U.S.C.A. § 793.
48. 29 U.S.C.A. § 794.
49. 442 U.S. 397 (1979).
50. 38 U.S.C.A. § 2012.
51. 29 U.S.C.A. § 621.
52. 29 U.S.C.A. § 633(a).
53. 29 U.S.C.A. § 206(d).
54. See, for example, *Shultz v. Wheaton Glass Co.*, 421 F.2d 259, (3rd Cir. 1970), cert. den, 398 U.S. 905 (1970).
55. 101 S. Ct. 2242 (1981).
56. § 703(h), the "Bennett Amendment."
57. Regulations under Executive Order 11246 are codified in various parts of Title 41 of the CFR. Also consult Uniform Guidelines on Employee Selection Procedures.
58. 20 U.S.C.A. § 1681.
59. See *Seattle University v. United States Department of HEW*, 621 F.2d 992, cert. gr. 449 U.S. 1009, (1980).
60. *North Haven Board of Education v. Hufstedler*, 629 F.2d 773 (2d Cir. 1980), cert. gr. 101 S. Ct. 1345 (1981).
61. For example, see the Comprehensive New Jersey Law Against Discrimination, N.J.S.A. 10:5-1 et. seq.
62. See, Note: Equal Rights Provisions—The Experience Under State Constitutions, 65 *Calif. L. Rev.* 1086 (1977).
63. Pa. Const. Art. I., § 28.
64. § 712.
65. *Personnel Adm'n. of Massachusetts v. Feeney*, 442 U.S. 256 (1979).
66. *Gay Law Students Assn. v. Pacific Tel. and Tel.*, 24 Cal. 3d 458, 156 Cal. Rptr. 14, 595 P.2d 592 (1979).
67. 427 U.S. 273 (1976).
68. 443 U.S. 193 (1979).
69. 29 CFR, part 1608.
70. 29 CFR, part 1604.
71. § 706(g).
72. See *Rios v. Enterprise Assn. Steamfitters, Loc. 638*, 501 F.2d 622 (2d Cir. 1974).
73. § 703(h).
74. 401 U.S. 424 (1971).
75. 426 U.S. 229 (1976).
76. 29 CFR, part 1607 (1979).
77. § 703(e).

78. 29 U.S.C.A. § 623(f)(1).

79. See 29 CFR 860.102(f)(1).

80. *Hodgson v. Greyhound Lines, Inc.*, 499 F.2d 859 (7th Cir. 1974), cert. denied 419 U.S. 1122 (1974).

81. *Diaz v. Pan American World Airways, Inc.*, 442 F.2d 385 (5th Cir. 1971).

82. *Dothard v. Rawlinson*, 433 U.S. 321 (1977).

83. See *Harriss v. Pan American World Airways*, 637 F.2d 1297 (9th Cir. 1980), (withdrawn from publication).

84. See § 703(h) of Title VII.

85. 450 U.S. 248, (1981).

86. 608 F.2d 563 (5th Cir. 1979).

87. *Supra* note 85.

88. 5 U.S.C.A. § 8147 et. seq.

89. 33 U.S.C.A. §§ 901-950.

90. N.J. Rev. Stat. 34:15-1 et. seq.

91. *Beam v. Chrysler Corp.*, 332 A.2d 143 (Del. 1975).

92. N.J. Rev. Stat. 34:15-36.

93. See *Tocci v. Tessler & Weiss, Inc.*, 28 N.J. 582, 147 A.2d 783 (1959).

94. N.J. Rev. Stat. 34:15-7.

95. *State Employees Retirement System v. Industrial Accident Commission*, 97 Cal. App.2d 3801, 217 P.2d 992 (1950).

96. 127 Colo. 385, 257 P.2d 423 (1953).

97. 526 P.2d 450 (Or. App. 1974).

98. *Mora v. Fowlerville Pub. School Sys.*, 37 Mich. App. 371, 194 N.W.2d 481 (1972).

99. *Cerniglia v. City of Passaic*, 50 N.J. Super 201, 141 A.2d 558, (App. Div. 1958).

100. 26 U.S.C.A. §§ 3301 et. seq.

101. 42 U.S.C.A. §§ 1101 et. seq.

102. 29 U.S.C.A. § 49.

103. *Texas Employment Com. v. Holberg*, 440 S.W.2d 38 (Tex. 1969).

104. See 26 U.S.C.A. § 3304(a)(11).

105. See, for example, *National Gypsum Co. v. Administrator, Louisiana Dept. of Education Security*, 313 So.2d 230 (La. 1975).

106. Penna. Stats. Annot. 43:801 et. seq.

# 7

# Administrative
# Topics in Brief

Parks, recreation, and leisure services, along with most other complex fields of endeavor, touches the law at many points. Lest this book become an encyclopedia, we have necessarily had to be somewhat selective. In this chapter we deal with several topics that are enormously complex and usually require the attention of legal specialists. Nevertheless, since they are of importance to leisure service we have tried to provide at least a minimal introduction.

## CRIMINAL LAW

Criminal law is a major area of legal responsibility with which parks and leisure services personnel have become all too familiar in recent years.

In addition to the unhappily familiar litany of crimes that affect all of society, there are, of course, crimes with specific application to parks situations. Among these are federal, state, and local laws dealing with criminal trespass, vandalism of monuments and natural resources, and the whole range of violations of fish, game, and firearm laws that plague national and state forests and parks.

For example, a federal statute provides:

Whoever, except in compliance with rules and regulations promulgated by authority of law, hunts, traps, captures, wilfully disturbs or kills any bird, fish or wild animal of any kind whatever, or takes or destroys the eggs or nest of any such bird or fish, on any lands or waters which are set apart or reserved as sanctuaries, refuges or breeding grounds . . . or wilfully injures, molests, or destroys any property of the United States on any such lands or waters, shall be fined not more than $500 or imprisoned not more than six months, or both.[1]

Another federal statute provides for penalties ranging up to a $10,000 fine or one year imprisonment for illegal transportation of wildlife in violation of state, federal, or even foreign laws.[2]

Because of the physical danger and specialized skills and technical knowledge required, parks employees, rangers, and police charged with enforcement of criminal laws must receive intensive training. The coordination of law enforcement functions with more traditional visitor services is more a matter of management and supervision than it is of law. Nevertheless, any park professional who is in regular contact with the public must be prepared for confrontation with some aspect of criminal behavior, if only as a witness. Park planners must keep crime prevention in mind as they develop facility master plans. And, as indicated above, at the higher levels of parks management, administrators may find themselves in a position where cooperation with police or even nominal supervision of law enforcement personnel is a routine aspect of their professional duties.

## Basic Criminal Law Principles

A useful guide to modern criminal law is the *Model Penal Code* published by the American Law Institute. This is the criminal law equivalent to the institute's restatements of common-law civil topics such as torts and contracts, but it is more reform oriented. The *Model Penal Code* contains not only modern and simplified definitions of crimes, but also proposed reforms and redefinitions of such vexing problems of criminal law as the insanity defense and the punishment of victimless crimes such as sexual deviation, prostitution, and gambling.

There are a number of serious offenses against person or property recognized as *felonies*, the most reprehensible form of individual antisocial behavior. These were first enunciated in the common law, although they have been codified in many states.

Common-law felonies include murder, arson, burglary, kidnapping, rape and robbery. Historically, there are complex definitional distinction between the various felonies. For example, robbery involved direct larceny from a person by force or threat of force. Burglary required the "breaking" and entering of a home or dwelling place at night for the purpose of committing a felony, usually larceny. In addition to felonies, most states define some offenses as *misdemeanors*, less serious crimes with suitably milder punishments. A familiar example would be the distinction between *grand* and *petit larceny*, the latter concerned with theft of small sums. Disorderly persons offenses and simple *violations* such as a parking violation or minor traffic offenses may be separately categorized. To add to the confusion, in some states felonies are known as *high misde-meanors.*

As indicated, definitions vary from state to state. For example, many states have two degrees of murder. *First-degree murder* includes premeditated killings and those that occur during the commission of other felonies in which there is a substantial likihood of violence. Under a *felony-murder* charge, a participant in a violent crime may be convicted even though he did not directly participate in the killing. *Second-degree murder* usually involves deaths resulting from intentional assaults and other actions that are sufficiently dangerous to threaten serious bodily harm, but do not imply an actual intent to kill.

Lesser but still obviously dangerous conduct leading to the death of another may be characterized as *involuntary manslaughter.* Examples include reckless or grossly negligent conduct such as driving at extreme speeds in a crowded area or taking target practice with live ammunition near a campground.

The degree of seriousness or the culpability of a perpetrator of a criminal act is, of course, a matter of substantial concern for criminal justice and penal officials. Length of sentence and conditions of incarceration depend, to a degree, on the peculiar nature of the act. This is not the prime responsibility of park officials, whose interest in protecting the public as well as park property is equally great whatever the motivation or the nature of the criminal.

### Criminal Law and Parks: Basic Procedural Problems

Although major crimes like murder and rape command the bulk of the attention of criminal law, they are still, fortunately, rare occurrences in most parks. Nevertheless, as recent studies indicate, fear of violent crime has resulted in underutilization of park facilities and a diversion of funds from leisure services to protective activities. Most of the illegal behavior of routine concern to park professionals may be regarded as breaches of regulations, minor misdemeanors, or disorderly persons offenses, but that does not mean such conduct is not serious in a collective sense. Littering, vandalism, graffiti, public drunkenness, and similar activities erode and destroy the values for which a park was created. These acts are not confined to poverty pockets and depressed urban parks; they may often be found in well-to-do suburban areas. In our urbanized national parks crime problems mirror the society as a whole. Even in wildlands and more remote national parks, improper fires, hiking in prohibited areas, snowmobiling or skiing in posted ecologically sensitive areas, improper sanitation practices, and illegal fishing and hunting all contribute to the destruction of the very qualities that justified creation of the parks in the first place.

Unquestionably, effective enforcement of ordinances and prosecution of violators is of critical importance to the future of the profession. Therefore, it is important to bear one overriding principle in mind. That is: *regardless of the magnitude or seriousness of the violation, the same basic standards of proof and constitutional protection apply.*

For example, it is universally accepted that the *state* (the term includes all levels of government from federal to local) must establish the guilt of a defendant charged with a violation of law *beyond a reasonable doubt.* Whether the maximum penalty is life imprisonment or a twenty-five-dollar fine, all material elements of an offense must be shown with proper, constitutionally appropriate evidence. Furthermore, all defendants are presumed to be innocent up to the moment of conviction.

The major differences between the legal treatment of serious crimes and minor infractions are largely procedural. States need not provide jury trials for petty offenses. Most minor violation prosecutions are not commenced with grand jury indictments; they are dealt with through the summons or "ticket." Nor are there complex arraignment and bail procedures. Furthermore, although there is always a right to counsel, the state need not provide an attorney to an indigent defendant where a jail term is not to be imposed.[3]

The basic fact of legal life, that the same *substantive rights* must be provided all defendants, often appears to escape those with responsibility for law enforcement. To be certain that violations are prosecuted and not dismissed, responsible parks officials should initiate and maintain policies to (1) clearly inform visitors of what the regulations require, (2) ensure that evidence of violations will be carefully documented and maintained, and (3) make certain that both eyewitnesses and the appropriate law enforcement personnel are present and properly prepared at hearings and trials along with the physical and documentary evidence.

Since park police and law enforcement officers are usually well aware of these requirements, it is most important that leisure services personnel understand and follow proper procedures for reporting crimes that they have witnessed or that they suspect may have taken place. Employees should take particular care in recording the names and addresses of potential witnesses, identifying and preserving evidence, and documenting the chain of custody of that evidence with signed receipts right up to the time of introduction at trial. Of course, prompt recording of the accounts and recollection of witnesses is also of vital importance.

## Notice

Because of the relatively minor nature of many violations related to the parks, judges are often reluctant to convict or impose sanctions on individuals. This is particularly true when they feel that the rule violated is not one which the ordinary person would be aware of or would take seriously. Most ordinances do not include specific language dictating the extent of understanding required to justify conviction and punishment, although terms like "willfully" may be utilized when the legislative body determines that something more than mere innocent volition is necessary to justify punishment, or when the punishment is relatively severe.

Nevertheless, many courts will accept as sufficient notification the formal posting of rules and regulations at principal entry points to a park. If it is not possible or practical to post all of the rules in a visible manner, it may suffice to warn visitors of the general nature of the rules to be followed and make full copies available at park headquarters, ranger stations, or other locations. Such general notices may be supplemented with specific warnings of critical problems. Thus, for example, a large sign posted at a park entrance might read.

*Notice*

*No firearms permitted.*

Hunting, fishing, solicitation are regulated. Licenses required.

Permits required for all camping and overnight hiking.

All visitors must observe Park Regulations.

Violators will be prosecuted.

Copies of the regulations governing this park are available at Park Headquarters located at _____ and at all ranger stations.

Although a proliferation of signs may be undesirable for esthetic, ecological, and economic reasons, there is no virtue in keeping the public in ignorance, particularly if a rule has an important safety function and is not merely a reflection of the park administration's idea of appropriate use. That is to say, signs should be limited to significant matters and those of the "No ballplaying, picnicking, sunbathing" variety should be avoided unless absolutely necessary.

## Vagueness

Another difficulty that has plagued criminal law enforcement in the parks has been the constitutional due process prohibition against convictions for violating a law that is so vague that the specific forbidden conduct cannot be ascertained. Such laws furnish police and other law enforcement officials almost unbridled discretion for selective interpretation and enforcement. As the Supreme Court put it in *Lanzetta v. New Jersey:*[4]

> A statute which either forbids or requires the doing of an act in terms so vague that men of common intelligence must necessarily guess at its meaning and differ as to its application, violates the first essential of due process of law.

Loitering, disorderly persons, and vagrancy ordinances are, by their very nature, subject to attack on vagueness grounds. Of course, these ordinances are rarely challenged in appellate courts. Vagrants, drunks, juveniles, and others likely to be selected for enforcement of such laws are rarely in a position to mount a legal counterattack. In many cases, the laws are simply cited by police in moving such individuals out of a park or public area with no intent to prosecute; or charges will be dropped after the victim has spent a night in jail or has been bailed out by family or friends. Nevertheless, when such ordinances are contested, they will often be found unconstitutional.

A perfect illustration of this matter is provided by the case of *Borough of Dumont v. Caruth.*[5] This case was extraordinary in that even though it was a lowly municipal court prosecution, Justice Morris Pashman of the New Jersey Supreme Court was temporarily assigned to hear the case, presumably so that the vexing problem presented by the prosecution could be dealt with at the source.

The Borough of Dumont had the authority of New Jersey statutes,[6] which among other matters delegated to municipalities power to "prevent loitering . . . lounging or sleeping in the streets, parks or public places." The municipality dutifully enacted an ordinance stating: "No person may remain, stay or loiter in the park between the hours of 11:00 P.M. and sunrise."

The court ruled that the ordinance was "unconstitutionally vague, in that it failed to provide a guide or standard by which it could be determined who was loitering." This could result in "arbitrary enforcement" and "the distasteful proposition that a police officer should have unlimited discretion to determine who is in violation of the law and who is not."

The limitation of specific hours of enforcement of closing of the park did not save the ordinance even without the loitering provision because "some warning to leave the park must be issued" and the Dumont ordinance contained no warning or notice provision. It would be far wiser for park authorities to enact narrowly drawn regulations aimed at specific conduct that threatens or disturbs the functions and property of the park and to require and provide appropriate notice of them. When drafting an ordinance the professional should avoid terms like "loitering," "disorderly conduct," "improper attire or conduct" or "disturbance of the peace."

### Due Process and the Rights of Criminal Defendants

Over the last twenty-five years, there have been several developments in criminal law that have been described as constituting a revolution in criminal procedure. In a number of landmark cases, the Supreme Court has utilized provisions of the Bill of Rights to limit the actions of police and prosecutors and to enhance the protection afforded criminal suspects and defendants. Although some of these developments concern practices at the trial and appellate level, others are aimed at conduct in the field and at the early stages of law enforcement. Since even park personnel who are not involved in law enforcement may be called upon to participate in the investigation and arrest processes, some understanding of the requirements is useful.

The public's perception of the evolution of defendant's rights has been filtered through political rhetoric and sensational editorializing. They leave the impression that when attorneys become judges, they tend to ignore the legitimate safety needs of law-abiding citizens. In fact, the recent procedural protections have a firm grounding in the Founding Fathers' beliefs that ultimately a free society has more to fear from abuse of power by those in government than it does from outcasts and criminals. Lawbreakers are individually dangerous, but they rarely pose an organized threat to destroy our rights. Thus, many of the provisions in the Bill of Rights concern themselves with the improper use of the criminal process. Nevertheless, it was only when the Supreme Court became convinced by the continued evidence of abuses by police and prosecutors of the rights of those presumed to be innocent that the Court took the drastic actions that have resulted in the release or dismissal of charges against so many apparently guilty criminals.

An example of the kind of abuses that prompted the Supreme Court's action is found in attempts to enforce the Fourth Amendment's prohibitions against unreasonable searches and seizures and the improper granting of warrants without "probable cause." The amendment's guarantees (applied to the states through the Fourteenth Amendment's due process clause) were rendered virtually meaningless by the refusal of prosecutors to bring actions against police who obtained evidence illegally. Furthermore, criminal defendants were rarely in a position to maintain or succeed in civil suits against authorities who abused their rights. Even the exclusion of such evidence from federal trials[7] was defeated by the practice of turning the material over to state officials who were not barred from introducing it in trials.[8] Finally in the case of *Mapp v. Ohio*[9] the Court ruled that exclusion of illegally seized evidence was the only effective way to ensure compliance with the Fourth Amendment. This exclusionary rule was ultimately extended to prevent the introduction of evidence obtained through any unconstitutional methods. Furthermore under a doctrine known as "the fruits of the poisonous tree," most evidence that is directly or indirectly derived from illegally obtained material is also excluded.

Of course, we are all sympathetic to the innocent family whose door is broken down by overzealous agents conducting a warrantless search for illegal drugs. On the other hand, it is very disconcerting to see a dangerous criminal go free because the gun he used in a crime or the material he stole may not be introduced into evidence against him. There are clearly instances when police are in a position where they feel that public safety demands that suspicious individuals must be apprehended and their possessions searched, even though the officers run the risk that successful prosecution will be jeopardized. The Supreme Court has recognized this dilemma and has carved out several exceptions to the exclusionary rule. In doing so, a number of contradictory and seemingly illogical distinctions have been made.

Two recent decisions rendered on the same day by the Supreme Court illustrate the confusing nature of these distinctions. In one case, *Robbins v. California*,[10] police had stopped an erratically driven car. They smelled marijuana smoke and proceeded to search the car. They found two packages wrapped in "opaque plastic" in the trunk. When the packages were unwrapped, marijuana was found. In an opinion written by Justice Stewart, a plurality of the Court ruled that the search was unconstitutional. The marijuana was a in a "closed container." The court rejected the argument that a plastic package was not a closed container like a locked suitcase. Since its contents were not in "plain view" and posed no danger to the arresting officer, the seizure was not justified.

In the second case, *New York v. Belton*,[11] a different group of justices joined in an opinion also authored by Justice Stewart upholding the seizure of evidence. In *Belton*, a policeman observed an auto traveling at an excess rate of speed. When the vehicle was stopped, the officer claimed that he smelled marijuana and saw an envelope on the floor of the car. He ordered the occupants out and arrested them. He then proceeded to search the passenger compartment and came across Belton's jacket. The officer unzipped the jacket pocket and found cocaine inside it. The court held that the jacket was "within [the] arrestee's immediate control" and therefore was subject to being searched in order to prevent the possibility of a concealed weapon being obtained or evidence being destroyed before a warrant could be obtained.[12]

There are a variety of search and seizure rules that may have a relationship to parks crime problems. As the preceding cases indicate, some leeway is permitted in searches of autos, because of their mobility, yet random stops of cars and detention of drivers for license-registration checks may be held unreasonable,[13] although spot checks including *all* vehicles at a roadblock may be justifiable. If material is in "plain view" or visible through a car window, the police need not ignore it. On the other hand, there is a zone of privacy that a person may reasonably expect to surround him even in a public place. Thus in one famous case, eavesdropping on a telephone conversation conducted from a public booth was held unconstitutional.[14]

It is even possible that under circumstances indicating substantial efforts to ensure privacy, a search of open areas might be considered improper without a warrant,[15] although this would seem highly unlikely in a public park.

Although such complex matters are not the day-to-day concern of parks professionals, they nevertheless provide the basis for an important principle. If you become suspicious that criminal activities are taking place, then, within the bounds of safety, observe, collect information and data, and, as promptly as possible, inform the appropriate law enforcement officials who may obtain proper search warrants. Blundering into a tent, demanding entry into a recreational vehicle in a campground, or seizing a backpack may not only be foolhardy and dangerous, it may also jeopardize a successful prosecution and leave you open to face civil actions for assault, false arrest, or false imprisonment.

Obviously there is a reasonable expectation of privacy in many camping and hiking situations. Any park employee who asserted authority would be found to be acting in a quasi-law enforcement capacity and would be subject to at least the same limitations as apply to the police, if not more.

In addition to the Fourth Amendment privileges, other rights have also been applied to protect criminal defendants both in federal and state prosecutions. These include the Fifth Amendment's privilege against self-incrimination[16] and the Sixth Amendment's right to the assistance of counsel at trial, including the appointment of a lawyer if the defendant cannot afford one.[17] These rights have been extended to apply to interrogations during custody.[18] Furthermore, police must give a suspect appropriate warnings of the right to remain silent and the right to counsel prior to "custodial interrogation." Failure to meet any of these standards will result in suppression of evidence and dismissal of charges.

In conclusion, it is somewhat ironic that the parks and leisure services profession, which is dedicated to the development and servicing of many of humankind's higher qualities and aspirations, must be so concerned with the meanest and most destructive of human practices. That is, unfortunately, a fact of life, as is the further irony that many of the most intractable of criminal and constitutional law problems, from the proper application of disorderly persons offenses to the special evidentiary and search and seizure issues presented by narcotics use and distribution cases, seem to surface in park settings. Certainly the desire of the parks professional to maintain high levels of service requires that diligent attention be paid to law enforcement problems and the manner with which they are dealt, even if prime responsibility for criminal law lies elsewhere.

## COPYRIGHT LAW

Leisure services is only one of several consumer-related industries to take advantage of the information explosion triggered, in part, by the development of sophisticated copying, recording, and communications equipment. Photocopies of books, journals, and magazine articles, tapes of shows, movies, and sporting events, and the almost limitless uses of cable television are helping recreation professionals expand and enrich the services they afford; at the same time, very few understand the rights of authors, publishers, and producers to the works that are so readily being reproduced and transmitted.

The general attitude appears to be that as long as the use of a copyrighted publication is limited, not for profit, and of public value, no one should or will object to its unauthorized reproduction. Obviously this is wishful thinking compounded by a widespread faith that most transgressions will go undetected.

What is the actual law on this subject?

First, the authorization for protecting "for limited Times to Authors and Inventors the exclusive Right to their respective Writings and Discoveries" is found directly in the Constitution.[19] The Founding Fathers recognized that economic and artistic exclusivity is necessary "To promote the Progress of Science and useful Arts . . . ."

Although the first copyright law was enacted in 1790 and has been modified numerous times since, a comprehensive modern revision only went into effect in 1978,[20] and many of its provisions have not yet been fully interpreted and understood. This law protects against unauthorized use of photocopying, computer and information retrieval systems, cable television, video and sound recording and tapes, as well as the traditional forms of publication. Most government publications may be reproduced freely.

Copyrighting has been made a simple process for authors. Creative works are protected from the moment of writing or production. Formal copyrights are issued by filing a form and payment of a small fee along with copies of the work in question with the Copyright Office of the Library of Congress in Washington. Thus, for example, if Joan Smith, a therapeutic recreation specialist in Central City, prepared a pamphlet of games and activities of her creation, not under the direction of her employer nor under contract to a publisher, she would have all copyrights from the time she put pen to paper even if her work were not published. By filing the form and a copy of her pamphlet (two copies if published) she would be able to maintain copyright infringement actions for damages and attorney's fees against anyone who reproduced her material without authorization. Under various sections of the act, she could recover actual damages and lost profits,[21] statutory damages of from $250 to $10,000[22] depending upon the court's evaluation of the seriousness of the infringement, and punitive damages up to $50,000[23] if the infringement is willful.

This is not the place to get into details of the ownership of copyright when a work is "prepared by an employee within the scope of his or her employment," or is "specially ordered or commissioned." Suffice it to say that any leisure services professional planning to write or otherwise create an original work that might conceivably be considered a part of her employment responsibilities should carefully consider the employer's publication policy, if any, and consult an attorney specializing in "intellectual property" if there are any potential questions concerning ownership of the creative product.

We should add that, under current law, the copyright on new works is extensive, lasting the owner's life plus fifty years, with other provisions for previously published materials and works created in the course of employment for "hire."

Once a work is copyrighted, the owner has exclusive rights of reproduction, distribution, recording, performing, and developments of derivative materials. Obviously, however, there must be some limitation to the control a copyright gives its owners. After all, much of the information in this or any textbook is derived from the work and ideas of others. Furthermore, an author would scarcely expect or desire that his work be read or viewed individually, in silence, with no discussion or debate or criticism. Therefore, there are two primary limitations on copyright. One is that, while the form of expression or the specific pattern used may be protected, the ideas expressed may not be. Secondly, the doctrine of *fair use*[24] provides practical limitations to copyrights.

The essence of fair use is that some reproduction for purposes of teaching, research, commentary, and criticism is both inevitable and appropriate, if properly attributed and limited in amount. (Generally this may be no more than 200 words, excluding poetry.)

Innocent infringement may cause an award to be reduced to a token $100; if librarians, archivists, or public broadcasters have an "honest belief" that their actions constitute fair use, statutory damages are precluded. Public recreation agencies are not among those named specifically in the fair use sections of the statute. Indeed, with regard to what is fair use for educational or public benefit purposes, the law and its legislative and judicial history are exceedingly complex, since much depends upon the motivation of the copier and the nature of the work. For example, in one important case, the reproduction of thousands of medical journal articles by the National Library of Medicine and the former HEW department[25] was held to be a fair use of copyrighted materials because the materials were needed for valid research purposes.

The basic rule to be applied is that reproduction or copying may not be a substitute for the purchase of a copyright work, and, of course, the copier may not sell reproductions for profit in any case. Suppose, for example that Joan Smith was offering a course in wheelchair basketball for the Central City Recreation Department and wished to use a particular instruction book that retailed for ten dollars. If Smith utilized techniques found in the book in her own teaching, that would clearly be a fair use. Quoting from the book or providing a couple of copies for the class to borrow would be permissible; and even reproducing a page or two of illustrated exercises would probably not be objectionable. On the other hand, reproducing a chapter or other substantial segments for each of the students in the class in order to save them the purchase cost of the whole book would be a clear violation of copyright. Similarly, if Smith were writing her own wheelchair basketball text, reproducing in her book even a page or two of text or illustrations from another's work without permission would violate the law. For example, a social scientist wrote a scholarly dissertation entitled "The Social Psychology of Romantic Love," which included a questionnaire or "scale," the answers to which supposedly would indicate the romantic quality of an individual's relationships. When a magazine used the scale as part of an article, the court of appeals ruled that although the learned material published in the dissertation was open to discussion, the direct use of the author's list of questions "affected plaintiff's market for the scales" and was an infringement.[26]

With regard to the uses of reproductions of telecasts through noncommercial equipment or commercially purchased or rented tapes of shows or motion pictures, not to mention both commercial cable systems and community antenna television (CATV), it is clear only that long and difficult battles lie ahead, although both the Supreme Court[27] and the new Copyright Act have made efforts to provide solutions to the cable television issue that would both protect the producers of shows and simplify matters for cable operators. The general thrust of the law has been to exempt noncommercial rebroadcasting or simple telecasting but not the direct commercial reuse of original programming. Nevertheless, just as this book was going to press, the Ninth Circuit Court of Appeals ruled that home videotape recordings for private use were copyright infringements which would subject the manufacturers and sellers of recording equipment to liability. The court acknowledged that the law did not really consider this problem and suggested that one possible solution would be a "continuing royalty" from the manufacturers to the producers and copyright owners of "telecast audiovisual material." The court did not suggest that the private noncommercial consumers should be held liable.[28]

Certainly with the growing availability and lessening cost of all manner of sophisticated copying and reproduction equipment, new methods for protecting an author's intellectual efforts and a producer's or publisher's investment must be devised. In the interim, a commonsense rule of thumb should be utilized by leisure service programmers: whenever the reproduction or display of copyrighted material is contemplated on a formalized, substantial, or commercialized basis, or when the use would deleteriously affect the value of the copyright owner's proprietary interest, knowledgeable legal advice should be sought before proceeding. On the other hand, the ordinary uses to which copyrighted materials are put within a recreation agency, such as the posting of articles or pictures on bulletin boards, the cutting out of pictures for use in arts and crafts classes, the playing of a new pop tune at a senior citizen's dance, and the like, are by custom and interpretation fair and appropriate use of copyrighted materials, and it is inconceivable that legal action would be taken to enjoin them.

## CONTRACTS

In the broadest sense, every agreement between human beings, enterprises, and agencies that seeks to regulate or dictate actions and behavior includes elements of contract. Political philosophers speak of the *social contract* between individuals that leads to the formation of governments. Parents contract with their children to pay weekly allowances in exchange for such services as lawn mowing, dishwashing, and (hopefully) taking out the trash. The purchase of a can of peas at the grocery store involves a fairly complex series of actions collectively called a *consumer contract*.

Obviously many of the subjects discussed earlier in this book, from the creation of parks by land acquisition in Chapter 2 through the employment relationship in Chapter 6, have important contractual components.

Individual employment contracts and property purchase or lease agreements are often highly formalized and ritualistic. For the most part, the role of parks and leisure service administrators in these contract areas is to work with their attorneys providing information on the substantive elements and conditions to be included. The lawyers will then incorporate these specifics into a legally binding and enforceable framework.

Our focus in this section is on those contract areas which concern recreation officials on a recurring if not continual basis. These include bidding and contracting for capital facilities, equipment, and materials, the franchising or "contracting out" of significant capital aspects of a parks development program to concessionaires, and similar relationships with providers of recreation services. First, however, we shall sketch some of the material elements of modern contract law.

### The Development of Contract Law

Like tort law, contract law is largely of common-law origin and has its roots in the ancient causes of action for *covenant* (documents which were sealed upon oath), *debt* (the requirement that the possessor of goods, money, or completed services pay for them), and *assumpsit* (payment of damages for the failure to fulfill a promised undertaking).

The common law of contracts developed through the experience of the courts in dealing with the customs and problems of merchants, traders, bankers, brokers, and commercial life in general.

There is a substantial difference between contracts and torts, however. The common law has not proven to be adequate to cope with the complexities of modern business. Furthermore, unlike torts, where the potential for varying fact patterns in accidents and injuries is virtually limitless and, therefore, suited to the flexibility of common law, most commercial transactions and problems are of a recurring nature and are suitable for statutory regulation.

Today, the *Uniform Commercial Code* has been adopted in all states except Louisiana. There are minor variations among the states, but the various U.C.C. articles cover all manner of business and commercial relations, including sales, negotiable instruments such as checks and bills and notes, banking practices, credit, warehousing and transfer of goods, investments, and secured commercial transactions. We will not discuss specific details of U.C.C. regulations with regard to such matters as notice, time limits, filing of documents, and other technical matters. Obviously recreation and leisure service agencies should not enter into significant commercial dealings without legal advice concerning the application of the U.C.C. Furthermore, although most park employees may rely upon common practice and agency policy in their dealings, those with major responsibility for the acquisition of goods and services should have a working knowledge of their state's applicable U.C.C. provisions and judicial interpretations as well as the specific bidding and contract rules relevant to their agency.

## Basic Contract Rules and Principles

**Elements of a Contract.**  Thre are three elements which are essential to most contractual relationships. These are: (1) the offer; (2) the acceptance; and (3) consideration (payment). Let us illustrate in the simplest form. Jane Doe, a Central City playground leader, is leading a group in volleyball. Suddenly the ball springs a leak and no replacement is available. Jane then unlocks her petty-cash drawer and comes up with a twenty-dollar bill. Jane sends one of the teenagers at the playground, Joey, around the corner to the Acme Sporting Goods store to purchase a new volleyball. Joey finds the section of the store where volleyballs are kept. He observes that a ball is stamped "$14.00," takes it up to the register, and receives six dollars in change. Joey returns to the playground with the change and the volleyball and the game continues.

In contract terms, we have had an *offer* made by the store to sell a volleyball for fourteen dollars as indicated by the stamped price on the ball. The offer has been *accepted* by Joey as signified by his coming to the cash register with the ball and *tendering* the twenty-dollar bill. The *consideration* of fourteen dollars changed hands and at that moment, *title* to the ball passed from the store to the Central City Recreation Division for whom Joey was acting as *agent*.

This simple transaction may give rise to a number of complications. Suppose Jane Doe was not authorized to purchase sports equipment out of petty cash. Can the recreation division revoke the purchase? Or is the *apparent authority* which Jane possessed as a playground leader sufficient to validate the contract to buy the volleyball? Wouldn't it be unfair to require the store to investigate before it sold the volleyball to Joey? Shouldn't the store be able to assume that those who offer money at the cash register have authority to make the purchase? Would your answer be different if young Joey tried to purchase a gross of volleyballs? Should it make any difference that Joey was a juvenile? As a general rule, contracts made with children for nonnecessities are not binding on the children. Does that mean that a child may purchase goods and return them (or *rescind*) at will? Could Joey be the one making the offer? Suppose the salesperson refused to sell him the ball?

Suppose that Jane Doe became aware that Acme was selling volleyballs for fourteen dollars through an advertisement in the newspaper, and when Joey went to purchase the balls the store was sold out or they claimed the price was in error and the actual cost was eighteen dollars. Could Central City Recreation demand the ball for fourteen dollars?

**The U.C.C. and Consumer Protection Laws.**    The U.C.C. is generally not geared to deal with the typical consumer problem. Many states have consumer protection statutes, and a Uniform Consumer Practices Act has been adopted in a few states.[29] Typically these statutes deal with deceptive advertising practices, improper debt collection, misleading warranties, unconscionable installment sales, franchise, and pyramiding schemes. The kinds of questions raised in our hypothetical situation will be answered by reference to these laws or to the common law of contracts. When large-scale purchases, capital improvements, and service contracts are being considered, the U.C.C. is more likely to offer an authoritative answer.

For example, historically contracts involving real estate have had to be in writing in order to be valid. Similarly, contracts for services or employment that could not be performed within a year also had to be evidenced by a formal written agreement.

These requirements were imposed by the *Statute of Frauds* originally enacted in Britain in 1677 and adopted in most states with numerous additions and variations.

Under the U.C.C., Section 2-201 states that with certain exceptions contracts for the sale of goods of $500 or more must be evidenced by a written contract. Under Section 1-206, most other contracts for the sale of personal property (not real estate) of more than $5000 in amount must also be in writing. Other sections of the U.C.C. (most notably Section 2-206) have liberalized formal rules concerning offers and acceptances to conform the law to actual commercial practices.

Normally when the terms of a contract are in writing, evidence of oral modification of the terms (called *parole* evidence) will be excluded by the courts.[30] Here again there are exceptions when written terms are ambiguous or when fraud, duress, or material mistake is alleged by one of the parties. Courts have been particularly reluctant to permit oral modification of contracts for the sale or lease of real property.

*Remedies and Damages.*    Obviously proof of breach of a contract is only of practical value to a litigant if there is an appropriate remedy available at law. In most cases, the innocent party to a breached contract may recover monetary damages measured by the losses sustained through the breach.

Depending on the circumstances, these may be determined on the basis of losses actually caused by the failure, the difference in value or cost between the contracted for services or goods and their replacement or, in some instances, an amount agreed upon in the original contract called *liquidated* damages. Various aspects of damages in commercial sales are detailed in U.C.C. Sections 2-701 to 725.

In some cases where the subject of the agreement is unique or impossible to duplicate, a court may require *specific performance.*[31] This is a remedy normally available in land purchase agreements, since all real property is considered unique. On the other hand, specific performance would almost never be required in personal service contracts, although individuals with unusual talents or attributes may be enjoined from performing their services for others as part of a remedy.

*Unconscionable or Illegal Contracts.*    Although courts generally stand ready to enforce contracts (or award damages for a breach) as agreed upon by the parties, they will not enforce those agreements that violate statutory or constitutional law. For example, courts will not enforce private agreements not to sell property to minority purchasers.[32]

More often there will be instances when courts find that contract provisions are "unconscionable,"[33] either because they are unfair, usually as a result of unequal bargaining power, or because the provisions violate public policy. Most often this will involve *contracts of adhesion* where an enterprise dictates the terms of a contract to an individual who has no choice but to accept the terms or do without an important service. (You will recall our discussion of contracts of adhesion as they related to releases from liability in Chapter 4.)

Leases of property and consumer sales contracts may contain unconscionable provisions. Unfair limits on warranty, excessive liquidated judgments, confessions of judgment (an agreement not to contest a legal action), or agreements to be represented by attorneys named by the other contracting party are among the unconscionable contract provisions which are eliminated by judicial or legislative action.

There are a variety of legislative and administrative schemes which modify the traditional approach to contracting for goods and services. *Caveat emptor* (let the buyer beware) is no longer an accurate phrase even in commercial arrangements. In addition to the provisions of the U.C.C. discussed above, such agencies as the Federal Trade Commission,[34] the Food and Drug Administration,[35] and the Consumer Product Safety Commission,[36] control various aspects of the safety and suitability of products and the fairness of commercial practices and advertising. The Consumer Product Safety Commission, in particular, has played a major role in determining standards for playground and other recreational equipment.

With this basic introduction to contract law generally, let us consider some contract related problems that are among the most significant and recurring in the leisure services field.

### Contracts in Recreation and Leisure Services

There is substantial evidence that budgetary restrictions throughout the United States are causing public and voluntary recreation and leisure service agencies to look for innovative ways to stretch their dollars. While all agencies utilize the contract process to acquire materials, supplies, and equipment, the use of independent and private organization contractors for services that have previously been performed by the parks department or recreation agency is a relatively new development. Recent surveys indicate that there is precedent for contractual services covering virtually all aspects of the leisure service delivery system.[37] An HCRS publication gives the following examples:

- training seminars
- parking lot staff

- special events coordinators
- minipark operation and maintenance
- ballfield maintenance
- street tree and median maintenance
- all accounting and bookkeeping services
- renovation and operation of tennis/racquetball facilities
- masterplanning
- architectural design
- construction management
- janitorial services
- turf maintenance
- fee recreation
- sports officials[38]

Obviously, various aspects of coaching, instruction, and program development may also be contracted.

There are a number of philosophical and practical considerations to be evaluated when the agency is deciding whether to use an outside agency to provide certain services, particularly when a private, profit-making contractor is utilized. While most of these considerations are matters of policy, politics, and management, a number of them have associated legal aspects. For example, the decision to use an outside contractor to maintain the recreation building might be a violation of the labor agreement that had previously been negotiated. The agency's decision to purchase playground equipment valued at $6000 may require advertisement for competitive bids or soliciting prices for the goods from several potential suppliers. When an agency tailors its proposal too closely to the products or services of one particular contractor, competitors may file charges of collusion and violation of bidding laws. Drafting of service agreements with independent contractors requires great care. The agency may find that tort liability and workers' compensation responsibilities are not readily avoided despite contractual agreements to the contrary.

Some departments may find that there are legal restrictions in their municipal charters or in the state code that limit their authority to contract. Even if legislation authorizes contracting, franchising, and the like, the laws may impose time limits and financial criteria that will discourage serious capital investment. For example, an entrepreneur would hardly be expected to invest in a new municipal stadium if a law limited franchises to a three-year period.

**Categories of Contracts.** The types of contracts used most frequently by parks and recreation agencies can be grouped into four categories: (a) purchase of supplies, equipment, and materials; (b) purchase of services; (c) construction contracts; and (d) concession, franchise, lease and sales contracts.

**Terms.**  The terms of a contract specify the performance requirements, the length of the contract time, who the parties to the contract are, what compensation is to be paid, and other salient details. Contracts that are the most successful in terms of meeting the expectations of both parties are those in which the terms are very specific, unambiguous, and mutually fair. There is no real value to either party in withholding pertinent information, misleading or misrepresenting the prospects for success, or generally taking advantage of ignorance or innocence. Unfair bargains are rarely fulfilled—a breached agreement will be costly to all sides. Let us give two examples.

A theatrical promotion company signed a contract with a county parks agency to construct and maintain a semipermanent tent theater. Part of the contractual obligation on the part of the promotors was a guaranteed rent or percentage of the gross revenues, whichever was greater. Furthermore, they agreed to keep the theater operational with professional, family-type entertainment throughout the warmer months of the year. Both the county parks department and the promotors invested substantial money, personnel, and effort in preparing and promoting the theater. Unfortunately, it soon became apparent that the park board in its zeal wildly exaggerated the potential audience for theater in the community. Within a few years, the theater deteriorated and the productions became sporadic and ceased altogether. The park system was left with a contract it could not enforce against a nearly bankrupt company (carefully and legally separated from the producers' more successful operations), rusting chairs, a dilapidated tent, and a general eyesore.

The second example involves a contract for tennis instruction and services at a private recreation facility. The club's board of directors decided to have first-class instruction, management, and supervision of its tennis facilities. It entered into a contract with a well-known local tennis professional. Rather than pay him a salary, the club agreed to let him have the exclusive use of one court and to keep all of his lesson fees. In return, the professional was to stock and operate the tennis pro shop for a percentage of the profits, set up tennis clinics, supervise court maintenance personnel, promote and manage tournaments, and so on.

Within a couple of months the professional realized that the pro shop could not generate a profit, so he essentially abandoned it. Since his income came exclusively from lesson fees, he concentrated on private instruction and gave short shift to his managerial duties. As a result, the courts and facilities deteriorated and the program of clinics and tournaments was poorly run. In retrospect, it seems obvious that the way in which the contract was set up virtually guaranteed that the club's goals would not be met.

The lesson from these examples is clear: contracts should be written so they are realistic, reasonable, enforceable, and understandable.

Another point of importance is financing. Today more than ever before, the needs of financial institutions must be considered in drafting agreements. An undercapitalized venture is likely to fail. For example, we once drafted a contractual agreement for the development of a paddle-tennis facility in a park system. The agreement protected the department financially so that no matter what happened to the entrepreneur and his business venture, if he defaulted or breached the contract in any way, the park system would get full control of the facility. The financial institution that was funding the enterprise rejected this agreement. They quite reasonably insisted that the park system guarantee their security interest in the facility. Until we redrafted the contract to take their interests into account, they wouldn't loan the money to build the courts.

The specifications of a contract should be detailed enough to guarantee the level of service that the agency needs and has determined would be reasonable. A contract saying that the concession stand should be open "a reasonable number of hours each day" is open to varying interpretations. If the contract specifies that the facility be open from ten a.m. to six p.m., or for "no fewer than eight hours per day" then the level of service is more likely to be that which the agency had in mind. At the same time, specifications should not direct the work efforts of contractual employees to such an extent that they become agency employees in the eyes of the law. In other words, you should specify the end results expected but only those means critical to the maintenance of necessary agency standards.

The length of the contract, the term for which the contract runs, is negotiable and will vary according to statutory limitations, agency policy, and the monetary commitment required from the contractor. Generally contracts for services and concessions, franchises, and leases, need to run for a long enough period for the vendor to recoup his investment by amortizing it over a period of years. As noted earlier, the greater the capital commitment, the longer the contract period which will be expected. At the same time, the agency desires the contract to be short enough to maintain control and to be able to replace an unsatisfactory vendor. Among the ways to handle this problem is to provide for a set of performance criteria within the contract, with clearly spelled out rights and responsibilities. Failure of the contractor to meet the most critical criteria may result in losing the franchise, while lesser criteria should have correspondingly lesser penalties. Again, the key factor is realism and fairness. Do not write criteria that represent unrealistic ideals.

**Bidding.** The basic purposes of the open and competitive bidding system are to reduce the temptation to award contracts to friends, relatives, or the influential, and to eliminate political maneuverings, favoritism, fraud, and corruption.

Most states have codes that regulate bidding and purchasing procedures for political subdivisions. There are also often local purchasing procedures and ordinances. Private and voluntary agencies also often "go out to bid" as a matter of policy on all purchases over a certain amount.

The bidding process for a public agency frequently works in this manner: A notice is placed in a newspaper or trade journal or is otherwise publicized. In many states there is a requirement that this notification be published a certain number of days before the bids will be received and opened. The notification indicates that the agency is planning to accept bids for a specific item or service. An interested party can pick up the specifications packet at the agency office. These bid documents detail the time and procedures for the sealed bids to be received and the criteria by which the bids will be evaluated. At the designated time the appropriate official opens the bids. This is frequently done at a formal public meeting, although in some jurisdictions the requirement may simply be met by notification of the time of opening of bids to interested parties.

Generally when an agency is purchasing goods or services it is required to accept the lowest qualified or "responsible" bid. While an agency would not be required to do business with a vendor who has been indicted and found guilty of fraud or one who has failed to meet business obligations, the agency must have substantial justification to disqualify a low bid from a legitimate source. The reasons should be carefully documented. Rejection must not be based on personal animosity or political differences.

When the agency is selling something—a surplus piece of equipment or the franchise to operate the pro shop, for example—the winning bid will be the qualifying party who offers the highest return to the agency.

Frequently the vendors who are bidding on a contract will be required to submit a *bid bond* with their bid. This security deposit indicates their ability to enter into a contract. The successful bidder is often required to furnish a *performance bond* which guarantees that he can complete the contract.

Obviously, not all contracts can be handled through the competitive bidding system. Agreements with neighborhood associations to maintain their vest-pocket parks, emergency situations where the replacement parts are needed tomorrow, contracts involving unique professional skills such as the ability to teach belly dancing, purchases that are too small to justify the time and expense of the formal bidding process are most often exempted. The terms of these contracts are developed through negotiation.

**Contract Administration.** Even though you have fine-tuned your specifications to the place where there can be no misunderstanding, there still must be someone whose primary function is to monitor or administer the various contracts. While this position might be viewed as an enforcer, the contract administrator can provide insight into problems with the contract, future considerations, and can clear up misunderstandings. Often negotiation and modification of terms by the parties to conform to their actual experience is much more productive than insistence on the letter of the contract.

For example, suppose a contract between a resort hotel and a bicycle rental company calls for the provision of fifty bicycles, "at least twenty-five of which are to be ten-speed racers." Furthermore, the shop is to be open nine a.m. to seven p.m. from April 15 to October 30. If, after a year of experience, the vendor complains that there is no business in the early morning hours until July and that most of the customers are elderly people who want traditional one-speed American bikes, the contract administrator should investigate, and if she finds the franchisee is accurate, there would be little reason to demand full compliance with the original terms. An appropriate modification would be in order.

## Conclusion

Obviously, contracting out of services and responsibilities is not a panacea for the problems of leisure service agencies. Often the financial constraints that lead an agency to seek cooperative ventures with entrepreneurs are also reflected in the private sector. Tight money, high interest rates, and inflation affect us all.

The decision to use outside contractors should, of course, be based on professionally justifiable management criteria. Unfortunately, some of the reasons that agencies have given are legally questionable. As noted earlier, courts take a dim view of agencies that try to avoid labor-management agreements and workers' compensation by utilizing independent contractors. Furthermore, agencies will not necessarily eliminate tort liability by contracting out their programming functions.

In short, the use of outside contractors should be limited to those occasions when the goals of the leisure services agency may best be met through that method.

Once the decision is made to use independent contractors, administrators should work with their lawyers to carefully draw contract specifications that will meet those goals and that will provide incentives to all parties to fulfill the contract terms. Last, but far from least, it is extremely important that contracts with franchisees provide for accurate means of monitoring receipts so that the agency may be certain it is receiving fair payment.

## NOTES

1. 18 U.S.C.A. § 41.
2. 18 U.S.C.A. § 43.
3. *Scott v. Illinois*, 440 U.S. 367 (1979).
4. 306 U.S. 451, 453 (1939).
5. 123 N.J. Super 331, 302 A.2d 566 (Dumont Mun. Ct. 1973).
6. N.J.S.A. 40:48-1. See also N.J.S.A. 40:12-6.
7. *Weeks v. United States*, 232 U.S. 383 (1914).
8. *Wolfe v. Colorado*, 338 U.S. 25 (1949).
9. 367 U.S. 643 (1961).
10. 101 S. Ct. 2841 (1981).
11. 101 S. Ct. 2860 (1981).
12. See *Chimel v. California*, 395 U.S. 752 (1969).
13. *Delaware v. Prouse*, 440 U.S. 648 (1979).
14. *Katz v. United States*, 389 U.S. 347 (1967).
15. See *Wattenburg v. U.S.*, 388 F.2d 853 (9th Cir. 1968).
16. *Malloy v. Hogan*, 378 U.S.1 (1964).
17. *Gideon v. Wainwright*, 372 U.S. 335 (1963).
18. *Escobedo v. Illinois*, 378 U.S. 478 (1964).
19. Art. I, § 8.
20. 17 U.S.C.A. § 101 et. seq.
21. § 504(b).
22. § 504(c).
23. § 504(c)(2).
24. § 107.
25. *Williams & Wilkins Co. v. United States*, 487 F.2d 1345, (Ct. of Cl. 1973), aff'd w/o opinion, 420 U.S. 376 (1973).
26. *Rubin v. Boston Magazine Co.*, 524 Patent Trademark and Copyright Journal A-6 (1st Cir. 1981).
27. *Teleprompter Corp. v. Columbia Broadcasting System, Inc.*, 415 U.S. 394 (1974).
28. *Universal City Studios v. Sony Corporation of America*, 50 U.S.L.W. 2238 (9th Cir. 1981), see also 17 U.S.C.A. § 106, § 111, and §§ 501-505.

29. Kansas, Ohio, and Utah.
30. See U.C.C. § 2-202.
31. See U.C.C. § 2-716.
32. *Shelley v. Kraemer,* 334 U.S. 1 (1948).
33. See U.C.C. § 2-302.
34. 15 U.S.C.A. §§ 41-77.
35. See Federal Food, Drug and Cosmetics Act, 21 U.S.C.A. generally.
36. See 15 U.S.C.A. § 2073.
37. See survey by HCRS and California State University, Hayward, June 1979, as reported in Heritage Conservation and Recreation Service's *Contract Services Handbook,* U.S. Department of the Interior, October 1979, and Martin P. Schwartz, "An Analysis of Innovative Fiscal Strategies in Local Public Recreation and Park Agencies," unpublished doctoral dissertation, Temple University, 1981.
38. Contract Services Handbook, *supra* note 37, at 7.

# Appendix A

# A Note on
# Legal Research

Genius has been described as being composed of 10 percent inspiration and 90 percent perspiration. Successful practice of law, and indeed, the use of the law as a meaningful element in any administrative and policymaking function would certainly call forth a similar equation. In law, the 90 percent perspiration would largely consist of the combined task of finding, compiling, and distilling the overwhelming mass of information available from courts, administrative agencies, and legislatures as reported, summarized, and analyzed by the clerks, students, and scholars of the law. This is not an easy task. Nevertheless, the nonlawyer should not be completely overwhelmed by the image cultivated by the embroidered autobiographies of attorneys who like to depict themselves as latter-day Merlins, able to conjure up an appropriate legal citation or devastating judicial quotation out of a vast and awe-inspiring reservoir of jurisprudential wisdom.

The fact of the matter is that most basic legal research is accomplished by law students and junior attorneys who can hardly claim to have accumulated a great storehouse of legal knowledge. Rather, what they have learned, usually in the first year of law school, are those essential techniques and tools of research that will permit them to tap a reservoir of appropriate legal information at short notice, even in areas of the law with which they may be unfamiliar. If a first-year law student can do this, it stands to reason that any literate and diligent person also may.

Every law library has pamphlets and books to help you find the law. Often these are published and distributed by major legal publishers and emphasize their own publications. Nevertheless, they are quite helpful. Law librarians are usually eager to furnish basic research assistance and are particularly helpful in locating government documents, new legislative enactments, administrative regulations, and other materials that, as will be demonstrated below, may be difficult for even the experienced legal researcher to rapidly locate.

There are also a number of books on legal research and writing that, although perhaps too detailed for the nonlawyer, may still be an invaluable tool. These include *Pollack's Fundamentals of Legal Research* by Jacobstein and Mersky, and Cohen's *How to Find the Law*. There are also several books aimed at beginning law students, such as Rombauer, *Legal Problem Solving*, and Statsky, *Legal Research, Hunting and Analysis: Some Starting Points*, which may serve as an introduction not only to research, but also to the task of effectively utilizing the results of research in problem solving. Most basic of all is a small paperback pamphlet periodically issued by the *Harvard Law Review* in conjunction with several other major legal publications. This work, entitled *A Uniform System of Citation*, and currently in its thirteenth edition, sets forth the correct way to cite all United States and most foreign legal materials and includes not only forms of citation but also appropriate abbreviations. Citation forms used throughout this text are based on the uniform system or "Harvard Blue Book" as it is popularly known. (Every so often the color of the cover of a new edition changes and the "blue book" becomes the "white book.")

In the early days of the development of American law, the critical bulk of the law was to be found in a few *treatises* or learned legal commentaries such as Kent's *Commentaries on American Law*, as well as a small number of volumes of collected cases and statutes. Today the amount of new law every month in cases, statutes, administrative regulations and rulings, not to mention interpretive materials in digests, articles, treatises, encyclopedias, and loose-leaf specialized services, is truly staggering. There is certainly more law in a week than formerly was published in a year, and probably as much in a year as in a good part of the nineteenth century. In addition to the tremendous number of important new volumes, computerization and miniaturization through the use of microfilm, microfiche, and sophisticated and expensive information retrieval systems have opened up whole new avenues of information. For example, the entire case histories including the briefs in major cases are now preserved and readily retrievable in major law libraries around the country. Previously there was only access to the final formal opinion and perhaps a brief summary of the arguments.

Despite this explosion of information and the inevitable complexity that comes with it, traditional legal research methods and tools are still efficient, accurate, inexpensive, and certainly serve for the great majority of research being conducted.

Most of the law you will ever need to know will be found in judicial decisions, state or federal statutes, administrative regulations, and in the commentaries, digests, treatises, law review articles, and legal encyclopedias that synthesize and interpret them. Unfortunately, materials that may be significant to park administrators, including local ordinances, copies of municipal court decisions, and local regulations, are the least likely to be found in law libraries. Although a few municipal charters and codes are formally published, even when they are found in law libraries they may not be indexed in a useful way. The best method to obtain a local ordinance or administrative order is to go to the clerk of the particular community or government agency and ask to read it. In most states, copies of ordinances must be made available to the public at reasonable cost.

State and federal administrative regulations and rulings also present considerable difficulty, although, unlike local law, persistence will generally result in obtaining necessary information. Research techniques for this material are considered later in this note.

## TOOLS OF LEGAL RESEARCH

Fortunately, the essential tools of legal research, those that encompass major state and federal judicial decisions and statutes, are also the most universally distributed and the simplest to use. They are as follows.

### The Judicial Case Reports

These include official United States Reports containing Supreme Court decisions and official state reporters, which may include the work of the state supreme court as well as separate volumes for selected opinions of lower state courts.

In addition to these government-sponsored official reports, there are a number of reporters published by West Publishing Company that include all major federal and state court decisions. These include the Federal Reporter, which covers the federal circuit courts; the Federal Supplement, covering federal district courts; and seven regional reporters (i.e., Atlantic, Pacific, Southwestern, etc.), which encompass state court decisions. The West Publishing Company reporting system is so universally used that the federal government doesn't publish an official reporter for its circuit and district courts, and several states have given up publishing their own reports.

In addition to the regional reporters, West publishes a California Reporter and a New York Supplement, which include all of the voluminous appellate (and many trial court) decisions of those two states. In addition to the official United States Supreme Court reports, West and the Lawyers Co-operative Publishing Company publish unofficial Supreme Court reporters.

What the researcher should bear in mind is that the actual reports of opinions in these various volumes are exactly the same whether they are found in the official or unofficial volumes. The only differences may be found in the preliminary summaries and annotations (called "head notes"), which, except when written by the court, do not form part of the actual case report but are intended as a research aid to the reader.

## Other Case Reporters

In addition to the official and West Publishing Company court reporters there are a number of other publishers who provide information on cases. Many of these are aimed at attorneys who need immediate reports of decisions. Although most reporter systems use paperback "advance sheets" to speed up the process of publication, it may still take months before a case is actually reported. Because of this there are local, state, and national law newspapers published on weekly or, in a few major cities, on a daily basis. By and large, these are not very useful to the lay reader. The most important of the fast reporting services is the *United States Law Week,* which publishes substantial portions of the text of major Supreme Court decisions and summaries of major state and federal opinions on a weekly basis. *Law Week* also provides the text of some statutes and other important legal news. The publisher of *Law Week* is the Bureau of National Affairs (not a government agency), which also publishes a number of other "loose-leaf" services, (so called because they can be inserted into a binder and later discarded when out of date). These provide surveys and summaries of cases, laws, and administrative decisions in a variety of specialized legal fields. Of greatest interest to those in parks and leisure services are the *Environmental Reporter* and the *Product Safety and Liability Reporter.*

Two other firms, the Commerce Clearing House (CCH) and Prentice-Hall Publishing Company, also publish a number of loose-leaf services. Most of these deal with highly technical matters, predominately tax law. CCH's *Consumer Product Safety Guide* and *Products Liability Reporter* may be of some interest to the parks and recreation professional.

One other significant publication should be mentioned here. This is the *American Law Reports* or *ALR* (also known as the Annotated Law Reports). This series publishes selected cases that its editors deem of special significance. The cases are followed by extensive annotations or commentaries summarizing the law in a particular area touched on by the reported case. If a researcher can find an ALR annotation on a case of interest, a substantial number of related cases will be discussed. There will also be citations to related annotations. Finally, through supplements and a "later case service," ALR annotations are kept current with brief citations and discussions of cases on the same topic that have been decided since the original annotation was published.

## Summaries and Commentaries on the Law

Beyond the reporters there are two important types of publications that summarize case law—encyclopedias and digests. Unfortunately, both have serious limitations as research tools. Probably best known to nonlawyers are the two major legal encyclopedias, *Corpus Juris Secundum,* published by West Publishing Company, and *American Jurisprudence,* published by the Lawyers Co-operative Publishing Company. These works share the problems common to all multivolume encyclopedias: they both oversimplify through generalization and overcomplicate by necessarily focusing on broad topics rather than on specific points of concern. Although a reader may get a broad introduction to an area of law, the mass of material, the extensive case citation, and the turgid style of the encyclopedias will seldom result in directly useful information.

The legal digests are even more difficult to read than the encyclopedias. Rather than having comprehensive articles or annotations, the digests are made up of brief one-sentence or short paragraph summaries of the points of law from the cases. These are often in very vague and general form. Most digests are published by West Publishing Company. There are federal, state, and regional digests; there is also a national digest system, the *American* or *"decennial digest,"* which is supposed to contain brief summaries of all significant cases decided in the United States, whether state or federal. A new decennial series has been published every ten years starting in 1897, covering all cases in the preceding decade. Thus the most recent series, the eighth, covering 1966-1976, was recently completed. They are to be published more frequently in the future. Prior to 1896, digests of cases are found in the *Century Digest* and until the next series is published, a general digest keeps matters up to date on a regular basis. To use the digests successfully, the researcher may have to plow through a great number of topics and subtopics before finding a digest note that will indicate a relevant case. Sometimes the notes will briefly summarize the facts, and this will aid in narrowing down the number of cases that must actually be read. At other times, the researcher may be forced to at least glance at tens or hundreds of cases of only marginal interest or relationship to the question of concern. Nevertheless, there are ways to make the use of digests more productive and efficient, and these will be described in the section on research methods below.

*Treatises* or legal texts on major subject areas of the law can be very useful both in providing general background in a readable form and also in pointing the way to specific information in the particular problem area being researched. Because treatises are usually the work of one author or a small number of authors, they tend to be much more critical and opinionated than the digests or encyclopedias, which are largely composed by committees. There are basically three types of treatises. First are classic multivolume works, such as Wigmore on Evidence and Corbin on Contracts, that teach and explain as much or more than they summarize. These texts tend to be regarded as sources of the law as well as authoritative expositions of the cases. There are single-volume works or "hornbooks" that summarize major areas and that are most useful to law students. Some of these texts, such as Prosser on Torts and more recently Tribe on Constitutional Law, not only explain the law in simplified fashion, but because of the extent of the authors' learning and the force of their arguments, have been very influential on lawyers and judges seeking answers to newly emerging legal questions. Finally there are more highly specialized works that fall somewhere between the traditional treatise and a specialized encyclopedia or digest. Larson on Workers' Compensation, Frumer and Freedman on Products Liability, and similar works give extensive reports and summaries on cases and laws with frequent supplements to update information along with critical discussions and comments. Whatever the topic area of research, it is always wise to check the catalogs to see if there are relevant treatises in the area. They can save a great deal of research time and provide ready access to relevant cases.

Approximately halfway between the digests and encyclopedias on the one hand and the treatises on the other are a series of multivolume works known collectively as *Restatements of the Law*. The Restatements are published by the American Law Institute, the membership of which consists of jurists, professors, and prominent attorneys. The Restatements in such areas as torts, contracts, property, and other common-law subjects attempt to "restate" the law as it has been generally interpreted by the courts in a series of rules or principles with comments and illustrations. There are critical notes written by the "reporters" for each restatement who are particularly learned scholars who prepare the drafts for approval by members of the institute. Cases are cited in the notes and there are also volumes of case citations to the narrow restatement sections. Given the often contradictory nature of the common law, virtually all of the restatement principles are subject to so many qualifying exceptions and distinctions that a lay reader may well emerge from a study of a restatement more confused about the rule of law than when he or she began. The Restatements are very important nevertheless, and are often cited and relied upon by judges in rendering decisions on common-law questions.

Of all the research tools, the most interesting, argumentative, and timely may be the articles and notes found in the *law journals* published by most American law schools. Articles are generally written by law professors, or, in the case of "notes" and "commentaries," by law students, although judges and practitioners are also represented among the authors. Largely student edited, the reviews or journals provide the forums for expressions of opinion on an incredibly wide range of law and law-related topics. There are also a number of periodicals published by bar associations or other professional groups and commercial publishers, but most of these are of little research interest. Many of the journals deal with a full spectrum of current legal topics, but others, such as the *Ecology Law Quarterly,* or the *Journal of Family Law,* restrict their coverage to specific areas of the law. The best source of access to the articles in the journals is the *Index to Legal Periodicals,* published monthly by the H. M. Wilson Company.


## Statutes

Statutory materials follow essentially the same pattern as case reports—that is, advance sheets, loose-leaf services, and annotated and official compilations. Because it may take some time before a newly enacted statute is codified, a researcher trying to locate a recent statute may have to seek a law librarian's aid in searching through state session laws or federal *Statutes at Large.* Rather than go into detail here, we will simply point out that there are unofficial codes in many states published by private publishers that contain annotations, including notes on the history of legislation, cross-references, brief discussions of cases that have interpreted the statute in question, and so on. Many states no longer publish official codes and have simply contracted with or adopted the codes of private publishers. For federal statutes, the *United States Code,* which is not annotated, is the best source for the unadorned text. The *United States Code Annotated* (U.S.C.A.), published by West, offers a tremendous amount of information, but if a law has been frequently cited it may be difficult for a researcher to focus on the statute's exact wording, since statute paragraphs may be separated by many pages of notes.


## Administrative Law

Administrative laws propounded by federal and state agencies, whether in the form of rules and regulations (statutory), administrative law decisions (judicial), or promulgations by executive officials, are among the most important and, in some ways, the most difficult to research. This is partly because of the jargon and bureaucratic language that makes much administrative law impenetrable, the sheer volume of materials, and the abominable indexing and editorial work. There is a *Code of Federal Regulations* (CFR), which roughly parallels the United States Code. It is hard to use and frequently out of date. The *Federal Register* is the administrative and executive equivalent to the Congressional Record. Just about every federal agency activity is set forth in detail in the Federal Register. There are summaries, updates, and tables to make it easier to work with these publications. Unfortunately, they do not always succeed, at least not for the casual or lay researcher. The best advice on administrative information is to keep close tabs on a loose-leaf service which covers your area of concern and become friendly with a competent government documents librarian.

As far as the judicial or case law aspects of administrative law, the loose-leaf services are also useful tools. A number of agencies, such as the National Labor Relations Board and the Federal Communications Commission, publish their decisions. Some general services, such as Pike and Fischer's *Administrative Law Service*, exist, but here again, unless one is intimately and continuously aware of the work of a particular agency, substantial research is best done with the aid of a professional librarian.

If research into federal administrative law is difficult, state administrative and executive determinations are often nearly impossible to find. A state law library or a county bar association library is the best source for such materials.

Although administrative research is often difficult, there are some mitigating factors. Many administrative regulations and decisions, particularly those that are significant or controversial, find their way into courts for judicial interpretation. Thus, even if it is hard to follow all of the developments in administrative law, the comparatively straightforward case law research system will provide access to important agency information.

## LEGAL RESEARCH METHODOLOGY

Now that we have described the major sources of American law and legal information, we must proceed to sort out the methods that make this mass of material comprehensible. In the future, it may be that a researcher will merely have to punch a few key words into a computer terminal in order to be instantly rewarded with all of the required information. In fact, computer-based legal research programs already exist; among them are LEXIS, WESTLAW, and JURIS. Their use is currently quite expensive, and they obviously will not play a major part in most student and nonlawyer research efforts for the foreseeable future. Fortunately, the existing research system, particularly for judicial opinions, is both relatively simple and, considering the amount of materials to be sorted through, quite fast and efficient.

The key to legal research is the efficient use of the various resources we have described earlier. The principal tools that aid in this process are *Shepard's Citations* and the West Key Number System.

The Shepard Citation system is based on a simple fact that in American law, every decision of a court has its roots in earlier decisions. That is, the principle of *stare decisis* and the need to justify judicial decisions on the basis of prior judicial wisdom, means that opinions will be full of citations to earlier opinions on the same or related subjects. The Shepard Citations list in columns all of the cases which cite the case the researcher is interested in; thus, once a researcher has found a case or two on the subject of interest, he can readily find other cases.

There are Shepard Citators for every case reporter, federal and state, official and unofficial, as well as state and federal statutes. There are specialized Shepard's for administrative and labor law, and even volumes concerning citations to law review articles. The Citators can be used to find out the procedural history of a case (i.e., was it affirmed or reversed), and through the clever use of a series of explanatory letters and numbers can tell you a great deal about the importance of the case you have started with and the validity of the principles of law upon which it relies. Let us illustrate.

Suppose we are interested in the case of *Diodato v. Camden County Park Commission,* 162 N.J. Super. 275, 392 A.2d 665 (Super. Ct. Law Div. 1978), a New Jersey parks liability case. As the *Uniform System of Citation* explains, the volume in which the case is found comes first, then the title, and then the page. Thus the *Diodato* case is found in Volume 162 of the New Jersey Superior Court Reports at page 275, and at Volume 392 of the second series of the Atlantic Reports at page 665. The first part of the citation refers to the official reporter, the second part to the unofficial West Publishing Company reporter. Remember that the actual report of this case is identical in both reporters. The remainder of the citation tells you the court that decided it (the law division or the basic trial court of the New Jersey Superior Court) and the date that the decision was rendered. Thus the complete citation of a case gives us the name of the case (as it appears at the head of the page at the beginning of the opinion in the official report), the exact volume and page where the case begins, the court that decided it, and the date of the decision.

Armed with this information we consult the Shepard's Citation for the New Jersey Courts commencing with the first volume published after the decision was rendered (1978), and then bringing the research down to the most recent Citation (usually just a slim paperback edition covering the last few months). In Shepard's we find the listing for 162 N.J. Super and we look down the column until we find -275-. Under this we find the following:

$$-275-$$
$$(392 \ A.2d \ 665)$$
$$80 \ N.J.^2 \ 403$$
$$f. \ 162 \ Su^{11} \ 402$$
$$163 \ Su^{13} \ 430$$
$$f. \ 163 \ Su^{13} \ 431$$

How do we translate this into useful information? First, the citation in parentheses is the unofficial or West citation to the *Diodato* case itself. Similarly, if we had looked for the case in the Atlantic Citations, the official citation would have been given first. Following this *parallel* citation would have come a series of citations indicating both the earlier and later history of the case, each citation prefaced by a letter explaining what happened to the case (a=affirmed, r=reversed, etc.). None of these are present in the *Diodato* case, so we know that, at least up to the publication date of the most recent Shepard's we have researched, there had been no decided appeal in the case. What then do the other citations mean? Most basically, that the *Diodato* case has been cited four times since its decision. At the time of this writing, *Diodato* had only been cited in one volume of Shepard's, so these four citations are all there were. The citations are to the exact page at which the reference to the Diodato case appears, thus you will note that the last two citations, 163 Su 430 and 163 Su 431 are on following pages of volume 163 of the New Jersey Superior Court Reports. Examination will show that these two citations are in the same case. Since this is a recent case, decided by a relatively low-level trial court, we would not expect to find a great many citations. However, if this were a very important case, there might be scores, even hundreds of citations. How do we avoid having to read all of the cited cases? This is where the preceding letters and superscripts come in.

At the beginning of each bound volume of Shepard's is a full explanation of these letter abbreviations, and we will not repeat them all here. The small *f*'s preceding the cited cases mean "followed," which signifies that the citing courts agreed with the viewpoint of the court in *Diodato*. If we had seen a *q* (questioned), a *c* (criticized), or an *o* (overruled), we would have recognized instantly that the opinion no longer represented good law or was, at least, dubious authority. The superscript numbers as in 80 N.J.[2] 403, are particularly significant in helping to make our research more efficient. These numbers represent the corresponding number in the head notes or prefatory summary of the major legal points of the case. The numbered head notes, in turn, correspond to numbers in the text of the case inserted by the editors to indicate the paragraph where the legal point reflected in the head note is actually discussed.

In *Diodato* there are thirteen of these numbered head notes. Their subject matter varies, although not as widely in *Diodato* as in many other cases. By limiting research to the reading of only those cases whose head note number in Shepard's Citations corresponds to a legal point we are interested in, we may substantially limit the number of cases we have to read to ensure that we have an accurate understanding of the law.

Shepard's is obviously not the final answer. Suppose our case is a very recent one, or one that passed without a great deal of notice. How then do we gain access to other cases on the same topic? This is where the West Key Number System becomes useful. West Publishing Company, in addition to the descriptive word index, has a system of "key numbers" (graphically illustrated with little keys—lawyers are certainly literal!). Each major topic in law is divided into minutely differentiated principles, and each principle is given a key number. All of the digests in the West System and all of the West case reporters use this system. Once a relevant key number is discovered, every American case making the same or similar point of law may be found by checking the appropriate key number and closely related key numbers. In the digests, there will be column after column of notes listed under succeeding key numbers. In the West Reporters, the key numbers are listed in the head notes. In the *Diodato* case in the New Jersey Superior Court Reports (which even though it is official is a West publication), the thirteen head notes have reference to three different key numbers. For example, one head note looks like this:

13.  Counties    ⟨⚷ KEY NUMBER SYSTEM⟩ 143

Accident at county-owned park, whereat plaintiff sustained serious injuries when he dove into river and struck partially submerged trash barrel, did not come within the immunity provided county and its park commission by the Tort Claims Act, since the injury producing condition was not a natural condition. N.J.S.A. 59:4-8

(The citation at the end of the note is to the statute—New Jersey Statutes Annotated, Title 59, Section 4, Paragraph 8.)

Thus, if we wanted to find cases on similar points in, for example, California, we would turn to the California or Pacific Digests and look up "Counties ⟨key number system⟩ 143".

There are, of course, all manner of other indexes, tables, legal dictionaries, and summaries of law to aid in research. The use of these various devices depends in part on the amount and type of information the researcher has to start with. For example, if one has a statute reference only, the proper place to begin research might be the annotated statutes for the particular jurisdiction. The researcher would then follow a pattern of reading cases cited under that statute, Shepardizing them, finding other cases, and so on. What the researcher should keep in mind is that the purpose of legal research is to find accurate information on particular questions of law, and that once entry is gained into the legal research system, whether through a case, a digest, or an ALR annotation, all of the tools discussed above can be used to rapidly gain complete information on the question. We must emphasize that in order to ensure accuracy, you must always bring research up to date through the most recently published supplements to the various research works; otherwise a major recent change in law might go undiscovered.

## A BRIEF SAMPLE RESEARCH PROJECT

In order to ilustrate more graphically how legal research can be done, let us follow a research project step by step.

The director of parks in Urban County, New Jersey, called the park attorney, Louise Jones. "Louise, we've got a problem I need help with. You know there are several ponds in the county park which freeze over in the winter. Every year or two, someone will fall through thin ice. We've used a flag system in the past, but I really can't afford to keep guards on these ponds. Are we going to be liable if someone falls through? What do I have to do legally to protect us?"

Here are the steps that Louise followed. First, she went to ALR to see if there was an annotation to give her general background and references to cases. Using the ALR2d and 3d series Quick Index, she looked up "ice," which referred her to "snow and ice." Under this heading she discovered nothing useful. Similarly, annotations under "skating" related to indoor and artificial rinks, so little of value was learned there.

Turning in the index to "parks and playgrounds," an annotation was found at 37 ALR3d 738 entitled "Tort Liability of Public Schools and Institutions of Higher Learning for Injuries due to Condition of Grounds, Walks, and Playgrounds." This annotation was found to have good background discussion of liability for hidden dangers and also for snow and ice on playgrounds. Louise made some notes on these, but finding nothing more specific on falling through ice in the note or in the updated supplement, she turned from ALR to the New Jersey Digest, a West publication. Here she looked up "Parks" and found:

Tort Liability
Counties ⟜🗝⟝ 143

Under the key number "counties 143," Louise found several notes to *Diodato v. Camden County Park Comm.*, discussed earlier. She also found references to the New Jersey Tort Claims Act and the New Jersey Landowner's Liability Act and its application to public entities. Another key number cited under "Tort Liability" was Municipal Corporations 851. Here she found the case of *Kleinke v. City of Ocean County*, 163 N.J. Super 424, 394 A.2d 1257 (Super Ct. 1978), which concerned liability for injury to a body surfer at a supervised beach. Note that to this time she had not found any cases directly relating to ice skating or ice pond accidents.

Frustrated so far, Louise read the *Diodato* case. In *Diodato* there was a reference to *Harrison v. Middlesex Water Co.*, 158 N.J. Super 368 (Super Ct. App. Div. 1978). This case involved an ice skating accident on a reservoir in a formerly rural area, now surrounded by housing developments. Louise read the Harrison case and it looked very promising for her employer. The court had held that where two fifteen-year-old boys fell through the ice of a town reservoir that had not been patrolled for the past several years the New Jersey Landowner's Liability Act specifically protected the rural landowners against liability. This protection was applicable even though the municipality knew the pond was used for skating. The *Harrison* case also cited an earlier case, *Odar v. Chase Manhattan Bank*, 138 N.J. Super 464, 351 A.2d 389 (1976), which also involved an ice skating accident.

Unfortunately, when Louise Shepardized the *Harrison* case, she found that it had been reversed by the New Jersey Supreme Court at 80 N.J. 392 (1979). The Supreme Court held that the burden of guarding against intermittent trespassers on the pond was not outweighed by the known risks when the area was developed for housing, and that the Landowner's Liability Act didn't protect the defendants because the area was no longer rural.

At this point we will leave Louise as she goes on to Shepardize other cases, reads the annotations under the N.J. Tort Claims Act, and so on. Although she has not yet resolved the original questions and, in fact, the questions may not be clearly resolved by the courts in New Jersey, she is gaining good insight into the probable judicial approach. She may now also go on through the key number system to see how cases in other states have dealt with similar issues. The point to be made here is that through the use of basic research tools and techniques, Louise has, in an elapsed time of less than an hour and a half, learned a considerable amount about a legal question concerning which she had little or no knowledge at the outset.

In order for you to become comfortable with legal research methods, you should attempt to research a problem of interest to you. A few hours spent in a law library seeking the solution to some questions will be profitable. Here are a few questions you might try.

1. Can a state park system refuse to permit religious solicitations in its parks?

2. Is a private commercial animal reserve liable to a visitor who is bitten by an animal when the visitor breaks a rule and rolls down his window?

3. May a municipality require a developer to dedicate a portion of her property as parkland?

# Appendix B

# Sample Memorandum of Law

When research into a legal problem is completed, it is important to summarize the results in a comprehensive and coherent form so that other persons will not have to repeat the same efforts when similar problems arise.

The basic form of reporting the results of the legal research is called a "legal memorandum." Unlike a legal "brief," the memorandum is a neutral statement of the issues and the research results, not an attempt to influence the reader by argument and manipulation of the facts and law.

Although styles may vary, the basic memorandum includes the following:

1. *Date* when research completed. This is very important since it will help future readers know how far back they will have to go in their research to update a memo.

2. A succinct statement of the *facts*.

3. A statement of the legal issues considered.

4. A brief *conclusion*, which is often placed at the *beginning* of the memo. The reason for this is so that the reader can determine the essence of the research at a glance.

In the body of the memo, it is important that *subheadings* be used liberally, so that the reader may focus on those matters most crucial to his or her interests.

Although this sample memo is very brief and not exhaustive, some memos are extensive and complex.

Case File:   Johnson v. United States                                    Res. Compl.

To:   Senior Partner                                                     15 Sept. 1978

From:   Research Associate

*FACTS:*

   Mr. William Johnson was severely injured by a wild grizzly bear while on a
trail hike in Glacier National Park, Montana. The hike was a popular one to Grin-
nel Glacier and was organized and guided by a United States Park Service ranger.
Mr. Johnson was trailing a group of 40 hikers when the bear suddenly appeared.
Johnson's injuries were suffered while attempting to protect his 11-year-old son.

   It is presumed that upon entering the park, Johnson paid the standard park
auto admission fee. He had received general written warning about grizzly bears
advising visitors to keep off closed trails. The ranger guiding the hike gave no
warnings and, in fact, indicated there would be no danger. The Park Service has a
bear management policy which involves removal of bears to remote areas.

*LEGAL ISSUES:*

   May the government be liable for Johnson's injuries under the Federal Tort
Claims Act?

   What, if any, duty is owed Johnson with regard to his status as a park
visitor?

   Under applicable Montana law, what, if any, defenses may be available?

*CONCLUSION:*

   The majority of cases hold that the United States is not responsible for attacks by wild animals in National Parks. In general, bear management is held to
be a discretionary function, not subject to liability under the Tort Claims Act. It
does appear that Johnson is a public invitee, and therefore is owed a duty of warnings of hidden dangers known to the government and also reasonable inspection
to assure safe conditions. Also, unlike the majority of cases it does not appear
that Johnson was contributorily negligent or voluntarily assumed the risk.
Therefore, whether Johnson may recover may depend upon the extent to which
the Park Service knew or should have known of the presence of grizzlies in the
hike area, and whether adequate precautions were taken.

   *Wild Animal Attacks in National Parks, Generally.*
   There have been several cases involving bear attacks in Yellowstone National
Park. Under the Tort Claims Act, 28 U.S.C. § 1346(b) liability depends upon the
law of the place where the alleged act of negligence occurred. There is nothing to
indicate that the law of Montana differs substantially from the general law of
negligence except as noted below. In *Hansen v. Brogan,* 145 Mont. 224, 400 P.2d
265, 21 A.L.R.3d 595 (1965), it was held that in Montana the law of negligence applies to keepers of wild animals, not strict liability.

   The majority of cases would appear to find no liability under the Tort Claims
Act when visitors have been attacked by animals in national parks. See *Martin v.*

*United States*, 546 F.2d 1355 (9th Cir. 1977); *Ashley v. United States*, 215 F. Supp. 39 (D. Neb. 1963), aff'd 326 F.2d 499 (8th Cir. 1964); *Rubenstein v. United States*, 338 F. Supp. 654 N.D. Cal. 1972), aff'd. 488 F.2d 1971 (9th Cir. 1973). However, the cases are not unanimous. *Claypool v. United States*, 98 F. Supp. 702 (S.D. Cal. 1951) involved a grizzly attack in Yellowstone which resulted in a holding favorable to the injured plaintiff. See also *Cowden v. Bear Country, Inc.*, 382 F. Supp. 1321 (D. S.D. 1974), in which a private wildlife park could not escape responsibility for a mountain lion attack on a child, even though the child's mother had ignored safety instructions. Related cases which are of significance include *Smith v. United States*, 546 F.2d 872 (10th Cir. 1975) aff'g 383 F. Supp. 1076 (D. Wyo. 1974), involving injuries to a child who fell through the crust of a thermal area in Yellowstone and *Middaugh v. United States*, 293 F. Supp. 977 (D. Wyo. 1968), in which plaintiff's decedent was killed by a falling lodgepole pine. These latter cases appear favorable to Mr. Johnson's position.

### The Status of Johnson in the Park and the Duty Owed to Him.

Under the Restatement (Second) of Torts § 332, Johnson is clearly a public invitee since the government obviously communicated its willingness to receive him and his family in the park and on the trail hike. Comment (d) to § 332 states that when one installs playground equipment on one's lot and opens it to children a child visitor's status would be that of invitee. The Restatement indicates that payment of a fee is not critical. The cases would appear to confirm this.

In *Middaugh*, the court placed some emphasis on decedent's purchase of a $7.00 Golden Eagle pass, but stated at 293 F. Supp. at 980-81, "The invitation extended to public invitees encourages visitors to enter upon the land with a sense of assurance that it had been prepared for their safety." The government is charged with a duty to inspect and guard against injury to "invitees." *Id.* at 980. Thus, liability resulted when a diseased tree whose unsafe character would have been revealed by inspection fell on decedent in a designated campsite. In *Ashley*, the district court found plaintiff to be an invitee without regard to the auto fee payment, 215 F. Supp. at 44, and required the government to keep the park reasonably safe and clear of hidden danger. In *Smith*, it was held that an unreasonable failure to warn of hidden dangers would be negligent under 28 U.S.C.A. § 2674 et. seq. *Rubenstein* and *Martin* do not contradict these positions. Rather, *Rubenstein* held that there was no specific undisclosed danger of bear attacks, and in *Martin*, plaintiff's decedent appeared to disregard the warnings he had received. Furthermore decedent had not paid an entrance fee nor gotten appropriate back country permits which may have rendered his invitee status doubtful although the decision didn't turn on that point. See 546 F.2d at 1357. Montana law on the subject of duties owed to persons on land is sketchy but conventional. See *Demaree v. Safeway Stores, Inc.*, 102 Mont. 47, 508 P.2d 570 (1973).

### Was the Government Negligent toward Johnson?

We are not possessed of sufficient facts to determine negligence. The mere fact he was attacked is insufficient to establish negligence. In *Rubenstein*, it was held "that a grizzly bear would embark on an unprovoked attack under these circumstances [within a campground] was totally outside the experience of park authorities." 338 F. Supp. at 657. In *Martin*, an attempt to prove negligence by attacking bear management policy generally failed as the court found that this was within the discretionary exception to the Tort Claims Act, 28 U.S.C.A. § 2080(a). It is noteworthy that in *Martin*, plaintiff's decedent had ignored warnings and was knowingly camping in an unauthorized area. In *Ashley*, plaintiff was bitten by a bear while sleeping in his car with his elbow on the sill of an open window. Plaintiff was obviously contributorily negligent in both *Ashley* and *Martin* and in both cases, there was no specific failure to warn. In *Rubenstein*, there was uncorroborated testimony that plaintiff's son was assured the campground was safe by a ranger. This parallels the general assurances given to Johnson. *Rubenstein* does seem the case most supportive of the government.

To avoid a negative result, Johnson must attempt to show that bears (hopefully this bear) had been seen in the area and that additional warnings and precautions should have been taken under the circumstances. The fact that this was a ranger guided hike may be particularly useful to Johnson. In *Claypool*, the most supportive case to his position, there had been a bear attack on a camper four nights previously, yet a park ranger assured plaintiff of the safety of the campground. See 98 F. Supp. at 704. Similarly in *Smith*, although plaintiff failed on the basis of contributory negligence, the circuit court indicated that failure to warn of hazards in a frequented area could be negligent. See 546 F.2d at 876 and 877 n.6.

There is no indication that Johnson's conduct was negligent in any way. Certainly under Montana's comparative negligence statute (Mont. Rev. Codes Ann. Sec. 58-607.1) Johnson would not be barred.

*Conclusion.*

It would not appear that the general assurances of safety given Mr. Johnson would be understood to negate the warnings and common understanding about the risks of attack by wild animals, but if it can be shown that grizzly sightings were frequent and/or recent in the area of the hike, the failure to take precautionary measures by the park rangers could result in a holding that the government was negligent.

# Appendix C
# Sample Activity Participation Form

Central College Recreation Association
Activity Participation Form

ACTIVITY DESCRIPTION: *Blue Mountain Backpacking Trip*

This is a 15-mile hike on the Blue Mountain Trail from the trailhead to Blue Lake (seven miles) where we will camp overnight, and out to the highway at Milepost 10. This is a moderately difficult hike which does not require any technical climbing ability, but does put stress on good physical conditioning. There are some steep slippery stretches both up and down hill. Weather conditions are usually variable, and the trail may become particularly difficult if there is a rain storm. Wildlife may appear at any time, and black bear are known to frequent the region. Rattlesnakes are also present in the area.

EQUIPMENT REQUIRED to be furnished by the participant:

a. Well broken-in hiking boots with lug-soles or other anti-slip soles;
b. rain gear, warm sweater, hat and gloves;
c. change of clothing appropriate for temperature range from below freezing to 75° F.;
d. sleeping bag (may be rented from Recreation Association).

EQUIPMENT SUPPLIED by the Recreation Association:

a. Backpacks (you may, of course, bring your own if you desire);
b. tents (two-person tents) (You may bring your own if you desire);
c. food, beverages, and utensils;
d. first-aid equipment, anti-snake venom.

NO alcoholic beverages, illegal substances, cigarettes, cigars, or pipes may be brought on this trip. This area is subject to forest fires.

Participant acknowledges that he/she has read and understands the aforementioned information. Participant further certifies that he/she is in good physical condition and is fit to participate in this activity. Participant understands that this is a wilderness recreational activity, that unexpected hazards may arise and that he/she must always be alert for dangers to themself and to other participants.

Signature of participant_____Date_____

Signature of parent or guardian (if under 18)_____

IMPORTANT!

I have the following physical condition(s) which may affect my ability to successfully participate in this trip or which may be significant in case of emergency or accident:
(If none, check here_____)

_____

_____

Date_____    Signed_____

# Table of Cases

# Index